the BookStore
at western

P9-CRH-224

Explore your store!

TEXTBOOKS

- We offer the largest selection of new and used textbooks for all courses.
- Textbooks are priced at the current Canadian list prices, provided by the publishers.
- Used textbooks are 25% off the new retail price.
- Payment options include Visa, MasterCard, American Express, Interac, cheque or cash.

EXPLORE BOOK SCAPES

- Over 20,000 general book titles, including reference and leisure books.
- Save 25% on The Globe & Mail and The New York Times current bestsellers lists everyday.
- Author events, book sales and special events throughout the year.

SCHOOL SUPPLIES AND WESTERN WEAR

- Check out **The Buck Store** to get quality school supplies for a buck or less.
- From T-shirts to school rings, The Book Store is the official source for Western clothing, giftware and accessories.

BOOKS PLUS

- Located at 1153 Western Road, beside Perth Hall. Open 7 days a week.
- Textbooks and reference material for Education, Communication Sciences and Disorders, Occupational Therapy and Physical Therapy.
- Full service copy centre, self-serve digital copiers, PC work station, fax service and report binding.
- Popular fiction, school supplies, and Western clothing and gifts.

VISIT WWW.BOOKSTORE.UWO.CA

Save a bag. Plant a tree.

Every time you reuse or decline a plastic bag at The Book Store, Campus Computer Store or Books Plus, we will make a donation to **ReForest London**. Money raised will be used to plant trees in London. See our store staff for details.

Present this **COUPON** at The Book Store and receive a **FREE** reusable bag.

Limit one per customer, valid until Oct 10, 2008 or while quantities last.

the Book Store
at western

University Community Centre • 519-661-3520 • www.bookstore.uwo.ca

WHAT IS SERVICE-LEARNING?

Service-learning is a form of experiential education in which students engage in structured community-based activities that are designed to enhance student learning and civic responsibility, while addressing community needs. Service-learning can occur inside or outside the classroom.

Curricular

This form of service-learning integrates service in the community with academic study. Faculty, in collaboration with community partners, design service-learning projects that meet community needs and deepen students' comprehension of course content. Reflective components are designed within the curriculum to help students see the conncection between their service work and what they are learning in class. Check the service-learning website for possible course choices!

www.servicelearning.uwo.ca

Co-curricular

This type of service-learning is part of the students' extracurricular experience. Programs give students the oppporunity to engage in meaningful service activities with their friends and apply what they are learning in class. These activities range in length from a

day to a week and may occur locally or internationally. It is your choice to determine the type of involvement you want to have. You can volunteer to work for a week in an orphanage in the Dominican Republic or build houses with Habitat for Humanity! Visit the alternative spring break web site for details: www.asb.uwo.ca

To contribute locally you can join over 300 students who participate annually in a day of service to benefit London community groups. More information can be found at www.westernserves.uwo.ca

Benefits of Service-Learning for Students

- Strengthens sense of social responsibility
- Increases understanding of the issues underlying social problems
- Deepens comprehension of course content
- Builds connections with the community
- Integrates theory and practice
- Enhances cognitive, personal and spiritual development
- Heightens understanding of diversity and inclusivity

"Service-learning gave me a chance to really see what my courses were teaching me. The meaning behind what I'm studying became very apparent, and it fueled my passion for helping others."

~ Western student

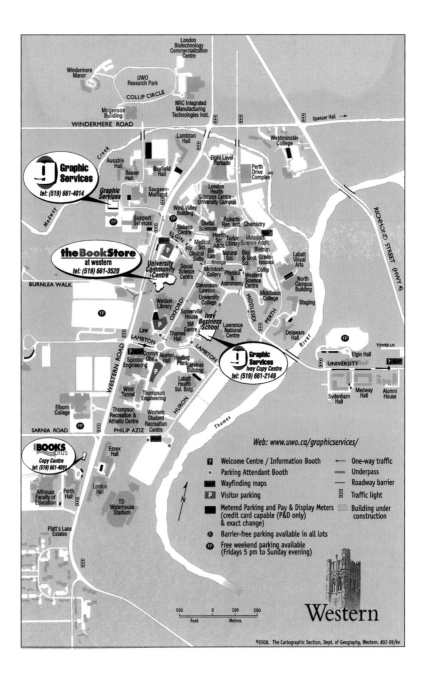

Graphic Services
tel: (519) 661-4014

theBookStore
at western
tel: (519) 661-3520

Graphic Services
Ivey Copy Centre
tel: (519) 661-2149

BOOKS plus
Copy Centre
tel: (519) 661-4091

Web: www.uwo.ca/graphicservices/

	Welcome Centre / Information Booth	←	One-way traffic
•	Parking Attendant Booth		Underpass
MAP	Wayfinding maps		Roadway barrier
P	Visitor parking		Traffic light
	Metered Parking and Pay & Display Meters (credit card capable (P&D only) & exact change)		Building under construction
	Barrier-free parking available in all lots		
fp	Free weekend parking available (Fridays 5 pm to Sunday evening)		

500   0   100   200
Feet
Metres

Western

©2008. The Cartographic Section, Dept. of Geography, Western. #02-09/kv

THE BRIEF PENGUIN HANDBOOK

Custom Edition for the University of Western Ontario

Lester Faigley • Roger Graves • Heather Graves

Taken from:
The Brief Penguin Handbook, Canadian Edition
by Lester Faigley, Roger Graves and Heather Graves

Custom Publishing

New York   Boston   San Francisco
London   Toronto   Sydney   Tokyo   Singapore   Madrid
Mexico City   Munich   Paris   Cape Town   Hong Kong   Montreal

Taken from:

The Brief Penguin Handbook, Canadian Edition
by Lester Faigley, Roger Graves and Heather Graves
Copyright © 2008 by Pearson Education Canada
Published by Longman
Toronto, Ontario
Canada

This special edition published in cooperation with Pearson Custom Publishing.

Printed in Canada

10 9 8 7 6 5 4 3 2 1

2008240357

BK

**Pearson
Custom Publishing**
is a division of

www.pearsonhighered.com

ISBN 10: 0-55501259-X
ISBN 13: 978-0-555-01259-8

Contents

PREFACE

The Canadian edition of *The Brief Penguin Handbook* is designed for students who are learning to write in a visual era. It begins with the idea that writing is a visual medium, even if this aspect of writing has, until recently, been neglected. It acknowledges that even low-cost computers now enable students to perform design and production tasks that once required an entire staff. And it understands, and stresses, the connections between the writing students do in post-secondary education and the writing (and presentations) they will undertake in their professional and public lives.

LOOKING AT WRITING IN A NEW WAY

The Brief Penguin Handbook presents writing visually. By taking a term or concept that may be unfamiliar or confusing to student writers, like *point of view*, and presenting it through images as well as words, *The Brief Penguin Handbook* enables students to actually see how the term is used.

Unique visual layouts provide vivid, concrete examples that help students see, understand, and apply key concepts in their own writing. By looking at the photographs, students can begin to see and understand the differences between the point of view taken by the writer in each written text.

20

Point of View in Verbal Texts

At the most basic level, point of view means selecting among first person (I, we), second person (you), and third person (he, she, it) when you write about your subject. Using *I* emphasizes the writer or the teller of the story in fiction. Using *you* puts the relationship between writer and reader in the foreground. Using *he, she,* or *it* keeps the focus more on the subject and diminishes the prominence of the writer.

Point of view is also determined by how you locate yourself in relation to your subject. Whether you write in first or third person, you can write about a subject from close, first-hand experience or you can place yourself at a distance from your subject, giving the sense of being an impartial observer offering an overview.

You can write about Niagara Falls as if you were looking across the gorge.

Niagara Falls actually consists of three falls: the American, the Bridal Veil, and the Canadian or Horseshoe Falls. The American Falls descends between 21 and 34 metres to the rock at the base. The Horseshoe Falls descends 52 metres into the Maid of the Mist Pool below. More than 168 000 cubic metres of water goes over the brink every minute during daytime hours. The flow is reduced at night, after peak tourist hours, to generate electricity. Water is removed from the river upstream to generate hydroelectricity for both Canada and the U.S. The total power generating capacity at the falls is about 4.4 million kilowatts.

You can write about Niagara Falls from the bottom.

Once the Maid of the Mist reached the foot of the falls, the spray had blotted out the sun, and we felt a steady, soaking mist on everything. Now we understood why the crew had insisted we all wear huge, black raincoats: otherwise we would have been drenched. The thundering of the water was deafening. We could see each others' lips move but heard only water. We caught magical glimpses of the secret world behind the waterfall.

WRITING FOR POST-SECONDARY EDUCATION AND BEYOND

In addition to the usual changes you might expect to see in a Canadian edition of a handbook, this edition includes two new chapters on writing about literature and writing about film and new media. "Writing about Film and New Media" is a completely new chapter that guides students through the strategies essential to planning and writing effective film, website, and video game reviews. "Writing about Literature" is an expanded chapter that offers more detailed guidance on how to develop an effective thesis statement from annotations in a reading journal and how to turn

---

154 **11d** Writing about Film and New Media

At this point in your writing process, pay attention to editing your draft and crafting your sentences (see Part 9, Effective Style and Language; Part 10, Understanding Grammar; and Part 11, Understanding Punctuation and Mechanics).

11d **SAMPLE *MISE EN SCÈNE* ANALYSIS OF *PRIDE & PREJUDICE***

The following paper presents a *mise en scène* analysis of the 2005 version of *Pride & Prejudice*, directed by Joe Wright and starring Keira Knightley and Matthew Macfadyen. It focuses on how the point of view shifts throughout the scene where Elizabeth Bennet and Fitzwilliam Darcy first meet at the assembly in Meryton to convey the instant attraction the two feel despite their protestations of dislike.

Calcagno 1

Vittoria Calcagno
Film 120
Professor Ebert
April 7, 2007

Shifting Viewpoints Reveal Lizzie and Darcy's Attraction

Pride & Prejudice, dir. Joe Wright. Perf. Keira Knightley and
Matthew Macfadyen. Focus Features. Universal
Studios, 2005.

Technical criteria used in the analysis: the shifting viewpoint so viewers see from third-person perspective as well as from Lizzie's and Darcy's perspective.

In the most recent adaptation of Jane Austen's *Pride and Prejudice* to the big screen, director Joe Wright uses the first meeting between Darcy and Elizabeth Bennet to show their instant attraction, despite the pride that keeps them apart. Wright relies on viewers being able to distinguish the camera angles that characterize sometimes Lizzie's gaze, more often Darcy's gaze, and other times an omniscient gaze, to communicate the emotional connections represented by this shifting gaze. We first see

> Annotated sample papers offer students complete model texts, illustrating informative and persuasive writing for academic purposes in a range of disciplines.

---

110 **8e** Writing to Inform

You may have gotten your job based on your technical skills but to keep it or be promoted, you need to have excellent communication skills, both written and spoken.

Need help improving your writing skills?
Call us. We can help you radically improve your writing skills after only a few hours of instruction.

Have several employees who'd love to promote it only they could write well?
Call us. We can make a significant improvement in their skills after only a few hours of one-to-one instruction or small group instruction.

Need piggmend writing resources on your company intranet?
Call us. We can create a series of tutorials for self-study tailored to the specific needs of your employees. Or use our website for a wealth of writing-related information and tips.

Need prompt and helpful feedback on a draft document?
Email us a draft. We will get comments back to you within 24 hours. Our response will identify both the strengths and weaknesses of your draft and provide you with specific suggestions for improvement.

G² Communications Unlimited

Contact us:
G² Communications Unlimited
Anna Green
Maurice Gauthier
234 King St.
Mississauga, ON
agreen@g2comm.com
mgauthier@g2comm.com

Visit us:
http://www.g2communications.com

Corporate writing instruction:
✓ Small classes
✓ One-on-one
✓ Online follow-up
✓ Internet resources

Specialized writing instruction for:
✓ Financial analysts
✓ Engineers
✓ Corporate management

Results guaranteed within four hours of instruction

Panel 5 is the first one the reader sees after the cover. The reader sees a series of questions that outline the kinds of services the consulting firm offers.

The back cover (panel 6) gives contact information and the website address.

The front cover (panel 1) uses a blend of right and left alignment for a distinctive appearance.

Small Classes (Max. 8 individuals)
✓ Classes tailored to needs of writers enrolled
✓ Work on current or upcoming projects
✓ Re-work previous projects
✓ Team writing/individual writing
✓ Learn to analyze corporate style, word choice, and genre conventions

Class length:
2 x 4 hr. sessions (recommended)
Variable, depending on writers' needs

One-on-One Instruction
✓ Make rapid progress with writing instruction tailored to your specific needs
✓ Understand and emulate the features of your industry's style and phrasing
✓ Express yourself concisely, clearly, and correctly

Length:
One to two hours per session
Number of sessions varies with individual

Online Resources
✓ Extensive online resources
✓ Tailored to your organizations' communication needs
✓ Self-directed tutorials on genres and discourse conventions for your industry
✓ Online consulting offers feedback and constructive criticism on works-in-progress
✓ Writing tutorials prepared for your writers that can be uploaded onto company intranet for multi-employee access

Follow-up
✓ Start a new project and have a few questions?
✓ Email us for answers
✓ Send us a draft and we'll provide quick, clear feedback

Need an hour or two face time to talk?
✓ Schedule an appointment
✓ Visit online chat

Why choose G² Communications?

"Klaus improved almost overnight from an employee on probation to one of the best writers in his group following several meetings with Mr. Gauthier."
Yvette, supervisor at Morningstar

"I met with another writing coach but couldn't capture the [company] voice, so I came to G2 Communications, and after two meetings began to understand the finer points of our style."
Noemi, financial analyst

"I've passed Mr. Gauthier's name around within my group and two of my co-workers have gotten equally great results as me working with Maurice."
Vladimir, financial analyst

"The class with G2 Communications was one of the most helpful professional development seminars that I've taken. We got limited writing instruction during the engineer program, so this course helped me to understand how to adapt my message to the audience. I learned so much in these eight hours I could hardly believe it. My writing has improved 100%."
Henry Whodini, nuclear engineer, Energy Canada

The inside panels (2, 3, 4) can be viewed together when the brochure is opened.

On the centre panel Gauthier highlights the online resources the consulting group has created as some of its innovative products and solutions.

> Illustrated examples show writing to inform and persuade in genres used outside the classroom, including brochures, magazine articles, and websites.

these ideas into a compelling literary analysis. Each chapter illustrates the discussion with a sample paper in an academic genre as well as an accompanying public or professional document to show how writing extends into the world beyond the classroom.

RETHINKING THE WAY HANDBOOKS TEACH DOCUMENTATION

The Brief Penguin Handbook aims to present information in ways that are visually accessible for today's students. Documentation style, in particular, is presented differently than in other handbooks.

In this edition, new visual source samples illustrate for students where and how to find key information for constructing citations. In the sample pages shown here, for example, an annotated title page and copyright page from an actual book show students exactly where to look to find the information they need to include when they are citing a book in MLA or APA style.

In addition, each source sample is accompanied by an annotated citation for the source being shown. A three-part colour scheme reinforces the idea that every citation has three main parts: author, title, and publication information. This colour scheme is used in all four documentation chapters, helping students to see that no matter which citation style they are using, they can almost always look for the same three main elements when they are citing a source.

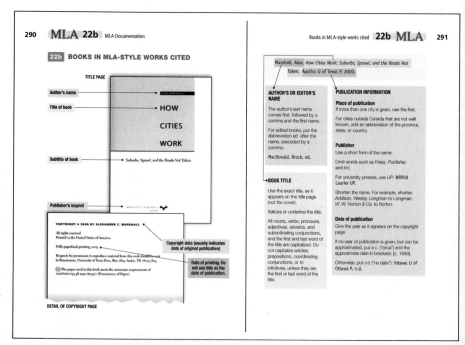

RESEARCHING AND WRITING WITH TECHNOLOGY

To conduct research effectively today, students need to understand how to locate, filter, and evaluate a wealth of information in both print and electronic environments. *The Brief Penguin Handbook* offers a new chapter on online research that includes the most extensive guidance in using library databases available in any handbook. Part 5 walks students through the entire research process, from planning to final revisions, understanding that students today typically begin their search process on the web.

FIGURE 18.3 Citing a database article from LexisNexis Academic

> Students often struggle when using and citing database sources. New annotated sample database screen shots help students see and understand what information they need to capture in their notes and citations.

To cite this article in both MLA and APA styles, you'll need the following information:

- Author, if any
- Title of article
- Name of periodical or news service
- Date of publication (and edition for newspapers)
- Section and page number, if applicable
- Name of database
- Date of access (the day you found the article in the database)

MLA style also requires you to provide the name of the library where you accessed the database and the URL of the vendor's homepage. In this case, you would give the name of the library you used (D. B. Weldon Library at the University of Western Ontario) and the URL of LexisNexis (www.lexisnexis.com). (The vendor's URL is sometimes on a link of "home" or "terms and conditions.") The citation for the article in Figure 18.3 would appear as follows in an MLA-style list of works cited (see Chapter 22).

Terazono, Emiko. "Addicted Online Gamblers to Be Offered Help Internet Betting." *The Financial Times* 17 June 2006, London ed.: 4. *LexisNexis Academic.* LexisNexis. D. B. Weldon Lib., U of Western Ontario. 24 Oct. 2006 <http://www.lexisnexis.com/>.

MAKING IT EASY TO FIND KEY INFORMATION QUICKLY

The Brief Penguin Handbook is designed to be browsed in addition to being accessed with its table of contents and index. A number of features are designed to help students find what is most important and to help them become familiar with the diverse kinds of information in a handbook.

---

456   frag   **33c** Fragments, Run-ons, and Comma Splices

COMMON ERRORS

Recognizing comma splices

When you edit your writing, look carefully at sentences that contain commas. Does the sentence contain two main clauses? If so, are the main clauses joined by a comma and coordinating conjunction *(and, but, for, or, not, so, yet)*?

INCORRECT   The concept of "nature" depends on the concept of human "culture," the problem is that "culture" is itself shaped by "nature." [Two main clauses joined by only a comma]

CORRECT   Even though the concept of "nature" depends on the concept of human "culture," "culture" is itself shaped by "nature." [Subordinate clause plus a main clause]

CORRECT   The concept of "nature" depends on the concept of human "culture," but "culture" is itself shaped by "nature." [Two main clauses joined by a comma and coordinating conjunction]

Treating the word *however* as a coordinating conjunction produces some of the most common comma splice errors. *However* is a conjunctive adverb that does not function grammatically like the coordinating conjunctions *and, but, or, nor, yet, so,* and *for* (see Section 32b).

INCORRECT   Commercials that depict women as sex objects to sell products are obviously demeaning to women, however the always-present man, off-screen, who represents the viewers' gaze is equally demeaning to men.

CORRECT   Commercials that depict women as sex objects to sell products are obviously demeaning to women; however, the always-present man, off-screen, who represents the viewers' gaze is equally demeaning to men. [Two main clauses joined by a semicolon]

Remember: Do not use a comma as a period.

For step-by-step discussion, examples, and practice of this common error, go to **www.pearsoned.ca/faigley/227**.

Writing teachers know that students typically make the same kinds of errors. Common errors boxes offer simple, robust principles for dealing with these frequent errors. Most common errors boxes link to the companion website for additional examples and practice in understanding and avoiding the error.

Graphic icons are used in tandem with key words to offer another way to navigate the book and locate needed material.

6b   Critical Reading and Viewing

THE BRIEF PENGUIN HANDBOOK COMPANION WEBSITE

The Brief Penguin Handbook is supported by an innovative website that offers a wealth of interactive exercises and activities that relate directly to material presented in the book.

> Integrated URLs linked directly to exercises, activities, and resources on the website allow students to extend their learning and practise strategies presented in the book.

 To see this student paper in its complete form, visit www.pearsoned.ca/faigley/220

Key features of *The Brief Penguin Handbook* Companion Website include

- **Student Writing Samples with Audio Commentary**, offering complete papers in a number of disciplines with additional audio commentaries by the author
- **Writing in the World Projects**, providing complete scenarios and situations for a variety of writing and research assignments. In addition, Writing and Researching Worksheets help students focus on particular stages of the writing, design, and research process and can be used independently or in conjunction with a specific project.
- **Creating a website tutorial,** providing current information on web design, authoring tools, and HTML coding
- **Help Desk**, presenting students with a friendly, illustrated guide to the Companion Website and responses to frequently asked questions about how to find things on the site
- **Common Errors Workbook**, providing additional exercises and activities directly related to the most frequent problem areas encountered by student writers
- **Common ESL Errors Workbook**, providing additional practice and exercises to help nonnative speakers and writers recognize common grammar and style problems
- **Punctuation Personality Quiz**, offering students an entertaining look at punctuation

SUPPLEMENTS

Accompanying *The Brief Penguin Handbook* are the following supplements:

- The Companion Website to accompany *The Brief Penguin Handbook* (at www.pearsoned.ca/faigley/). References to this useful, consistently relevant website can be found throughout the handbook; URLs are provided throughout that link directly to specific pages within the Companion Website.

- An e-book of *The Brief Penguin Handbook* is now available within Pearson Education Canada's premier composition website, *MyCanadianCompLab*. In *MyCanadianCompLab*, students and teachers will have access to the best multimedia resources for grammar, writing, and research in one easy-to-use site. Added to this, the e-book of *The Brief Penguin Handbook*, with hyperlinks to websites and video and audio clips, updated by Jill Jackson of the University of Windsor, provides a complete, engaging multimedia learning experience for students. Tour the site at www.pearsoned.ca/ highered/mycanadiancomplab/.

- An *Instructor's Resource Manual*, updated by Sue Adams of Sheridan College, offers guidance to new and experienced teachers for using the handbook and its ancillary package to the best advantage. To download a copy of this supplement, please visit the book's online catalogue page, which can be accessed at http://vig.pearsoned.ca.

ACKNOWLEDGMENTS

When once asked what it is like to write a handbook, I replied that it's like walking across Europe and Asia. The journey is long and lonesome. Without a great deal of help along the way, I could not have completed it. I most appreciate the dedication, patience, and sound judgment of my editor, Lynn Huddon, who has supported the project from the beginning and carried it to fruition in two editions. Her creativity, conceptual vision, and attention to detail are evident throughout the book. My guide for the second edition has been Michael Greer, the brilliant development editor who has been a co-author and friend throughout.

I would like to thank the many students who provided feedback and who gave us suggestions for this new edition of *The Brief Penguin Handbook*, particularly the students from Grand View College, Caldwell Community College, Del Mar College, Iowa State University, Lander University, Pima Community College, and Colorado Christian University.

I am especially grateful to Ellen Crowell, who made major contributions to the documentation chapters and elsewhere in the book. Kristin Cole, Susan "George" Schorn, and Nathan Baran have been extraordinary in creating new material for the Companion Website. I thank the students I have been fortunate to teach at Texas and who produced the splendid work that is included in this edition. Colleagues Julie Allen and Frank Whigham were generous in contributing photographs. Michele Ostrow and Alexia Thompson-Young of the University of Texas Libraries gave me valuable advice. I also appreciate the help and support of numerous colleagues in the Division of Rhetoric and Composition and in the Undergraduate Writing Center at Texas.

Special thanks go to Paul and Aya Matsuda, who have brought a new, global perspective on English as a contemporary language. Today speakers and writers of English come from many diverse cultural and linguistic backgrounds, complicating the notion of distinguishing between "native" and "non-native" speakers. Paul and Aya have written a new section on English as a global language (Section 31a) and a new chapter on writing in second language (Chapter 48), as well as other contributions in Part 10.

I thank my kayaking, climbing, and trekking companion of thirty years, Jim Witte (who appears in Chapter 4), for getting me to some of the greatest places on earth, and, more important, getting me back. I've learned a great deal about photography from Frank Whigham, who constantly encourages me. My greatest debt of gratitude is to my wife, Linda, whose enduring support has allowed me to complete this journey with good humor intact.

Lester Faigley

We would like to thank Colleen Fraumeni and Patty Riediger for involving us in this project, creating a Canadian edition of *The Brief Penguin Handbook*. Writing this edition brought us into contact with some things about Canadian history and culture that we didn't know before and sharpened our sense of what it is to be Canadian after our time in the U.S. We also appreciate the guidance and good ideas offered by our developmental editors, Charlotte Morrison-Reed and John Polanzsky, during the process of revising this book. Others at Pearson who have contributed their wisdom and experience are Söğüt Y. Güleç, Production Editor; Janis Raisen, Production Coordinator; Lisa Berland, Copy Editor; and Rob Giannetto and Sharon Kirsch, Proofreaders.

We are especially grateful to Don and Naureen Brodie, Erin Graves, Eric Graves, and Lisa Locascio for graciously allowing us to use some of their written and visual materials as building blocks for a number of these chapters.

We were fortunate to have the benefit of a wonderful group of reviewers, who were not only perceptive in their suggestions but were supportive of a handbook that breaks new ground. They are Anita Agar, Sheridan College; Matthew Beedham, Malaspina University-College; Garry Engkent, Seneca College; Mary Findlay, Seneca College; Norma Kathleen Greenfield, McGill University; Peggy Lynn Kelly, University of Ottawa; Shannon Lewis-Simpson, Memorial University of Newfoundland; Wendy Shilton, University of Prince Edward Island; Kathleen Wall, University of Regina; and Leland Young, Dawson College.

We also want to thank Buster, who came in part way through this project, and who helped keep us focused on the important things in life: long walks, good food, and rousing games of Frisbee-chase.

Heather Graves
Roger Graves

CREDITS

1 COMPOSING IN A VISUAL ERA

With a personal computer and powerful software, individuals today can publish high-quality documents with visuals, create sophisticated multimedia presentations, and produce websites that tens of millions of people around the world can view.

Writing in the World Project

Volunteering as a Writer: The Toronto Symphony

Many organizations have ongoing needs for capable writers to create all kinds of documents. The Toronto Symphony website contains a volunteer job descriptions page that lists descriptions for volunteers to write letters, contribute newsletter articles, and oversee the production of marketing and public relations materials.

Check out the descriptions yourself at their website: www.tsvc.on .ca/job_descriptions.htm.

 Visit *The Brief Penguin Handbook* Companion Website at
www.pearsoned.ca/faigley/

MyCanadianCompLab
Where writing and research help is a click away.
MyCanadianCompLab may be packaged with your textbook.
If not, it can be purchased from your college or university's bookstore.
Go to www.pearsoned.ca/highered/mycanadiancomplab/
for a tour.

INTRODUCTION

Writing for Different Purposes in Different Media

Learning how to write well is a critical part of your post-secondary education. Many surveys that ask graduates what they most value about their education report that they rank writing and communication skills far above anything else they learned. If you write well, you will become more confident and more successful in whatever you do.

In your lifetime, digital technologies have profoundly changed what it means to write well. With a personal computer and powerful software, individuals today can publish high-quality documents with visuals, create sophisticated multimedia presentations, and produce websites that tens of millions of people around the world can view. Nevertheless, the new literacies made possible by digital technologies haven't replaced the old literacies of pencil, pen, printing press, and paper. New technologies have simply added more choices, raising the ante for being an effective communicator in the digital era. Let's look at an example of what an educated professional does in a typical day.

A DAY IN THE LIFE OF AN EDUCATED PROFESSIONAL

Linda Petch, the president and founder of Petch & Associates of Victoria, B.C., specializes in working with boards of directors to strengthen corporate governance structures and practices. That may sound imposing, and the work can be, but one of the advantages of starting your own company is that you can work out of a home-based office. The commute to the office takes only seconds and it immerses her in a world of reading, writing, and communicating in person, on paper, and through email.

A typical day working from home

When Linda Petch gets up in the morning she goes to the office to turn on her computer before returning to the kitchen to put on the coffee. When she returns to the office she logs on to her computer, checks for email and voice messages, and reads online the *New York Times* and Google News. She then reads *The Globe and Mail* and *Victoria Times Colonist* newspapers. Her intent in doing all this reading is "just to know what is going on in the world." Mornings are her prime working time, a time when she is able to focus intently on the various projects she is working on and respond quickly and thoughtfully to email and voice messages. On any one morning you'll find her carrying on email conversations with clients in Ontario and British Columbia simultaneously. She'll work from six or seven in the morning until about noon to prepare presentations and work on reports, manuals, and all manner of other documents. In her emails, she exchanges documents and information to be included in the reports that she is writing. This is her prime researching, writing, and composing time. In the afternoons, she will schedule meetings, read, garden, or even go biking.

Long-term projects

Petch's work changes from project to project. On one long-term project for the Ontario Safety Service Alliance (OSSA), she began by flying to Toronto for a series of meetings with key personnel and staff. After the initial meeting in Ontario, she went to work reading two three-inch binders full of information that the previous writer had gathered from wherever he could. The previous writer suffered a stroke and could not finish the document. After reading through this material, Petch put together a presentation and workshop on best practices on governance. She needed to gather material from previous presentations, tailor it to the specific needs of OSSA, and then spend a day with the board to get agreement on where this project was headed and why. Once she had established the direction for the manual through this presentation, she revised it from the ground up. For each financial policy and procedures section, OSSA would email it; she would re-write it; Petch and OSSA would each edit it; OSSA would proofread the final version at their end; and finally she presented the document to OSSA and conducted a training session for the board on how to use the information.

The entire process took one year. Dozens of people were involved in creating the document—other consultants wrote material that was then incorporated into the larger document. Petch had no trouble working from a distance because of the technologies available to her: she created PDF files of the draft document and zipped the document when it got large (several hundred pages). She used telephone and voice mail to talk with the other writers, and she used email extensively to consult and exchange drafts of the document.

One-day workshop: Group writing day

But not all of Petch's writing projects are such long-term, complex projects as the manual for the OSSA. For example, Petch also created a strategic plan for the Downtown Victoria Business Association (DVBA). Starting with the vision and mission statement DVBA had already created, she guided them through the stages of creating a strategic plan: establishing the main challenges the board felt they faced; identifying goals for DVBA; creating themes or objectives for DVBA; and finally creating measurable objectives for the next 12 months. This plan helped to distinguish between the kinds of activities the board should be involved in and the duties of the general manager of DVBA. Petch used a variety of technologies to assist this group in writing this document: paper, flipcharts, and markers; a laptop computer and projector; and presentation software. The result was a one-page plan that the group could easily refer to and use to guide their decisions. They created the document, revised it, and agreed to it before leaving the workshop. As the lead editor, Petch helped them brainstorm, phrase, and organize ideas to bring all this text together into one document that the participants could see up on the screen at the end of the day.

Petch's days are typical of those of many professional people. Writing is a large part of her professional and personal life. Petch lives in an information economy. Her primary product on the job is information presented in several forms—reports, memos, letters, visuals, and oral presentations. She uses the information resources of the internet to remain current and for a variety of other uses, such as making airline reservations.

THE COMPLEX WRITING DEMANDS OF THE DIGITAL ERA

Linda Petch's day represents the complexity of writing in a digital era. People who can write effectively are far more successful in their professional and civic lives than those who can't. In large companies and organizations, often the only way others know you is by what you write. Similarly, if you expect to be able to influence decisions that affect you and your community, you most often have to communicate in writing. Let's look at what is demanded of you.

- **Writers today use a variety of writing technologies.** People do not throw away their pencils and ballpoint pens when they buy a laptop computer. Each writing tool is well suited to particular uses; it's hard to top a pencil for jotting down a grocery list, although some people may be equally comfortable using PDAs for such daily writing tasks.
- **Writers today do many different kinds of writing:** letters, reports, memos, newsletters, evaluations, articles, charts, websites, computer-assisted presentations, press releases, brochures, proposals, resumés,

agendas, users' manuals, analyses, summaries, and email. Each kind of writing has its own special set of demands.

- **Writers today have multiple purposes.** An email may convey both business strategies and personal news. A proposal may have as its unacknowledged purpose the request for a new job or wider responsibilities. Even a simple memo often conveys many unstated messages, such as the attitude of the writer toward her co-workers.
- **Writers today have multiple audiences.** Often documents are read by readers who have different interests. The speed of digital media allows many points of view to be expressed simultaneously. Skilled writers in the digital era know they must negotiate among these many points of view.
- **Writers today know how to find and present information relevant to their purposes.** They are efficient researchers who can locate, evaluate, and present information clearly and ethically to their readers. Most readers prefer well-selected information to a barrage of unfiltered data.
- **Writers today often work in teams.** They communicate with colleagues to achieve a common goal, so the ability to collaborate effectively may be an unanticipated need in writing effectively.
- **Writers today know that it is critical to emphasize what is important.** They understand that readers face an overdose of information, have little patience, and want to know quickly what is at stake.
- **Writers today recognize that an active and personal style free from errors is often most effective.** Readers in general prefer a personal and accessible style.
- **Writers today communicate visually as well as verbally.** Computers and digital media give writers the ability to use pictures and graphics in addition to text. Knowing how to communicate visually is important to your success in the digital era.

CHAPTER 1

The Rhetorical Situation

COMMUNICATING IN THE WORLD

Roberto de Nobili

In May 1605, a Portuguese ship arrived at the colony of Goa on the west coast of India, the administrative centre for Portuguese trade in the East. On the ship was a young Italian aristocrat, Roberto de Nobili, who had abandoned his inherited title and wealth to become a Jesuit missionary. He found the wealth of Goa dazzling, but it did not take long for de Nobili to discover that the spiritual mission of the Jesuits had failed. After nearly a hundred years of occupation, almost all the converts to Christianity were either the servants of the Portuguese or under their direct control.

Roberto de Nobili quickly learned Tamil, the language spoken in much of southern India. His talents made him the ideal candidate for an attempt to convert the people in India who lived in the interior. He was sent to Madurai, a provincial capital in southern India, where his predecessor had failed to make a single convert in 11 years. Over time de Nobili came to understand why the record of success had been so poor. The Portuguese ignored the basic values of the local people, such as the prohibition on eating beef; consequently, the people in India regarded the Portuguese as subhuman beings.

De Nobili decided that he needed to take a different approach. He wore the clothing of a Hindu holy man, ate one meal a day of herbs and rice, observed local customs, and preached in Tamil. Gradually, de Nobili drew many visitors and became the first European to learn Sanskrit, giving him access to Hindu religious texts. With this knowledge he could draw parallels between certain Hindu and Christian beliefs. He gained widespread acceptance among the upper castes of Hindu society. Even though his dream of converting much of India to Christianity did not come to pass, de Nobili taught us how people from vastly different cultural backgrounds might engage in dialogue.

1a   THE RHETORICAL TRIANGLE

The lessons that Roberto de Nobili learned still apply today. He recognized that the message alone is inadequate for effective communication. If de Nobili were to convince anyone in southern India to convert to Christianity, he would first have to convince the people that he was a person worth listening to. De Nobili realized that to gain respect he would have to respect the values of the community.

All too often, as was the case with de Nobili, we become aware of how communication works only when communication breaks down. De Nobili understood that communication is more than the message—that the speaker and the audience are also essential components of communication. These components are often represented with a triangle.

The rhetorical triangle (Figure 1.1) depicts two important points about any kind of communication. First, all three elements—speaker, subject, and audience—are necessary for an act of communication to occur. Even if you are talking to or writing to yourself, you still have an audience. Second, the three elements are in a dynamic relationship, which the example of Roberto de Nobili illustrates. De Nobili had to change his dress, his eating habits, his language, and indeed, his entire way of living in order to convince his audience that he was a person of good will with their best interests in mind. Few people ever go to these extremes to communicate, but every one of us makes adjustments depending on our audience (think of how you talk to small children). Similarly, just as speakers adjust to

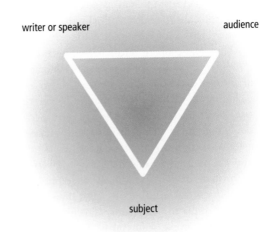

writer or speaker   audience

subject

FIGURE 1.1 The rhetorical triangle

audiences, audiences continually adjust to speakers (think of how your attitude toward speakers changes when they are able to laugh at themselves).

Persuasive appeals

The ancient Greeks recognized that the dynamic nature of the rhetorical triangle is the key to understanding how an audience is persuaded. The most important teacher of rhetoric in ancient Greece, Aristotle (384– 323 BCE), defined rhetoric as the art of finding the best available means of persuasion in any situation. He set out three primary tactics of persuasion: appeals based on the trustworthiness of the speaker (*ethos*); appeals to the emotions and deepest-held values of the audience (*pathos*); and appeals to logic, reasoning, and evidence (*logos*). These appeals likewise can be represented using the rhetorical triangle (Figure 1.2).

Let's take a practical example of persuasion. Imagine that you drive every day on Lakeside Boulevard, a four-lane highway divided in two by a narrow grass median strip. You've read in the newspaper about numerous accidents on Lakeside Boulevard, many of them fatal. You yourself have witnessed two horrible accidents, when cars skidded across the median and collided head-on with traffic in the opposite lanes. You want your city council to vote to erect a concrete barrier that will prevent these frequent head-on collisions. One approach would be to use logic and evidence, documenting that Lakeside Boulevard has far more fatal accidents per kilometre than other streets in your city (logos). Another would be to invite an expert on traffic safety to speak to

Ethos
appeals to the character and expertise
of the writer or speaker

Pathos
appeals to the beliefs and values
of the audience

Logos
appeals based on logic, reasoning, and
evidence concerning the subject

FIGURE 1.2 Persuasive appeals

FIGURE 1.3 *Ethos.* "At 24, I became the second youngest champion in NASCAR history."

FIGURE 1.4 *Pathos.* "As young people, you have a fresh perspective."

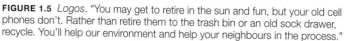

FIGURE 1.5 *Logos.* "You may get to retire in the sun and fun, but your old cell phones don't. Rather than retire them to the trash bin or an old sock drawer, recycle. You'll help our environment and help your neighbours in the process."

the city council (ethos). A third way would be to appeal to the council about the unnecessary loss of life caused by the unsafe street (pathos). Often you will use all of these appeals to gain the support of an audience.

The larger context

The rhetorical triangle is useful for understanding how an act of communication works at a particular time. What is missing, however, is a sense of how the participants happened to be talking about that particular subject at that time in that place. Roberto de Nobili did not arrive in southern India by accident. He was part of an expanding Portuguese empire that extended from Macao off the coast of China, across south Asia and Africa, to Brazil in South America. De Nobili was also a priest who represented the Roman Catholic Church. Likewise, the people of the higher castes in southern India, whom de Nobili was attempting to convert, were not vegetarians because they had suddenly decided to stop eating meat; they were following a centuries-old Hindu religious tradition of not taking the lives of animals.

We do not think much about long-standing cultural traditions when we talk to people who live in our own culture, but we often become aware of the historical dimensions of particular subjects for particular audiences. For example, you might know that certain species of sharks are becoming increasingly rare. Large coastal sharks are vulnerable to overfishing because they grow slowly and have a slow reproductive rate. Nonetheless, it's much harder to convince a general audience that sharks need protection than it is to argue for the protection of a cuddly species like the panda. Most people have seen too many movies like *Jaws* and read too many accounts of shark attacks to think of sharks in the same way they think of pandas.

Any act of communicating is never quite the neutral situation that a simple rhetorical triangle implies. Speaker, subject, and audience each bring histories to a particular rhetorical situation (Figure 1.6). People who know how to communicate effectively use those histories to their advantage. They understand that many people have spoken and written about the subject before them and that they are entering an ongoing conversation.

The writing situation

When the rhetorical situation changes from speaking to writing, it becomes more complex. It might seem that we can simply substitute "writer" for "speaker" and "readers" for "audience" in the rhetorical triangle, but it's not that simple. While every healthy person above infancy can speak and listen, people can read and write only if they are taught. Writing requires a system of representation, in which symbols stand for sounds or

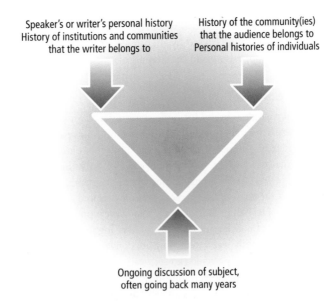

Speaker's or writer's personal history
History of institutions and communities
that the writer belongs to

History of the community(ies)
that the audience belongs to
Personal histories of individuals

Ongoing discussion of subject,
often going back many years

FIGURE 1.6 Social and historical contexts of the rhetorical situation

words. Writing requires an instrument for writing, even if it is only your finger making letters in the sand at the beach. More important, writing changes the dynamics of the rhetorical triangle because usually writer and reader are separated by time and space. Writing changes the nature of the audience and the nature of the speaker in more ways than merely substituting written words for those spoken.

1b A WRITER'S AUDIENCE

On occasion you may write to a person who is close enough to talk to. For example, in a large lecture class you might write a note to the person sitting beside you. At other times, even though the person isn't present, you know the person so well that writing seems almost like speaking, such as when you send email to a member of your family. You know your family member shares much in common with you and will pick up on your tone and meaning when you write "Aunt Suri made her mystery samosas once again."

At other times your audience may consist of many individuals whose knowledge is relatively uniform and similar to yours. If you write an article for a journal in your major field, you can assume that your readers are familiar with the terms and concepts in that field even though your readers are different as individuals. When you can easily characterize the knowledge and attitudes of your audience, the audience can be called a **simple** audience.

Frequently, however, the issue of audience is much more complicated when you write. When an accountant writes a financial analysis for a bank, different people—officers of the bank, other employees, shareholders, government regulatory officials, financial analysts, and potential investors—might read that analysis for different reasons. This kind of complex audience—people with different backgrounds who read the same document for different reasons—is called a **multiple** audience. When you write for multiple audiences, you need to consider differing levels of knowledge about your subject, as well as differing attitudes toward both you and the topic you are writing about.

Critical to what you write is your audience's knowledge of your subject. If you know that your readers will be unfamiliar with your subject, you should provide background information and connect your new information to what your readers already know. Another critical factor is the level of expertise of your audience. If you are writing for an audience of experts in a field, you can use the technical language of that field. If you are unsure how much your audience knows, you may need to explain technical terms. For example, a newspaper article about the options for connecting to the internet from home should explain key concepts such as kilobits per second, the measure of connection speed. If your audience knows nothing about your subject, then you may have to convince them that they should be interested.

1c A WRITER'S ETHOS

Your school newspaper may print guest editorials by fellow students and others connected with the institution on the editorial pages. When you glance through its columns, you make quick decisions about what to read. When you read an editorial, you form an opinion about how much the writer seems to know about the subject. And if the writer urges you to do something—such as vote for a candidate or initiative—you will decide whether the writer has your best interests in mind before you act.

A perusal of any newspaper illustrates two key principles about a writer's ethos. Writers must convince their readers that the writers

- Are knowledgeable about the subject
- Have their readers' needs in mind

If a writer fails on either count, readers either stop reading or do not believe that what they have read has any relevance to them.

Some writers begin with credibility because of who they are. If you wonder what foods compose a balanced meal for your dog, you will probably take seriously the advice of a veterinarian. If you want to develop a powerful backhand in tennis, you might read carefully advice from Venus Williams in a tennis magazine. Most writers, however, do not begin with an established ethos. They have to convince their readers to keep reading by demonstrating knowledge of their subject and concern with their readers' needs. No matter how much you know about a subject or how good your ideas are, your ethos as a writer will be destroyed by sloppy, error-filled writing. Perhaps people should not make strong negative judgments on the basis of a few mistakes, but in the workplace and in public life they often do.

1d A WRITER'S PURPOSE

The starting point for effective writing is determining in advance what you want to accomplish. You may want to reflect on your experience or the experience of others. You may want to inform your readers about a subject. Or you may want to change your readers' attitudes about a subject or persuade them to take action. Your purpose will determine the tone and presentation of your message. You will find more about these purposes in Chapters 8, 9, 10, and 11.

To give one example, imagine that you are invited to contribute a guest editorial to the newspaper at your post-secondary institution. Your purpose is to convince your readers that government should subsidize one bus route that loses money transporting students to your school. Your position is that these students will have no affordable alternative if the route is cut, so tax dollars are justified in supporting this group.

First, you have to establish your ethos by doing your homework. You know the route only carries 70 passengers a day, costing taxpayers nearly $100 000 a year, but the distance is too far to ride a bike, especially during the winter months. You feel that the taxpayer loss is justified because it will enable these students to become affluent, contributing members of society if they are able to graduate. You also locate three other cities in Canada that subsidize transit routes for various reasons.

But you know from the outset that not everyone on your campus will agree if he or she is unaffected by the route cancellation. Some of your readers will feel strongly that public money should not be used to subsidize transportation for a few less affluent students. You can anticipate that critics will argue that these students should move to housing closer to the school. You will have to deal with that point. Anticipating points of view different from yours and stating them in a way that is recognizable to those who hold those different viewpoints is a means of building your ethos. Even though you know from the outset that you will not convince everyone, if you can get your readers to consider your position seriously you will have succeeded.

CHAPTER *2*

Words, Images, and Graphics

2a MULTIMEDIA WRITING

For the past few hundred years in Western culture, people typically communicated using one medium at a time. The more highly valued the communication, the more likely they would use only one medium. The most valued writing, such as great literature, academic books and articles, and legal contracts, had dense pages of print with no illustrations. Great art was limited to a few materials—oil on canvas or chiselled stone. Great music likewise was performed on orchestral instruments by formally dressed musicians.

With the development of mass media, people have increasingly been exposed to communication that involves more than one medium. In the nineteenth century magazines were illustrated with drawings; in the twentieth century they used photographs as well. Silent films relied on written words to accompany images; later, when sound was added to films, it became possible to combine images, music, and dialogue.

Recent developments in personal computers and software have made it possible for individuals to create multimedia texts that formerly required production staffs. Today, word processing programs not only permit you to control type styles and size but also allow you to insert pictures, add tables and other graphics, print in colour, and prepare sophisticated visuals for oral presentations. The problem today is not whether you can add images and graphics but when to add them and for what effects. Just as for other rhetorical situations, it finally comes down to what you hope to accomplish—your purpose for communicating.

2b COMMUNICATING WITH WORDS, IMAGES, AND GRAPHICS

Knowing when to use images and graphics and when to use words requires you to think about them as media—as different means of conveying information and ideas. The word *writing* makes us think of words, yet in our daily experience reading newspapers, magazines, advertisements, posters, and signs, we find words combined with images and graphics. Similarly, the dominant visual medium of our time, television, uses words extensively (think of the words you see on commercials when you have the sound off and the running text across the bottom of the screen on news, sports, and financial programs).

Many ideas and concepts can be explained more effectively with a combination of words, graphics, and images. One example is the creation of the Waterpocket Fold, a nearly 160-kilometre-long wrinkle in the Earth's crust, a major landmark in Utah in the southwestern U.S. (See the following pages.)

Newspaper Rock, Utah, U.S.A. People communicated with images long before recorded history.

Verbal explanation

The Waterpocket Fold is a classic monocline: a regional fold with one very steep side in an area of otherwise nearly horizontal layers. A monocline is a "step-up" in the rock layers. The rock layers on the west side of the Waterpocket Fold have been lifted more than 7000 feet higher than the layers on the east. Major folds are almost always associated with underlying faults. The Waterpocket Fold formed between 50 and 70 million years ago when a major mountain building event in western North America, the Laramide Orogeny, reactivated an ancient buried fault. When the fault moved, the overlying rock layers were draped above the fault and formed a monocline.

More recent uplift of the entire Colorado Plateau and the resulting erosion has exposed this fold at the surface only within the last 15 to 20 million years.

—U.S. National Park Service

Visual explanation

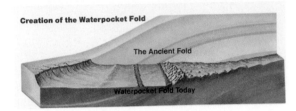

The creation of the Waterpocket Fold

Images

Unless you have seen the Waterpocket Fold, it's hard to imagine what it looks like without a photograph.

Aerial photography enables us to take in large features like the Waterpocket Fold.

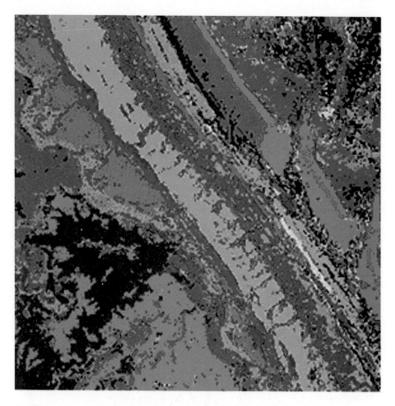

Satellite images provide yet another way of seeing. This image uses colour to identify specific kinds of rock.

Organization in Verbal Texts

Organization is the path the writer creates for readers to follow. Even in a reference book like this one, in which readers consult particular chapters and sections according to their needs, there still is a path from beginning to end. Sentences, paragraphs, sections, and chapters are the writer's materials in constructing the pathway. The various subjects the writer treats are the places along the pathway. If the trail is well marked and the places identified, the reader can follow without getting lost and can revisit particular places.

Mapping of ideas

Some kinds of writing demand particular kinds of organization. A short memo in an office typically begins with an announcement of the subject. But in other kinds of writing, the organization is not so predictable. How you begin and how you take the reader along a pathway depend on what you are trying to achieve. Thinking about your purpose often helps you to map out the organization.

Titles, headings, and paragraphs

Titles and headings combine verbal and visual indicators of levels of importance and major divisions in subject matter. Paragraphs give visual cues to the progression of ideas in verbal texts. Other visual indicators such as boldface and italics provide emphasis at the level of words and phrases. Print, after all, is a visual as well as a verbal medium.

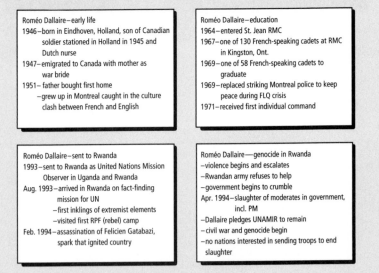

Roméo Dallaire—early life
1946—born in Eindhoven, Holland, son of Canadian soldier stationed in Holland in 1945 and Dutch nurse
1947—emigrated to Canada with mother as war bride
1951—father bought first home
 —grew up in Montreal caught in the culture clash between French and English

Roméo Dallaire—education
1964—entered St. Jean RMC
1967—one of 130 French-speaking cadets at RMC in Kingston, Ont.
1969—one of 58 French-speaking cadets to graduate
1969—replaced striking Montreal police to keep peace during FLQ crisis
1971—received first individual command

Roméo Dallaire—sent to Rwanda
1993—sent to Rwanda as United Nations Mission Observer in Uganda and Rwanda
Aug. 1993—arrived in Rwanda on fact-finding mission for UN
 —first inklings of extremist elements
 —visited first RPF (rebel) camp
Feb. 1994—assassination of Felicien Gatabazi, spark that ignited country

Roméo Dallaire—genocide in Rwanda
 —violence begins and escalates
 —Rwandan army refuses to help
 —government begins to crumble
Apr. 1994—slaughter of moderates in government, incl. PM
 —Dallaire pledges UNAMIR to remain
 —civil war and genocide begin
 —no nations interested in sending troops to end slaughter

Index cards are a traditional method for mapping ideas.

Source: From Roméo Dallaire, *Shake Hands with the Devil: The Failure of Humanity in Rwanda* (Toronto: Vintage Canada, 2003).

Organization in Visual Texts

Organization is often called *composition* by photographers, artists, and designers. The materials for photographers and artists are objects placed in space.

Both of the pictures below are of the same subject. Which do you find more appealing, the image on the left or the one on the right?

Static versus dynamic

The image on the left is a typical snapshot. The person is placed at the exact centre, and the horizon is about at the midpoint. Putting the subject in the exact centre is what happens when people take snapshots without thinking about how they are composed. The effect is static because the focus is on the object.

The image on the right moves the person away from the centre and places him in relation to a large rock illuminated by the setting sun. Instead of focusing on the man, we now see him in relation to objects on the beach and the sea and sky behind.

If the picture is divided into thirds horizontally and vertically, we can see that the prominent rock and the man are placed at the intersections of these imaginary lines. This principle of organization is known as the "rule of thirds." Although there is no beginning and ending in a photograph, principles of organization still apply.

Point of View in Verbal Texts

At the most basic level, point of view means selecting among first person (I, we), second person (you), and third person (he, she, it) when you write about your subject. Using *I* emphasizes the writer or the teller of the story in fiction. Using *you* puts the relationship between writer and reader in the foreground. Using *he, she,* or *it* keeps the focus more on the subject and diminishes the prominence of the writer.

Point of view is also determined by how you locate yourself in relation to your subject. Whether you write in first or third person, you can write about a subject from close, first-hand experience or you can place yourself at a distance from your subject, giving the sense of being an impartial observer offering an overview.

You can write about Niagara Falls as if you were looking across the gorge.

Niagara Falls actually con-sists of three falls: the American, the Bridal Veil, and the Canadian or Horse-shoe Falls. The American Falls descends between 21 and 34 metres to the rock at the base. The Horseshoe Falls descends 52 metres into the Maid of the Mist Pool below. More than 168 000 cubic metres of water goes over the brink every minute during daytime hours. The flow is reduced at night, after peak tourist hours, to generate electricity. Water is removed from the river upstream to generate hydroelectricity for both Canada and the U.S. The total power generating capacity at the falls is about 4.4 million kilowatts.

You can write about Niagara Falls from the bottom.

Once the Maid of the Mist reached the foot of the falls, the spray had blotted out the sun, and we felt a steady, soaking mist on everything. Now we understood why the crew had insisted we all wear huge, black raincoats: otherwise we would have been drenched. The thundering of the water was deafening. We could see each others' lips move but heard only water. We caught magical glimpses of the secret world behind the waterfall.

Point of View in Visual Texts

Where we choose to stand when we take a photograph makes all the difference in how the audience sees the subject. The photographer gives the audience a vantage point to take in the subject by allowing the audience to see what the photographer sees, creating an effect comparable to the use of *I* in writing. But photographers can also diminish the immediacy of a photograph by placing subjects at a distance or photographing them in stereotypical ways.

Three views of a landscaped garden

These photos show a sunken garden from the top of the quarry, from the base of the lookout in the garden, and through a close-up of flowers in one of the beds. What difference does point of view make in how we see the garden?

Photographers also create a *you* relationship with their subjects. Photographing people at close range creates a sense of interaction between subject and photographer.

Focus and Frame in Verbal Texts

When you write, maintain focus on one subject at a time. You achieve focus by what you choose to include and what you choose either to leave out or to postpone until later.

When you write about a complex subject, often you think about many things at once and try to get them all into your prose.

Our era is not unique as a time of uncertainty. In the past the Four Horsemen of the Apocalypse—war, disease, famine, and death—represented uncertainty. Today much of the risk is produced by humans. Science and technology are both the cause of and the solution to our problems. In the past spirits or demons took the blame for catastrophes; today the blame circles back on us. The media tell us that things go wrong because we choose the wrong lifestyle or the wrong partner or the wrong kind of food or the wrong occupation, and it's our responsibility to fix what is wrong.

When you write about a complex subject, sort the issues and present them one at a time.

Our era is not unique as a time of uncertainty. The Four Horsemen of the Apocalypse—war, disease, famine, and death—have been the daily reality for most humans in times before modernity and for many living now. There are two major differences between uncertainty today and in the past.

First is the degree to which risk is produced by humans. Science and technology are both the cause of and the solution to our present risks. Every new technology brings associated risks; trains brought the risk of train wrecks, airplanes brought plane crashes, automobiles brought traffic accidents and smog, nuclear power brought radiation leaks, the internet brought rapidly spreading computer viruses.

Second is the absence of traditions to account for risks. In the past spirits or demons took the blame for catastrophes. Today the blame circles back on us. We chose the wrong lifestyle or the wrong partner or the wrong kind of food or the wrong occupation. When things go wrong, it is the individual's responsibility to seek counselling, to retrain herself, to pull himself up by his bootstraps.

Focus and Frame in Visual Texts

Just as in writing, make the subject of your images clear to the viewer. Beginning photographers tend to see only what is at the centre of the viewfinder. More experienced photographers pay attention to the edges of the frame because they know the frame is critical to how the viewer sees the subject.

What's the subject of this picture? The soccer players? The spectators? The two kids playing behind the spectators?

If the subject is soccer, then change the frame to one that focuses on the action.

Most of the time you should aim for simplicity in images.

When your subject is complex, you can still achieve simplicity by paying close attention to point of view and frame.

Interest in Verbal Texts

Readers will plow through pages of boring writing if they have a strong purpose for reading, such as a financial report for a company they plan to invest in. Most of the time, however, you have to create and hold readers' interest if you expect them to finish what you write. When you create interest, you also build your credibility as a writer.

Details make writing lively.

Tavistock is typical of the small farming communities of southwestern Ontario: well kept, prosperous, a curious blend of past and present. The sprawling farms give way to city lots with neat houses—19th-century yellow brick, 20th-century vinyl-sided split- or bi-levels, and 21st-century cement brick two-storeys. No malls or box stores: only houses and a convenience store, a gas station, a Tim Hortons, a hardware store. At the only stoplight, county road 26 intersects 24, 59, and Maria Street. Beyond the light, residential streets cross CR 26, but one or two blocks down the houses give way again to corn and soybean fields.

Dialogue brings people to life.

In the cramped waiting room of Xiaolan Zhao's Toronto clinic, boxes of herbs vie for space with stacks of old-fashioned file folders. Nothing is high-tech here. Patients sit on mismatched, straight-backed chairs waiting for acupuncture or massage. . . . After a brief consultation with Xiaolan . . . she had a close look at my puffy kneecap. "Have you ever had acupuncture?" she asked. "No, but one of my horses did," I said. "Ahh, you take better care of your animals than you do yourself." Bingo. In one treatment, my knee was better. "One hundred per cent!" I enthused. "No," Xiaolan said patiently, "80 percent."

—Barbara Righton, "Healer to the Stars," *Maclean's*, 9 Jan. 2006: 36.

Humour rewards readers and can make points memorable.

Large, naked, raw carrots are acceptable as food only to those who live in hutches eagerly awaiting Easter.

Inhabitants of underdeveloped nations and victims of natural disasters are the only people who have ever been happy to see soybeans.

—Fran Lebowitz, *Metropolitan Life*

Interest in Visual Texts

Interest in visual texts is created by composition and subject matter. Some subjects possess inherent interest, but the photographer or artist must build on that interest. Kittens and puppies are cute, but viewers' interest fades quickly if the images are predictable.

Even potentially interesting subjects can be rendered boring if they are photographed in stereotypical ways.

Children often express a spontaneity lacking in adults, which provides visual interest.

Lines

Lines create interest in photographs. Strong diagonal lines can create dynamic photographs. Curved lines can produce graceful images.

2c WHERE IMAGES AND GRAPHICS WORK BEST

"A picture is worth a thousand words" is an old cliché. We could just as easily turn around the cliché to say that certain words such as *justice, truth,* and *faith* are worth a thousand pictures. It's not that images are necessarily more powerful than words but that images and words are different media. Our eyes and brains are able to take in a great deal of visual information and sort that information for relevance. People have little difficulty distinguishing familiar faces in a crowd or recognizing familiar patterns.

For example, we've now become accustomed to deciding whether we'll need to wear a sweater outdoors tomorrow by looking at the colours on a weather map. But even then, we depend on words to tell us whether the forecast is for today or tomorrow, and what each colour signifies. Visuals are typically used in combination with text. Visuals work well when they

- Deliver spatial information, especially about spatial relationships
- Represent statistical relationships
- Produce a strong immediate impact, even shock value
- Emphasize further a main point you've made in words

2d WHERE WORDS WORK BEST

Words can do many things that images cannot. Written words work best when they

- Communicate abstract ideas
- Record information
- Report information
- Persuade using elaborated reasoning
- Communicate online using minimal bandwidth
- Adapt to specific users' needs (Words can be converted from oral to written language for those who are hearing impaired, or from written to oral for those who are visually impaired.)

If you've ever visited a website that opens with a glitzy Flash screen that takes forever to load and then discovered there was no significant content behind the opening screen, you know the problem of style without substance. While more of our communication in the digital era will take advantage of the multimedia capabilities of new technologies, these technologies will not replace the need for effective writing.

PART TWO

Planning, Drafting, and Revising

- What kind of paper am I expected to write? (3a)

- How can I come up with ideas for my paper? (3b)

- What's the best way to write an effective thesis? (3c)

- How do I create strong transitions between my ideas? (4e)

- What do I look for when I start revising my draft? (5b)

3 Planning and Drafting

4 Composing Paragraphs

5 Rewriting, Editing, and Proofreading

2 PLANNING, DRAFTING, AND REVISING

Good writers begin by asking questions: Who will read what I write? What am I trying to accomplish? How will my readers respond to what I write? Such experienced writers also understand the value of drafting and then rewriting rather than trying to get everything exactly right in one try.

Writing in the World Project

Writing an Editorial to Your Local Newspaper

Read 5 to 10 editorials that have been posted on the web or in print. Visit two or three of these sites, or read some local and national newspapers.

- www.canadianculture.com/Canadian_editorials.html
- www.mapleleafweb.com
- www.canada.com/nationalpost/news/editorialsletters/index.html
- www.theglobeandmail.com/opinions/editorials

Identify common features of these editorials: How long are they? What kinds of evidence are used to support the writer's arguments? What kinds of topics do they cover? What types of sources do they use?

Here is a brief analysis of an editorial:

- A summary of the topic, putting the issue in context
- Statement of a thesis or argumentative position
- Evidence offered to support position, including examples, statistics, and qualifiers
- A conclusion that restates the original thesis

Once you've identified the kinds of evidence and arguments that your sample of editorials contains, write one yourself, taking a position on an issue that is important on your campus or in your community.

Visit *The Brief Penguin Handbook* Companion Website at
www.pearsoned.ca/faigley/

MyCanadianCompLab
Where writing and research help is a click away.
MyCanadianCompLab may be packaged with your textbook.
If not, it can be purchased from your college or university's bookstore.
Go to **www.pearsoned.ca/highered/mycanadiancomplab/**
for a tour.

CHAPTER 3

Planning and Drafting

Good architects begin by asking who will use a building and what they will use it for. Good writers ask similar questions: Who is likely to read what I write? Why should they be interested in reading what I have to say? What am I trying to accomplish? How do I anticipate that readers will be influenced by what I write? Will they know something they didn't know before? Will they think about something familiar in a different way or at least acknowledge that other viewpoints exist? Will they consider taking some action based on what I have written?

Even if you are writing a diary only for yourself, you still ask these questions in some form. If, for example, you are writing a journal during a trip, you might record where exactly you went, how long it took to get there, and how much money you spent. Or you might concentrate on describing in detail what you saw and whom you met. Or you might focus on your reactions to particular places and people. Thinking about how people will use a building guides a successful architect in drawing blueprints and in supervising construction. Thinking about how you want readers to respond helps you make a global plan about what to write and helps you carry out that plan, revising it when necessary.

3a ESTABLISH YOUR GOALS

When you are writing for post-secondary classes, your instructor is generally your primary audience and your goal is to convince the instructor that you are an effective writer. Nevertheless, your instructor is aware that the goal of your course is to prepare you for other kinds of writing you will do in higher education and later in life. Likely you will be asked to think about audiences besides your instructor, including members of your class, your school community, and others beyond the campus.

Your instructor will give you specific suggestions about how to think about your audience and topic. Two ways to make your task simpler are:

- Be sure you are responding to the assignment appropriately
- Select a topic that both fits the assignment and appeals to you enough to make you want to write about it

Look carefully at your assignment

When your instructor gives you a writing assignment, look closely at what you are asked to do. Often the assignment will contain keywords such as *analyze, compare and contrast, define, describe, evaluate,* or *propose* that will assist you in determining what direction to take.

- **Analyze:** Find connections among a set of facts, events, or readings, and make them meaningful.
- **Compare and contrast:** Examine how two or more things are alike and how they differ.
- **Define:** Make a claim about how something should be defined, according to features that you set out.
- **Describe:** Observe carefully and select details that create a dominant impression.
- **Evaluate:** Argue that something is good, bad, best, or worst in its class, according to criteria that you set out.
- **Propose:** Identify a particular problem and explain why your solution is the best one.

A specific audience might be mentioned in the assignment. If you are writing for a specific audience, what will those readers know about your topic? What attitudes are they likely to have about your topic? If you are still unclear about what the assignment calls for, talk with your instructor.

Find a topic you care about

If you do not have an assigned topic, a good way to find one is to look first at the materials for your course. You may find something that interests you in the readings for the course or in a topic that came up in class discussion. It's hard to write about something that doesn't engage you, so start by writing down things that do. If your assignment gives you a wide range of options, you might write more than one list, starting with your personal interests. Think also about campus topics, community topics, and national topics that intrigue you. Your lists might resemble these:

Personal

1. Benefits of weight training
2. Wit and humour in Mike Myers movies
3. History of hairstyles

Campus

1. Pros and cons of charging computer fees
2. Should food services provide more alternatives for students with food allergies?
3. Should my school require a program-related internship?

Community
1. Fundraising for community food banks
2. ESL education and literacy programs
3. More bike lanes to encourage more people to ride bicycles
4. Shortage of doctors in the community

Nation/World
1. Funding and training of Canadian athletes
2. Separatism in Quebec and the West
3. Private vs. public healthcare clinics
4. Pollution caused by fish farms

Often you will find that, before you can begin writing, you need to analyze exactly what you mean by a phrase like "private healthcare clinics." For example, do you mean patients pay cash out of pocket, or the government pays the owners of the clinic based on the patients they have treated?

- Put a checkmark beside the topics that look most interesting or the ones that mean the most to you.
- Put a question mark beside the topics that you don't know very much about. If you choose one of these issues, you will have to do research.
- Select two or three topics that look the most promising.

3b EXPLORE YOUR TOPIC

Once you have identified a potential topic, the next step is to determine what you already know about that topic and what you need to find out. Experienced writers use many strategies for exploring their knowledge of a topic and how interesting it really is to them. Here are a few.

Ask questions

These classic reporter's questions will assist you in thinking through a topic:

1. *Who* is doing it?

2. *What* is happening or at issue?

3. *When* is it happening?

4. *Where* is it happening?

5. *How* is it happening?

6. *Why* is it happening?

Freewrite

Another method you can use to find out how much you know about a topic is to **freewrite**: Write as quickly as you can without stopping for a set time, usually five or ten minutes. The goal of freewriting is to get as much down as possible. Don't stop to correct mistakes. Let your ideas flow wherever they take you, even if they take you well outside the boundaries of your topic. The constant flow of words should generate ideas—some useful, some not.

If you get stuck, write the same sentence over again, or write about how hungry you are, or how difficult freewriting is, until thoughts on your selected topic reappear. After you've finished, read what you have written and single out any key ideas.

Freewrite on problem bears

Didn't know there was a problem until my uncle was telling us about a black bear that ripped their screen door off the hinges and came into the kitchen to check out what was for dinner. Bear made off with several things from the fridge, which it ate out in the yard. Over the summer read several news articles on hikers and bears. Woman killed by a black bear near Algonquin Park in Ontario. Further north, arctic communities having problems with polar bears coming into town. Polar ice is melting and their hunting range is shrinking. Solutions I've seen: educate hikers/campers about carrying food and storing it properly, shoot and kill bears that are nuisance, trap and transport them hundreds of kilometres away further north.

Ideas to Use

1. *Human casualties from bear encounters.*
2. *Killing bears is an extreme solution.*
3. *Bears are a problem in many parts of the country.*

You may want to use a keyword or idea as a starting point for a second freewrite. After two or three rounds you will discover how much you already know about your topic and possible directions for developing it.

Brainstorm

An alternative method of discovery is to **brainstorm**. The end result of brainstorming is usually a list—sometimes of questions, sometimes of statements. You might come up with a list of observations and questions, such as these for bear encounters:

- Bears make hiking and camping unsafe.
- Where did tame bears come from all of a sudden?
- How can bears be discouraged?
- What are local governments doing to control bear populations?
- How widespread is the problem?

Use subject directories

Online subject directories such as Yahoo divide big subjects into subtopics. They can help you narrow the focus of a subject down to a topic that is manageable (see Section 16c). Likewise, your library's online resources often divide big subjects into more manageable segments. For example, if you type "genome" in a subject search in your library's online catalogue, you will get several more specific subtopics. (See Figure 3.1.)

SUBJECT INDEX Search Results

(Records 1 - 10) For Brief Records, click on number.

YOUR SEARCH: GENOME has no exact match. The next entry is:

1 Genome mapping. --1 item(s)

2 Genomes --20 item(s)

3 Genomes--Computer programs. --1 item(s)

4 Genomes--Congresses. --7 item(s)

5 Genomes--Data processing. --4 item(s)

6 Genomes--Data processing--Congresses. --1 item(s)

7 Genomes--Data processing--Periodicals. --2 item(s)

8 Genomes--Nomenclature--Congresses. --1 item(s)

9 Genomes--Periodicals. --5 item(s)

10 Genomes--Research--International cooperation. --2 item(s)

FIGURE 3.1 A subject search for "genome" in a library's online catalogue generates a list of subtopics that may point to a more manageable, specific topic.

Make an idea map

Still another strategy for exploring how much you know about a potential topic is to make an **idea map**. Idea maps are useful because they let you see everything at once, and you can begin to make connections among the different aspects of an issue—definitions, causes, effects, proposed solutions, and your personal experience. A good way to get started is to write down ideas on sticky notes. Then you can move the sticky notes around until you figure out which ideas fit together.

Let's go back to the topic of problem bears. If you decided to write on this topic, you would need to find out more. Since the topic is quite current, newspaper sources are important. Your library has tools that can help you to find recent articles in newspapers from around the country. Figure 3.2 shows what your idea map on bear encounters might look like.

Make a storyboard

Filmmakers, multimedia designers, and web designers all use storyboarding as a primary tool for planning. Storyboards are a series of rough sketches of successive screen contents (see Figure 3.3). In film, video, and animation,

Reasons for attack
- Bears feel threatened (e.g., mothers & cubs).
- Adolescent male bears making trouble
- Bears are hungry and need food.
- Bears are used to humans and know easy food sources available around humans (i.e., garbage, food supplies).

Extent of problem
- 800 000 black bears in North America
- 60 000 brown bears
- number of attacks and nuisance incidents increasing each year
- Stephen Herrero, bear environmentalist at U of Calgary, estimates, "Bears kill three people and seriously injure five to fifteen a year in North America."

The problem
- Campers and hikers mainly affected by bear attacks
- Also residents living in bear territories
- Bear attractions around residences

Bear encounters

Solutions
- Educate residents on how to bear-proof their property.
- Educate campers and hikers on how to avoid bears and how to repel an attack.
- Trap and transport troublesome bears hundreds of kms away from communities.
- Shoot and kill human-hunting bears.

Experts' view
- Nothing unusual in these attacks
- Bear business as usual
- Marc Gibeau, Parks Canada bear specialist, says, "When you're in bear country, you should always be aware."

Safety advice if you meet a bear
- Avoid bear if possible.
- Convince bear you aren't a threat by backing away; don't run.
- Former wisdom said to play dead, but now experts say if you play dead, you will end up dead.
- Pepper spray, sprayed directly into the bear's face, increases your chances of survival to 75%; then get away from the area while the bear is still stunned.
- Gun is best defence: aim for heart to kill. Wounded bear even more dangerous

How to avoid bears
- Avoid back country during spring when bear activity is at its height.
- Residents: secure garbage in bear-proof containers.
- Don't leave food outside.
- Don't let pets roam: supervise dog when outside to do its business.
- Clean barbecue after each use.
- Clean up windfall fruit and garden harvest promptly and regularly.

FIGURE 3.2   Idea map on bear problems

the sketches represent the script, something like a comic book without speech bubbles. Storyboards for websites also include the links that are required from one page to others.

Read about your topic and take notes

Most of the writing you do in post-secondary education will be linked to texts you are reading. Find time to read about your topic before writing about it. Even if you know quite a bit about your topic, it's always worthwhile to

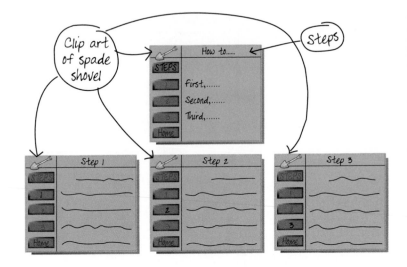

Sketch for part of a
gardening website

FIGURE 3.3 Web designers use storyboards to envision how the content will be placed on different pages and how the pages will be linked.

explore what has been written about it. Reading will often give you ideas on where to begin writing and will help you to think of ways of developing your ideas. Chapters 17 and 18 give you ways of finding material about your topic.

What you focus on when you annotate and take notes depends on your purpose in reading. Sometimes you will want to annotate in a general way; it is always useful to highlight key points and write keywords and phrases in the margins when you read. At other times, when you are reading after you have formulated a **thesis**, or main idea, your notes will be more specific.

"Talking" to a text by writing questions and comments about it will help you feel at home with it. What would you say to the author if he or she were on the other side of the table from you? Writing down responses to a reading can bring that text to life. It can also help you realize that the author is, like you, a person with a point of view.

Keep a journal

Freewriting and idea mapping can help you to discover what you know about a topic at a given time. Keeping a journal, by contrast, allows you to keep a record of ideas you come up with over time, perhaps even over many years. Whether its lifespan is long or short, a journal gives you a chance to see how your ideas grow and shift. A journal can be a sourcebook for essay ideas. Or it can be written simply for its own sake—for the satisfaction of recording your experiences and observations, and exploring your thoughts. Your teacher may ask for a particular type of journal, but even if the topic or kind of writing is assigned, usually you have more freedom in a journal to try out ideas or writing styles. Be bold and experiment.

Talk and listen

Writing requires concentration, which for many people depends on quiet and solitude. Nevertheless, many ideas come from conversation, and all ideas are born from other ideas. When we talk and listen, we discover. Productive writers are engaged in a community where ideas are discussed. Your writing class is a writing community. To make the community as useful as possible, it is important to ask your peers for specific and genuine feedback on your drafts and to pay close attention to your classmates' writing as well.

If any of your class communication is done through email or online discussion, you will already have a head start on your assigned writing. Emails and online discussions can be used the way journals and freewrites are—as material for essays. When you are planning your essay, you may find that you already have a wealth of written material to draw from.

You can get one-on-one help in developing your ideas, focusing your topic, and revising your paper at your writing centre.

3c WRITE A WORKING THESIS

The initial stage of the planning process involves finding ideas, expanding and broadening your thoughts, and recording ideas from written sources and conversations. The next stage of thinking, after you have decided on a topic, is *narrowing* your focus to a specific topic. Having a specific focus is the key to writing a strong essay.

Use questions to focus a broad topic

Childhood obesity is certainly a current and interesting research topic, but it is too broad. Ask questions that will break the big topic into smaller topics.

- Why are children becoming obese?
- Why are children today more obese than children of past generations?
- How has the food industry contributed to childhood obesity?
- What changes in Canadian culture have contributed to childhood obesity?
- What are the adverse health effects of childhood obesity?
- What strategies are effective for preventing childhood obesity?

Consider other angles to expand a narrow topic

Too-narrow topics are rarer than topics that are too broad. Although candy consumption is certainly one factor contributing to obesity in children, this narrow focus overlooks many other factors that together lead to childhood obesity. For instance:

- Why do some children eat large amounts of candy yet maintain a healthy weight?
- Children have always eaten candy. Why are children today more obese than children of past generations?
- Even when parents keep kids away from candy, some still gain weight. Why?

If you cannot seem to find enough information on your topic to construct an argument, your topic might be too narrow.

Turn your topic into a thesis statement

Your thesis states your main idea. Much of the writing that you will do in higher education and later in your career will have an explicit thesis, usually stated near the beginning. The thesis announces your topic and indicates what points you want to make about that topic.

Your thesis should be closely tied to your purpose—to reflect on your own experience, to explain some aspect of your topic, or to argue for a position or course of action.

A REFLECTIVE THESIS	My experiences of watching wildlife over a long time have taught me that they spend much of their time competing with other members of their own species for territory and food.
AN INFORMATIVE THESIS	The spread of the suburbs has created new habitats for wild animals that can adapt to living near people, such as coyotes and bears.

A PERSUASIVE THESIS	Anyone camping or hiking in the Canadian wilderness should regularly review safety information about encountering bears and carry equipment to help repel an attack.

Evaluate your working thesis

Ask yourself these questions about your working thesis.

1. Is it specific?
2. Is it manageable in the length and time you have?
3. Is it interesting to your intended readers?

Consider the following examples.

EXAMPLE 1

The Canadian cod fishing industry collapsed in 1990 because of over-fishing.

Specific? The thesis is too narrow. It states a commonly acknowledged fact.

Manageable? A known fact is stated in the thesis, so there is nothing to research. The general topic of overfishing is too complicated for essay-length treatment.

Interesting? The decline of cod stocks on the Grand Banks is interesting to Atlantic fishermen, but Canadians living inland would need an angle that is appealing.

REVISED THESIS

The Department of Fisheries and Oceans must ban dragger nets as soon as possible before all Canadian fishing stocks are depleted.

EXAMPLE 2

People who live and vacation in the Canadian wilderness must learn how to protect themselves from dangerous wildlife to minimize their chances of being attacked.

Specific? The thesis is too broad. How are we defining "dangerous wildlife"? Is the wolverine something we should protect ourselves against? Elk?

Manageable? Because the thesis is not limited to a particular species of dangerous animal, it cannot be researched adequately.

Interesting? The topic is potentially interesting, but most people know that wildlife can be dangerous. If you chose this topic, what could you tell your readers that they don't know already?

Persuasive? This thesis leans a bit too far toward being an informative rather than a persuasive thesis. Make sure you take a clear stand on the issue.

REVISED THESIS

When we kill bears as a solution to bear–human encounters, we are addressing the symptom rather than the cause of the problem: the solution starts much earlier when we educate people who vacation or live in Canada's wilderness areas about how to remove a bear's desire to interact with humans.

These examples suggest that the key to writing an effective thesis is finding a topic that is neither too vast nor too narrow, and one that is not obvious. You may have to adjust your working thesis more than once as you plan and begin drafting.

3d   PLAN A STRATEGY

People who write frequently on the job or who make their living by writing have many different ways of producing a successful piece of writing. Some may plan extensively in advance, either individually or as a team, specifying exactly what will go in each section. **Advance planners** don't start writing until they know what will go into each part. They believe that detailed planning cuts down on the need for rewriting.

Other writers find that putting ideas into words often changes the ideas and generates new ones. These writers know that writing drafts is a way of discovering their subject, and they count on one or two or more rewrites to get their document into shape. **Deep revisers** trust that the structure of what they write will evolve during the process of writing, and they realize that they can make major changes if necessary. No matter what their style of composing, successful writers are aware of what they will need to do to complete a writing task, and they have strategies for when they get stuck or encounter the unexpected. Even more important, they have a good sense of the writing situation. (See Chapter 1.)

Consider making an outline

At some point in school you may have been required to produce a formal outline to submit along with a paper. A **formal outline** typically begins with the thesis statement, which anchors the entire outline. Each numbered or lettered item clearly supports the thesis, and the relationship among the items is clear from the outline hierarchy.

Thesis statement: When we kill bears as a solution to bear–human encounters, we are addressing the symptom rather than the cause of the problem: the solution starts much earlier when we educate people who vacation or live in Canada's wilderness areas about how to remove a bear's desire to interact with humans.

I. Bear–human encounters increase every year, resulting in more serious attacks.
 A. 800 000 black bears in North America, 60 000 brown bears (including grizzlies).
 B. Stephen Herrero, "bears kill three people and seriously injure 5 to 15 a year in North America."
 C. Nothing unusual in these attacks, according to Marc Gibeau, "When you're in bear country, you should always be aware."
II. People unfamiliar with bears can unwittingly trigger attack.
 A. Invading bear's personal space can make it feel threatened (e.g., mothers and cubs).
 B. In early May adolescent male bears can be troublemakers.
 C. Food-conditioned bears approach humans hoping to scavenge their food.

Consider using a working outline

A working outline is more like an initial sketch of how you will arrange the major sections. Jotting down main points and a few subpoints before you begin can be a great help while you are writing. If you have made an idea map (see Figure 3.2), you can easily work from the map to produce a working outline. You can read the complete essay that developed from these outlines in Section 9d.

How to avoid bear encounters

Section 1: Begin with friend's experience with the bear that tore out the car window to get at the sandwiches her mother was making during childhood camping trip in Banff National Park.

Section 2: Talk about food conditioning as a motivator for human-bear encounters.

Section 3: Explain current responses to problem bears (shoot and kill; trap and transport; etc.).

Section 4: Examine better solutions: study bear behaviour to better understand their psychology; educate humans (hikers, campers, residents) to reduce risk of encounters.

Section 5: Explain how a publicity campaign would inform newcomers and motivate established residents to bear-proof their property to avoid attracting bears into the city.

Section 6: Support making information on bear safety more readily available at tourist centres across Canada in areas that bears inhabit.

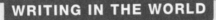

WRITING IN THE WORLD

Discipline-specific organization

Pay attention to writing conventions when you move from one discipline to another. The expectations for writing in your biology class or in your psychology class are not the same as those in your English class. Disciplines in the social sciences, sciences, and engineering typically specify the organization you should follow for particular kinds of writing. At first, you may think such writing is too rigid, but the creativity comes in the questions that you explore and the results that you discover. Coming up with a structure for your paper is not the challenge.

A lab report in the sciences and engineering typically will have the following organization with these distinct parts:

- Abstract (gives a summary of the report)
- Introduction (gives the purpose and background of the experiment)
- Methods and Materials (refers to the lab manual used)
- Procedure (describes what was actually done in the experiment)
- Results (states results in both sentence and graphic form)
- Discussion (includes an analysis of what can be explained from the results)
- Conclusion (states what is known from the experiment)

If you are unfamiliar with how writing is organized in different disciplines, ask your instructor to recommend examples for you to use as possible models.

3e COMPOSE A DRAFT

A common misconception about successful writers is that they write a finished piece in one sitting without having to go back and change anything. Nothing is further from the truth. The best writers know that nobody gets everything right the first time. They know that the most efficient way of writing is not to become obsessed with getting everything in final form as you are writing. They aim at producing a good draft—not a perfect draft. They know that they can go back and revise later.

Essays typically contain an introduction, body, and conclusion. You do not have to write these parts in that order, though. In your **introduction**, you can offer a short example that illustrates the problem being discussed. You can state a surprising fact. You can begin with a fascinating quotation.

Your aim is to interest the reader and to let the reader know the topic of the paper, if not necessarily the thesis.

The **body** of the essay consists of the primary discussion. Remember to guide readers through the discussion by letting them know where you are going. If your discussion is a road, your readers need road signs to tell them where the road is taking them. Road signs are transition words and phrases such as "consequently," "the third reason is . . . ," and "on the other hand."

The last section, the **conclusion**, often repeats what has already been said. If the essay has been long and complex, sometimes this repetition is necessary, but usually the repetition is just that—annoying redundancy. The final paragraph does not have to repeat the main point. It can give a compelling last example or propose a course of action. It can ponder the larger significance of the subject under discussion. It can pose an important question for the reader to think about.

Use drafting strategies to overcome writer's block

1. **If you have an outline, put it on the computer screen or place it beside you.** The outline will give you prompts to help get you started.
2. **Begin writing what you know best.** If you don't know exactly where you are headed, the introduction can be the hardest section to write. The introduction can wait until last.
3. **Resist the urge to revise too soon.** It's more important to keep moving forward. If you stop to polish a section, you will lose momentum, and in the end you may discard that section anyway.
4. **If you get stuck, try working on another section.** Look again at your notes or outline.
5. **If you are still stuck, talk to someone about what you are trying to write.** If your campus has a writing centre, talk to a consultant. Reading more about your subject can also help you to get moving again.

3f WRITE AS A MEMBER OF A TEAM

Almost without exception people in occupations that require post-secondary education write frequently on the job, and much of that writing is done in collaboration rather than alone. The better you understand how to write effectively with other people, the more enjoyable and more productive the process will be for you.

You can become a member of a successful writing team by understanding how a team works effectively.

Determine the goals and identify tasks and roles.

- Write down the goals as specifically as you can and discuss them as a team.
- Determine what tasks are required to meet those goals. Be as specific as you can. Write down the tasks and arrange them in the order they need to be completed.
- Decide whether the team has the skills and resources to perform those tasks. If you do not possess the necessary skills and resources, adjust the goals to what you can realistically expect to accomplish.

Make a work plan.

- Make a timeline that lists the dates when specific tasks need to be completed and distribute it to all team members. Charts are useful tools for keeping track of progress.
- Assign tasks to team members. Find out if anyone possesses additional skills that could be helpful to the team.
- Revisit the team's goals often. To succeed, each team member must keep in mind what the team aims to accomplish.
- Decide on a process for monitoring progress. Set up specific dates for review and assign team members to be responsible for reviewing work that has been done.

Understand the dynamics of a successful team.

- Teamwork requires some flexibility. Different people have different styles and contribute in different ways. Keep talking to each other along the way.
- It may be desirable to rotate roles during the project.

Deal with problems when they come up.

- If a team member is not participating, find out why.
- If team members have different ideas about what needs to be done, find time to meet so that the team can reach an agreement.
- Get the team together if you are not meeting the deadlines you established in the work plan and devise a new plan, if necessary.

Have realistic expectations about the pluses and minuses of working as a group.

- The major benefit of working in a group is that you can potentially accomplish a great deal more than you could by working alone. Participating as a team member can be personally rewarding.

- Working in groups can have disadvantages. Groups can require more time because people bring different perspectives that need to be discussed. Two perennial problems with groups are maintaining focus on clearly articulated goals and handling team members who aren't doing their share.

3g STAY ORGANIZED

If you work on paper, use file folders for your notes, freewrites, drafts, and research. If you work on a computer, label your files and put them in a folder. Develop a system for naming your files of drafts, so you will know which is the most recent (one way is to put a date in the file name). If you decide to cut a section out of a draft, make a new file and save it with a file name such as "assignment1-extra." Or make a folder and label it "assignment1-old" and put the earlier versions in it. You may change your mind later and decide you want to use what you have set aside.

CHAPTER 4

Composing Paragraphs

The word *paragraph* derives from a symbol (¶) that was used in medieval manuscripts and later in print to indicate a small shift in topic. It took centuries for the notion of a paragraph to evolve into its modern form—a short block of text set off by indentation or space, with all sentences connected in some way to a single topic.

You may have heard a paragraph defined as a unit of thought, but that definition is incomplete. A paragraph is also a device to help readers. If you have ever picked up a book by a classic writer of the nineteenth century (for example, Charles Darwin), you likely found paragraphs that ran on for pages. Most readers today cringe at the sight of paragraphs that fill entire pages, and, as a result, paragraphs have become shorter over the past hundred years. Most important, readers expect that the sequence of paragraphs will set out a line of thought that they can follow.

4a FOCUS YOUR PARAGRAPHS

Readers expect sentences in a paragraph to be closely related to one another. Often writers will begin a paragraph with one idea, but other ideas will occur to them while they are writing. Paragraphs confuse readers when they go in different directions. When you revise your paragraphs, check for focus.

In the following example, notice how much stronger the paragraph becomes when we remove the sentences in green. They distract us from the subject, Royal Chitwan National Park in Nepal and how it is different from Western national parks.

> Like everything else in Nepal, Royal Chitwan National Park is different from Western notions of a park. It is a jungle between two rivers, with grass twenty to twenty-five feet tall growing in the swampy land along the rivers. Several rare or endangered species live in the park, including leopards, crocodiles, royal Bengal tigers, and the greater one-horned Asian rhinoceros. **In fact, we saw several rhinos during our weeklong visit to the park. To my relief we saw all but one from the safety of an elephant's back.** But the boundaries of the park restrict neither the Nepalis nor the animals. The Nepalis cross the river into the park to gather firewood and the tall grass, which they use to make their houses. Some even live within the park. The rhinos and deer raid the Nepalis' fields at night, and the leopards prey on their dogs and livestock. To keep the truce between these competitors, the army patrols the park, mostly to prevent poachers from killing the tigers and rhino. But confrontations do occur; the animals lose habitat and the Nepalis lose their crops and lives.

When to use explicit topic sentences

You were probably taught to begin a paragraph with a topic sentence. Topic sentences alert readers to the focus of a paragraph and help writers stay on topic. Topic sentences should explain the focus of the paragraph and situate it in the larger argument. However, topic sentences do not have to begin paragraphs, and they need not be just one sentence. You will decide what placement and length will best suit your subject.

Topic sentences at the beginning of a paragraph will quickly orient readers, preparing them for the sentences to come. Each sentence that follows elucidates the topic sentence.

TOPIC SENTENCE AT THE BEGINNING

We live in a world of risks so much beyond our control that it is difficult to think of anything that is risk free. Even the most basic human acts involve risk—having sex in an era of AIDS, eating in an era of genetically altered food, walking outdoors in an ozone-depleted atmosphere, drinking water and breathing air laden with chemicals whose effects we do not understand. Should we eat more fish in our daily diet? Nutritionists tell us that eating fish reduces the risk of heart disease. Other scientists, however, tell us that fish are contaminated with a new generation of synthetic chemicals.

When a paragraph builds to make a particular point, the topic sentence is more effective at the end of the paragraph.

TOPIC SENTENCE AT THE END

We are continually being summoned to change ourselves for the better—through fitness programs, through various kinds of instruction, through advice columns, through self-help books and videos—and somehow we never quite measure up. The blame always comes back on us. If we had eaten better, or exercised more, or paid more attention to our investments, or learned a new skill, or changed our oil every 5000 kilometres, then things would have turned out better. Very rarely do we ask how a different social organization might have made things better. **Our society incorporates critical thinking without being much affected by the consequences of that thinking.**

When to use implicit topic sentences

In some cases, particularly in narrative prose, writers omit explicit topic sentences because they would clash with the tone or style of the paragraph. Instead, these paragraphs use tightly connected, focused sentences to make the topic implicitly clear.

IMPLICIT TOPIC SENTENCE

By the mid-1970s in the United States, the temporary advantage of being the only major power with its industries undamaged following World War II had evaporated, and rust-belt industries failed one after the other against competition from a revived Europe and an emergent Asia. The United States seemed to be going the way of other historical world powers, where efficient trading nations beat out bloated military regimes. Japan appeared to be the model for a fast and light capitalism that the rest of the world would imitate. Just a few years later, however, the American decline reversed. The United States again became the economic leader of the world in the 1990s.

The implicit topic sentence is something like "The United States' economy appeared to be in rapid decline in the 1970s, only to bounce back to world leadership in the 1990s."

Description

Description is a common strategy for informative and narrative writing. Providing concrete details—sights, sounds, smells, textures, and tastes—gives the reader a sensory memory of your subject.

Topic sentence

Details convey a dominant impression.

> The airport at Kathmandu resembles one-gate airports in Canada, with a small waiting room and baggage area, except that it is deluged with international tourists. Busloads of young people lug bright nylon rucksacks and duffle bags emblazoned with names like "Australian Wilderness Adventures" and "South Korean Dhaulagiri Winter Expedition." Mingled with them are traders from India and Nepal—some dressed in suits, some in peasant clothes—carrying bulky goods like folding chairs, drums of cooking oil, and boxes of medicine.

This descriptive paragraph relies on a comparison to a place Canadian readers will probably recognize.

As in descriptive writing, in photographs close attention to detail is essential.

The example paragraphs about Nepal are adapted from Lester Faigley, "Nepal Diary: Where the Global Village Ends," *North Dakota Quarterly* 57.3 (1989): 106–29.

Narration or Process

Narrative paragraphs tell a story for a reason. Organized by time, narratives relate a series of events in the order they occur. This approach is useful when the temporal order of ideas or events is essential to their logic, such as in how-to writing.

The ascent goes easier than they expected. In two hours they reach the yak pastures where they will make the high camp. The view from the high camp is spectacular, with Dhaulagiri in clouds above them and the three sunlit summits of Nilgiri across the valley, with snow plumes blowing from their tops. Jim and Lester drop their packs at the campsite and continue walking to scout the route above the camp that they will follow in the darkness of early morning the next day. They find a steep path that parallels a fern-lined gorge, now rich in fall colour. It is the lushest forest they have seen in Nepal. They congratulate each other on their decision to attempt the climb to the Dhaulagiri icefall, unaware that they will soon experience the mountain's furious weather, even on its lower slopes.

Verbs establish the sequence of events to orient the reader in time.

Narrative paragraphs often include description to orient the reader in space.

Comparison and Contrast

Paragraphs of comparison assess one subject in terms of its relation to others, usually highlighting what they have in common. Contrasting paragraphs analyze differences between things.

You can organize a comparison or a contrast in two ways: by describing one thing and then describing another, or by moving back and forth between the two items point by point. Often the latter strategy highlights contrasts, as the following paragraph illustrates.

Nepal was closed to Europeans from 1843 to 1949 and missed the colonial influences of the British. Consequently, Kathmandu remains a medieval city at heart, with a thin overlay of the last two decades of trendy Western culture: Tibetan women dressed in traditional clothes weave rugs on antique looms while humming Sting tunes; a traffic jam on Kathmandu's only wide street is caused by bulls fighting in an intersection; restaurants play U2 and serve tough buffalo steak under the name *chateaubriand*; coffee houses serve cappuccino across the street from women drying rice by lifting it into the air with hoes; nearly naked children wearing burlap sacks grab cake slices out of the hands of gawking tourists emerging from a Viennese pastry shop.

Establishes the terms of the comparison.

Each phrase shows the medieval "heart" and the "thin overlay" of Western culture.

This comparison/contrast also uses a cause/effect pattern to help organize it. The word *consequently* in the third line is the transition from the cause to the effect.

Definition

Much writing in post-secondary education depends on establishing the definitions of key terms. Consequently, writers often use entire paragraphs for definitions. Paragraphs organized by definition usually begin with the term and then go on to list its distinguishing features, sometimes using examples. Writers may begin with a standard definition and then qualify or add to that definition in unexpected ways.

Definitions are critical to persuasive writing. If your audience accepts your definitions of key terms, usually you will be convincing.

Tranquility in Western countries is usually equated with getting away from it all. Its synonyms are *calmness, serenity,* and *peace of mind,* and no wonder: We live in a world where it is increasingly difficult to get completely away from human-produced noise. In the Hindu and Buddhist traditions, however, tranquility is thought of as an internal quality that is gained when a person no longer is controlled by worldly desires. While this definition of tranquility may seem foreign to us, the internal state of tranquility is evident when you are in the presence of someone who possesses it.

Usual definition

Extended definition adds a new dimension.

Examples and Illustrations

If you want to prove a point or bring an issue to life, an organization based on examples and illustrations may work well. This structure usually begins with the main idea or point, and then moves to a vivid explanation of one or two examples that illustrate the main idea. Examples and illustrations also can work well in opening and concluding paragraphs.

Point

Illustration

> When religious principles clash with practical realities, ingenuity often comes to the rescue. Upon entering Braga, a Buddhist village built into a cliffside high in the Himalayas, Jim and Lester noticed that the men of the village surrounded two yaks, wrestled them to the ground, and tied their feet together. By a stone wall on the side of the field, an old bearded man read from a holy book while the yaks were stabbed in the heart. They lay panting, bleeding little, taking a long time to die. Three young men poured water down the throats of the yaks, while the other men chanted in their Tibetan dialect. As Buddhists, the people of Braga are forbidden to kill animals, yet the environment demands that they eat meat to survive. They resolve the dilemma by helping the animal to assume a higher form when it is reincarnated.

Cause and Effect

Cause-and-effect paragraphs are structured in two basic ways. The paragraph can begin with a cause or causes, then state its effects, or it can begin with an effect, then state its causes. Insightful analysis often requires you to look beyond the obvious to the underlying causes.

The loss of the world's forests affects every country through global warming, decreased biodiversity, and soil erosion, but few suffer its impact more than Nepal. Deforestation in Nepal has led to economic stagnation and further depletion of forest resources. The immediate cause of deforestation is the need for more fuel and more farmland by an increasing population. The loss of trees in Nepal, however, has been accelerated by government policies. During the eighteenth and nineteenth centuries, Nepal taxed both land and labour. Farmers could avoid these high taxes for three years if they converted forests to farmland. Others could pay their taxes in firewood or charcoal. While these taxes were reduced in the twentieth century, the government required farmers to register their land, which encouraged clearing of trees to establish boundaries. Furthermore, the stagnant economy led to families' wanting more children to help in the fields at home and to send abroad to find jobs as another source of income.

Effects

Obvious cause

Underlying cause 1

Underlying cause 2

Underlying cause 3

Classification and Division

Classification and division are valuable strategies for analyzing and explaining a topic. Classifying places items into categories according to their similarities. Dividing takes a single item or concept and breaks it down into its component parts.

Category

Characteristics of specific category

Classifying

Nepal is classified as one of the poorest and least developed countries in the world. The average annual income of $220 a year places Nepal alongside the poorest nations in Africa. Only 27% of the population is literate, and over 40% of the population lives below the poverty line. The infant death rate of 76 per 1000 births is one of the highest in the world.

Item

Parts of item

Dividing

Nepal is divided into three distinct regions. In the south is the Terai, the flat river plain of the Ganges, occupying 17% of the country. The central hill region is the largest, containing 64% of the land, including the Kathmandu Valley, the country's urban centre. The rugged Himalaya mountain region in the north is above 4000 metres (13 120 feet) and features 8 of the 10 highest mountains in the world, including the tallest, Mt. Everest at 8850 metres (29 028 feet).

4b ORGANIZE YOUR PARAGRAPHS

Well-organized paragraphs in essays usually follow a pattern similar to that of a well-organized paper, but in miniature. Seven strategies for effectively organizing sentences within a paragraph have been illustrated in the examples on pages 46–52. Remember, the form of the paragraph should follow its function in the paper. Chances are you'll use a combination of these strategies within paragraphs in order to get your point across.

4c MAKE YOUR PARAGRAPHS COHERENT

Your teachers may have told you that your paragraphs should flow. Paragraphs that don't flow make readers struggle to understand how sentences relate to one another, often forcing readers to backtrack. Sentences clash rather than mesh together.

But what exactly does *flow* mean? Writing that flows is coherent. To achieve coherence you must make all the separate parts fit together as a whole. At the level of the paragraph, your task as a writer is first to determine how your sentences fit together. Sometimes you know how your sentences relate to each other as you write them; at other times these relationships become clearer when you are revising. In either case, reiterating key phrases and using transitional terms help writers achieve that elusive quality called flow.

Reiterate key terms and phrases

When you repeat key terms and phrases within paragraphs, your reader will be able to trace major ideas and stay situated in your argument. In the following paragraph, notice that the writer refers back to two central terms, *grass roots activism* and *battleground*. Notice too, that the paragraph isn't repeating itself. Repetition without forward momentum is self-defeating.

> The web has become the primary medium for **grass roots activism**. Among thousands of websites created by individuals are many pages devoted to media criticism and parodies of advertising. **This activism** has come at a time when the internet has become the **battleground** for the deregulated corporate giants. On **this battleground**, control of the coaxial cable and fibre-optic conduits represents only a small part of the potential fortunes to be made from an array of services carried through the pipe.

Signal relationships with transitional terms

Transitional terms act like warning signs for readers, preparing them for whatever is around the bend. Notice how transitions in the following paragraph make it easier to read by preparing you for what is coming.

In spite of all the talk about the internet as cyberspace and a virtual world, the materiality of the internet as a medium is unavoidable. You sit in front of a machine that has to be turned on and connected to the net. And if you want to access the resources of the World Wide Web, you need an internet service provider, a modem, and a computer with enough memory to support the current versions of Netscape or Internet Explorer. In Canada the lines do not go to every neighbourhood, and in the rest of the world almost the entire continent of Africa outside South Africa is not online. At present the internet continues the one-way flow of information from the First to the Third World. Can the internet be a factor in promoting a two-way flow between the margins and the centre?

Transitional terms

Be sure to use transitional terms accurately in order to signal the relationships between your sentences:

- **To enumerate:** again, also, and, as well, finally, furthermore, first, second, third, in addition, last, moreover, next, too
- **To generalize:** commonly, in general, for the most part, on the whole, usually, typically
- **To offer an example:** for example, for instance, indeed, in fact, of course, specifically, such as, the following
- **To situate in time:** after a month, afterward, as long as, as soon as, at the moment, at present, at that time, before, earlier, followed by, in the meantime, in the past, lately, later, meanwhile, now, preceded by, presently, since then, so far, soon, subsequently, suddenly, then, this year, today, until, when, while
- **To situate in space:** above, below, beyond, close to, elsewhere, far from, following, here, near, next to, there
- **To conclude:** as a result, hence, in conclusion, in short, on the whole, therefore, thus
- **To contrast:** although, but, even though, however, in contrast, conversely, in spite of, instead, nevertheless, nonetheless, on the one hand, on the contrary, on the other hand, still, though, yet
- **To compare:** again, also, in the same way, likewise, similarly
- **To signal cause or effect:** as a result, because, consequently, for this reason, hence, if, so, then, therefore, thus
- **To sum up:** as I said, as we have seen, as mentioned earlier, in conclusion, in other words, in short, in sum, therefore, thus
- **To concede a point:** certainly, even though, granted, in fairness, in truth, naturally, of course, to be fair, while it's true

4d CONSIDER PARAGRAPH LENGTH

Paragraph breaks can signal various kinds of shifts:

- A new concept
- The next step in an argument
- The end of the introduction
- The beginning of the conclusion
- A new speaker in dialogue
- A shift in time or place
- A logical pause that gives the reader a breather

What is the ideal length for a paragraph? It depends on what sort of paragraphs you are writing. Business letter writers strive for short paragraphs so their readers can see the essential information at a glance. Fiction writers construct paragraphs of various lengths to produce dramatic effects. For instance, Jack Kerouac's description of staying up all night in a skid row movie theatre goes on for 32 sentences in *On the Road*. But Margaret Atwood includes a five-word paragraph—*Women were not protected then.*—in *The Handmaid's Tale*. Paragraphs in academic essays tend to be about 150 to 200 words long. Academic writers need space to make and support arguments in depth. As a general rule, readers' eyes glaze over when they see paragraphs in an essay that stretch beyond one page. Nevertheless, too many short paragraphs are a sign that the piece lacks either weighty ideas or sufficient development.

WRITING IN THE WORLD

Paragraph length and line length

Newspapers and other documents that use narrow column formats tend to use short paragraphs to increase readability.

Text on websites often has short paragraphs for the same reasons. Except for those who have big-screen, high-resolution monitors, text is generally harder to read on the screen than on paper.

To some extent the length of paragraphs is in proportion to the length of lines.

If the column is extremely narrow—five words or fewer—expect nearly every sentence to be a paragraph.

4e LINK ACROSS PARAGRAPHS

Transitions at the beginnings and ends of paragraphs guide readers. They explain why a paragraph follows from the previous one. They offer writers the opportunity to highlight the turns in their thinking.

Write strong transitions

Thin content is a common source of weak transitions. When writing doesn't progress from paragraph to paragraph, but merely reiterates the same point, transitions have no work to do. Be aware of transitions in your writing. Ask yourself why one main idea leads into the next. What step or shift takes place between paragraphs? How does this step or shift fit into the overall development of the piece? The answers to these questions can become your transition.

The same strategies that make a paragraph coherent will make links between paragraphs coherent. Notice how the repetition of central terms and phrases in the following paragraphs helps the reader track the development of ideas from one paragraph to the next. The first paragraph sets up a dichotomy between "real" families and "virtual" players. The second paragraph redefines the "virtual" players as "real"—flesh-and-blood friends. This redefinition explodes the initial analogy that online gaming is addictive by explaining that gamers participate in a social activity with other real people. The third paragraph reintroduces the addiction analogy by analyzing the nature of the attraction and the fact that gamers neglect their physical needs to continue playing.

> Is online gaming an **addictive** curse or benign social entertainment? Gamer widows complain that their 20-something husbands are spending **every free moment** playing online games like *World of Warcraft*, to the neglect of their **flesh-and-blood families**. The only time they have their gamer's undivided attention is when the power goes out or the server crashes.
>
> Gamers respond that while online they interact with many **flesh-and-blood players**—in fact, some go online to "hang out" with friends whom they cannot easily visit in person. Playing online becomes a way to **stay in touch**. Realtime chat, as well as microphones, allows gamers to exchange information or news and plan strategy. The interaction is goal-driven, as players plan and execute strategies to complete quests. They **help one another** by exchanging tips and loot, by helping lower-level players move up in the hierarchy.
>
> Experts suggest that the games become **addictive** when the fantasy worlds are experienced as more attractive and rewarding than real life. While players may not enjoy power and prestige in their real lives, they can measure their characters' improvement after one evening of earning increased skill levels and better-quality weapons. At what **physical cost**, when they barely leave the machine to eat or use the washroom?

4f WRITE EFFECTIVE BEGINNING AND ENDING PARAGRAPHS

Beginning and ending paragraphs of essays should behave like a smart suitor meeting "the parents" for the first time: Dress well; start with a firm handshake; show you are thoughtful and personable; close on a strong note. Because readers are more likely to remember beginning and ending paragraphs, they are your best opportunity to make a good impression.

Understand what beginning paragraphs do

Effective beginning paragraphs convince the reader to read on. They capture the reader's interest and set the tone for the piece. In essays they often state the thesis and briefly map out the way the writing will progress from paragraph to paragraph. Sometimes the work of the beginning paragraph might be carried through three or four paragraphs. A writer might start with a memorable example, then use the example to launch the rest of the essay.

Start beginning paragraphs with a bang

Getting the first few sentences of an essay down on paper can be daunting. Try the following strategies to ease your struggle. Get your reader's attention by beginning with one of the following.

A QUESTION

How valuable are snow leopards? The director of a zoo in Darjeeling, India, was fired when its snow leopard caught a cold and died.

A HARD-HITTING FACT

Poaching is big business—to be exact, a six-billion-dollar business. The only illegal trade that's larger is drugs.

A PITHY QUOTATION

"That the snow leopard is," writes Peter Matthiessen, "that it is here, that its frosty eyes watch us from the mountains—that is enough." And it has to be enough because, while snow leopards are here now, they may not be here much longer.

IMAGES

Tonnes of animal pelts and bones sit in storage at Royal Chitwan National Park in Nepal. The mounds of poached animal parts confiscated by forest rangers reach almost to the ceiling. The air is stifling, the stench stomach-churning.

AN ANECDOTE

The snow leopard stood so still in the frosty bushes, it wasn't until the goat squealed that we saw it. Its mottled white fur was now spattered with the goat's blood. Steam rose from the animal's wounds. We fumbled for our cameras, hoping to capture this terrible beauty.

A PROBLEM

Ecologists worry that the construction of a natural gas pipeline in Russia's Ukok Plateau will destroy the habitat of endangered snow leopards, argali mountain sheep, and steppe eagles.

A CONCISELY STATED THESIS

If the governments of China and Russia don't soon act decisively, snow leopards will be extinct in a few years.

A CONTRADICTION OR PARADOX

Snow leopards are tremendously versatile animals, strong enough to kill a horse and fast enough to chase down a hare. What they can't do is hide from poachers in Nepal and India. And this may be their downfall.

An ODD, RIDICULOUS, OR UNBELIEVABLE FACT

Caterpillar fungus is a hot commodity. Traditional healers and their clients are willing to pay handsomely for illegally harvested ingredients for their treatments. As a result, demand for the fungus, along with other poached items like rhinoceros horns and snow leopard bones, drives a lucrative and destructive black market in endangered species.

Essays that begin with obvious, overly general, or exaggerated sentences dampen the readers' interest immediately. Use the first sentence to tell readers something they don't know. Begin with a fresh idea, fact, or image.

Understand what ending paragraphs do

Ending paragraphs remind readers where they've been and invite them to carry your ideas forward. Use the ending paragraph to touch on your key points, but do not merely summarize. Leave your readers with something that will inspire them to continue to think about what you have written.

Conclude with strength

The challenge in ending paragraphs is to leave the reader with something provocative, something beyond pure summary of the previous paragraphs. The following are some strategies for ending an essay:

ISSUE A CALL TO ACTION

Although ecological problems in Russia seem distant, students like you and me can help protect the snow leopard by joining the World Wildlife Fund campaign.

DISCUSS THE IMPLICATIONS OF YOUR ARGUMENT

Even though the extinction of snow leopards would be a sad event, their end is not the fundamental problem. Instead, their precarious position is a symptom of a larger dilemma: environmental damage throughout developing nations in Asia threatens their biodiversity.

EXPLAIN THE APPLICATIONS OF YOUR ARGUMENT

This study of snow leopard breeding behaviour can inform captive breeding programs in zoos.

MAKE RECOMMENDATIONS

Russia's creditors would be wise to sign on to the World Wildlife Fund's proposal to relieve some of the country's debt in order to protect snow leopard habitat. After all, if Russia is going to be economically viable, it needs to be ecologically healthy.

SPECULATE ABOUT THE FUTURE

Unless Nepali and Chinese officials devote more resources to snow leopard preservation, these beautiful animals will be gone in a few years.

TELL AN ANECDOTE THAT ILLUSTRATES A KEY POINT

Poachers are so uncowed by authorities that they even tried to sell a snow leopard skin to a reporter researching a story on endangered species.

DESCRIBE A KEY IMAGE

As they watched the pile of confiscated furs and bones burn, Nepali forest rangers flashed proud smiles that seemed to say, "This time we mean business."

OFFER A QUOTATION THAT EXPRESSES THE ESSENCE OF YOUR ARGUMENT

Too often, developed nations impose their high-flown priorities, like protecting snow leopards and tigers, on developing nations. A Russian

farmer summed up the disjunction succinctly. Tigers ate 2 cows in his herd of 50. When he was compensated for the two he asked, "What's this? Can't the tiger come back and eat the remaining forty-eight?"

ASK A RHETORICAL QUESTION

Generally the larger and more majestic (or better yet, cute) an endangered animal is, the better its chances of being saved. Bumper stickers don't implore us to save blind cave insects; they ask us to save the whales, elephants, and tigers. But snow leopards aren't cave bugs; they are beautiful, impressive animals that should be the easiest of all to protect. If we can't save them, do any endangered species stand a chance?

Resist the urge to end on a bright note if what comes before doesn't warrant it; you don't want your ending to ring hollow.

 C H A P T E R 5

Rewriting, Editing, and Proofreading

Skilled writers know that the secret to writing well is rewriting. Even the best writers often have to revise several times to get the result they want. To be able to revise effectively, you have to plan your time. You cannot revise a paper or a website effectively if you wait until the last minute to begin working. Allow at least a day to let what you write cool off. With a little time you will gain enough distance to "re-see" it, which, after all, is what revision means.

You also must have effective strategies for revising if you're going to be successful. The biggest trap you can fall into is starting off with the little stuff first. *Don't sweat the small stuff at the beginning.* When you see a word that's wrong or a misplaced comma, the great temptation is to fix it. But if you start searching for errors, it's hard to get back to the larger concerns.

5a SWITCH FROM WRITER TO READER

Begin your revision by pretending you are someone who is either uninformed about your subject or holds an opposing view. If possible, think of an actual person and pretend to be that person. Read your draft aloud, all the way through. When you read aloud, you will probably hear clunky phrases and outright errors, but do no more in this stage than put checks in the margins so you can find these things later. Once again, you don't want to get bogged down with the little stuff. What you are after in this stage is an overall sense of how well you have accomplished what you set out to do.

Use these questions to evaluate your draft. Note any places where you might make improvements.

Does your paper or project meet the assignment?

- Look again at your assignment, especially at the keywords, such as *analyze, define, evaluate,* and *propose.* Does your paper or project do what the assignment asks?
- Look again at the assignment for specific guidelines, including length, format, and amount of research. Does your work meet these guidelines?

Does your writing have a clear focus?

- Does your project have an explicitly stated thesis? If not, is your thesis clearly implied?
- Is each paragraph related to your thesis?
- Do you get off the track at any point by introducing other topics?

Are your main points adequately developed?

- Do you support your main points with reasons and evidence?
- Can you add more examples and details that would help to explain your main points?
- Would additional research fill in gaps or make your case stronger?

Is your organization effective?

- Is the order of your main points clear to your reader? (You may want to make a quick outline of your draft if you have not done so already.)
- Are there any places where you find abrupt shifts or gaps?
- Are there sections or paragraphs that could be rearranged to make your draft more effective?

Do you consider your potential readers' knowledge and points of view?

- Do you give enough background if your readers are unfamiliar with your subject?
- Do you acknowledge opposing views that readers might have?
- Do you appeal to common values that you share with your readers?

Do you represent yourself effectively?

- To the extent you can, forget for a moment that you wrote what you are reading. What impression do you have of you, the writer?
- Does "the writer" create an appropriate tone?
- Has "the writer" done his or her homework?
- Is the writing project visually effective? Has "the writer" selected an attractive and readable font? Does "the writer" use headings and illustrations where they are helpful?

Do you conclude emphatically?

- Conclusions that only summarize tend to bore readers. Does your conclusion offer more than a review of ideas you have already fully discussed?
- Could you use your conclusion to discuss further implications?
- Could you conclude by making recommendations for change or improvement, or by imploring readers to action?
- Have you left your audience with a final provocative idea that might invite further discussion?

When you finish, make a list of your goals for the revision. You may have to write another draft before you move to the next stage.

5b   LEARN STRATEGIES FOR REWRITING

Now it's time to go through your draft in detail. You should work on the goals you identified in your review.

1. Keep your audience in mind.   Step back and assess your paper from a reader's perspective. Paragraphs with strong, engaging openers keep an audience's attention, establish a writer's credibility, and above all intrigue readers so that they want to read on. Reread each of your paragraphs' opening sentences and ask yourself whether the language is strong and engaging enough to keep your reader interested in your argument from paragraph to paragraph.

2. Sharpen your focus wherever possible.   You may have started out with a large topic but find now that most of what you wrote concerns only one aspect. For example, you may have started with the large topic of privacy, but your focus now is on the current practice of some retailers' selling their customer databases to companies that build junk mail lists. Revise your thesis and supporting paragraphs as needed.

Check to see that your focus remains consistent throughout the essay. For example, let us say you started out with the large topic of privacy and wrote a whole paragraph about libraries' using filters on their computers to prevent minors from accessing pornography. Then you shifted your focus to states' selling databases. You should then cut the discussion of libraries' use of filters.

3. Check that key terms are adequately defined. What are your key terms? Are they defined precisely enough to be meaningful? Consider this example:

> If people are just in their initial actions (i.e., going to war), they will tend to act justly throughout the situation. If people are unjustified in their initial actions, however, they will have no reason to act justly throughout the rest of the situation. In the Six Day War, the Israelis were justified in going to war and fought a just war throughout. In Vietnam, the Americans had no justification for going to war, and thus they fought unjustly throughout.

What do the words *just* and *unjust* mean in this paragraph? Evidently whatever the writer wants them to mean. This paragraph is a true hall of mirrors. If your argument depends on a critical distinction such as the difference between "just" and "unjust," you are obligated to be as specific as possible in defining these terms.

4. Develop where necessary. Key points and claims may need more explanation and supporting evidence. Look for opportunities to add support without becoming redundant.

Perhaps you are writing about the hardships experienced by an immigrant family: "The Ruhigira family has a hard life," you begin. "They do not have enough money, and they have transportation problems." Each generalization needs a supporting detail to show the reader what you mean.

> The Ruhigira family has a hard life. When Hélène walks the seven blocks to the grocery store, she has enough money for rice and beans, but she must choose between meat and cheese. Toothpaste is too expensive. Hélène's walk home is difficult carrying two heavy bags of groceries. She hopes that when Justin gets paid next week, they will have enough to buy a new alternator for their car.

5. Check links between paragraphs. Transitions between paragraphs allow readers to connect your ideas. Carefully crafted transitions accomplish two things: they explain to your reader why a paragraph logically follows the previous one, and they express the twists and turns of your thinking.

Look for any places where your ideas seem to shift abruptly, and work to make these transitions smoother or more logical. If you are struggling with your transitions, try this quick diagnostic: underline the first and last sentences of each paragraph in your paper and then read these underlined sentences aloud to a friend. Do these sentences together make a logical and coherent argument? If not, spend more time figuring out the relationships between your ideas. Often writers can express these relationships more clearly by choosing accurate transitional phrases such as *although, for example, on the other hand, in contrast, similarly,* and so on (see Section 4e).

6. Consider your title.   An effective title makes the reader want to read what you have written. Be as specific as you can in your title, and if possible, suggest your stance. "Use of Instant Messaging" as a title is vague and bland, and it suggests a topic far too large to be handled well in a few pages. A stronger title would be "Does Instant Messaging Isolate or Connect Adolescents?"

7. Consider your introduction.   In the introduction you want to get off to a fast start and convince your reader to keep reading. If your subject is the use of instant messaging among high school students, don't start with an empty sentence like "Too much messaging can distract students from homework." Cut to the chase with a sentence such as "Not all adolescents waste their time instant messaging; many use online chat to help one another with homework assignments—the equivalent of 'getting together to study.'"

Then you might follow with a sentence that indicates how you will approach your topic: "My experiences as a high school student gave me insight into innovative ways that instant messaging can improve academic performance: adolescents collaborate on school projects and tutor one another in difficult subjects such as calculus and physics." In two sentences you have established your topic and your own authority to write about it.

8. Consider your conclusion.   Restating your claim usually isn't the best way to finish; conclusions that offer only summary tend to bore readers. The worst endings say something like "in my paper I've said this." In contrast, effective conclusions remind readers where your argument has taken them and then invite further discussion. Try to leave your reader with something interesting and provocative. Think about whether there is an implication you can draw, or another example you can include that sums up your position. You might briefly discuss the implications of your argument, or argue why your readers' ideas or beliefs should change because of your findings. If you are writing a proposal, your ending might be a call for action.

The essay "Reminding Residents to Be Bear Aware" (see Section 9d) ends with a proposed solution to the problem (advertise hazards and safety information more widely), a rebuttal of a likely objection to the solution of a publicity campaign (the expense), and a final reason for the solution based on ethics (humans create problem bears; we all share responsibility for eliminating the problem). This conclusion is strong because it follows logically from the discussion that comes before and drives home the proposed solution by appealing to the audience's higher values.

9. Improve the visual aspects of your text. Does the font you selected look attractive? (See Section 12d.) Do you use the same font throughout? Are you consistent if you use more than one font? Do you include headings and subheadings to identify key sections of your argument? If you include statistical data, would presenting it in charts be effective? (See Section 13e.) Would illustrations help to establish key points? For example, a map could be very useful if you are arguing about the location of a proposed new highway.

5c RESPOND TO OTHER WRITERS' DRAFTS

Your instructor may ask you to review your classmates' drafts. Writing a response to the work of a fellow student may make you feel uncomfortable. You may think you don't know enough to say anything useful. Remember that you are only charged with letting the writer know how you—one of many potential readers—react.

But you do have to put forth your best effort. Responding to other people's writing requires the same careful attention you give to your own draft. To write a helpful response, you should go through the draft more than once. Before you begin, number the paragraphs, if the writer has not already done so.

First reading

Read at your normal rate the first time through without stopping. When you finish you should have a clear sense of what the writer was trying to accomplish.

- **Main idea:** Write a sentence that summarizes what you think is the writer's main idea in the draft.
- **Purpose:** Write a sentence that summarizes what you think the writer was trying to accomplish in the draft.

Second reading

In your second reading, you should be most concerned with the content, organization, and completeness of the draft. Make notes as you read.

- **Introduction:** Does the writer's first paragraph effectively introduce the topic and engage your interest?
- **Thesis:** Where exactly is the writer's thesis? Note in the margin where you think the thesis is located.
- **Focus:** Does the writer maintain a focus on the thesis? Note any places where the writer seems to wander off to another topic.
- **Organization:** Are the sections and paragraphs ordered effectively? Do any paragraphs seem to be out of place? Do you note any abrupt shifts? Can you suggest a better order for the paragraphs?
- **Completeness:** Do any sections and paragraphs lack key information or adequate development? Where do you want to know more?
- **Sources:** If the draft uses outside sources, are they cited accurately? If there are quotations, are they used correctly and worked into the fabric of the draft?

Third reading

In your third reading, turn your attention to matters of audience, style, and tone.

- **Audience:** Who is the writer's intended audience? What does the writer assume the audience knows and believes?
- **Style:** Is the writer's style engaging? How would you describe the writer's voice?
- **Tone:** Is the tone appropriate for the writer's purpose and audience? Is the tone consistent throughout the draft? Are there places where another word or phrase might work better?

When you have finished the third reading, write a short paragraph on each bulleted item, referring to specific paragraphs in the draft by number. Then end by answering these two questions:

1. What does the writer do especially well in the draft?
2. What one or two things would most improve the draft in a revision?

5d   EDIT FOR PARTICULAR GOALS

In your final pass through the text of your paper, you should concentrate on style and eliminate as many errors as you can.

1. Check the connections between sentences. Notice how your sentences are connected. If you need to signal the relationship from one sentence to the next, use a transitional word or phrase. For example, when you find two sentences that are closely connected, you should ask what the relationship is. If you need to signal the relationship, use a transitional word or phrase:

> *Silent Spring* was widely translated and inspired legislation on the environment in nearly all industrialized nations. *Silent Spring* changed the way we think about the environment. →

> *Silent Spring* was widely translated and inspired legislation on the environment in nearly all industrialized nations. **Moreover**, the book changed the way we think about the environment.

2. Check your sentences. If you noticed that a sentence was hard to read or didn't sound right when you read your paper aloud, think about how you might rephrase it. Often you can pick up problems with verbs (see Chapters 34 and 35), pronouns (see Chapter 36), and modifiers (see Chapter 37) by reading aloud. If a sentence seems too long, you might break it into two or more sentences. If you notice a string of short sentences that sound choppy, you might combine them. If you notice run-on sentences or sentence fragments, fix them (see Chapter 33).

3. Eliminate wordiness. Writers tend to introduce wordiness in drafts. Look for long expressions that can easily be shortened ("at this point in time" → "now") and unnecessary repetition. Remove unnecessary qualifiers (*rather, very, somewhat, little*). See how many words you can take out without losing the meaning (see Chapter 27).

4. Use active verbs. Any time you can use a verb besides a form of *be* (*is, are, was, were*) or a verb ending in *-ing,* take advantage of the opportunity to make your style more lively. Sentences that begin with "There is (are)" and "It is" often have better alternatives:

> It is true that exercising a high degree of quality control in the manufacture of our products will be an incentive for increasing our market share. →

> If we pay attention to quality when we make our products, more people will buy them.

Notice too that the use of active verbs often cuts down on wordiness (see Chapter 26).

5. Use specific and inclusive language.   As you read, stay alert for any vague words or phrases (see Chapter 29). Check to make sure that you have used inclusive language throughout (see Chapter 30).

EXAMPLE OF SENTENCE-LEVEL EDITING

~~It is a widely believed opionion that computers have greatly influenced the lives of the latest generation. I agree with this opinion. I remember back w~~ *W*hen I was in the fourth grade, we had a computer *literacy* class every Friday. ~~The classroom held about~~ *in a room equipped with* 20 Apple IIe computers. Besides learning how to type correctly, we were also given simple graphic programming assignments. ~~Thus, I along with m~~ *M*y fellow classmates~~,~~ *and I* were assigned to input VLIN (Vertical Line) and HLIN (Horizontal Line) commands followed by a colour and coordinates~~. When we finished we would have~~ *that created* a picture on the monitor. ~~This was not a photographic quality image by any means.~~ Because the pixels were only slightly smaller than sugar cubes~~;~~ and ~~we were~~ limited to 16 colours, these images made ~~the~~ *our* Nintendo Entertainment System's graphics ~~at~~ *output* look like the ~~graphic output~~ *quality* of a Hollywood studio production *by comparison*.

5e   PROOFREAD CAREFULLY

To proofread effectively, you have to learn to slow down. Some writers find that moving from word to word with a pencil slows them down enough to allow them to find errors. Others read backward to force themselves to concentrate on each word.

1. Know what your spelling checker can and cannot do.   Spelling checkers are the greatest invention since peanut butter. They turn up many typos and misspellings that are hard to catch. But spelling checkers do not catch wrong words (e.g., "to much" should be "too much"), missing endings ("three dog"), and other, similar errors. You still have to proofread carefully to eliminate misspellings (see Chapter 45).

2. Check for grammar and mechanics.   Nothing hurts your credibility with readers more than a text with numerous errors. Many job application letters get tossed in the reject pile because an applicant made a single, glaring error. Issues of grammar are treated in Chapters 32 through 37. The conventions for using punctuation, capitalization, italics, abbreviations, acronyms, and numbers can be found in Chapters 38 through 47. Get into the habit of referring to these chapters.

5f LEARN TO EDIT THE WRITING OF OTHERS

Editing someone else's writing is easier than editing your own. In your own writing you know most of the time what you meant to say and often you don't notice where a reader might be stopped or jarred. But editing someone else's writing is also harder because you want to give the writer useful feedback without taking over the writer's task.

1. Make comments in the margins. If you find a sentence hard to read, let the writer know. If you think a sentence is repetitive, let the writer know. If you think a word was left out, say so in the margin. Also let the writer know when a sentence is especially successful.

Word missing here?

Same point as sentence 1?

Can you join this sentence with the previous sentence?

Vivid description!

2. Use symbols to indicate possible problems. Draw a wavy line under any phrase or sentence where you think there may be a problem. Even if you are not sure what the problem is, you can ask the writer to look carefully at a particular sentence. If you think a word is misspelled, draw a circle around it. If you think words can be deleted, put parentheses around them.

A webcam is a webpage that hosts images or even live video streams served by a digitel camera attached to a computer. Webcams serve as surveillance, entertainment, control, and many other services. Webcam technology has become quite popular with people since the first webcams hit the World Wide Web.

WRITING IN THE WORLD

Standard proofreading symbols

More advanced editing requires learning standard proofreading symbols. Authors, editors, and printers use proofreader's marks to indicate changes. Standard proofreading marks are used in pairs. One mark goes in the text where the change is to be made and the other goes in the margin, close to the change.

Mark in the margin	Mark in the text
ℒ	Delete: take it out
◡	Close up: foot ball
∧	Caret: insert here
#	Insert a space: a word
⟨tr⟩	Transpose: the in beginning
⌃	Add a comma: moreover we
⌄	Add an apostrophe: Ellens books
⌄ / ⌄	Add double quotation marks: James Joyce's Clay
:	Add a colon: 3 45 p.m.
;	Add a semicolon: concluded however, we
⊙	Add a period: last call Next we
¶	Begin a new paragraph
No ¶	No new paragraph
sp	Spell out: 7 dwarfs => seven dwarfs
stet	Ignore correction: in the beginning

PART THREE

Writing in Post-Secondary Education and Beyond

- How do I go about *reading* a visual text? (6d)

- How should I organize a *rhetorical analysis* paper? (7c)

- What are some good ways to organize an informative essay? (8c)

- How do I find good reasons for my argument? (9c)

- How do I write a good thesis statement for my literary analysis paper? (10b)

- How do I write a review of a computer game? (11e)

6
Critical Reading and Viewing

7
Analyzing Verbal and Visual Texts

8
Writing to Inform

9
Writing to Persuade

10
Writing about Literature

11
Writing about Film and New Media

Appendix
Writing Essay Examinations

3 WRITING IN POST-SECONDARY EDUCATION AND BEYOND

Writing in post-secondary education requires you to reflect in depth on what you read and to analyze verbal and visual texts. In college and university and beyond, writing can serve different purposes: to analyze, to inform, or to persuade. These purposes shape the kinds of papers, documents, and presentations made in a variety of settings.

Writing in the World Project

Homelessness in Canada: An Informative Essay

How are homeless people in Canada depicted? What kinds of stereotypes are used in presenting images of the homeless in various Canadian media?

Using Google or another search engine, search for images of "homelessness in Canada." Examine a number of the images that you find.

Select several images from among the many that you find, and do a critical analysis of these elements. Use the critical viewing techniques outlined in this section, and then present your analysis and conclusions in an informative essay.

Visit *The Brief Penguin Handbook* Companion Website at
www.pearsoned.ca/faigley/

MyCanadianCompLab
Where writing and research help is a click away.
MyCanadianCompLab may be packaged with your textbook.
If not, it can be purchased from your college or university's bookstore.
Go to **www.pearsoned.ca/highered/mycanadiancomplab/**
for a tour.

CHAPTER *6*

Critical Reading and Viewing

When you write about any major topic, you will be entering ongoing written conversations to which many others have contributed. Consequently, most writing you will do in post-secondary education requires you to reflect in depth on what you read, to engage in a process called **critical reading**. This critical awareness does not stop with reading. Courses at post-secondary institutions often ask you to engage in critical viewing, to think in depth about what you see—whether it be in the form of photographs, drawings, paintings, graphics, advertising, television, film, or the World Wide Web.

Courses at post-secondary institutions may or may not ask you to do reflective writing. When we write to reflect, we consider an idea or experience, and through this consideration come to an understanding of its significance. Your goal in this type of writing should be to allow your readers to share your discovery of the significance of the experience. It should not be to vent pent-up feelings, necessarily, or to expose secrets. Reflective writing can present a way for you to move from interpreting and understanding your personal experience to the more impersonal analysis and interpretation that characterizes much of the academic writing you will do at your post-secondary institution. This section of the handbook focuses primarily on the skills of critical analysis and interpretation with the goal of presenting your insights as informative and persuasive documents. For more detailed information about organizing and writing reflective papers, please visit **www.pearsoned.ca/faigley/**.

6a TWO KINDS OF READING AND VIEWING

Many familiar words are used in slightly different ways in higher education, and reading is one of them. Reading can mean what you normally think of as sitting down with a book, newspaper, or magazine. But reading can also mean thinking about and interpreting almost anything—tattoos, a clever commercial on television, a fashion trend, or a controversial museum exhibit. Reading does not have to mean simply reading words.

Let's take an event as an example. Imagine you are with several friends visiting the career centre at your school to investigate possible volunteer opportunities. Your school has a new general requirement that every student engage in 20 hours of community service each term to graduate. As you are crowded around the computer screen looking at results pulled up from your search, the conversation drifts from what you did on the weekend (besides study) to the opportunities available. Someone cracks a joke about one of the positions, while someone else complains that the location of one opening that she might be qualified for would take forever to reach on the local bus system. For the sake of convenience, let's describe this kind of viewing of the volunteer openings as **ordinary reading** or viewing.

If you observe people carefully, you know that there is no such thing as "ordinary" viewing. One friend will make jokes about every opening; another will consider the location first, the type of work second; and a third is only interested in a position that will help her get a paying job later. Even though viewing behaviour varies, ordinary viewing in this situation means that people don't attempt to do much interpreting beyond learning about the opportunities that are available. Suddenly you note, "My uncle fought against this service learning requirement, you know. He says that our volunteer work reduces the number of paid jobs for union employees." One of your friends starts talking about how unfair it is that the school requires students to donate their time to non-profit organizations when most students get paid little more than minimum wage to support themselves and their school expenses. Another agrees, noting that she needs these volunteer hours to earn money to pay her rent. A third friend says that your uncle has a point because his mother was able to find a grant writer who would do fundraising for the women's shelter on a volunteer basis when she thought she would otherwise have to hire someone to do it. A fourth argues, "At the food bank, it would close if Dave had to pay each of us for our time. Money goes for gas in the trucks to collect the donations around town and pay the building utilities. If I didn't volunteer, a lot of children in our area would stay hungry." All of a sudden your friends aren't making jokes or worrying about bus routes but are thinking about it in terms of economics. They are still reviewing the volunteer opportunities, but they are viewing the school requirement quite differently—in a way that might be termed critical reading or viewing.

The discussion of mandatory service learning as a graduation requirement suggests the different strategies you use for different kinds of reading. When you engage in ordinary reading, one time through is enough. While waiting for a haircut you pick up a magazine and thumb through it. An article catches your eye and you start reading. You get a sense of content and form an initial impression: whether what you are reading is interesting, whether the author has something important to say, whether you agree or disagree. But when you finish, you put the magazine back on the stack, and it's unlikely that you will read the article again.

When you read for a specific purpose, you use different strategies. You no longer read just to form a sense of the overall content. Often you look for something in particular. You might reread a historian's account of the Riel Rebellion to find out the fate of children whose parents participated. You might reread your car insurance coverage to double-check the amount of your deductible for a new windshield. This second kind of reading—often literally a second reading—is critical reading. Critical reading doesn't mean just criticizing what you read, although certainly that can be one result of critical reading. Critical reading begins with questions and specific goals.

6b CRITICAL READING

Nearly all the reading required in post-secondary courses is critical reading. You cannot get far into an academic discipline with ordinary reading. When you read the work of several people in the same discipline, you quickly realize that they do not have the same point of view—they may not even agree on basic facts. And you also quickly realize that their work builds on the work of others; thus you have to have a sense of how they are interpreting the work of others before you can evaluate their claims.

You can become a more effective critical reader if you have a set of strategies and use them while you read.

Previewing

Preview a reading by considering its context first, before reading closely (see Section 1a for a discussion of context). When previewing, begin by asking the following questions:

- Who wrote this material?
- Where did it first appear? In a book, newspaper, magazine, or online?
- What is the topic or issue?
- Where does the writer stand on the topic or issue?
- What else has been written about the topic or issue?
- What social, political, and economic forces and influences can be identified in this piece of writing?
- Why was it written?

When you come to an understanding of the context, certain details take on additional meaning.

Summarizing

Make sure you understand exactly what is at issue, usually a claim or question. If the claim or question is not overtly stated, note where you think it is being made or asked. Circle any words or references that you don't know and look them up. You may get a sense of the main points the first time through, or you may have to read the piece slowly a second time. Then summarize by asking yourself these questions:

- What is the writer's main claim or question? (You should be able to paraphrase it in your own words.)
- If you do not find a specific claim, what is the main focus?
- What are the key ideas or concepts that the writer considers?
- What are the key terms? How does the writer define those terms?

Analyzing

On your second reading, start analyzing the structure, using the following questions:

- How is the piece of writing organized?
- What does the writer assume the readers know and believe?
- Where is the evidence? Does this evidence support the thesis and main claims? Can you think of contradictory evidence?
- Does the writer refer to expert opinion or research about this subject? Do other experts see this issue differently?
- Does the writer acknowledge opposing views? Does the writer deal fairly with opposing views?
- What kinds of sources are cited? Are they from books, newspapers, periodicals, or the web? Are they completely documented?
- How would you characterize the style?
- How does the writer represent herself or himself?

Responding

As you read, write down your thoughts. Something you read may remind you of something else. Jot that down. Ask these questions:

- What points does the writer make to which you should respond?
- What ideas do you find that you might develop or interpret differently?
- What do you need to look up?
- What else should you read before writing?

Photocopy the reading and make notes in the margin: ask questions about what you are reading; contradict the author's point of view; think of other examples or points the author had ignored; mark sentences or short paragraphs that you might quote or paraphrase to support your own per-spective. Your responses will help generate ideas when you begin writing.

Critical response

Let's start by imagining a fine Persian carpet and a hunting knife. The carpet is twelve feet by eighteen, say. That gives us 216 feet of continuous woven material. Is the knife razor sharp? If not, we hone it. We set about cutting the carpet into thirty-six equal pieces, each one a rectangle, two feet by three. Never mind the hardwood floor. The severing fibers release small tweaky noises, like the muted yelps of outraged Persian weavers. Never mind the weavers. When we're finished cutting, we measure the individual pieces, total them up—and find that, lo, there's still nearly 216 square feet of recogniz-ably carpet-like stuff. But what does it amount to? Have we got thirty-six nice Persian throw rugs? No. All we're left with is three dozen ragged fragments, each one worthless and commencing to come apart.

Quammen begins with the analogy of a Persian carpet.

He develops the analogy with sensory details and humour.

The point of the analogy is that many scraps do not add up to a whole.

Now take the same logic outdoors and it begins to explain why the tiger, *Panthera tigris*, has disappeared from the island of Bali. It casts light on the fact that the red fox, *Vulpes vulpes*, is missing from Bryce Canyon National Park. It suggests why the jaguar, the puma, and forty-five species of birds have been extirpated from a place called Barro Colorado Island—and why myriad other creatures are mysteriously absent from myriad other sites. An ecosystem is a tapestry of species and relationships. Chop away a section, isolate that section, and there arises the problem of unravelling.

Quammen turns to extinct species.

Why does he give Latin names?

The direct connection of the analogy is made with a metaphor: an ecosystem is a tapestry.

—David Quammen, *The Song of the Dodo:
Island Biogeography in an Age of Extinctions*, 1996

6c VERBAL FALLACIES

Reasoning depends less on proving a claim than it does on finding evidence for that claim that readers will accept as valid. The kinds of faulty reasoning called logical fallacies reflect a failure to provide sufficient evidence for a claim that is being made. Among the most common fallacies are the following:

- **Bandwagon appeals.** *It doesn't matter if I copy a paper off the web because everyone else does.* This argument suggests that everyone is doing it, so why shouldn't you? But on close examination, it may be that everyone really isn't doing it—and in any case, it may not be the right thing to do.

- **Begging the question.** *People should be able to say anything they want to because free speech is an individual right.* The fallacy of begging the question occurs when the claim is restated and passed off as evidence. In fact, there are many things we cannot and should not say, such as threatening to kill people.

- **Either-or.** *Either we increase corporate taxes or else individuals will have to pay higher taxes.* The either-or fallacy suggests that there are only two choices in a complex situation. Rarely, if ever, is this the case. (In this example, the writer ignores the fact that individuals may have to pay higher taxes even if the government raises corporate taxes.)

- **False analogies.** *Japan quit fighting in 1945 when the Allies dropped nuclear bombs on them. Maybe NATO should use nuclear weapons against other countries.* Analogies always depend on the degree of resemblance of one situation to another. In this case, the analogy fails to recognize that circumstances today are very different from those in 1945, and it is easy to point out how the analogy fails.

- **Hasty generalization.** *We have been in a drought for three years; that's a sure sign of a climate trend.* A hasty generalization is a broad claim made on the basis of a few occurrences. Climate cycles occur regularly over spans of a few years; climate trends must be observed over centuries.

- **Name calling.** *Green party candidates are rabid environmentalists; the Bloc Québécois are self-absorbed separatists; Conservatives are rapacious capitalists.* Name calling is frequent in politics and among competing groups. Unless these terms are carefully defined, they are meaningless.

- ***Non sequitur.*** *A university that can raise a billion dollars from alumni should not have to raise tuition.* A *non sequitur* (which is a Latin term meaning "it does not follow") ties together two unrelated ideas. In this case, the argument fails to recognize that the money for capital campaigns is often donated for special purposes, such as centres for excellence, and is not part of a university's general revenue.

- **Oversimplification.** *No one would run stop signs if we had a mandatory death penalty for doing it.* This claim may be true, but the argument would be unacceptable to most citizens. More complex, if less definitive, solutions are called for.

- **Polarization.** *Easterners don't care what happens west of the Ontario-Manitoba border.* Polarization, like name calling, exaggerates positions and groups by representing them as extreme and divisive.

- *Post hoc* **fallacy.** *The stock market goes down when a Northeast division team plays in the Stanley Cup finals in an even year.* The *post hoc* fallacy (from the Latin *post hoc ergo procter hoc*, which means "after this, therefore because of this") assumes that things that follow in time have a causal relationship.
- **Rationalization.** *I could have finished my paper on time if my printer had been working.* People frequently come up with excuses and weak explanations for their own and others' behaviour that avoid actual causes.
- **Slippery slope.** *If we allow same-sex couples to marry, then next people will want to marry their pets or farm animals too.* The slippery slope maintains that one thing will inevitably lead to another.
- **Straw man.** *Loggers won't be satisfied until they clear cut every mountainside in British Columbia.* A straw man argument is a diversionary tactic that sets up another's position in a way that can be easily rejected. In fact, logging all of the trees would put the lumber industry out of business.

6d CRITICAL VIEWING

Critical viewing is similar to critical reading, although it may be a skill less often practised. Let's take an example. Usually photographs come in a context—in a book with a caption, in a family photo album, in a magazine advertisement—that tells us a great deal about why the photograph was taken and what purpose it is intended to serve. But even without the external context, there are often clues within a photograph that suggest its origins.

Figure 6.1 shows an early homestead on the Canadian prairie. We could guess the approximate date of the photograph based on the shack and accompanying tent and wagon as late nineteenth or early twentieth century. We see no signs of gasoline-powered vehicles or roads, suggesting this homestead predates this technology. The low scrub on the hills suggests the foothills of Alberta or the hilly country of northern Saskatchewan. In fact, this photograph was taken in 1910, and it appears as the frontispiece for Georgina Binnie-Clark's book, *A Summer on the Canadian Prairie.* Journalist Binnie-Clark described her efforts to develop her own farm in the Saskatchewan Qu'Appelle Valley in this book. While single and married men were entitled to free land for their homesteads, single women were not: Binnie-Clark had to buy her farm, compounding the difficulty of achieving financial success.

One approach to critical viewing is to examine a photograph in terms of its composition. In the photograph accompanying *A Summer on the Canadian Prairie*, the shack, tent, and wagon—all manufactured structures—

FIGURE 6.1　A typical prairie homestead

are dwarfed by the steep hillside behind and the tangle of brush that covers the land. The edge of the farm, which runs to the foot of the hills, splits the picture roughly in half with the wilds of nature dominating the scene. The pale grey sky and white tent contrast with the dark landscape.

Another approach to critical viewing is to analyze the content. In 1910 settlers were still breaking ground for what would become some of the world's most bountiful agricultural land. Many of these settlers moved from established communities in Eastern Canada, and like Binnie-Clark, left behind family and professional careers to break sod in the West. They moved from cities like Toronto to these primitive accommodations. The hours were long, the work back-breaking, and the winters harsh and long. We also know that if we put this image of the farmstead against our knowledge of Binnie-Clark as its builder (a relationship known as **juxtaposition**), we can come to a new appreciation of the effort and sacrifice made by these settlers—including single women. The broader context for this image helps it serve as an ironic commentary: adding to the general hardship, Binnie-Clark had to pay for what her male counterparts received as a gift.

No one set of questions can cover the great variety of images, but a few general questions can assist you in developing a critical response.

Previewing

Critical viewing requires thinking about the context first. Begin by asking yourself the following questions:

- Who created this image (film, advertisement, television program, and so on)?
- Why was it created?
- Where did it first appear?
- When did it appear?
- What media are used? (Websites, for example, often combine images, text, and sound.)
- Who sponsored it?
- What has been written about the creator or the image?

Analyzing

The following analytical questions apply primarily to still images. Animations and motion pictures also provoke questions about their narrative structure.

- What can you say about the composition of the image? See Chapters 2 and 11 for ways to analyze composition.
- Where do your eyes go first? If there is an attention-grabbing element, how does it connect with the rest of the image?
- How is colour used?
- How does the image appeal to the values of the audience?
- How does the image relate to its context?
- Was it intended to serve a purpose besides art or entertainment?

Responding

Make notes while you view the image and after, with these questions in mind:

- What was your first impression of the image (film, advertisement, television program, and so on)?
- After you have thought more and perhaps read more about it, how has your first impression changed or expanded?

6e VISUAL FALLACIES

Misleading images

The era of digital photography has made it possible to create images of almost anything imaginable, including lifelike dinosaurs chasing humans, interactions between people now living and those long dead, and human feats that defy human limits and the laws of physics. Viewers of action films today care little whether stunts are filmed live or digitally generated, and readers of newspapers no longer are shocked to find that some news photos are digitally manipulated.

The photograph in Figure 6.2 circulated on the internet for a while in 2001, purporting to show a shark attacking a British Navy diver. In fact, the photo was created by combining two different and unrelated pictures (see Figures 6.3 and 6.4). Figure 6.3 shows a great white shark snapped by Charles Maxwell, a South African photographer, while Figure 6.4 is a photo of an HH-60G Pave Hawk helicopter from the 129th Rescue Wing, Moffett FAF (a California National Guard unit). It was taken by Lance Cheung. The bridge in the background is the Golden Gate Bridge in San Francisco. You can easily see how the two photos could be superimposed to produce the "shark attack."

Pictures are not always what they claim to be. Critical viewers ask the same questions about images that they do about texts.

Misleading charts

A special category of visual fallacies is misleading charts. For example, the fictitious company Glitzycorp might use the chart in Figure 6.5 to attract investors. The chart shows what looks like remarkable growth from 2001 to 2003 and projects additional sales for 2004. But is the picture quite as rosy as it is painted?

FIGURE 6.2   This photograph, showing a shark attacking a British Navy diver, is a hoax, created by combining two real but unrelated pictures.

FIGURE 6.3   A photograph of a great white shark taken off the coast of South Africa by Charles Maxwell.

FIGURE 6.4   A photograph of a helicopter from a California National Guard Reserve Unit, taken by Lance Cheung, with the Golden Gate Bridge in San Francisco in the background.

Notice that the bars in this bar chart start at 20 rather than at 0. The effect is to make the $22 million sales in 2002 appear to double the $21 million sales of 2001, even though the increase was less than 5 percent. Three years is also a short span to use to project a company's future profits. Figure 6.6 shows the sales of Glitzycorp over seven years, and it tells quite a different story. The big growth years were in the late 1990s, followed by a collapse in 2000 and slow growth ever since.

Glitzycorp's sales charts illustrate how facts can be manipulated in visual presentations.

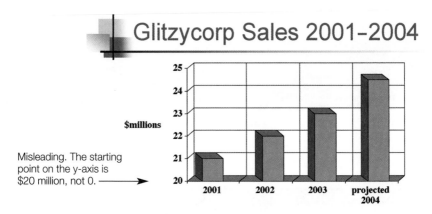

Misleading. The starting point on the y-axis is $20 million, not 0. ⟶

FIGURE 6.5   This figure is misleading because the y axis does not start at 0, exaggerating the increase in sales over a short period of time.

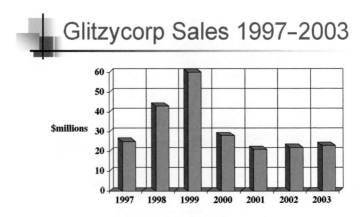

FIGURE 6.6   This figure provides an accurate view of Glitzycorp's previous sales, by including a longer time span and starting the y axis at 0.

CHAPTER 7

Analyzing Verbal and Visual Texts

7a THE AIM OF ANALYSIS

Whereas critical reading and viewing are general skills, **analysis** is a more specific process in which those critical reading and viewing skills are applied to particular subjects. Analysis involves dividing a whole into parts that can be studied both as individual entities and as parts of the whole. The classic scientific discoveries were made when scientists broke down processes into parts. Fire, for example, was once thought to be caused by phlogiston, a property inherent in flammable things. In the 1770s, Antoine-Laurent Lavoisier rejected the idea of phlogiston and identified oxygen as the necessary component in combustion. Lavoisier was one of the founders of modern chemistry although his approach was that bodies can be understood only when their constituent substances are analyzed and classified.

    Rhetorical analysis is a kind of analysis that divides a whole into parts to understand how an act of speaking or writing conveys meaning. Thus the goal of a rhetorical analysis is to understand how a particular act of writing or speaking influenced particular people at a particular time. Rhetorical analysis is not limited to speaking and writing. The tools of rhetorical analysis have been applied to understanding how meaning is made by other human creations, such as art, buildings, photographs, dance, memorials, websites, music, advertisements—any kind of symbolic communication.

    Writing a rhetorical analysis (also called "critical analysis" or "textual analysis") is a frequent assignment in post-secondary education. Rhetorical analysis is often a part of research-based and persuasive writing as well. A rhetorical analysis requires you to step back from a text and consider it from multiple perspectives. Writing a rhetorical analysis can give you a heightened awareness of a text and a better appreciation of what the author accomplished.

    Understanding how communication works or fails to work is a worthy goal by itself, but rhetorical analysis has other benefits. It enables you to think about a text in more depth, to better understand the arguments it makes, and to appreciate how it is put together. In turn, this knowledge helps you in writing your own text. You have a much better sense of what has been said and written about your subject and where you have opportunities to contribute your own ideas.

7b   ANALYZE THE CONTEXT AND THE TEXT

Rhetorical analyses typically run on a continuum between considering the **context**—the relationship between the piece of writing or speaking and the larger society surrounding it—and the **text** itself—what it is about and how it is designed. We can think of the context, which lies at one end of the continuum, in two senses. First, the **immediate context** refers to where the text was written and read or heard. For example, on January 19, 1914, Nellie McClung argued for voting rights for women in Manitoba by acting as a female premier denying suffrage to a male delegation in a play staged at the Winnipeg Theatre. Second, the **broader context** refers to the larger cultural and historical circumstances in which a text is produced and read. The broader context for "The Women's Parliament" was Premier Roblin's earlier dismissal of a female delegation petitioning for enfranchisement in the Manitoba legislature, and the larger backdrop of the women's suffrage movement in North America and England in the early 1900s. McClung's satire helped to change her contemporaries' minds about voting rights for women, contributing to a Conservative government defeat and passage of a bill allowing women to vote in Manitoba by 1916.

At the other end of the continuum lies the text itself. We can consider a text as if it were a piece in a museum, where we closely scrutinize it. For example, Nellie McClung recounted "The Women's Parliament" in *Purple Springs* where, if you examine the language of Pearl Watson's speech, you begin to see how the humour highlights the contradiction in the period's sentiments about women. Watson notes to the men petitioning for suffrage,

> Man's place is to provide for his family, a hard enough task in these strenuous days. . . . Would letting politics enter the home help matters? Ah no! Politics would unsettle our men. Unsettled men mean unsettled bills—unsettled bills mean broken homes—broken vows— and then divorce. Man has a higher destiny than politics. What is a home without a bank account? The man who pays the grocer rules the world. (283)

She suggests that men do not need to vote because they already have power in their role as breadwinners (i.e., equal but different to women). She then suggests that men are superior to women (i.e., their higher destiny than politics). These are contradictory positions, yet they are classic arguments that Premier Roblin had used to justify disenfranchising women in 1914.

Often in the back and forth movement between text and context, you gain surprising insights about how a text achieves certain effects. These questions will help you get started in composing a rhetorical analysis.

Questions for a rhetorical analysis

What is the context?

- Why was this text written or spoken at the particular time?
- What else had been said or written previously about the subject?
- What was the purpose?
- Can you identify social, economic, and cultural influences of the larger context?

Who is the audience?

- What attitudes would the audience have about the subject?
- What attitudes would the audience have about the author?
- What did the author assume the audience knew or believed?

Who is the author?

- How does the author represent himself or herself in the text?
- How does the author establish a credible ethos?
- What else did the author compose?

What is the medium and genre?

- What is the medium: print? website? handwriting? voice recording?
- What is the genre: speech? essay? letter? poem? advertisement?

What is the subject?

- Can you summarize the main idea?
- How is the main idea supported?
- How is the text organized?
- How does the writer/speaker appeal to reason (logos) or to emotion (pathos)?

How would you describe the style?

- Is the style formal? informal? academic?
- Does the writer/speaker use humour or satire?
- What metaphors are used?
- Can you identify any patterns in the sentences?
- How is the style related to the purpose?

7c DEVELOP AND ORGANIZE A RHETORICAL ANALYSIS

Writers have countless options when choosing topics for rhetorical analysis. Maybe you have chosen to analyze how a famous public speech altered the course of history. Or you might analyze how a magazine ad uses rhetoric to persuade readers to buy its product, or how well a federal party candidate's website uses written and visual strategies to attract voters. No matter whose persuasive rhetoric you choose to analyze, following a few simple guidelines will make your analysis stronger.

Choosing details

- **Identify** your text's intended audience. All rhetoric is aimed at a particular audience; an argument that persuades one group of people might not persuade another. Spend some time thinking about the text's implied or explicit audience, and include an analysis of audience in your rhetorical analysis.
- **Analyze** your text's use of rhetorical strategies. What is the writer's rhetorical goal? What does he or she want to change in the audience's beliefs, feelings, or actions?
- **Demonstrate** how your text uses rhetoric to persuade. Use direct quotations to illuminate a writer's main points or claims. Choose passages that show how your text uses rhetorical appeals based on credibility (ethos), emotion (pathos), and logic (logos).
- **Evaluate** how well these rhetorical arguments might work for your text's intended audience.
- **Justify** your rhetorical analysis. Ask yourself why your readers should care about how well your chosen text uses rhetoric to persuade its intended audience. Spend some time thinking about the historical or cultural significance of your text.

Organizing your ideas

The main section of any rhetorical analysis addresses how a text uses rhetorical strategies to persuade an intended audience. However, readers may need background information before they can understand your arguments. You might decide that your analysis requires some historical background. Caleb Inouye begins his analysis of the rhetorical strategies used by Teresa Migwans, Chief of Whitefish Lake First Nation, in her presentation to the Renewal Commission of the Assembly of First Nations, by giving his readers some background about the Assembly of First Nations and the Renewal Commission's purpose. He wants his readers to understand that Migwans' audience is other administrative and political figures associated with the Assembly of First Nations. Clearly describe the text's intended audience for your readers. For example, if you are analyzing an advertisement for *Maclean's Guide to Canadian Universities*, your analysis will be stronger if you describe the magazine's readers (news junkies, educated professionals, parents of university-eligible children) before you analyze how the ad uses rhetorical strategies to persuade that audience.

Once you have established a context for your analysis, you can turn to the main body of your argument: how the text you are analyzing uses rhetoric to persuade. You will need to make a claim, which you will then support. Caleb Inouye makes his claim in these two sentences:

Migwans uses language from both mainstream business and Ojibway cultures to show her membership and establish her credibility to speak about the need for change in how First Nations peoples manage their lives. She establishes her credibility to add weight to the logical point that she wants to argue: that the AFN assume the Department of Indian Affairs' current role to create a "true Indigenous administration."

Spend some time thinking about how to organize your paper to support your claim. Although there are three main elements of rhetoric—ethos, pathos, and logos—the text you analyze might use one element more than another. Or it might fail to use one aspect of rhetorical persuasion successfully. In addition, each rhetorical appeal a writer uses to persuade an audience is intimately connected to another. Think about how each rhetorical appeal works with others to create an overall effect on an audience. Are all of your text's rhetorical appeals equally effective? Do they build on each other, until the final appeal tips the audience one way or another? How might your answers to these questions alter your transitions? Paying attention to how a text's rhetorical appeals overlap can help you develop an outline and establish transitions between ideas. (See Sections 4c and 4e on transitions.)

7d **SAMPLE RHETORICAL ANALYSIS**

Inouye 1

Caleb Inouye

Professor Janis

English 100

4 May 2007

Rhetorical Strategies in Teresa Migwans' Submission

to the Renewal Commission of the

Assembly of First Nations

Inouye's opening provides background to help readers understand the broader context for Migwans' submission.

The Assembly of First Nations (AFN) is a national lobbying organization founded to advance the political interests of First Nations peoples. The First Nations peoples signed treaties and other agreements that established a relationship between them and the British Crown in the years before Confederation, and they argue that this pre-existing association affects their relationship with the Canadian federal government today. The First Nations peoples see themselves as independent nations within Canada rather than as Canadian subjects, and they created the Assembly to help reinforce this position. The AFN is a democratic organization representing over 630 communities and over 700 000 First Nations citizens both on and off reserve lands. As part of the process of renewing this organization and improving its effectiveness, the AFN established a renewal commission to gather input from groups across the country. These meetings were intended to gather ideas about what issues are important to the membership and how the organization might be altered to make it more effective. Teresa Migwans submitted her speech as part of her

Inouye 2

responsibilities as the newly elected Chief of the Whitefish
Lake First Nation.

The renewal process documents that Migwans'
submission responds to clearly draw from business jargon
and processes. For example, on the webpage that describes
the renewal process, the document refers to the group's
inability to "strategically plan a process from conception
to implementation." This line could come out of any
organization's correspondence. Also, the formal schedule
of meetings across the country, the fact that transcripts of
the meetings are available, and the publication of printed
submissions to the commission seem in line with the way
a large corporation would conduct its business. Migwans'
presentation to the commission also uses language that is
clearly borrowed from the corporate, business-process
setting, but she combines this with language that seems
drawn directly from Ojibway culture. Migwans uses
language from both mainstream business and Ojibway
cultures to show her membership and establish her
credibility to speak about the need for change in how First
Nations peoples manage their lives. She establishes her
credibility to add weight to the logical point that she
wants to argue: that the AFN assume the Department of
Indian Affairs' current role to create a "true Indigenous
administration."

Migwans begins by thanking the commission, in
Ojibway, for the opportunity to communicate with them,
"*chi-migwiitch.*" She then identifies herself as part of the
Ojibway Nation before giving her Ojibway name, "*Giiwadin
Waasgoonai* (Northern Flower)," and clan affiliation, "Elk."

> This paragraph uses
> examples to show
> how Migwans
> establishes her
> credibility as an
> experienced
> administrator by
> drawing on
> language from
> corporate culture.

Inouye 3

Inouye shows how Migwans also establishes her identity as an Ojibway member and chief, which authorizes her to speak in support of an indigenous administration.

She then notes that she is the newly elected Chief of the Whitefish Lake First Nation. These rhetorical moves are important because they establish her credibility (ethos). Before the Commission could take any of her ideas seriously, they would need to know who the speaker is. Since Migwans could not be present physically, she has the added burden of trying to establish her credentials for speaking only through her written words. Her first strategy, then, is to identify herself as a First Nations citizen through her use of the Ojibway language, through her clan affiliation, and through her status as Chief.

Inouye notes that only after Migwans thoroughly establishes her credentials does she begin to advance her main argument.

Migwans' second way of establishing her ethos or credibility comes through the next two paragraphs where she gives details describing her educational background. These two paragraphs read like something out of a corporate brochure: the phrases "My background presently is public administration . . ." and "My previous work experience prior to being elected" are both very formal and use words like "presently" and "prior" that do not often occur in informal speech. Migwans' goal seems to be the same: to establish her ethos or credibility, but in this paragraph the credibility seems directed more toward her competence as an administrator rather than derived from her identity as a First Nations citizen. This also seems like a very important part of her text because the whole process of renewal that the AFN is engaging in here seems very business-oriented. By using some of the business language and phrasing, she is demonstrating that she is capable and knowledgeable in financial affairs.

Inouye 4

Having established that she should be listened to because of her qualifications and identity, Migwans then provides some context for the main argument she will advance in her submission. She writes briefly about the Whitefish Lake First Nation before introducing some key historical facts. In 1850, Chief Shawenakeshick signed the Robinson-Huron Treaty, which she stresses is a "pre-Confederation" treaty. This is a crucial point because she then argues that "Being a First Nation that is an original signatory to the 1850 Robinson-Huron Treaty affords us with a special relationship to the Crown, a Nation-to-Nation relationship." This is the heart of the argument she will make in the remainder of the submission. In Canadian law, precedent is an important aspect that affects rulings. Migwans must know this, and she is using this knowledge of the law against the power of the Canadian government to argue for a peer-to-peer relationship between her Ojibway First Nation and Canada. This argument clearly is based on logic or logos: if our nation existed before Canada was even created, then it cannot be part of Canada if it was not specifically invited into Confederation. Consequently, Canada must treat us as another nation and not as just another subordinate group of Canadian citizens.

This paragraph outlines Migwans' logical argument that the Whitefish Lake First Nation is entitled to a "Nation-to-Nation" relationship in negotiating with the Canadian government.

Toward the end of the submission Migwans extends this logical argument. If the Ojibway First Nation exists in a nation-to-nation relationship with Canada, then it should have the right to self-govern. To set up the grounds for this point, she notes that the Whitefish Lake First Nation "administers the Indian Act and its assimilative

Shows how Migwans expands argument to claim that the Whitefish Lake First nation should be allowed to self-govern and help its citizens progress both collectively and individually.

policies. We run our elections under the Indian Act meaning that we have a councillor for every 100 people; we have two-year terms. We run band business as per the policies of the Indian Act." In this section she underlines that the band is competent and functional as an administrative body. As a result, the next stage of development or "renewal" would be to create "a true Indigenous administration related to the federal government that provides financial and administrative support." This "third order of government" would allow First Nations people to create more vibrant, more sustainable communities and to make "progress." Migwans defines "progress" as "knowing who you are as an individual, in my case *Anishinabe-qwe,* and taking that knowledge and applying it to your everyday life and life's happenings, and once you are able to do that then are you better prepared to work as a collective and as a collective are we able to succeed." She ties the idea of her community's ability to be successful with her belief that this grows from knowledge of identity, especially cultural identity.

Inouye uses examples to support his point that Migwans also develops an effective emotional appeal through her word choice and word order.

Migwans does not rely only on credibility (ethos) or logic (logos). Throughout her submission, she takes care to use emotion (pathos) to make her argument forceful and memorable. Using the Ojibway greeting and giving her Ojibway name are part of this appeal to emotion, but she also uses inspired language toward the end of the submission: "We must hold on to our lands, our cultures, our Freedom" is one phrase that uses the repetition of "our" for emphasis. She follows that with a quotation from the AFN charter that she puts in bold face type: "The rights and responsibilities given to us by the Creator will not be altered or taken away by any other nation." By invoking a spiritual belief as a basic idea that is not negotiable, she is not relying on logic but rather on an emotional charge to "never surrender." In this way, Migwans underscores her logical argument with challenging the renewal commission members to remember that their work carries a religious significance beyond its administrative duties.

Work Cited

Migwans, Teresa. "Submission to Renewal Commission of the Assembly of First Nations 2004." 6 October 2004. Assembly of First Nations Renewal Commission. 22 September 2005 <http://www.afnrenewal.ca/english/hearings.htm>.

7e   ANALYZE IMAGES AND OTHER KINDS OF VISUAL TEXTS

The word *text* typically brings to mind words on a printed page. But in the sense that anything that can be "read" can be a text, then nearly everything is a text. Consider, for example, the designs of the two pairs of athletic shoes pictured in Figures 7.1 and 7.2. While shoe designs are not texts in the same way that the dialogue from "The Women's Parliament" is a text (because they are not made of words), they can still be analyzed for their meaning and rhetorical strategies. Like other kinds of texts, the meaning of these designs can be analyzed in their context. In this case, the move to blur the difference between athletic shoes and "active wear" is a key element of this context. In the twentieth century, athletic shoes were developed for use in sport or exercise; in the last 10 years athletic shoe companies have developed shoes that borrow the look of athletic shoes but are meant for everyday use. Consequently, many who purchase "athletic" shoes do not play sports or exercise. Nor are shoes designed primarily for a particular activity (some are, but we are focusing on the ones marketed as fashion items). Then what motivates people to buy these shoes? The people who design the shoes believe they carry messages for the people who buy them. Puma's website announces that one of their shoes—the "Motion Spike"—was inspired by track spikes and designed for "attention-hungry urbanites."

The blue shoes (Figure 7.1), with their stylized cleats, snug fit, and light weight, allude to track shoes, although their owner likely is not an athlete. These shoes announce their wearer through both colour and artistic detail—the baby blue shade grabs the eye, making this footwear hard to miss. The asymmetrical design, with the leaping puma on one side and the black stripe on the other, rewards the longer gaze by defying expectation.

FIGURE 7.1 Visual design contributes to the differing messages that athletic shoes convey. The style of the Pumas (left) is quite different from the Adidas (right).

FIGURE 7.2 With the Goodyear name and the Adidas stripes, these shoes conjure images of the race track.

No words appear on the shoes: observers are expected to recognize the brand from the logos (the puma and the stripe). The cultural messages these images carry mean something to the wearer and to other "attention-hungry urbanites": I'm cool, we share similar tastes in clothing, we share similar views on society and our place in it as middle-class consumers.

The black shoes (Figure 7.2) present a more subtle statement: black on black with accents of silver. Produced as a collaboration between Adidas and Goodyear, these shoes allude to the car racing scene: the soles are tire treads, made of tire rubber. Of course, the wearer of such shoes is unlikely to be a race car driver. These shoes display the name of the shoe manufacturer on the tongue (Adidas) and the Goodyear Tires company name and logo on the outside edge of the sole. Advertised as the "fastest thing on two heels," these shoes may be the closest a teenager will get to driving a car, let alone a racing vehicle. The blue shoes borrowed from the cachet that track athletes enjoy; these faux racing "boots" borrow adjectives from Formula 1 drivers: suave, masculine, powerful, fast.

That shoes communicate cultural meaning is no recent development. Back in the 1990s, when Michael Jordan wore his red and black "Air Jordans" in a basketball game for the second time, the Chicago Bulls were fined $1000 for "non-uniformity of uniform." *Chicago Journal* sports writer Steve Ascheberner wrote, "Michael Jordan is not the most incredible, the most colourful, the most amazing, the most flashy, or the most mind-boggling thing in the NBA. His shoes are." This was exactly the attitude that Rob Strasser, a central builder of Nike, had hoped for: "Fight the law, he always said, break the rules."

These shoes function as images that carry meaning just as much as words do, and being able to analyze or read images will help you understand both people and the objects they associate with themselves.

Quotations in this section are from J.B. Strasser and Laurie Becklund, *Swoosh: The Unauthorized Story of Nike and the Men Who Played There* (New York: Harper-Collins, 1993).

CHAPTER 8

Writing to Inform

Much of what you read in post-secondary school is informative. Even before you enter the institution, you read about how to apply, and, after you are accepted, how to register for courses. When you begin courses, your textbooks inform you about particular subjects, and you learn more about those subjects by reading in the library and on the web. You read about what is happening on campus in your school newspaper, and you learn about other campus activities by reading. Likewise, many of the writing tasks assigned in post-secondary education are informative—from lab reports and essay exams, to analyses of literature, research reports, and case studies.

The emphasis on writing to inform in post-secondary education is not surprising because nearly every occupation that requires a post-secondary degree or diploma requires informative writing. The communication product of many professionals, including accountants, engineers, scientists, journalists, and business consultants, to name a few, is a written report. Informative writing has four primary functions: to report new or unfamiliar information; to analyze for meaning, patterns, and connections; to explain how to do something or how something works; and to explore questions and problems.

8a FIND AN INFORMATIVE TOPIC

At the beginning of any post-secondary assignment, especially one that asks for informative writing, it is critical to understand what kind of information your instructor expects. Look at your assignment for keywords such as *study, analyze, explain*, and *explore*, which indicate what kind of writing you are expected to produce (see Section 3a).

Reporting information

Reporting information takes many forms, ranging from reports of experimental research (see Section 23f) and reports of library research to simple lists of information. Writing to persuade (Chapter 9) also reports information. The main difference is that the focus of a report and other informative kinds of writing is on the subject, not on changing readers' minds or on getting them to take action. Writers of reports usually stay in the background and keep their language as neutral as possible, giving the impression of an objective, impartial observer.

Analyzing meaning, patterns, and connections

Writers not only report what they read and observe. They often construct meaning through selecting what and what not to include and in organizing that information. Sometimes this construction of meaning is made explicit as **analysis**. You may have experience in analyzing literary texts (see Chapter 10). Writing in and after post-secondary school requires you to analyze more than literature. The complexity of the world we live in requires making connections. For example, scientists now agree that the earth has become warmer over the last few decades, but to what extent this warming has been caused by the burning of fossil fuels remains controversial. Advertisers know that certain kinds of ads (for example, ones that associate drinking beer with social life) sell the product, but often they do not know exactly how these ads work or why some ads are more effective than others. Historians debate the importance of certain historical events (for example, the Treaty of Versailles following World War I) and how those events led to subsequent events (World War II).

Explaining how

Often what you know well is difficult to explain to others. You may know how to solve certain kinds of difficult problems, such as how to fix a malfunction in your car's electrical system, but if you have to tell someone else how to do it over the phone, you may quickly become very frustrated. Often you have to break down a process into steps that you can describe in order to explain it. Explaining a process sometimes requires you to think about something familiar in a new way.

Exploring questions and problems

Not all informative writing is about topics with which you are familiar or ones that you can bring to closure. Often post-secondary writing involves issues or problems that perplex us and for which we cannot come to a definitive conclusion. The goal in such writing is not the ending but the journey. Tracing the turns of thought in a difficult intellectual problem can result in writing far beyond the ordinary. Difficult issues often leave us conflicted; readers appreciate it when we deal honestly with those conflicts.

Finding a topic

When your general subject is specified in your assignment, you can make your work more enjoyable by choosing a specific topic that is either more familiar to you or that you find particularly interesting. Here are some guidelines you can use when choosing a topic:

- Choose a topic you will enjoy writing about.
- Choose a topic that readers will enjoy reading about.
- Choose a topic that you know something about or can readily find information about.
- Choose a topic for which you can make a contribution of your own, perhaps by viewing something familiar in a new way.
- If you choose an unfamiliar topic, you must be strongly committed to learning more about it.

8b NARROW YOUR TOPIC AND WRITE A THESIS

A central difficulty with writing to inform is determining where to stop. For any large subject, a lifetime may be insufficient. The key to success is to limit the topic. Find a topic you can cover thoroughly in the space you have. Broad, general topics are nearly impossible to cover in an essay of five pages. Look for ways of dividing large topics such as "the social problems created by online gaming" into smaller categories and select one that is promising. "How online games break up marriages" is a topic that you are more likely to be able to cover in a short paper.

Often your readers will lack initial interest in your topic. If you ignore their lack of interest, they in turn likely will ignore you. Instead, you can take your readers' knowledge and interest into account when you draft your thesis. For example, someone who knows a lot about birds in the parks of your city might write this informative thesis:

> Watching birds in urban areas is interesting because unusual birds often show up in city parks.

It doesn't sound like a topic that most young adults would find as interesting as the writer does. But if the writer puts the audience's attitude in the foreground, challenging them to consider a subject they likely have not thought much about, a traditional post-secondary school audience might read beyond the title:

> Although most post-secondary students think of bird watching as an activity for retired people, watching birds gives you a daily experience with nature, even in urban areas.

This thesis also gives the writing a stance from which to approach the topic.

8c DEVELOP AND ORGANIZE YOUR IDEAS

Successful reporting of information requires a clear understanding of the subject and clear presentation. How much information you need to include depends on your audience's knowledge of and potential interest in your topic.

Introducing your subject to your audience

Consider these questions about your audience:

- What does my audience already know about the subject?
- What questions or concerns might they have about my subject?

- What is their attitude toward the subject? If it is different from mine, how can I address the difference?

If your audience is unfamiliar with your subject, you will need to supply background information. If key terms are unfamiliar, you should define them.

Organizing your information

The organization of informative writing varies according to the subject. If you are writing about a topic that occurs over time, often a **chronological organization** works best.

Most analyses require you to identify the major aspects of a subject and to discuss each. **Conceptual organization** requires you to make decisions before you start about what is most important and how those concepts relate to each other. Idea maps can help you determine what the key concepts are and how they relate to each other (see Section 3b). Andrea Chen used a conceptual organization in her report on the health risks of manure disposal, moving from an overview of the types of micro-organisms that can cause illness to the ways that these micro-organisms can contaminate food or water supplies (see Section 8d). A useful strategy for deciding how to organize your information is to make a working outline that sets up the key points (see Section 3d).

If you are reporting on two similar or different things, a **compare and contrast organization** is likely appropriate. The simplest procedure is to describe one thing and then describe the other, ending with a conclusion that summarizes the similarities and differences. However, it is often more effective to proceed point by point, explaining how each is similar or different in each aspect.

8d SAMPLE INFORMATIVE ESSAY

Andrea Chen was given the following essay assignment in her environmental biology class: *Report on this issue with broad implications in environmental health and microbiology: the disposal processes for manure from intensive farming operations. Write on one aspect of the problem and cover your topic completely. Include an account of how you located your information.*

Chen chose to write about the human health risks from micro-organisms associated with manure disposal. After doing several internet searches, as well as visiting the library to locate scientific articles, Chen wrote this report. Her instructor requires papers prepared according to APA style, using its documentation system. (See Chapter 23 for a full explanation of APA style.)

1

Andrea Chen

Biology 106

November 30, 2006

Manure Disposal and Human Health:

A Survey of Human Health Risks from

Pathogens Associated with Manure Disposal

The thesis is placed early in the report.

Manure disposal in North America is a growing concern because it involves factory farms with a large concentration of animals in a relatively small area. The treatment, use, and disposal of their waste becomes more important as these operations grow larger and more numerous (Wallinga, 2004).

Introduction

Manure disposal has repercussions for the health of the environment and the people who live around the farm or rely on water sources connected to farmlands. The major risks to human health resulting from improper manure disposal practices are

- Pathogenic micro-organisms
- Chemical compounds and nutrients

This report focuses on pathogenic micro-organisms. Most human health risks associated with pathogenic micro-organisms in manure can be reduced and controlled through following standard regulations and proper hygiene. As farming operations grow, these practices become more important.

Methods of collecting information are set off in their own paragraph.

The research for this report began with searching Canadian government websites, followed by a general search to gain an overview of the major issues associated

2

with human health and manure disposal. Several articles from the library added the scientific perspective to balance the farming policy view of earlier documents. The articles provided information about characteristics of pathogenic micro-organisms that link manure disposal and human disease.

Micro-organisms

The major health concern associated with disposing of manure is the pathogens contained in it. Safe disposal means minimizing the number of potential pathogens released into the environment, while also considering environmental conditions, like rainfall amount, soil type, and geographical conditions, (e.g., location of nearby ground and surface water; Manitoba Agriculture, Food and Rural Initiatives, 2005). These conditions affect how quickly pathogens migrate into the water supply (Wallinga, 2004). The speed of migration and soil environment affect how many pathogens reach water sources and the level of risk they pose to people (Wallinga, 2004).

Types of Organisms

A wide range of potential human pathogens are shed in livestock manure (Atwill, 1999). A few micro-organisms have a clear, proven connection between their presence in livestock manure and human disease, and even more have uncertain but suggestive connections (Atwill, 1999). Table 1 compares the prevalence of enteric pathogens in humans, cattle, pigs and poultry (Olsen, 2000).

> Link between pathogens in manure, contamination of water supplies, and risk to human health established at beginning.

3

Table 1. Prevalence of enteric pathogens in humans, cattle, pigs and poultry.

	Human	**Cattle**	**Pigs**	**Poultry**
Salmonella spp	1%	0–13%	0–38%	10–100%
E. coli 0157:H7	1%	16%	0.4%	1.3%
Campylobacter jejuni	1%	1%	2%	100%
Yersinia enterocolitica	0.002%	<1%	18%	0%
Giardia amblia	1–5%	10–100%	1–20%	0%
Cryptosporidium spp.	1%	1–100%	0–10%	0%

Source: Olsen, 2000.

 Cryptosporidium parvum and *Giardia duodenalis* are protozoa shed by a wide range of livestock, and they have been implicated as the cause of disease when they are present in drinking water (Atwill, 1999). These organisms have a two-stage life cycle—the trophozoite and the oocyst (*Cryptosporidium*) or the cyst (*Giardia*) (Atwill, 1999). While the protozoa themselves can only reproduce inside a host, the cyst or oocyst stages are long-lived and resistant to chemical disinfectants, including those used to treat drinking water (Madigan, Martinko, & Parker, 2004, p. 663). Filtration effectively removes them from water, but many treatment facilities do not filter water (Madigan et al., 2004). Because these protozoa can survive the treatment process, it is important to minimize their entrance into source waters. Some of the symptoms associated with protozoa infection are diarrhea, headache, vomiting, and fever (Fleming, 2004).

 Besides protozoa, livestock manure also contains shed bacteria that are human pathogens (Atwill, 1999). *Escherichia coli* and *Campylobacter* are organisms of major

Using a conceptual organization, Chen subdivides micro-organisms into protozoa and bacteria and then describes the main types.

4

concern (Atwill, 1999; Wallinga, 2004). Both can cause food- or water-borne infections (Wallinga, 2004). *E. coli* has been strongly linked to beef manure and causes approximately 73,000 infections a year in the U.S. (Wallinga, 2004). Symptoms of *E. coli* infection include bloody diarrhea, abdominal cramping, and occasionally kidney failure (Centers for Disease Control & Prevention, 2005).

Especially associated with poultry manure, *Campylobacter jejuni* causes 24 million infections a year in the U.S; 130 people die (Wallinga 2004). Symptoms include abdominal pain, diarrhea, and fever (Madigan et al., 2004, p. 941).

Transmission

Contaminated Water

Micro-organisms from manure that contaminate surface and groundwater are usually released into the environment by intentional spreading of the manure on fields as fertilizers or by accidental leaks from manure holding pits (Atwill, 1999). Both of these release pathogens into the soil surrounding the livestock farm.

This section details the methods by which the micro-organisms are transmitted from the manure to the food and water supplies.

Regulations governing the processing of manure before it goes onto fields help to minimize health risks (Atwill, 1999). Before manure is applied to fields, it sits in lagoons or storage pits. The length of time that it sits is based partly on chemical decomposition and partly on the concentration of pathogens (Atwill, 1999). The number of viable pathogens decreases exponentially the longer it sits, effectively minimizing the health risks (Wallinga, 2004). When manure goes onto fields, however, it is not pathogen-free, and the more manure that is spread, the

5

higher the concentration of pathogens added to the soil in that area. Pathogens can move freely through the soil with water, meaning that any micro-organisms present can leach through the soil and into either ground or surface water (Wallinga, 2004).

Another source of soil contamination from livestock farms is manure runoff from holding pits (Wallinga, 2004). Manure can also leak out of pits into the surrounding soil and eventually reach ground water (Wallinga, 2004). An American study showed that many of these storage pits were built without regard for the location of local drinking water sources. Many pits sit directly above aquifers, making the water source especially vulnerable to contamination (Wallinga, 2004).

Once the micro-organisms have been released into the soil, the type of soil and environmental conditions determine how quickly and how many organisms leach out and reach local water sources. One study found that both fecal coliforms and coliphages leached into subsurface water through a tile drainage system as it percolated through the soil, mostly composed of clay loam (Malik, Randall, & Goyal, 2004).

Contaminated Food

Food becomes contaminated through contact with polluted water or with manure used as fertilizer (Cote & Quessy, 2005). The nutrients present in manure make it a good fertilizer, but the micro-organisms also deserve consideration (Wallinga, 2004). A recent study found that *E. coli* could survive in sandy loam for 56–70 days (Cote & Quessy, 2005). *Salmonella* was detected in the soil for

Chen identifies three ways that food can become contaminated.

6

54 days after manure application (Cote & Quessy, 2005). The manure went on the fields in June, but when vegetables grown there were harvested, no *E. coli* or *Salmonella* was found on any of them (Cote & Quessy, 2005).

This study shows that these pathogens persist in the soil even after all regulations are followed. Variations in time of manure application, type of crop grown, type of soil, and amount of rain during the growing season all affect the persistence and viability of pathogens in the soil.

A third source of crop contamination is soil organisms that feed on micro-organisms. *Diploscapter,* a thermo-tolerant, free-living, bacteria-eating nematode can transfer the pathogens to the surface of pre-harvest fruits and vegetables (Gibbs, Anderson, Beuchat, Carta, & Williams, 2005). Found in compost and sewage across the U.S. (and presumably Canada), *Diploscapter* can survive in composted turkey manure; it ingests and disperses food-borne pathogens (Gibbs et al., 2005). This study indicates additional health risks in the interactions between pathogens in the manure and micro-organisms in the soil.

Conclusions

The human health risks associated with manure disposal hinge largely on good management, good storage design, and appropriate regulations. As long as guidelines are followed, there is minimal risk of human health effects resulting from the handling or disposal of manure (Atwill, 1999). Continued research into pathogen longevity and mobility in soil, as well as their viability over time under different environmental conditions, will be able to help further reduce human health risks from manure spread on fields.

Chen recaps the main points: health risks are minimized when farmers follow the guidelines for safe disposal; additional research will help to reduce risks further.

7

References

Atwill, E. R. (1999). Is livestock manure a risk to public health? *Advances in Pork Production, 10,* 75–80.

Centers for Disease Control & Prevention, Department of Health & Human Services, Division of Bacterial & Mycotic Diseases. (2005, October). *Escherichia coli* 0157:H7. Retrieved November 26, 2005, from http://www.cdc.gov/ncidod/dbmd/diseaseinfo/ escherichiacoli_g.htm

Cote, C., & Quessy, S. (2005). Persistence of *Escherichia coli* and *Salmonella* in surface soil following application of liquid hog manure of production of pickling cucumbers. *Journal of Food Protection, 86,* 900–905.

Fleming, R. (2004, April). *Cryptosporidium: Could it be in your water?* Factsheet. Ontario Ministry of Agriculture, Food & Rural Affairs. Retrieved November 25, 2005, from http://www.omafra.gov.on.ca/ english/engineer/facts/04-015.htm

Gibbs, D. S., Anderson, G. L., Beuchat, L. R., Carta, L. K., & Williams, P. L. (2005). Potential role of *Diploscapter sp.* strain LKC25, a bacteriavorous nematode from soil, as a vector of food-borne pathogenic bacteria to preharvest fruits and vegetables. *Applied & Environmental Microbiology, 71,* 2433–2437.

Madigan, M. T., Martinko, J. M., & Parker, J. (2003). *Biology of Microorganisms* (10th ed.). Upper Saddle River, NJ: Pearson Education.

8

Malik, Y. S., Randall, G. W., & Goyal, S. M. (2004). Fate of *Salmonella* following application of swine manure to tile drained clay loam soil. *Journal of Water & Health, 2,* 97–101.

Manitoba Agriculture, Food and Rural Initiatives. (2005, January). Living with livestock-land application of manure. Retrieved November 20, 2005, from http://www.gov.mb.ca/agriculture/livestock/ publicconcerns/cwa01s06.html

Olsen, M. E. (2000.) Human and animal pathogens in manure. Retrieved November 27, 2005, from http://www.stopthehogs.com/pdf/pathogens.pdf

Wallinga, D. (2004, August). *Concentrated animal feeding operations: Health risks from water pollution.* Institute for Agriculture and Trade Policy—Food and Health Program. Retrieved November 20, 2005, from http://www.environmentalobservatory.org/library. cfm?refID=37390

8e AN INFORMATIVE BROCHURE

Most businesses, organizations, and clubs use informational documents to tell audiences about themselves and to describe their products, services, and activities. The most common printed documents are brochures, form letters, flyers, and newsletters. Recognizing the need for an informational document is often the first step in writing one. Knowing a document is needed, however, is not the same thing as identifying exactly for whom it is to be written and what the document is intended to achieve. Begin with these questions:

Audience

- Is there a specific target audience?
- What do I know about their age, gender, ethnicity, educational level, and knowledge of the document's subject?

• Is there a broader or secondary audience who might also read the document?

Purpose

• What does the audience need to learn?
• What background information do they need?
• If they are to perform a task, what instructions do I need to give?

Context

• How does the document fit into the overall mission of the business or organization?
• How will the document be used? Will people be required to read it?
• Are there possible legal issues to consider?
• How much time do I have to produce the document? Will others help me?

Creating a brochure

Newsletters, brochures, and other informational documents that used to be difficult to produce are now easy to make using word processing tools and are inexpensive to print or photocopy. Some programs have templates that give you a choice of formats for brochures, letters, and newsletters, into which you put your content.

Brochures are one of the most useful informational documents because they can be produced using the front and back of a sheet of paper. They fit into standard #10 envelopes and are handy for distribution on tables or racks. Even if you don't use a ready-made template, six-panel brochures are straightforward to design.

1. **Develop a layout.** A typical brochure has six panels—three on the front and three on the back. Take two pieces of standard paper, place them together, and fold them into three sections. Separate them, lay one page above the other, and label the sections by number, so you will know which panel fits where (Figure 8.1; see page 110 for a sample brochure).

2. **Make a sketch of what you want to put on each panel.** Draw boxes where you want to insert art.

3. **In your software program, open a blank page and change the orientation to horizontal.** In Word, select **Page Layout** under **View**, which will allow you to see the graphics. Under the **File** menu, select **Page Setup**, then select **Landscape**, which will change the orientation of your page.

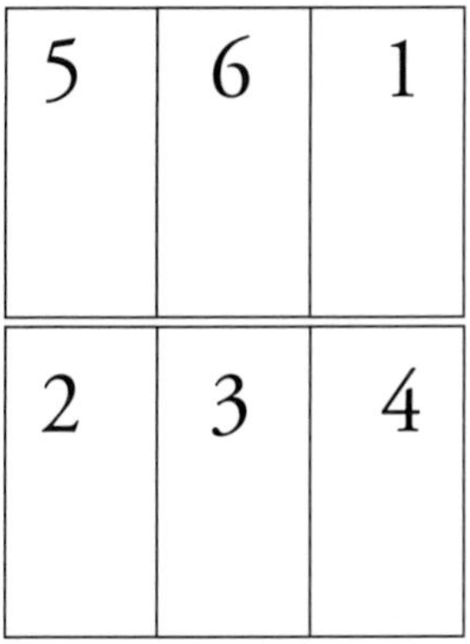

5	6	1
2	3	4

FIGURE 8.1

4. **Create a text box.** Under the **Insert** menu, select **Text Box**. Your pointer will change to a cross tool, which if you click and drag, creates a box. You can resize the box by clicking on its edges. Make three boxes for the panels on each side. Alternatively, create a three-column, one-cell table and place your text and images inside the table cells. Reset page margins to 1 cm on all sides.

5. **Format the text box.** Under the **Format** menu, select **Text Box**. You will find options that allow you to change the size, colour, and layout of the text box.

6. **Insert images.** You can insert images and other graphics into text boxes by selecting the options under **Picture** in the **Insert** menu.

7. **Check the formatting.** When you finish you will have two pages with three panels each. Place them together and fold them to make sure the panels are in the correct order. Also, check the alignment of the panels and the readability of the text. If you have extra space, consider enlarging the type and inserting blank space to set apart key points.

8. **Edit and proofread.** Errors destroy the effect of an otherwise handsome brochure.

Sample brochure

Maurice Gauthier created the brochure *G2 Communications Unlimited* for an assignment in a document design course. This informational brochure offers a visual and verbal introduction to a new consulting business that his parents had started. Gauthier chose background colours drawn from the shades in the illustrations.

You may have gotten your job based on your technical skills but to keep it or be promoted, you need to have excellent communication skills, both written and spoken.

Need help improving your writing skills?
Call us. We can help you radically improve your writing skills after only a few hours of instruction.

Have several employees you'd love to promote if only they could write well?
Call us. We can make a significant improvement in their skills after only a few hours of one-to-one instruction or small group instruction.

Need improved writing resources on your company intranet?
Call us. We can create a series of tutorials for self-study tailored to the specific needs of your employees. Or use our website for a wealth of writing-related information and tips.

Need prompt and helpful feedback on a draft document?
Email us a draft. We will get comments back to you within 24 hours. Our response will identify both the strengths and weaknesses of your draft and provide you with specific suggestions for improvement.

Contact us:
G² Communications Unlimited
Arva Green
Maurice Gauthier
234 King St.
Mississauga, ON
agreen@g2com.com
mgauthie@g2com.com

Visit us:
http://www.g2communications.com

G² Communications Unlimited

Corporate writing instruction:
✓ Small classes
✓ One-on-one
✓ Online follow-up
✓ Internet resources

Specialized writing instruction for
✓ Financial analysts
✓ Engineers
✓ Corporate management

Results guaranteed within four hours of instruction

Panel 5 is the first one the reader sees after the cover. The reader sees a series of questions that outline the kinds of services the consulting firm offers.

The back cover (panel 6) gives contact information and the website address.

The front cover (panel 1) uses a blend of right and left alignment for a distinctive appearance.

Small Classes (Max. 8 individuals)
✓ Classes tailored to needs of writers enrolled
✓ Work on current or upcoming projects
✓ Re-work previous projects
✓ Team writing/individual writing
✓ Learn to analyze corporate style, word choice, and genre conventions

Class length:
2 x 4 hr. sessions (recommended)
Variable, depending on writers' needs

One-on-One Instruction
✓ Make rapid progress with writing instruction tailored to your specific needs
✓ Understand and emulate the features of your industry's style and phrasing
✓ Express yourself concisely, clearly, and correctly

Length:
One to two hours per session
Number of sessions varies with individual

Online Resources
✓ Extensive online resources
✓ Tailored to your organizations' communication needs
✓ Self-directed tutorials on genres and discourse conventions for your industry
✓ Online consulting offers feedback and constructive criticism on works-in-progress
✓ Writing tutorials prepared for your writers that can be uploaded onto company intranet for multi-employee access

Follow-up
Starting a new project and have a few questions?
✓ Email us for answers
✓ Send us a draft and we'll provide quick, clear feedback

Need an hour or two face time to talk?
✓ Schedule an appointment
✓ Visit online chat

Why choose G² Communications?
"Klaus improved almost overnight from an employee on probation to one of the best writers in his group following several meetings with Mr. Gauthier."
Yvette, supervisor at Morningstar

"I met with another writing coach but couldn't capture the [company] voice, so I came to G2 Communications, and after two meetings began to understand the finer points of our style."
Noemi, financial analyst

"I've passed Mr. Gauthier's name around within my group and two of my co-workers have gotten equally great results as me working with Maurice."
Vladimir, financial analyst

"The class with G2 Communications was one of the most helpful professional development seminars that I've taken. We got limited writing instruction during the engineer program, so this course helped me to understand how to adapt my message to the audience. I learned so much in those eight hours I could hardly believe it. My writing has improved 100%."
Henry Windsor, nuclear engineer, Energy Canada

The inside panels (2, 3, 4) can be viewed together when the brochure is opened.

On the centre panel Gauthier highlights the online resources the consulting group has created as some of its innovative products and solutions.

CHAPTER 9

Writing to Persuade

Persuasive writing can take many forms, ranging from simple advertisements to entire books that advance a thesis with many pieces of evidence. Persuasive writing in post-secondary education is often called **argument**. When you imagine an argument, you might think of two people, or two groups of people, with different views, engaged in a heated exchange—maybe even shouting slogans. In post-secondary courses, in public life, and in professional careers, written arguments are aimed at readers who will not immediately accept or reject a **claim** expressed as a slogan. Extended written arguments attempt to change people's minds by convincing them that a new idea or point of view is valid, or that a particular course of action is the best one to take. Written arguments not only offer evidence and reasons, but also often examine the assumptions on which they are based, explore opposing arguments, and anticipate objections.

9a FIND AN ARGUABLE TOPIC

Probably you know at least a few people who will argue about almost anything. If you think long enough, you too can find ways to argue about almost anything. Some topics, however, are much better suited than others for writing an extended argument. One way to get started is to make a list of topics you care about (see Section 3a). Limited, local topics tend to work better for short papers than ones that are vast and have long histories. Try one or more of the invention strategies in Section 3b to identify a topic.

Position arguments and proposal arguments

How you develop a written argument depends on your goals. You may want to convince your readers to change their way of thinking about an issue or perhaps get them to consider the issue from your perspective. Or you may want your readers to take some course of action based on your argument. These two kinds of arguments can be characterized as **position** and **proposal arguments.**

In a position argument you make a claim about a controversial issue. You

- define the issue,
- take a clear position,
- make a convincing argument, and
- acknowledge opposing views.

WRITING SMART

Finding arguments on the web

Because the web is a grassroots medium with millions of people putting up websites, it's no surprise that the web has turned out to be a vast forum for arguments. Many organizations and individuals have taken advantage of the low cost of the web to publicize their stands on issues. To get a sense of the range of interest groups that use the web to publicize their views, go to Yahoo! (www.ca .yahoo.com). Under Yahoo! Web Directory, click on Canada, where you'll find under the "Society and Culture" heading, a subheading on "Issues and Causes." As you will see from the list, the issues extend from abortion to brain drain, to conservation, to weight and nutrition, to xenotransplantation.

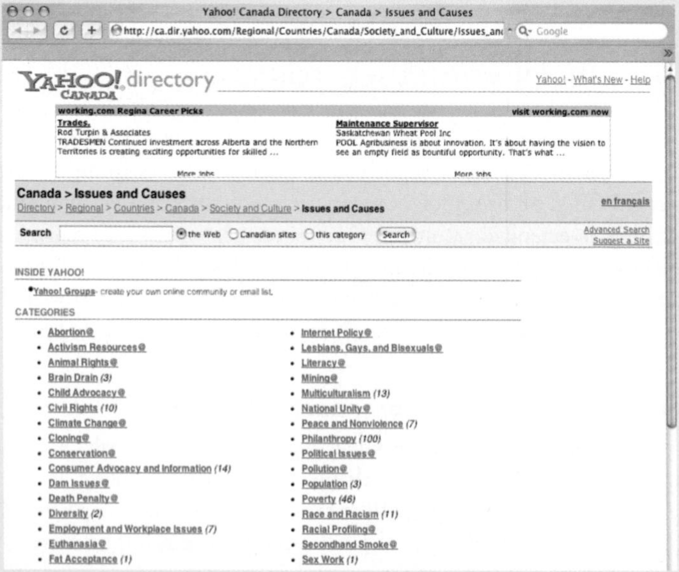

FIGURE 9.1   Yahoo Canada's Issues and Causes index (http://ca.dir.yahoo.com/Regional/Countries/Canada/Society_and_Culture/ Issues_and_Causes/)

In a proposal argument you propose a course of action in response to a recognizable problem. The proposal says what can be done to improve the situation or change it altogether. You

- define the problem,
- propose a solution or solutions, and
- explain why the solution will work and is feasible.

Topics that are not easily argued

Certain topics can be argued only in limited ways.

- **Statements of fact.** Statements of fact are usually not considered arguable since they can usually be verified by research. You can easily verify that Pierre Trudeau was the twenty-second prime minister of Canada. Claims of fact are arguable only if you can challenge the basis of the fact. For example, since Pierre Trudeau served two nonconsecutive terms, he might be considered the twentieth and the twenty-second prime minister. If you argue for counting him only once, he becomes the twentieth prime minister. Additionally, several men before him served as prime minister more than once, so if you argue for counting *them* only once, then Pierre Trudeau becomes the fifteenth prime minister.
- **Personal taste.** Another category of claims that are not arguable is claims of personal taste. If you hate peas, no argument can convince you that you like them. But just as some statements of fact turn out to be arguable, so too do many claims of personal taste turn out to be value judgments based on arguable criteria.
- **Claims of belief.** Many claims rest on **belief** or **faith.** If a person accepts a claim as a matter of faith or religious belief, that claim is true for that person and cannot be refuted. Of course, people still argue about the existence of God, and which (if any) religion reflects the will of God. But those who hold to irrefutable beliefs will not be convinced by those arguments.

9b MAKE AN ARGUABLE CLAIM

Slogans versus arguable claims

The difference between a slogan, such as *Vote for candidate X*, and an arguable claim, such as *Vote for candidate X because she will lower taxes and improve schools*, is the presence of a reason linked to the claim. A reason is typically offered in a ***because* clause**, a statement that begins with the word *because* and provides a supporting reason for the claim. The word *because* signals a **link** between the reason and the claim.

FIGURE 9.2

Regardless of their sloganizing, many bumper stickers still can be considered as starting points for written arguments. For example, the bumper sticker in Figure 9.2 offers the beginnings of an arguable claim.

We have to do some work to unpack this bumper sticker. First, we may want to know exactly what the writer means by *Buy Canadian,* since the components to many products are made overseas and assembled here. Second, we need to know exactly what the writer means by *It's our future.* Presumably the phrase means that if people in Canada buy products made in Canada more jobs will be created, which in turn will lead to greater prosperity. When we start fleshing out what the bumper sticker might mean, we find a proposal argument.

Supporting claims with reasons

To move beyond simple assertion—or a shouting match—a claim must have one or more supporting reasons, and the reasons must be linked to the claim in order to be accepted by readers. An argument in post-secondary writing, therefore, consists of a claim and a series of appropriately linked supporting reasons:

Buy Canadian　　　　because　　　　it's our future.

CLAIM ◄——— *LINK (because)* ◄——— REASON

The problem lies in convincing a reader to accept that the reasons provided are linked to the claim. A reader might challenge the bumper sticker's claim by asking *How? So what?* or *Why?*

Buy Canadian　　　　because　　　　it's our future.

CLAIM ◄——— *LINK (because)* ◄——— REASON

CHALLENGES *(How? So what? Why?)*

The argument should not end simply because it is challenged. Instead, you often must generate a **series of claims**, each of which is supported by evidence that your readers will accept:

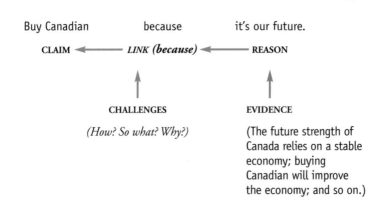

Claims must be specific and contestable

In addition to being supported by reasons that are appropriately linked to it, your claim must also be *specific*. Broad general claims such as *Canada lacks sufficient skilled workers* are nearly impossible to argue effectively. Often general claims contain more restricted claims that can be argued, such as *Canada should increase immigration quotas for educated, professionally trained applicants* or *The federal government should make tribal councils accountable for the funds they receive to maintain First Nations communities.*

Your claim must also be contestable. Your claim that you like sour cream on a baked potato is specific, but it is not contestable. No matter how many times you are told that a baked potato is less fattening without sour cream, the fact that you like sour cream won't change. You may stop eating the sour cream, but you won't stop wanting to eat it.

9c DEVELOP AND ORGANIZE GOOD REASONS

Thinking of reasons to support a claim is not hard. What *is* hard is convincing your audience that your reasons are good ones. When you create an argument, you should imagine critical readers—people who are going to listen carefully to what you have to say but who are not going to agree with you automatically. Whenever you put forward a reason, they will ask *So what?* You will have to have evidence, and you will have to link that evidence to your claim in ways they will accept if they are to agree that your reason is a good reason.

Think about your audience

A good reason works because it includes a link that your readers accept as valid. Your readers are a jury, passing judgment on your good reasons. If your audience accepts your reasons, and if they cannot think of other, more compelling reasons that *oppose* your position, then your argument will convince them. Thus, you need to learn as much as possible about your audience before you begin to construct your argument so that you can decide, first, whether or not it will be possible to persuade them and, second, how you can gather the best information for your subject. Here are a few questions you should ask about your audience:

- What does my audience already know about the topic?
- What is my audience's point of view about the subject?
- Does my audience already agree or disagree with my position?
- What are the chances of changing the opinions and behaviour of my audience?
- Are there any sensitive issues I should be aware of?

Most important, if your audience disagrees with your position, make sure you know why they disagree so that you will be able to develop an effective counter-argument.

Think about possible lines of argument

In the course of developing your arguments, get in the habit of asking a series of questions. If you ask these questions systematically, you will probably have more good reasons than you need for your arguments.

1. **Can you argue by definition—from "the nature of the thing"?**
   - Can you argue that while many (most) people think X is a Y, X is better thought of as a Z?

     Most people think of deer as harmless animals that are benign to the environment, but their overpopulation devastates young trees in forests, leading to loss of habitat for birds and other species that depend on those trees.

   - Can you argue that while X is a Y, X differs from other Ys and might be thought of as a Z?

     While geology is usually classified as a physical science, John McPhee's books on geology show how dependent geologists are on language and metaphors for their understanding of the earth.

2. **Can you argue from value?**
   - Can you grade a few examples of the kind of thing you are evaluating into good, better, and best (or bad, worse, and worst)?

     There were many important leaders in the suffragists' movement, but none had the quick wit, earnest passion, and eloquence of Nellie McClung.

- Can you list the features you use to determine whether something is good or bad and then show why one is most important?

  Brian Mulroney is often reviled for negotiating the extremely successful free trade agreement and bringing in the GST, but his most spectacular failure, the Meech Lake Accord, is nearly forgotten by the present generation.

3. **Can you compare or contrast?**
   - Can you think of items or events or situations that are similar or dissimilar to the one you are writing about?

     Television viewing in Great Britain is not plagued by frequent commercials because television programming is financed through a flat-rate fee rather than through advertising.

   - Can you distinguish why your subject is different from one usually thought of as similar?

     Psychologists argue that video games are as addictive and harmful as alcohol and cigarettes, but these games have no chemical component that alters brain chemistry; gamers play online to participate in an enjoyable activity while socializing with their friends.

4. **Can you argue from consequence?**
   - Can you argue that good things will happen if a certain course of action is followed, or that bad things will be avoided?

     If post-secondary students can secure a credit card with a modest limit, they can begin establishing a credit record that will enable them to buy a car or rent an apartment without their parents' co-signature.

   - Can you argue that while there were obvious causes of Y, Y would not have occurred had it not been for X?

     The Conservative Party may have won the election in part because the Liberals ran a poorly organized and reactionary campaign; the Conservatives could not have won if they hadn't also presented a platform that many Canadians found acceptable.

   - Can you argue for an alternative cause rather than the one many people assume?

     The one- or two-degree increase in temperature in the world's oceans has been blamed on human environmental pollution, but some scientists suggest that the warming trend is due to cyclical changes in the earth's atmosphere, caused by cosmic events in our solar system.

5. **Can you counter objections to your position?**

- Can you think of the most likely objections to your claim and turn them into your own good reasons?

  Some parents forbid their teens from attending parties because they fear their children will succumb to temptation, but the only way for those teens to develop their maturity and judgment is by encountering temptation and exercising that judgment.

- Can the reverse or opposite of an opposing claim be argued?

  New medications that relieve pain are welcomed by runners and other athletes who put their joints and muscles under extreme stress, but these drugs also mask important signals that our bodies send us, increasing the risk of serious injury.

Think about your organization

A typical organization of an argument essay contains three elements. Sometimes they are set out in one-two-three order, but sometimes the writer's position is not given until the background and opposing views have been addressed (see the sample paper in Section 9d for an alternative organization). The three elements are

1. **Introduction:** Captures the reader's attention, defines the issue or problem, and expresses the writer's thesis or indicates the writer's stance.
2. **Body:** Supports the writer's thesis in paragraphs that present reasons, facts, examples, and expert opinions. Opposing views are raised and discussed.
3. **Conclusion:** Presents a summary or strong conclusive evidence—logically drawn from the arguments—that underscores the writer's thesis.

Consider opposing views

You can use several strategies to strengthen your argument and address opposing viewpoints effectively:

- Use facts and examples rather than opinions to support your argument.
- Refer to respected authorities on your topic.

- If the opposition has a good point, admit it. Then show why the point is still not enough to sway your opinion. This is called *conceding a point,* and it will strengthen your credibility.
- Use polite and reasonable language rather than biased or emotionally charged words.

9d SAMPLE PROPOSAL ARGUMENT

In her wildlife management class, Stéphine Arsenault was assigned an essay persuading the local town council to consider a new solution to an ongoing local wildlife problem. The problem of newcomers to Kamloops who are unfamiliar with the town's Bear Aware program was still fresh in her mind, so she decided to research the problem and propose a solution to send to members of the city council and possibly publish in the *Kamloops Daily News*. Notice that she signals her stance early in the paper, but she does not state her position or her solution until she has defined the problem, given some background, and outlined efforts to solve the problem. The paper uses APA documentation style.

Arsenault 1

Stéphine Arsenault

Professor Jonas

Wildlife Management 307

21 November 2006

Reminding Residents to Be Bear Aware

A friend from the east recently confided an incident from a childhood vacation to Banff National Park. While parked at a picnic area, her mom was making sandwiches for lunch on a cutting board on her lap in the passenger seat. The window was half down so she could enjoy the summer breezes. She was assembling sandwiches of ham and mustard and had them piled up on one side until she had made enough. My friend's dad pointed out a black

> The vivid story lets even readers without a close encounter imagine the experience. Arsenault then signals that she will complicate a simplistic evaluation of the event.

Arsenault 2

bear that had ambled out of the woods and over to the garbage can about three metres from their car. The kids in the back seat all jostled at the window to get a better view, until the bear walked past the can and on toward their car. The kids drew back in puzzlement. Their mom kept making sandwiches, until suddenly she looked up and there was the bear sniffing the sandwiches. The mom shrieked and started cranking up the window, when suddenly the bear's claws reached into the crack and snapped the window off right at the door frame. The mom screamed even louder, then, threw the cutting board with everything on it out the window. It landed a metre or two from the car, and the bear ambled after it, while the dad revved up the engine and drove off. No harm done, just a great story for them all to tell for the rest of their lives. Or was it?

Arsenault provides background, citing experts on human-bear interactions. She uses parenthetical citations in the text that refer to the references list. See Chapter 23.

Stephen Herrero, an environmental scientist at the University of Calgary, estimates there are 800 000 black bears in North America, ranging across Canada and all but seven U.S. states, and about 60 000 brown bears, which includes grizzlies. He states that generally, "bears kill three people and seriously injure five to 15 a year in North America" (Sefton, 2000), but he notes that the number of bear attacks was higher than in the previous 28 years of recording-keeping. A Canadian Press story from May 2005 reported at least five bear attacks on one weekend in Alberta ("Troublemakers," 2005). Marc Gibeau, a Parks Canada bear specialist, says that increased use of wilderness areas by humans (especially during nice spring weather) increases the chances of bear-human interaction:

Arsenault 3

"There's no reason for additional warning. When you're in bear country, you should always be aware" ("Troublemakers," 2005). But what about people who don't know how to "be aware"?

Those of us who have lived all our lives in the backcountry know that feeding wild animals such as bears is a bad idea (not to mention illegal in B.C.). It teaches them that humans are a viable source of food; it emboldens them to approach humans looking for food. But my friend's family didn't know enough about bears to realize that when the bear passed the garbage can toward their car, they should have driven away instantly. We regularly read newspaper accounts of similarly inexperienced hikers' and campers' encounters with bears, and some of these end tragically, with the death of first the humans, then the bears. There are three solutions to problem bears: capture them and transport them hundreds of kilometres away; hunt them down and kill them; bear-proof your property and, if you hike or camp, educate yourself on bear safety and carry pepper spray or a gun for personal protection.

> This paragraph identifies the problem and three possible solutions.

Transporting bears means they just become a nuisance elsewhere: they will still approach human communities for an easy meal. Bears that attack or threaten humans are generally hunted down and killed. In fact, millions of tax dollars have been spent and thousands of black bears and grizzlies have been killed in British Columbia over the past 10 years without actually solving the problem (Bear Aware British Columbia, 2006). These bears have been taught by humans that approaching them results in easy food.

> After elaborating on the problem, Arsenault evaluates three possible solutions.

Arsenault 4

Killing the bear ends its life; a dead bear can't learn different habits. Eventually a new bear will come along and, if the humans have continued their same habits—leaving garbage outside, letting meat juices collect on their barbecues, and leaving windfall fruit rotting on the ground—the new bear will also follow the same pattern, creating another problem bear. Programs like *Bear Aware* (2006) attempt to educate people about how to bear-proof their property and to encourage us all to develop and pursue prudent food disposal habits. Various government websites as well as regular media stories also offer advice on how to respond if you encounter a bear in the wilderness.

This paragraph introduces Arsenault's proposal: a regular publicity campaign to reach newcomers and motivate established residents.

Newcomers to the city can visit the *Bear Aware* website to learn how to bear-proof their property, but what if they don't realize the potential for such a problem in the first place? But it's not just newcomers that pose a potential problem. Not all established residents are aware of or bother to bear-proof their property either. They believe that because they haven't seen any bears in their immediate neighbourhood, there is little danger of one appearing. However, a bear can smell garbage or other attractive odours over a kilometre away, so a bear that hasn't come that far into the city may be encouraged by rotting crabapples to move further in for more abundant and easy food sources. For these reasons, the city council needs to run a regular publicity campaign educating and informing people about the hazards of attracting bears and ways to discourage them from entering the city.

The publicity campaign should include brochures targeting newcomers to the area and television and radio

Arsenault 5

spots that air regularly all year to motivate all residents to
maintain a basic standard of bear safety around their
residences. If people are aware of the issue, they will be
more likely to take precautions around their own
residences or if they decide to hike or camp. The publicity
should elaborate these steps that residents can take to
bear-proof their property:

* collecting grease and cleaning the barbecue
  immediately after each use;
* harvesting fruit and vegetables from gardens or trees
  early and collecting and safely disposing of windfalls
  every day;
* storing garbage and pet food inside the house;
* putting birdfeeders out after the first snowfall and removing them at the end of winter;
* maintaining compost so there is no odour (Bear Aware
  British Columbia, 2006)

Another topic to include in this campaign is a review of
experts' advice on how to respond to a bear attack. Herrero
(2002) has published a book that could serve as the basis
for a second brochure that could be made available in the
tourist centre and the information booths of local and area
parks. We can reduce the number of people being seriously
injured or killed by bears in our area if we ensure that
members of and visitors to the community are educated on
avoiding and surviving a bear encounter.

These preventive strategies will cost money to prepare
and distribute, but hunting and transporting problem bears
is an even more expensive (and ineffective) response,
having already cost millions without actually addressing

This paragraph identifies methods to reach the city's target audience and the main points that the campaign should cover.

In her conclusion, Arsenault addresses concerns that her audience might have about the feasibility of her proposed solution.

Arsenault 6

the larger cause. Experts note that bears don't naturally seek out human contact: if they gain no reward for foraging in cities, they will remain in the wild. Bears with no experience with humans will be more likely to avoid them if they can, also reducing the possibility of attack in the wilderness. Simply shooting problem bears is not a viable solution. Humans must take responsibility for their part in creating problem bears in the first place. An important step is encouraging everyone in Kamloops to accept this responsibility.

The last sentence is a direct address to the audience.

Arsenault 7

References

Bear Aware British Columbia. (2006). Retrieved February 1, 2006, from http://www.bearaware.bc.ca

Herrero, S. (2002). *Bear attacks: Their causes and avoidance* (Rev. ed.). Guilford, CT: Lyons.

How to survive a bear encounter. (2005, June 6). *CBC News Online*. Retrieved January 19, 2006, from http://cbc.ca/printablestory.jsp

Sefton, D. (2000, October 1). Experts revisit advice on bear attacks. MSNBC. Retrieved January 19, 2006, from http://www.bears.org/pipermail/bearfolks/ 2000-October/000447.html

"Troublemakers" blamed for Alberta bear attacks. (2005, May 31). CTV.CA. Retrieved January 20, 2005, from http://www.ctv.ca/servlet/ArticleNews/story/ CTVNews/ 1117589489880_64/?hub=SciTeh

FIGURE 9.3 The homepage for the Canadian Lung Association makes a number of visual and verbal arguments.

9e A PERSUASIVE WEBSITE

Many non-profit organizations use websites to persuade people to take action on particular issues. Not surprisingly, the key issue for the Canadian Lung Association is air quality. The association uses its website to raise awareness about both the dangers of smoking and the benefits of clean air. On the website (Figure 9.3), you will find both visual and verbal arguments that work together to persuade viewers. For instance, images of blue skies and green fields, which make the viewer crave fresh air, are reinforced by a series of links on lung health.

9f A PERSUASIVE LETTER OF APPLICATION AND RESUMÉ

When you apply for a job, most often you send a **letter of application** (also called a **cover letter**) with your **resumé**. Together, the letter and the resumé are a proposal argument with the goal of a specific action—getting an interview. Letters of application and resumés use different tactics toward the same end. Resumés convey much information about your experience and skills in a small space. Letters of application favour depth and focus over coverage; they allow you to call the employer's attention to your key strengths as an applicant.

Letters of application

In writing a letter of application, don't fall into the trap of emphasizing why the job would be good for you. Successful letters focus on why you are good for the job, placing the reader's needs first. Show the reader that you are a competent, dynamic professional and a pleasant person. Here are some suggestions.

- Limit yourself to one page.
- In the inside address and salutation, use the name and title of the person doing the hiring whenever possible. If you don't know, call the organization to ask for the person's name, its correct spelling, and the person's official title. When responding to a help-wanted advertisement that lists only a post office box, begin the first paragraph after the inside address, omitting the salutation.
- In the first paragraph, explain your purpose for writing and name the position for which you are applying. List two of three qualifications that you have that you feel make you qualified for the position.
- In the second paragraph, elaborate the qualifications listed in your opener, and add evidence to support your claims for being qualified. Draw the evidence from prior experience, education, and skills (these should be listed on your resumé).
- In the third paragraph, describe additional qualifications or experience that you have that distinguishes you from other possible candidates. Do some research and demonstrate some familiarity with the company as you suggest ways you can help out the organization.
- Finally, mention that you've enclosed your resumé or add an enclosure line after the end of the letter. Express interest in speaking to the interviewer. Describe your availability for an interview. Give your contact information.

Resumés

You should start thinking about what kind of job you want long before you graduate. You may be able to arrange an internship or apply to a co-op program in your chosen field while you are still in school and get paid while gaining valuable experience. When you begin the serious job search, finding the right job depends on writing a successful resumé—one of the most important pieces of writing you will ever compose. The secret of a successful resumé is understanding its purpose. Above all, the purpose of your resumé is to get interviews with potential employers. Great jobs often attract many applicants. A successful resumé will place you among the small group of candidates to be interviewed.

Focus on the employer's needs. Begin by imagining that you are the person who will decide which candidate to hire. It is likely that person will be either the head of or a key member of the team that you hope to join. From that person's perspective, what qualities would the ideal candidate have? What would distinguish that candidate from other well-qualified candidates? Make a list of those qualities and put checks beside the ones you believe are most important. Then assess your own qualifications. What abilities and experiences do you have that match those of the ideal candidate?

Elements of a successful resumé

Many people think of a resumé as a life history beginning with elementary school. Nothing could be duller or less effective in a highly competitive job search. Instead, think of your resumé as an advertisement for yourself. In a very short space, you have to convince the prospective employer that you are competent, energetic, and collegial with co-workers. Some people think you only need one version of your resumé that you use for every application. Consider reorganizing sections of your resumé, depending upon the qualifications of the job advertisement, to highlight the matches between your experience and the organization's requirements. In some fields, an objective section is required in a resumé: visit your career centre to determine whether your field expects one or not. Similarly, some fields looks for an overview of the candidate's major qualifications and experience.

In the objective section target the position you are applying for: name the position, identify the location, and list the two most important qualities for excelling in that position. Instead of vague phrases like *an entry level position that presents new challenges and will fully utilize my talents,* be brief and focused:

> Credit reviewer in Central or South America where familiarity with local banking systems and fluency in Spanish and Portuguese are essential.

The overview section consists of short statements of the most important qualifications you bring to the position. How you structure this section depends on what you have to offer. List your education in reverse chronological order, beginning with certificates or degrees earned. List work experience in reverse chronological order, focusing on your more recent jobs and including details of your duties and accomplishments, as in the following:

Two years of experience analyzing computer system requirements and designing computer system specifications based on projected workloads.

Supervised, trained, and assessed the work of staff (1 to 4) involved in audit assists.

Reviewed real estate investments and loan portfolios for documentation, structure, credit analysis, risk identification, and credit scoring.

You can conclude with *References available upon request,* but this line is not necessary. You should never include the actual names and addresses of your references, but instead take them on a separate sheet to the interview.

Sample Job Advertisement

The letter of application should be tailored to the job advertisement. Figure 9.4 reproduces the advertisement to which the sample letter and resumé respond.

PAID INTERNSHIP

Employer: Digital Workshop Inc.

Job Title: Junior System/Network Administrator

Work Location: Edmonton, AB

Successful applicant must grasp knowledge of network infrastructure to resolve users' issues quickly without interrupting company operations. He or she must meet project-oriented deadlines and accept additional assignments to improve his or her professional development. After three weeks of training in Edmonton, candidate will be placed in St. Louis, Missouri, for the rest of the term. Must have a Canadian passport.

Required skills:
- Excellent communication, both oral and written
- Able to learn technical and professional skills
- Able to act calmly in critical situations
- Self-motivated

Preferred requirements: Knowledge of these operating systems:
- MS Windows (2000, XP)
- Sun Solaris 9
- CISCO IOS
- Linux

Knowledge of the following network protocols:
- TCP/IP
- HTTP(s)
- (t)FTP
- SSH

Knowledge of following hardware platforms:
- Intel x86
- Sun SPARC

Email resumé to Fergus Blackwell, fblackwell@dwi.com

FIGURE 9.4 A sample job advertisement. Target your application letter to the qualifications described in the advertisement.

Sample letter of application

---

937 2nd Ave NW
Calgary, AB T2N 0E7

February 2, 2007

Fergus Blackwell
Digital Workshop Inc.
7914 59th Street
Edmonton, AB T6B 3C3

Dear Mr. Blackwell:

Please consider my application for the internship position of junior network administrator at Digital Workshop Inc. recently advertised online at the career centre on the University of Calgary's website. My major qualifications for your position include some experience setting up and maintaining a small secure wireless network, my coursework so far towards a Bachelor of Applied Science in computer engineering from the University of Calgary, excellent written and oral communication skills, and authorization to work in the United States.

In this paragraph, Park applies to the job, identifies the position, explains where he saw the advertisement, and states his major qualifications for the job.

I have some experience with setting up and maintaining a network, having set up secure wireless networks for various friends and relatives, which has given me a strong basic knowledge of TCP/IP, SSH, (t)FTP, and HTTP(s). I have also gained experience with Linux and Windows operating systems through several assignments in electrical and computer engineer classes offered through my program. My communication skills are also quite strong: in my final year of high school the Senior Prose English Award was given to me for an essay entitled "Experience." Although I am a Canadian citizen, I grew up in the city of Chicago, and I have retained my permanent resident card while I am attending post-secondary school in Canada. Therefore, I am authorized to work in the U.S. so travelling to St. Louis, MO, and working there for several months would be no problem for me.

In this paragraph, Park elaborates the three major qualifications in the first paragraph, providing evidence to show his strength as a candidate.

My interest in computer hardware and software has been ongoing. I have read and experimented with computer components and software for many years. This experience will be valuable as it will make me able to respond quickly and efficiently to the various problems that you assign me as a network administrator at Digital Workshop. If I don't know how to do something, I can calmly and easily find out whatever I need to know to finish whatever type of project you might assign me as part of the innovative approaches to database management that helped Digital Workshop win recognition as one of the top 200 fastest-growing companies in Canada.

I look forward to meeting with you in an interview where we can further discuss the qualifications in my resumé (enclosed) and the ways in which I can use these skills and education to help Digital Workshop develop additional database management applications. My schedule is flexible this term, so you can reach me either through email at tspark@yahoo.ca or on my cell phone at 403-123-4567 to schedule an interview any afternoon during the week or anytime on the weekend.

Sincerely,

Terrence S. Park

Sample resumé

Terrence S. Park
937 2nd Ave NW
Calgary, AB T2N 0E7
tspark@yahoo.ca
403-123-4567

SKILLS
Extensive knowledge regarding PC hardware quality, installation, maintenance, etc.
Quick and efficient learner
Self-motivated and able to work well both independently and in groups
High level of experience with Windows 98/2000/XP
Knowledge of Ubuntu Linux
High degree of experience with Microsoft Office, including Excel and Word
Object-oriented C# programming experience and interest
Experience with wireless and local area networking

EDUCATION
2003–2007 B Sc (Applied), Computer Engineering
University of Calgary, Calgary, AB

EXPERIENCE
2004–2007 Help Desk, University of Calgary
Stationed at help desk 10–15 hours a week, solving users' problems as quickly and efficiently as possible. Also troubleshot issues with LAN, computer classrooms, and public labs.
2002–2003 Wait Staff, Swiss Chalet, Calgary, AB
Waited on tables, some food preparation, cleaning as necessary. Won "Wait Person of the Year" in 2003.

AWARDS
Senior Prose English Award for non-fiction essay (high school)
Placed seventh in high jump at the 2004 Canadian Junior Track and Field Championships in Saskatoon, SK

INTERESTS
High jump: dedicated year-round training 3 days a week. Will continue training for the high jump with the goal of representing Canada at the 2012 Olympics Games in London.
Computer hardware: recently built personal computer with heavy emphasis on performance-to-cost ratio, which required extensive research into every hardware component
Electronics: including radios, televisions, small appliances, wireless devices, modified video game consoles and how they work
Writing: mostly prose essays, with occasional short stories

WORK AUTHORIZATION
Citizenship: Canadian
Other: U.S. Permanent Resident Card holder

WRITING IN THE WORLD

Resumés

Most resumés are loaded directly into an electronic database in one of two ways: the applicant cuts and pastes information into a web form, or attaches a word-processed file. Applications are made online by cutting and pasting the relevant information into the correct area of the online form. You may also be asked to append a traditional version of your resumé as a document attachment to the form. The traditional resumé should include bullets, italics, boldfacing, and different type sizes. It must look attractive and highlight the most important information about your experience and qualifications. The blocks of plain text that you submit on the application form go into a database that the company uses to search for qualified applicants when new positions become available.

The information from your resumé that you submit to the database must contain words that can be scanned, sorted, and retrieved by a search engine. The employer will do keyword searches on the resumé database, so it's critical to anticipate which keywords the employer might use to find you. For example, an employer might search for *Oracle RDBMS* and *data modelling*. If you have *Oracle RDBMS* and *database administration* but not *data modelling* on your resumé, you will be overlooked. The best strategy is to include as many different nouns as possible that might describe you. Think about which nouns best represent your experiences and abilities and work them into your job descriptions or collect them together into a keywords section. Include not only nouns central to your areas of expertise and experience but also some personal qualities that signal your ability to work well with others: *team-player, self-motivation, independent learner,* or *detail-orientation.* The more matches your resumé can make with the terms under consideration, the greater the chance that you will come up as a viable candidate for interview.

If you are asked to submit a traditional copy of your resumé as a supplement to the online form, make sure it covers all the traditional elements of a resumé, including your work history. If you are not asked to submit a traditional resumé, but you do get an interview, make sure to bring along a copy printed on good-quality paper to refer to during the interview and to leave behind when the interview is over.

CHAPTER *10*

Writing about Literature

Less experienced readers sometimes believe that literature is a game played between writers and readers. The writer of literature hides the "real meaning" of a text beneath layers of symbols, images, metaphors, and other fancy literary tricks, daring the reader to find it. Literature is not three-card monte. Literary texts strive to open ground where your imagination and intellect can roam. Instead of hunting for the author's secret meaning, concentrate on developing a reading of your own. Experienced readers read texts several times before they become comfortable with them. They read methodically, recording their ideas in marginal notes or a reading journal.

10a BECOME A CRITICAL READER OF LITERATURE

Reading literature requires a set of practices different from those you might use while reading the Sunday paper or a memo from your boss. Think of yourself as an active critical observer. Your goal is not merely to soak up the text as you might a magazine article. Instead, carry on a dialogue with the text using marginal notes. Resist the urge to use a highlighter; highlighted text will help you identify passages that seemed significant during a previous reading, but it won't help you remember *why* they seemed so. Alternatively, consider keeping a reading journal, in which you record significant phrases (with page numbers) and your responses to these points. Although writing in the margins or a journal as you read may seem like extra work at first, you will soon discover that it saves time and, before long, sharpens your reading skills. Keeping a record of your reading will force you to engage with a text; being an active, critical reader gives you practice toward being a thoughtful reader. And marginal comments will be your best source from which to generate a paper topic.

The following is a partial list of aspects of a literary text you may want to note as you read:

- your gut response
- questions or points of confusion
- shifts in tone, plot, or character

- patterns
- contradictions
- word choice
- repeated words, sounds (alliteration), images, or motifs
- the effect of the narrative technique
- imagery and interesting metaphors
- allusions to other works

When reading poetry you may also want to note:

- rhyme scheme
- metre
- line breaks
- punctuation
- stanza breaks

"My Last Duchess," by British Victorian poet Robert Browning, is reproduced below, with annotations added by an active, critical reader in preparation for writing an English literature assignment that asked students to analyze how the Duke of Ferrara reveals more than he intends to through his dramatic monologue.

My Last Duchess

Ferrara

That's my last Duchess painted on the wall,

What, she wasn't a wonder when alive? (2)

Looking as if she were alive. I call

That piece a wonder, now: Frà Pandolf's hands

Work'd busily a day, and there she stands.

Will't please you sit and look at her? I said   5

Her expression is noteworthy—she is captivated by whatever she's looking at. (7–8)

"Frà Pandolf" by design: for never read

Strangers like you that pictur'd countenance,

The depth and passion of its earnest glance,

He controls who looks at her now, and therefore thinks he controls who/what she looks at now? (9–10)

But to myself they turn'd (since none puts by

The curtain I have drawn for you, but I)   10

And seem'd as they would ask me, if they durst,

How such a glance came there; so, not the first

Are you to turn and ask thus. Sir, 'twas not

The root of the problem: her typical response to anything that pleases her, apparently (according to the duke). (13–15)

Her husband's presence only, call'd that spot

Of joy into the Duchess' cheek: perhaps   15

Frà Pandolf chanced to say "Her mantle laps

Over my lady's wrist too much," or "Paint

He thinks that she saw any compliment as a courteous statement that needed response. How else might she have explained her behaviour? (19–20)

Must never hope to reproduce the faint

Half-flush that dies along her throat:" Such stuff

Was courtesy, she thought, and cause enough   20
For calling up that spot of joy. She had

> Was she too appreciative of other people? Should she be more aloof? (22–24)

A heart—how shall I say?—too soon made glad,
Too easily impress'd; she lik'd whate'er
She look'd on, and her looks went everywhere.
Sir, 'twas all one! My favor at her breast,   25

> A key point: She didn't single out his gift to show it was more significant than others'. (25–34)

The dropping of the daylight in the West,
The bough of cherries some officious fool
Broke in the orchard for her, the white mule
She rode with round the terrace—all and each
Would draw from her alike the approving speech,   30
Or blush, at least. She thank'd men,—good! But thank'd
Somehow—I know not how—as if she rank'd
My gift of a nine-hundred-years-old name

> He's obviously blaming her for not making him feel special. (34–35)

With anybody's gift. Who'd stoop to blame
This sort of trifling? Even had you skill   35
In speech—(which I have not)—to make your will
Quite clear to such an one, and say, "Just this
Or that in you disgusts me; here you miss,
Or there exceed the mark"—and if she let

> She should obey instantly, without questioning or explaining her actions. (39–41)

Herself be lesson'd so, nor plainly set   40
Her wits to yours, forsooth, and made excuse,

> It is "stoop[ing]" to blame her, so he does stoop, when it suits him. (42–43)

—E'en then would be some stooping; and I choose
Never to stoop. Oh sir, she smil'd, no doubt,
Whene'er I pass'd her; but who pass'd without

> He had her killed because she didn't obey him. (46)

Much the same smile? This grew; I gave commands;   45
Then all smiles stopp'd together. There she stands
As if alive. Will't please you rise? We'll meet

> Does she appear alive because she's still smiling? The painting enshrines this behaviour. How ironic. (46–47)

The company below, then. I repeat,
The Count your master's known munificence

> He's scrounging for a dowry for the next girl. Is he revealing his real motive? (49–53)

Is ample warrant that no just pretence   50
Of mine for Dowry will be disallow'd;
Though his fair daughter's self, as I avow'd
At starting, is my object. Nay, we'll go

> Duke insists they walk down together. Men are equals, women are subordinates? (53–54)

Together down, sir. Notice Neptune, though,
Taming a sea-horse, thought a rarity,   55
Which Claus of Innsbruck cast in bronze for me!

—Robert Browning

COMMON ERRORS

Confusing narrator or speaker with author

It's easy but incorrect to assume that the narrator of a work of fiction or the speaker of a poem is the author. *Narrator, speaker,* and *author* are not interchangeable. Think of the narrator as you think of other characters: the author's creative construction. For example, Robert Browning creates the character of the Duke of Ferrara, the speaker in "My Last Duchess," to communicate to us the excesses of absolute power. Refer to the speaker of a work of literature as the narrator (in a work of fiction) or the speaker (in a poem) rather than as the author.

Remember: Do not refer to the narrator as the author.

 For step-by-step discussion, examples, and practice of this common error, go to **www.pearsoned.ca/faigley/216**.

10b   DEVELOP AN ORIGINAL ARGUMENT

Assignments for English classes tend to be more open-ended than writing assignments in other disciplines. Use the freedom that an open-ended assignment offers to focus on an aspect of the text that interests you. Take a stand. Develop an original idea. Your job is to enlighten readers with your analysis of a literary text. Challenge conventional readings. Show readers something they may not have noticed, or offer a new analysis of an old observation. Ideally your audience will see the text differently after reading your argument.

Opinion versus argument

Papers about literature are often called *critical analyses*. Don't let the term trip you up. *Critical* in this sense doesn't mean judgmental. The fact is, your understanding of the text is much more interesting to a reader than whether you like it or not. Avoid making an argument about your opinion of a text unless the assignment specifically asks for one. Instead, develop a complex argument that illuminates some aspect of the text. Based on a topic that interests you, develop a thesis, or statement that conveys an interesting and controversial stance about the literary work, a statement that needs expansion and defence to be convincing. Harvey Birenbaum summarizes what makes a thesis good: "A good thesis statement cannot be self-evident; it is controversial and risky, crying out for a good defense"

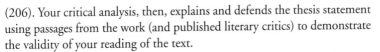
(206). Your critical analysis, then, explains and defends the thesis statement using passages from the work (and published literary critics) to demonstrate the validity of your reading of the text.

Source: Harvey Birenbaum. *The Happy Critic.* Mountain View, CA: Mayfield, 1997.

Simple versus complex arguments

Simple arguments are usually obvious and basic: for example, the Duke of Ferrara wants his listener to know that he's a jealous man who doesn't like his women to pay attention to other people or things; he also reveals that he's petty and insecure. This thesis isn't risky; even a superficial reading of the poem would communicate this point about the duke. You could add evidence to explain this thesis more clearly, but your reader wouldn't know much beyond what he or she could get from just reading the poem. Because such arguments lack the meatiness of a complex argument, they tend to read like a list; each paragraph simply piles up more evidence to prove the same point (the duke's pettiness and insecurity). Simple arguments tend to fall into generalizations about broad topics or offer observations about a text without developing it into an analysis. They may be well supported, but they won't compel the reader to view the text in a new way.

Complex arguments don't rest with easy or obvious answers. By concentrating on a sufficiently narrow topic, they can go into depth. While simple arguments generate black-and-white answers, complex arguments delve into grey areas. Each paragraph plays a role in unfolding an original analysis. Notice in the following example that the simple argument doesn't go beyond initial observation. The writer will be stuck illustrating the same idea again and again. The complex argument, on the other hand, refuses to accept tidy generalizations. Instead, it delves into the poem's subtleties.

SIMPLE ARGUMENT

In "My Last Duchess," the Duke of Ferrara shows the emissary the painting of his last wife as a warning to be passed along to the new bride about his expectations for her behaviour. When he tries to justify getting rid of her, his reasons reveal that he is petty and insecure.

COMPLEX ARGUMENT

Despite the duke's efforts to demonstrate how he ultimately took absolute control over his previous wife's behaviour to the emissary of his future wife, the fact that his last duchess continues to smile graciously at whomever he displays the painting to undercuts his image of himself as "Neptune . . . taming a sea-horse." The very characteristic in his late wife that he found so objectionable he has, ironically, enshrined forever in the portrait on his staircase. The big question becomes, who is Neptune, and who is the seahorse?

This thesis statement makes some surprising claims about the duke and the details in the poem that arrest your attention and intrigue you: you want to read on to find out what elements of the poem motivated these controversial and risky claims about what the duke is communicating to the emissary and to us, as readers.

Develop a complex argument

One way to develop a complex argument is to return to your marginal notes or reading journal and review the points that sparked your comment. Look for patterns or a connecting thread among the comments. Ask yourself *what*, *how*, and *why* questions to expand these ideas. These questions lead you from observation, to exploration, to an argument.

Observation: What's going on in the text?

If your assignment is open-ended, then examine your notes to see what you observed in the text that was unexpected, odd, powerful, or central. What questions did you ask? Wonderful arguments frequently evolve from a question or confusion about the text. If your assignment is more focused, such as the one reproduced in this chapter, then you might need to reread the text with the assignment in mind to spark some ideas related to that topic.

For example, in the marginal notes to "My Last Duchess," the reader has already noted an unexpected and contradictory point related to the assignment focus: the duke claims that he "choose[s] never to stoop," yet he clearly chose to "stoop to blame / This sort of trifling." Why does he stoop in one instance but choose not to in another? Are there other instances in which he also stooped?

Here are some other examples of intriguing questions that could be expanded into complex and controversial thesis statements:

Why does the concluding scene of *Pride and Prejudice* feature the Gardiners, two secondary characters?

Why do two chapters entitled "Night" bookend *The Handmaid's Tale*?

Although you won't have an argument at this stage, answering *why* questions will help you narrow your focus to a potentially fruitful topic for argument.

Exploration: How does the text do what it's doing?

The answer to this question may consider technical, stylistic, or thematic aspects of the text. At this point you'll begin to develop the first stages of your argument.

How does the duke convey his intentions to the emissary? He confides that he chooses never to stoop, yet he stoops both in being petty about his previous wife's behaviour and in revealing to his future bride (for her edification) what he refused to reveal to the past one—the cause of his dissatisfaction. Browning has him communicate more than he intends to in these statements: he stoops when it benefits him.

How does Austen feature the Gardiners in the last scene of *Pride and Prejudice*? Throughout the novel Austen shows us strained or broken marriages, but the Gardiners are an exception. She presents them as a well-matched, well-adjusted couple.

How do the two chapters called "Night" serve to set up and conclude the plot in *The Handmaid's Tale*? The first chapter describes the heroine's anxious uncertainty about the future prior to reaching the commander's household. The last chapter describes her exit, which is also anxious and uncertain.

Analysis and argument: Why does the text do what it's doing?

Consider to what end or for what purpose the text functions as it does. What are the ultimate implications of this feature of the text? Frequently, answers will fall into one of the following lines of inquiry:

1. It advances or complicates a major theme of the text.
2. It engages in commentary about larger political, social, philosophical, or literary issues of the author's day.
3. It reflects the influence of another writer or text.
4. It advances the plot or adds depth to a character.
5. It's attempting to be technically innovative. It highlights a capability or limitation in the author's choice of theme, genre, structure, stylistic elements, or narrative technique.

The following exploration draws on number 4 above.

Why does Browning want us to recognize that the duke will stoop when it suits him? It alerts readers as to the duke's real motives in his serial marriages. For example, the duke switches the conversation abruptly from his last duchess to negotiations about the dowry for the next duchess. He notes that the count's reputation for generosity satisfies him that whatever amount is requested the count will grant. Secondarily, he notes that the girl, not the money, is his real goal. Again, an abrupt change of subject when he indicates a bronze statue of "Neptune . . . / Taming a sea-horse, thought a rarity." Is it the statue itself that is rare or the act of successfully taming a seahorse? And did the duke "tame" his last duchess, when she can still smile indiscriminately at the servant to whom the duke "introduces" her?

Why does the end of *Pride and Prejudice* feature secondary characters, the Gardiners? The Gardiners exemplify successful marriage. By ending the novel with them, Austen lends a note of hope for Elizabeth and Darcy's union. The novel, then, is not a condemnation of marriage as an institution but of the social forces that promote bad matches. We can analyze Austen's characterization of the Gardiners to better understand the kind of marriage making she wants to advocate.

Why do two chapters entitled "Night" bookend *The Handmaid's Tale*? The first chapter describes how the girls' identities have been stripped away by their training as handmaidens, but it ends by showing how, under cover of night, the girls reinforce their personal identities. In the last chapter, the heroine's personal identity may be restored to her as she is removed from the household under cover of night. Infected by the paranoia of the society that has oppressed her, however, she fears either the freedom or the slavery that may await her.

10c SUPPORT YOUR ARGUMENT

Using the text as evidence

Have you ever worked to use the text as evidence in your paper only to have your instructor write in the margins "Don't summarize"? The trick is to employ the text in a way that creates analysis rather than summary. First, keep your audience in mind. Those who have already read the work will be bored by plot summary. Instead of summary, use quotations or paraphrased passages to advance your argument. Second, never use the text as evidence without analyzing it. Your analysis should be a close reading of the text that explains *how* the passage you've chosen illustrates your argument. A close reading looks at the details of the text; refer to the list in Section 10a for elements of the text you may want to discuss in a close reading.

Incorporating literary criticism

When you tackle an assignment that asks you to address literary criticism, you take on an additional responsibility in your argument. If you're writing about *Hamlet*, for instance, you have to enter a conversation among critics that has been going on for several hundred years.

If your instructor doesn't select critical sources for you, your first task is to narrow your scope to the point where the body of criticism you must address is not intimidating. Do some preliminary research on your topic to make a list of the major critical books and articles. Ask your instructor to review the list to identify the most important ones and to recommend any that you may have missed. You can use the critical works to help you select a compelling topic or to help you elaborate your chosen topic as points of support or disagreement.

As you read the critical works, identify common concerns, points of contention, and issues of interpretation. Once you understand the critical works, figure out how to use them in an argument. Your goal should be to contribute to the ongoing critical conversation, not merely to affirm or oppose it. Consider ways you can advance or revise the conversation about your topic. Does your interpretation of the text advance or complicate an existing critical perspective? Is there a scene or aspect of the text that the critics don't consider but should? Are the critics taking the historical, political, or social context of the work into account sufficiently? By developing original responses to these questions, you can enter the critical conversation.

Using the literary present tense

The disciplinary convention in English is to employ the literary present tense. The literary present tense requires the use of present tense when analyzing any literary text such as a poem, a play, a work of fiction, an essay, or a sermon. Also use the present tense when discussing literary criticism.

INCORRECT	In *Song of Myself* Walt Whitman **tempered** his exuberant language with undercurrents of doubt about whether language **could** do all he **asked** of it.	Past tense
CORRECT	In *Song of Myself* Walt Whitman **tempers** his exuberant language with undercurrents of doubt about whether language **can** do all he **asks** of it.	Present tense

However, you should employ the past tense when discussing literary history. The author's life, the creation of the text, the text's publication, and the critical reception of the text all exist outside the work itself and require the past tense. The following passage uses the past tense to discuss the publication history and critical reception of *Leaves of Grass*.

Beyond doubting whether his audience would understand the spirit of his verse, Whitman **worried** that *Leaves of Grass* would never reach an audience at all. He **was** so concerned, in fact, that he **published** reviews of the book under false names to drum up publicity.	Past tense

WRITING SMART

Electronic resources for writing about literature

While libraries are still the best places for literary research, you can find a number of handy resources online.

- **Bartleby.com** (www.bartleby.com) features free e-texts of well-known poetry, prose, and reference works, including the *Cambridge History of English and American Literature*. (continued next page)

- **Library and Archives Canada** (www.collectionscanada.ca) has an extensive and searchable collection of literary texts and criticism featuring Canadian (and other types of) literature.
- **MLA Bibliography** is an expansive searchable bibliography (available through the online reference site of most research libraries) of literary criticism.
- **Oxford English Dictionary** (dictionary.oed.com/entrance.dtl) is an electronic version of the OED, as it's commonly called, which records the history of a word's meaning, tracking where it first appeared and how its definition has changed through the years.
- **Project Gutenberg** (www.gutenberg.net) offers free e-texts of hundreds of works of literature.

`10d` SAMPLE LITERARY ANALYSIS

The following student paper responds to this assignment topic: "Writing early in the twentieth century about Robert Browning's poetry, R. V. Routh (in *Towards the Twentieth Century* [Cambridge, Eng., 1937]) noted that his 'best effects are produced by a kind of dramatic irony, by which the speaker reveals himself as infinitely better or (more often) worse than he supposes himself to be' (107). This quotation clearly applies to the speaker, the Duke of Ferrara, in Browning's dramatic monologue, 'My Last Duchess.' Analyze how the Duke reveals much more than he intends about himself and his relationships. Whether you want to argue that his revelations show him to be 'infinitely better or . . . worse than he supposes himself to be' is up to you, but incorporate related critical scholarship to support your own analysis and interpretation of the poem on whichever view you choose."

This essay uses close reading of the text to propose a new interpretation of the ending of the poem. It draws on appearance versus reality, a common topic in literary analysis, as a principle of organization. While it appears that the duke enjoys absolute control, the circumstances reveal that in reality he has compromised his positions. The essay uses MLA documentation style.

Keith 1

Drew Keith

Professor Hunt

Literature and Culture

March 28, 2006

His Last Duchess Tames the Duke

Robert Browning's dramatic monologue, "My Last
Duchess," ends with the Duke of Ferrara pointing out to
the emissary of his future father-in-law a bronze casting of
"Neptune, . . . / Taming a sea-horse, thought a rarity /
Which Claus of Innsbruck cast in bronze for me" (Browning
54–56). This statue of the Roman god of the sea subduing
a seahorse colours the previous conversation in which the
duke explicitly describes the type of behaviour he expects
in his future bride. There is some disagreement among
critics about whether or not the duke is consciously
revealing instruction for his prospective new bride. In
"Browning's Witless Duke," B.R. Berman argues against
this interpretation, but the evidence he offers against it
relies mostly on emphasizing the duke's proud character.
Other critics, including Laurence Perrine, argue that the
duke's obvious pride should be no prohibition against him
also being shrewd. It seems reasonable to regard this
apparently offhand reference as intended to apply
simultaneously to his future matrimonial prospects and his
past experience, casting the duke as Neptune and the
future (and past) duchess as the seahorse, being schooled
in his expectations of proper wifely behaviour. At least,
this is how the duke expects the emissary to understand
this reference and his veiled instruction to the prospective
bride. But, as eavesdroppers to the lesson, readers have

Opening paragraph
starts with key
moment in the
poem. Critics with
opposing
viewpoints on the
duke's intelligence
highlight contrary
interpretations.

gained a whole new perspective on the duke's relationship with his "last" duchess.

The duke draws the curtain so the emissary may gaze on his "last" duchess, and then he explains the origin of the expression captured in the painting as his justification for ordering the apparent execution of this engaging woman: "Sir, 'twas not / Her husband's presence only, call'd that spot / Of joy into the Duchess' cheek" (13–15). The reader notes that his presence, in fact, may have drawn this spot of joy into her cheek, so it was not that she failed to appreciate her husband and respond demonstrably to his attention. However, the duke continues by noting that

> Sir, 'twas all one! My favor at her breast,
> The dropping of the daylight in the West,
> The bough of cherries some officious fool
> Broke in the orchard for her . . .
> Would draw from her alike the approving speech,
> Or blush, at least (25–31).

Readers see that his dissatisfaction arose, not from her blushing in response to other men, but blushing over many things that gave her pleasure in life. He felt that she should treat his gifts differently, tempering her pleasure over anything that did not come from him: "she rank'd / My gift of a nine-hundred-years-old name / With anybody's gift" (33–34). We see that he was both petty and jealous that she did not attend particularly to making him feel special.

The next step in the duke's argument is to explain that this indiscriminate response in his late wife justified

Summary underscores the flaws in the duke's justification for eliminating his previous wife: she was not unfaithful, just too egalitarian in her responses.

Keith 3

her removal: "I gave commands; / Then all smiles stopp'd together. There she stands / As if alive" (45–47). In fact, in this portrait, the duke has captured for all eternity the very indiscriminate and intimate smile that so provoked him when she was alive. He has noted to the emissary that "none puts by / The curtain I have drawn for you, but I" (9–10), implying that he now has control over at whom his last duchess smiles. That may be true, but she still continues to smile *in the same way* (intimately and indiscriminately); he has tried to gain ultimate and absolute control over her behaviour, but in fact this portrait has captured for all eternity the very characteristic in his late wife that he found so objectionable. She may be dead, but her undiscriminating smile lives on. On these grounds we can ask, "Did he really tame her?"

> This paragraph unpacks the key element of the assignment: interesting points the duke reveals about himself that he did not intend.

In enumerating the problem with his previous wife, the duke himself acknowledges that his complaint may have been petty: "Who'd stoop to blame / This sort of trifling?" (34–35), he notes. His word choice here foreshadows his later proud claim that he "choose[s] / Never to stoop" (42–43) to explain why he chose not to allow her the chance to amend her behaviour. Berman takes the duke's assertion at face value: "Petty wrangling, even polite suggestion that she might not spread her personality so thin, would have been beneath his dignity, he insists—and we believe him. . . . It seems unlikely, therefore, that he would consciously unbend to tell 'strangers' like the emissary, directly or even subtly, what he expects of this new woman" (Berman 492). In contrast, Perrine notes that the duke's skill with words,

> In the last two paragraphs he brings in critical support for the point that the duke is *not* too proud to stoop when it suits him.

demonstrated throughout the poem, justifies judging him as both proud and shrewd: "[I]f the Duke can 'stoop' to state plainly what he expects in dowry, why should he not state subtly what he expects of a wife?" (Perrine 159). To further support this reading, one has only to point to the poem itself, where the duke clearly labels blaming her as a species of "stooping." Why might he stoop in one instance but choose not to in another? Evidence from the poem does support interpreting the message embedded in his story about the last duchess as a communication to the next duchess: he wishes to reveal to her what he refused to reveal to the past one—the cause of his dissatisfaction.

This paragraph links the point that the Duke has been tamed by his last duchess and that he cares more for the dowry than the girl.

Why does Browning want us to recognize that the duke will stoop when it suits him? It alerts readers to consider what might be the duke's real motives in his serial marriages. For example, the duke switches the conversation abruptly from his last duchess to negotiations about the dowry for the next duchess. He notes that the count's reputation for generosity satisfies him that whatever amount is requested the count will grant. Secondarily, he notes that the girl, not the money, is his real goal. Again, the subject changes abruptly when he indicates a bronze statue of "Neptune . . . / Taming a sea-horse, thought a rarity" (54–55). Is it the statue itself that is rare or the act of successfully taming a seahorse? It also raises that question about whom we should see as Neptune and whom as the seahorse. When his last duchess can still smile intimately and indiscriminately at the servant to whom the duke introduces her, is she really tamed? And the fact that the duke must "stoop" to

Keith 5

revealing this side of himself to both the emissary and his prospective bride makes us wonder if, in fact, it is not he who has been tamed by his "last duchess."

Works Cited

Berman, B.R. "Browning's Witless Duke." *PMLA* 72.3 (June 1957): 488–93.

Perrine, Laurence. "Browning's Shrewd Duke." *PMLA* 74.1 (March 1959): 157–59.

CHAPTER *11*

Writing about Film and New Media

In many ways, writing about film and new media is a lot like writing about literature: you need to develop a critical perspective on the film, game, or website that you are writing about. Just as good readers of literature will re-read a text (or parts of a text) several times, so, too, will film critics view a film more than once. They might even re-view related films by the same director or involving some of the same actors if they feel that this would help them write a more nuanced and informative critique. Critical essays based on games and other new media demand that the writer have extensive experience with the game and perhaps with similar games on the market now or games from the previous generation or competing platforms. This kind of research helps writers build context for their comments and extends the scope of their writing beyond the instance of the particular film, game, or media product under consideration. Ultimately, this kind of knowledge makes your writing more sophisticated and informative.

11a BECOMING A CRITICAL VIEWER

To view films or new media critically requires you to create distance between yourself and the film or media you are evaluating. How do you do that? One way is to view a film several times; after the second or third viewing, you become less conscious of the plot because you know what is going to happen. You then become more conscious of other aspects of the film, such as the acting, wardrobes, sets, camera angles, and so on. Re-viewing a film allows you to step outside the flow of action that tends to dominate a first viewing. The same can be said for video games: the first few times you play, your attention probably focuses on trying to stay alive (in the case of first-person shooter games) or active. After you've become adept at the game, you can attend to other aspects of it: the quality of the graphics, the cleverness of the plot and storyline, and the relative challenges that the game poses for various levels of players. If you have had experience with previous versions of a particular game—or similar games from other manufacturers that are in the same genre—then you can draw upon that experience, too, when you evaluate or comment.

11b LEARNING THE GENRE: FILM REVIEWS

One way to learn what makes for a good review of films and media is to read the reviews others have written. To find reviews of films, visit these internet sites:

- Rotten Tomatoes (www.rottentomatoes.com; see Figure 11.1)
- Internet Movie Database (www.imdb.com; see Figure 11.2)
- Movie Review Query Engine (www.mrqe.com/lookup)
- Yahoo Movie Review page (dir.yahoo.com/Entertainment/ Movies_ and_Film/Reviews/)
- UC Berkeley library film studies resource page (www.lib.berkeley .edu/MRC/filmstudies/reviewslist.html)
- Roger Ebert (rogerebert.com)
- Filmcritic.com (www.filmcritic.com)

Criticism and analysis tend to differ from film reviews, however, so you should be aware of the distinctions your professors may make between these kinds of writing assignments.

You've probably read film reviews when trying to decide whether or not—or which—film to watch. The reviews tend to be short—between 500 and 1000 words—and focus pretty much exclusively on the movie being reviewed, although they sometimes include brief references or comparisons to sequels or movies from the same genre. Reviews also tend to be

FIGURE 11.1 www.rottentomatoes.com

FIGURE 11.2 www.imdb.com

specific, personal evaluations of one particular film. Another key point about reviews is that they are written for readers who have not yet seen the film. Readers read movie reviews to evaluate whether they should spend their time and money viewing this particular film.

In writing about a horror movie such as *Slither,* for example, reviewers will comment only on that film. While reviewers may mention other films that the director worked on or that some of the actors appeared in, these references are brief, often parenthetical, notes. The introduction to a review takes some innovative aspect of the film—in *Slither*'s case, the word itself— and then places the film in the genre of horror films by alluding to previous classic films. A plot summary appears early in the review, followed by comments evaluating some important aspects of the film, such as pacing, character development, plot development, and special effects. Generally, a film review does not "give away" the ending.

11c LEARNING THE GENRE: FILM CRITICISM

As a student in a film course, you may be asked to respond to films in a variety of ways besides reviews. An important component of these responses will be analysis. An analysis differs from a review in that you assume the reader has seen and understood the film and is interested in a new interpretation (which your analysis offers). Since your reader is familiar with the film, you can reduce the amount of plot summary in your analysis to include just the details needed to provide a context for your points of analysis. There are a number of genres that you may be asked to write, depending on what your instructor feels is important in understanding a film. They tend to fall into the categories listed below.

In a film class, you may be asked to write a *mise en scène* analysis. **Mise en scène** refers to analyzing a particular scene or cut in a film using established criteria. Some of the criteria that may be used in a *mise en scène* analysis are as follows:

- Production design (sets, props, costumes)
- Colour (production design and lighting)
- Lighting
- Actors' movement/blocking
- Framing (depth of field, height, angle)
- Sound
- Black and white or colour film, fine-grain or grainy texture

If you were writing a *mise en scène* analysis of a scene—for example, the opening of *Pride & Prejudice* (2005)—you might decide to discuss the details of the costume worn by Keira Knightley as she finishes reading her book and arrives home. You might also assess the framing of the book, over her shoulder, and the final page before she closes it. As you can see, *mise en scène* analysis parallels "close reading" in literary analysis because both techniques ask you to focus on what is in the scene or the text. In your *mise en scène* analysis, you would take each (or some) of the characteristics above and comment on how each one contributes to your understanding of a particular scene in the film and its significance.

One complication that may come up is that *mise en scène* can also refer to a style of filmmaking in which the entire film is made up of scenes, and each scene is one shot. This style contrasts with the montage style, a style dominated by frequent cuts to different angles, the sort of style associated with many fast-paced music videos. Check with your instructor to confirm that the assignment is limited to *mise en scène* analysis or that *mise en scène* style is just one of several aspects you are being asked to evaluate.

Sequence analysis asks you to focus specifically on a set of shots within a smaller part or sequence within a film. In this kind of analysis, you would begin the process of researching the essay by identifying all of the shots within a sequence. You would then write an essay explaining how these shots make sense or are joined together for viewers as the sequence proceeds. Why does one shot lead to the next? What does each shot add to the narrative of the sequence—does it provide a reaction, a confirmation, a contrast? What are the borders of this sequence? How is this sequence related to other sequences in the film? How is sound used both within the sequence itself and as a transition into and out of the sequence?

Critical analysis essays take the specific techniques within a film—the *mise en scène* and sequence techniques described above—and add to them an understanding of the cultural context of the film. Here are some of the key questions a critical analysis attempts to answer:

- When was the film made? What was going on economically and politically?
- What other films were made at that time? Is this film part of a genre or specific kind of film?
- What is the quality of the screenwriting? Is the dialogue realistic or didactic?
- Who made the film? What other films did this person make?
- How was the film received by critics and the public when it was first released?
- Does the film make connections to other films, to historical events, and/or to people?

This kind of essay resembles the kind of researched essay described in the Writing about Literature chapter and in Part 5: Researching (Chapters 16–21). You will need to find out something about the film in question.

Look for information about these types of related subjects:

- Reviews of the film at the time it was released
- Some news stories pertaining to cultural, economic, and political events at the time
- Biographical information about who made it
- Other films made at the time that may have influenced the director

Consider starting your research process with these sources:

- *On the Screen*: A film, television, and video research guide
- *The Oxford Guide to Film Studies*
- *Film Literature Index*
- FIAF International FilmArchive Database
- International Index to the Performing Arts
- *International Index to Film Periodicals*
- *Retrospective Index to Film Periodicals*
- *Canadian Film Encyclopedia* (www.filmreferencelibrary.ca/; see Figure 11.3)

View the films you are studying several times, making notes about the structure, themes, techniques, and your own reactions to them. Do some

FIGURE 11.3 www.filmreferencelibrary.ca

Electronic resources for writing about film

Here is a list of post-secondary writing programs that offer useful advice to students on writing about films. Visit some of them to help you get started.

- Dartmouth Writing Program: www.dartmouth.edu/~writing/ materials/student/humanities/film.shtml
- George Mason University Writing Program: www.gmu.edu/ departments/writingcenter/handouts/film.html
- Langara College: www.langara.bc.ca/writingcentre/handouts/ film.html
- Sandhills Community College: www.sandhills.cc.nc.us/english/ shared/160guidelines.html

research about the directors, producers, and actors, and the cultural, political, and economic events at the time the film was made and shown. As you read, look for connections or disjunctions between techniques, for example, and technological developments. When did colour become possible for films? When were hand-held cameras developed? How did these (or other) technological developments affect what ended up on the screen? These are just some of the kinds of connections you could make as you try to put the film you viewed into a critical context for your reader. By making these kinds of connections, you are creating new knowledge and a new perspective on the film you are studying.

Once you have done your research, start working on a rough draft. Try writing out longer, more coherent explanations of the connections and disjunctions you have noticed. Think about how one idea or explanation can be linked to other ideas or developments. Then join those paragraphs. As you are writing these explanations, try writing a thesis statement: in a sentence describe the overall pattern or argument that you see emerging, based on your viewing and reading.

Try out your rough draft on other readers—classmates, your professor, a writing centre tutor, a friend—to get their reactions. Listen carefully to what they say. Note how they react and what connections they make that you might then explore further. Based on their responses, you might do some more research into a particular political event or person, for example. In this way you can develop your thoughts and understanding of the film from first impressions to making broader connections. As you gain a more nuanced perspective on different films, your understanding may lead to more sophisticated claims (i.e., thesis statement) about the film you are analyzing.

At this point in your writing process, pay attention to editing your draft and crafting your sentences (see Part 9, Effective Style and Language; Part 10, Understanding Grammar; and Part 11, Understanding Punctuation and Mechanics).

11d SAMPLE *MISE EN SCÈNE* ANALYSIS OF *PRIDE & PREJUDICE*

The following paper presents a *mise en scène* analysis of the 2005 version of *Pride & Prejudice*, directed by Joe Wright and starring Keira Knightley and Matthew Macfadyen. It focuses on how the point of view shifts throughout the scene where Elizabeth Bennet and Fitzwilliam Darcy first meet at the assembly in Meryton to convey the instant attraction the two feel despite their protestations of dislike.

Calcagno 1

Vittoria Calcagno

Film 120

Professor Ebert

April 7, 2007

Shifting Viewpoints Reveal Lizzie and Darcy's Attraction

Pride & Prejudice, dir. Joe Wright. Perf. Keira Knightley and
Matthew Macfadyen. Focus Features. Universal
Studios, 2005.

Technical criteria used in the analysis: the shifting viewpoint so viewers see from third-person perspective as well as from Lizzie's or Darcy's perspective.

In the most recent adaptation of Jane Austen's *Pride and Prejudice* to the big screen, director Joe Wright uses the first meeting between Darcy and Elizabeth Bennet to show their instant attraction, despite the pride that keeps them apart. Wright relies on viewers being able to distinguish the camera angles that characterize sometimes Lizzie's gaze, more often Darcy's gaze, and other times an omniscient gaze, to communicate the emotional connections represented by this shifting gaze. We first see

Calcagno 2

Darcy in the Assembly Hall in Meryton through Elizabeth's eyes. He looks distinctly uncomfortable in the crowd and, when coupled with the information about his circumstances, suggests to both Elizabeth and the audience that his discomfort grows from a sense of superiority and pride. In contrast, when he looks at Elizabeth, he sees (and we see) a lively, intelligent young woman who interacts freely and comfortably with her friends and family. She suffers none of the shyness or awkwardness felt by Mr. Darcy even when meeting new acquaintances.

The scene opens with an omniscient or third-person perspective while we are still looking at a full-frontal view of Longbourne, framed by two huge deciduous trees. A lively jig attracts our attention before the camera shifts to the eagerly anticipated ball at the Assembly Hall. We attend the ball as villagers, hearing the music before entering the room. We stand before the closed doors, which swing open to admit us. The music, laughing, clapping, and dancing greet us even before the door is fully open, and we are thrust into the lively entertainment. Onlookers and participants in the dance throng the hall.

For a few seconds we see only strangers, and then we notice Lydia among the dancers, and just behind her, Charlotte, Lizzie, and Jane. The camera pans back to the dancing crowd. This sequence signals the liveliness of the entertainment and the obvious enjoyment of the participants. In fact, it is not until we locate the rest of the Bennets that we find people who are not enjoying themselves: Mr. Bennet looks bored and resentful; Mary, eyes closed, looks disengaged; Mrs. Bennet, glass in hand, surveys the crowd. She looks old and tired.

> The third-person omniscient view allows viewers to revise their perceptions of the relationships between the characters.

With the camera, we turn back to the crowd, still inhabiting a third-person perspective, and we locate Lizzie and Jane. They are neither bored nor disengaged, but affectionately teasing one another. Lizzie predicts that by evening's end all of the men in the room will be in love with Jane. Jane reprimands Lizzie gently for castigating all men as "poppycocks," noting that when Lizzie finally finds a man she likes, she won't be able to criticize them all so liberally. This scene foreshadows Lizzie's imminent meeting with Darcy, which ends up being much more complex than Jane predicts.

The camera shifts to a full-length view of the room, filled with revelling dancers. Suddenly, three figures step into the foreground. We see them from the back, the two men in shadow and the woman illuminated so we can see details of her dress: it is white, stylish, and accented with elbow-length white gloves. Her elegance is immediately apparent, making every one else seem dowdy. As the newcomers are noticed, the dancing stops and the music fades. Several seconds of silence follow, while the villagers and the newcomers coolly assess one another. The crowd parts for Sir William Lucas, who, as the highest-ranking aristocrat in the crowd, has the honour of welcoming the newcomers. While his rank may be signalled by his role as the master of ceremonies, we see from our omniscient viewpoint that Sir William Lucas pales in significance compared to the elegance and splendour of his guests.

Calcagno 4

Necks crane everywhere to see the trio. Charlotte's, Lizzie's, and Jane's are among the heads that come into the frame for a view of the newcomers. This scene signals that the viewpoint is about to change.

Now we have our first encounter with Mr. Darcy, and the viewpoint shifts to that of Lizzie. He fills the upper centre of the screen, the focal point. Mr. Lucas's head obscures Mr. Bingley's face, heightening the suspense, since he is the individual that the Bennets have all been taught to anticipate. In this first view, Darcy is frowning, fully disapproving of the scene before him. Lizzie comments on how miserable he looks, and Charlotte notes that he is a very rich man. Along with Lizzie, in light of this comment we interpret Darcy's expression as arrogance and pride. The crowd now parts, and we (with Elizabeth) have a full-length view of Mr. Darcy in the centre of the screen. Mr. Bingley is revealed between Darcy and Sir Lucas, but viewers quickly realize (through Lizzie's eyes) that the real centre of the mystery is Darcy and not Bingley, who is unpretentious, agreeable, and uncomplicated.

> We first see Darcy through Lizzie's eyes. We view Darcy's behaviour as arrogant and superior because of the filter that Lizzie's point of view provides.

With the camera still focused on Darcy, we hear Charlotte's voice filling Lizzie and Jane in on Mr. Darcy's personal circumstances, while Lizzie jokes at his expense. A quick cut to Lizzie's face changes back to third-person where we see an impish grin. The stately trio walks passed, and she joins the mass curtsey, while the camera remains focused on Lizzie's downcast eyes. Suddenly she looks up, and her eyes lock with Mr. Darcy's. A spark passes between them and they both look away in confusion. Lizzie recovers first, laughing off her agitation, while the newcomers continue their stately walk the length of the room. This vantage point assures viewers that Lizzie has the upper hand.

The music starts again, the crowd regroups for the dance, and the ball continues. The camera periodically cuts to Mr. Darcy so that we can see his humourless face at the back of the sea of revelling dancers. The Bennets approach and Mr. Lucas introduces them. In this exchange, we see the action from Elizabeth's point of view. We note how Mr. Bingley looks mainly at Jane during the introduction, and he clearly approves of what he sees; Mr. Darcy continues to look as if he wishes he were somewhere else, his eyes darting briefly to the Bennets when he is the object of the introduction; while Caroline looks arrogant, casting a sidelong glance at Darcy, hopeful that he shares her disapproval of the Bennets.

After a brief interlude tracking the younger Bennets, the third-person viewpoint cuts to the dance floor where we see Jane and Bingley dancing. He can't take his eyes off her as the dance progresses; she steals brief glances at him. The camera notes for us the moment when their hands touch in the dance. Then it cuts to Lizzie and Darcy, standing side by side watching the couple. Lizzie, attempting to be polite, asks Darcy if he likes to dance. He appears to read her comment as a ploy for an invitation, and he cuts her off rudely by declaring, "Not if I can help it." Elizabeth notes the rebuke and is puzzled, but then she smiles briefly to herself. As we view this response, the camera reveals that she reads his response as evidence of her earlier judgment that he is arrogant.

Calcagno 6

The camera cuts briefly to Jane and Bingley, who are getting along famously, then back to Elizabeth and Darcy, where the climate is significantly cooler. Lizzie sniffs in response to Darcy's comments, smiles to herself, and then walks away. Darcy watches her go, and his face is neutral, rather than frowning. He glances down, and we wonder what he is thinking: Is he pleased at repulsing her or is he angry with himself for being so abrupt? He looks up and the camera follows his gaze: He watches Lizzie walk away. He watches longer than he should for someone who doesn't interest him.

> The camera assumes Darcy's point of view. His gaze suggests that Lizzie has piqued his interest.

The camera cuts to a third-person perspective from under the bleachers, where various people are seated, drinking and talking. Beyond the bleachers, we see and hear Bingley and Darcy conversing as they walk. Although Elizabeth does not witness this segment, we assume her vantage point from under the bleachers. We hear Mr. Bingley encouraging Darcy to join the festivities. Darcy notes that Bingley's partner (Jane) is "the only pretty girl in the room." Bingley replies that her sister, Elizabeth, is also very attractive, implying the Darcy should take an interest in her. Charlotte and Lizzie appear in the foreground of our view from under the bleachers, a short distance from where Darcy and Bingley stop. At this point we watch the tableau unfold: Lizzie cannot avoid overhearing Darcy's reply, the unforgiveable comment that Lizzie is "tolerable but not handsome enough to tempt me." We see Lizzie snap to attention. She turns to glare at Darcy as he admonishes Bingley to return to Jane. The expression on Lizzie's face is priceless—a mixture of pride,

Calcagno 7

outrage, contempt, and pain. She glances at Charlotte, who tries to comfort her. Lizzie looks down in humiliation, and she vows never to dance with Mr. Darcy. The third-person perspective on this scene allows viewers to see the crucial connections being made between the characters and their responses to each other.

At this point, the camera shifts from neutral third person to the dance floor from Mr. Darcy's point of view. We see Charlotte dancing with Mr. Bingley, both of them grinning wildly. We see Lizzie also dancing, but we never see her partner. She is in the centre of the frame to show the viewer that she has gained an inordinate hold on Mr. Darcy's focus of interest. The gaze shifts again, and at the back of the hall we see Mr. Darcy and Caroline looking on. Caroline looks disdainful, but Mr. Darcy looks bereft and forlorn. As the dance continues, Mr. Darcy is always present in the centre back of the frame, watching. The camera focuses on the dancing women, Charlotte, then Lizzie, then Jane. We see that Lizzie is not laughing and smiling as broadly as earlier. In the background, Mr. Darcy continues to watch her dancing. We see what, presumably, Darcy sees: Lizzie looking remarkably lively and full of fun. We also see that Lizzie is still mortified by the comment she overheard, an insight we gain that Darcy does not.

The final scene in their first meeting ends when Mrs. Bennet barges in between Bingley and Charlotte as the dance ends. The point of view here is unclear for a minute. It may be Darcy's from the back of the room, observing as Mrs. Bennet compliments Bingley on his fine dancing and notes Jane's superior ability. We realize the viewpoint is

Our perception of Lizzie is mediated by Darcy's perspective. Third-person perspective gives us insight into the attraction between Lizzie and Darcy, despite their verbal sparring.

Calcagno 8

third person as Jane, who is standing beside them, looks embarrassed and Lizzie amusedly exasperated by her mother's lack of subtlety. When Mrs. Bennet starts to discuss Jane's previous suitors, we see that both Caroline and Darcy are present for this conversation. Jane is humiliated and glances pleadingly at Elizabeth. Lizzie derails her mother by making a joke about poetry and love. Her comment sparks Darcy's interest: he asks her what she recommends to encourage love, if poetry will kill it. She admonishes him sharply with this comment: "Dancing, even if one's partner is barely tolerable." Their eyes lock for a moment, and then Lizzie curtseys, turns, and walks away. Mr. Darcy's face goes out of focus as Lizzie's face stays in view. She looks a bit smug at her own retort. However, as she retreats, she takes a deep breath, as if having barely survived a deadly ordeal. In the background, Mr. Darcy is visible over her right shoulder. Then the crowd closes in and when it clears, Lizzie has left the frame, and Mr. Darcy is no longer in view at the back of the hall.

The shifting camera perspectives highlight the scenes where Darcy and Elizabeth connect. While the words they speak suggest their disdain for one another, the amount of time Darcy spends looking at Elizabeth and her obvious emotional responses when she interacts with him in this first meeting reveal an undeniable spark between the two. What follows is hardly surprising, given the strength of connection that Wright underscores in this scene.

11e   WRITING ABOUT NEW MEDIA

In the same way you might be asked to write about films or literature, you may be asked to write about new media: video games, web-based information sites, art installations, blogs, bots, and (cy)borgs. New media attempt to create an experience in ways similar to a film or literary work. They aim to create an intellectual or emotional viewing or reading experience. The new media—computer-based CDs, internet-based multiple-player games, television-based gaming consoles—often combine elements of the "old" media to create these new experiences. For example, World of Warcraft, an internet-based multi-player dungeon (MUD), combines rich visual imagery with text-based chat features and real-time voice-over internet chat using an earpiece and microphone. Players meet online to organize "instances" or quests that the group will undertake together at a certain time and place. Each player brings the character that he or she has created and built by gathering items and defeating robots (bots) that the creators of the game have deployed throughout it. By combining the ability to speak as well as write to other players in real time, the creators of this game have created a new experience.

How can we talk about the relative quality or success of these new media? In this part of the chapter, we will focus on how to write an essay critiquing a video game experience.

Writing a video game review

Before reviewing a video game, one of the first things you should do is read a variety of reviews. Online sources for reviews are available at these sites:

- Game Rankings.com (www.gamerankings.com)
- Video Game Review (www.videogamereview.com; see Figure 11.4)
- AMG All Game Guide (www.allgame.com)
- Yahoo UK & Ireland Video Game reviews (uk.videogames.games .yahoo.com)
- GameSpot.com (www.gamespot.com/reviews.html)
- Metacritic.com (www.metacritic.com/games)

Reviews tend to vary widely from a fill-in-the-blank type form to full-blown essays topping 4000 words. Make sure that the requirements for the assignment you are asked to write differentiate between these two kinds of reviews.

Some of the general criteria for evaluating new media experiences include these concepts:

- Difficulty level (first-time player; experienced player of previous versions)

FIGURE 11.4   www.videogamereview.com

- Gameplay and strategy (character development, environments, gear)
- Graphics (realistic; smoothly transforming during play)
- Sound (quality; variety; appropriateness)
- Narrative (consistency within and across storylines)
- Authenticity (the degree to which the virtual world is consistent within itself)
- Transparency (the degree to which players can lose themselves in the virtual world and look through the interface rather than noticing it)

Structuring your review

Video game reviews generally address the same kind of audience as film reviews: readers who have not tried the game but are wondering whether it is worth the investment to buy it. Game reviews also follow the same general pattern as film reviews. The introductory paragraph offers an overview of the game's strengths, identifies the genre of game (e.g., role playing, shooter, racing), establishes brief links to the other games that this company has published, and evaluates the experience of playing it. The next paragraphs take readers through strategies for getting the game started. For example, many games offer a variety of choices for players as they build their virtual character. These paragraphs help readers understand the implications that these choices may have when they are 100 hours into playing the game and it is too late to change their minds.

The next paragraphs describe some of the different paths that players could take through the game. Many games create a virtual geography or landscape that players move through; these paragraphs describe how these landscapes are distinct and what kinds of encounters you are liable to find there. Finally, these reviews end with one or two paragraphs that detail improvements in the game.

Writing a website review

Another kind of text you might be asked to create is a review or analysis of a specific website or kind of website. Just as there are classes or kinds of films and games, there are various genres of website: news organization–sponsored websites (www.cbc.ca), educational sites (www.ontariosciencecentre.ca), social organizations and online communities (www.facebook.com), educational organization sites (www.uwo.ca), personal sites (publish.uwo.ca/~rgraves3), blogs (www.blogscanada.ca), and more. Your first task is to distinguish among these various kinds of webpages by determining what kind of social activity they support. Are they help sites? Teaching sites? Places to meet people?

Once you have established the kind of site you are reviewing, you can evaluate the site by asking some of these questions (see Chapter 15 for details):

- Is the information broken into readable chunks?
- Does the site organize information into columns so that lines of text do not flow across the entire screen?
- Does the site have a clear visual theme?
- Can you identify the audience for the site?
- Can you move around the site easily?
- How deep or how much content is provided on the site?
- How useful and how many links are on the site?

Once you have evaluated the site for both formal (design) and content aspects, start writing your analysis or review. As in film and literature essays, the scope of your essay will depend on the assignment. Are you asked to review a newspaper site only in the context of that site alone (as a kind of *mise en scène* analysis) or are you asked to critically review it in the context of newspaper sites within Canada or across the U.S. (ca.dir.yahoo .com/News_and_Media/Newspapers)? Should you be comparing the different ways the same story is represented in Calgary and Ottawa? Halifax and Houston? What you might say about each site will depend on the scope of the assignment that your instructor provides.

11f   A SAMPLE GAME REVIEW

The review below was written in response to the following assignment:

Select a computer-based video game that has been released in the last year. Write a review of that game using the criteria listed above. In your review, make sure you comment on previous games by the same creative group or company and indicate how this game fits with the other games that this group or company has produced.

Park 1

Terrence Park

Media Studies 120

Professor R. Brown

April 27, 2006

Review of *The Elder Scrolls IV: Oblivion* by

Bethesda Softworks LLC, a ZeniMax Media Company

Oblivion is the fourth game of the Elder Scrolls series from Bethesda Softworks. Like its predecessors (Arena, Daggerfall, and Morrowind), Oblivion is a single-player role-playing game (RPG) set in the massive medieval world of Tamriel. However, each game takes place in a different province with different plot and characters. Oblivion is set in the capital of the empire, Cyrodiil. This works nicely for the central plot, which involves the assassination of the emperor and his heirs, throwing the empire into disarray and creating a very interesting environment to explore. The most remarkable aspect of Oblivion (aside from the amazing graphics) is that it is entirely open-ended, allowing players unlimited freedom to explore the detailed world and complete quests as they see fit, or to focus on the main quest line immediately, something that has rarely been done in other series.

Introduction identifies the game, outlines its genre and related games by Bethesda, and evaluates the game's unique features.

Park 2

Outlines game's unique features and how they improve the quality of the game experience.

The reason most linear RPGs avoid an open-ended structure is that they depend on killing creatures for the player to gain "experience," "level up," and become more powerful. Oblivion uses a refined version of the innovative levelling system from previous Elder Scrolls games that allows players to go up a level by increasing their skills. Each character class (the game has 21 predefined classes and the option to create your own custom class) is specialized in Combat Arts, Magic Arts, or Stealth Arts. The chosen specialization is the overall focus of the class, but unlike most RPGs does not lock the player in to one particular play style. Each specialization has seven skills, and those skills start off higher, and are easier to increase, than skills outside the chosen specialization. Each class has seven major skills, which start significantly higher, and are easier to increase, than the other skills (minor skills). Ten increases in any combination of major skills allow the player to level up, regardless of how many monsters have been killed. Going up a level allows the character to increase attributes (which govern skills), health, and overall power. This innovative levelling system can take some getting used to, especially when creating a custom class, but overall is much more rewarding than choosing a stock class and slaughtering creatures mindlessly in order to level.

Another interesting aspect of character creation is race. There are 10 unique races (including lizard-like Argonians, cat-like Khajiit, 3 types of elves, and 4 types of humans), each with different skill bonuses and unique abilities. Each race has different looks and flavour

Park 3

(fully customizable, via the use of copious amounts of sliders and options) and different starting attribute scores, something lacking in almost all other games of this genre.

What is truly amazing about Oblivion is the incredible detail and realism of the graphics, which are evident during character creation. On the higher visual settings, hair looks lifelike. This is the first video game I have ever played that accurately portrays such minute detail. This multitude of options makes for some very interesting gameplay combinations and allows for some truly unique characters.

The graphical strength of Oblivion evident in character creation carries over to the environment. The trees and grass of the forests and the architecture of the buildings in the environment are amazingly detailed. This attention to background detail seems like a minor feature, but when compared to other video games it becomes huge. Most video games have trouble creating believable trees and natural scenery, because they are not naturally composed of straight lines. When a video game does create a believable model of natural objects, too often there are about three tree models used, which really detracts from the experience. Oblivion uses an engine specifically for creating natural foliage and curving, believable trees. When in town, the effects are just as stunning. Buildings are architecturally believable for the time period and extremely well done (the buildings on a rural farm are one storey, with grass-thatched roofs, surrounded by a low wall made of rocks to keep the wandering sheep in). Non-player characters (NPCs) look almost lifelike and have realistic

Explains the improved graphics and character behaviours that make the game more realistic.

Park 4

facial expressions and mouth movement during dialogue. In fact, Oblivion uses a new artificial intelligence system called Radiant AI, developed by Bethesda, that gives each NPC individual priorities and a daily schedule. It is common to walk by and witness two NPCs engaged in small talk, before one excuses himself and heads to the pub for a drink. This system could still use refining, as there will be disjointed conversations that do not make total sense and break the experience of the game. However, I would rather witness occasional bizarre behaviour in NPCs than have them behave in a uniformly dull manner all of the time. All in all the Radiant AI system is an improvement, but still not quite ready for primetime.

This paragraph elaborates further improvements to the game.

The gameplay itself is improved over Oblivion's predecessors. In Morrowind, melee fighting consisted of beating something until it died, using only one button. The melee fighting in Oblivion has been reworked, with new moves and a blocking button added. In addition, parries and power attacks are now possible, greatly changing the melee experience. In Morrowind, skills were simply static modifiers that changed the chance of successfully completing an action. In Oblivion, new skill perks are obtained upon reaching certain skill levels. For example, when characters obtains skill level 25 in Armourer (repairing weapons and armour), repair hammers last twice as long before breaking. When they reach skill level 50, they gain the ability to repair magic items. Upon reaching skill level 75, they can fortify weapons and armour, making it more effective. When characters reach

Park 5

skill level 100 (the highest level), repair hammers never break for them. This skill perk mechanism provides further incentive to increase skill levels and adds interesting flavour to each character. Further gameplay improvements include a new fast travel option (to eliminate much of the horrible "fetch these" quests that other RPGs rely on), the ability to ride horses, and more guilds and organizations than previous games.

Despite all of the innovative ideas in Oblivion, it is not perfect. There are a lot of reported glitches (although less than its predecessors), and the interface is kind of cluttered. The font size of the inventory window may seem too big to some, and it causes a lot more scrolling than needed. In order to achieve the amazing graphics with no in-game load screens, the draw radius for grass and high-quality texture is somewhat small. This means distant objects are poorly rendered, and the grass suddenly appears 30 metres away from the character. Because every line in the game is spoken by voice actors (including Patrick Stewart and Sean Bean), a lot of the characters sound the same. Also, some of the lines spoken by the beggars exhibit perfect English while others have a thick lowbrow accent. This discontinuity is startling and takes away from the experience.

> This paragraph summarizes flaws or areas in the game that need some improvement.

All in all, The Elder Scrolls IV: Oblivion is an incredibly innovative game with great graphics and gameplay but is not without its flaws. Most of its flaws are minor and excusable, but they do tend to detract a little from the overall experience.

A P P E N D I X

Writing Essay Examinations

If you are a student who groans at the prospect of an essay exam, take heart. Writing essay exams is a skill you can learn. Your ability will improve with practice and careful preparation.

PREPARING FOR THE EXAM

The key to preparing for an essay exam is to use common sense. Get a good night's sleep. Eat breakfast. Don't wait until the last minute to study. And most of all, be prepared. The following steps will help you prepare for an essay exam.

1. **Learn what to expect.** Ask the instructor to describe the format of the exam. How much time will you have? How many points will each portion of the exam be worth? What qualities is the instructor looking for in an essay? Can you look at any sample questions or old exams? If you need a dictionary, can you bring one?

2. **Study early and often.** Material studied regularly over a period of time has a much better chance of staying in your long-term memory than material crammed in between gulps of coffee the night before the exam. Review your notes and assigned readings for the major concepts and terms being tested. Practise explaining, applying, and analyzing them. Think about how the texts or concepts relate to one another. Form a study group with a few equally serious classmates, divide up the concepts likely to appear on the exam, and practise explaining them to each other.

3. **Anticipate possible questions.** Generate essay questions you think might appear on the exam, then outline possible responses. Almost all essay questions will ask you to prove your ideas about certain concepts using specific examples. In your outline, list examples you might use and note how they illustrate the concept. If you're working with a study group, critique and strengthen each other's questions and outlines.

4. **Make a plan.** You can reduce your anxiety about taking an essay exam if you have a plan for budgeting your time and approaching the questions. Decide in what order you will answer questions. You may want to tackle those worth the most points first to ensure you'll have enough time to do them well. Allow time to plan, pre-write, revise, and proofread in addition to actually writing the essay.

WRITING A SUCCESSFUL EXAM

After *be prepared,* the best piece of advice for writing essay exams is *don't panic.* It's easy to feel pressured as you hear the clock ticking away during an exam. Too often that pressure leads students to rush into an essay, dumping all the information they can remember into a few rambling paragraphs. Although time is limited, don't forsake the writing process when you write an essay exam.

Plan

After you read the essay question, breathe deeply and think. Take a few minutes to sketch an outline of your answer. Decide what argument you want to make. Break the argument into manageable chunks, logical steps, or categories. Note the examples you want to analyze in order to illustrate each chunk of the argument.

Write the essay

An essay exam is not the place to be subtle. Highlight your argument clearly at the beginning of the essay and map out the upcoming paragraphs. In the body of the essay write clear transitions that link paragraphs. Relate the point of each paragraph clearly to the larger argument. Offer examples to support your argument, and remember that examples aren't self-explanatory. Analyze your examples to prove that they illustrate the argument. Then write a conclusion that repeats your argument and the steps you took to prove it.

Revise and proofread

While your instructor won't expect essay exam answers to be as polished as other types of writing, your prose still affects your credibility. Reserve time at the end of the exam period to revise your essay, expanding on explanations, adding any examples that strengthen your argument, and clarifying muddled sentences. Then read the essay for errors in spelling, punctuation, and grammar.

4 DESIGNING AND PRESENTING

Today, writing demands an attention to design and presentation. Even basic writing projects may include options for layout and may include tables and charts. New media and visual projects like flyers, brochures, and webpages require a knowledge of design principles and strategies.

Writing in the World Project

An Informational Brochure for a Campus Club

Create an informational brochure that encourages students at your school to join a campus club. Find out who is running the club, and interview him or her in person, by email, or through an instant messaging program. Attend a club meeting and take photos or download images from the club's website to use as illustrations for your brochure. Interview two or three club members to assemble useful quotations and information about their experiences as members of this club. Include these perspectives in your brochure to encourage others to join. When you begin writing the brochure, consider using a design template from your word processing software or a program designed for creating brochures and newsletters.

Visit *The Brief Penguin Handbook* Companion Website at
www.pearsoned.ca/faigley/

MyCanadianCompLab
Where writing and research help is a click away.
MyCanadianCompLab may be packaged with your textbook.
If not, it can be purchased from your college or university's bookstore.
Go to **www.pearsoned.ca/highered/mycanadiancomplab/**
for a tour.

C H A P T E R *12*

Design Basics

Changes in writing technology have changed design expectations for writers. Before typewriters, for example, writers needed to worry about only the legibility of their handwriting. And typewriters required only setting the width of the margins and choosing single or double spacing between lines. Few writers paid attention to design because they had so few tools to work with.

Today the situation is radically different. When type is too small to read or a page is visually confusing, readers blame the writer, not the tools. But if you pay attention to design basics, the design can emphasize your main points and readers will appreciate the look and the clarity of your presentation.

12a CREATE VISUAL RELATIONSHIPS

Good design depends on creating effective visual relationships. In one of the most common design tasks—creating a flyer—attention to visual relationships can attract readers' attention and compel them to examine your subject. For example, the flyer in Figure 12.1 advertises a spring break trip to London sponsored by a drama club. The designer of this flyer uses a typical beginner's strategy—centre everything. This design does nothing to support the message.

The flyer in Figure 12.1 has exciting content but it is rendered in a boring way. The destination, London, gets no more attention than the sponsoring club. The list of attractions is not visually sorted. The white space isolates rather than enlivens the information. The typeface is Helvetica, a clean, modern typeface (see Section 12d), but it is one that has been overused and now seems a little dated. Overall, the visual effect is blah. The trip might be a lot of fun, but you do not get this impression from the flyer.

The first questions to ask when creating a design are

1. What are the elements of the design?
2. Which element is most important?

On the flyer, there are four elements: the title, the description, the contact information, and the image. Clearly the destination—London—is most important, yet the name is buried in the text. The picture on the flyer is one of the most frequently used images of London, yet it appears to be an afterthought.

Together *London* and the image are a powerful combination. The revised design in Figure 12.2 (on page 175) lets the name and image work together:

> # The Drama Club is sponsoring a Spring Break trip to London
> ## February 17–25, 2007
>
> You'll see six outstanding plays, including the Royal Shakespeare Company. During the day you'll see the famous sights of London, including Buckingham Palace, the Tower of London, Westminster Abbey, St. Paul's Cathedral, the Houses of Parliament, Big Ben, and 10 Downing Street—the residence of the Prime Minister. We will also visit the National Gallery of Art, the new Tate Modern, the restored Globe Theatre, and the British Museum.
>
> For more information please contact
> Karen Clark, President
> Drama Club
> 405 Memorial Union
> 482-1564
>
>

FIGURE 12.1   Novice designers typically centre everything.

the name appears in the upper left, where readers begin, and the image has been cropped to align with other elements on the page.

In the revised flyer, more than one typeface is used. *London* is set in Old English Text MS for a traditional look that contrasts with the other typefaces on the page. The attractions of London are divided into three categories with headings. The contact information is set off by ample white space, making it both easy to find and visually appealing.

12b   MAKE SIMILAR ITEMS LOOK SIMILAR

Use design principles to create visual relationships between elements on a page. For example, readers increasingly expect writers to divide long stretches

London

Spring Break
February 17–25, 2007

You'll see

Plays
Six outstanding plays, including a performance by the Royal Shakespeare Company

Sights of London
Buckingham Palace, the Tower of London, Westminster Abbey, St. Paul's Cathedral, the Houses of Parliament, Big Ben, 10 Downing Street—the residence of the Prime Minister

Museums
National Gallery of Art, the new Tate Modern, the restored Globe Theatre, the British Museum

Sponsored by the Drama Club

For information contact
Karen Clark, President
Drama Club
405 Memorial Union
482-1564

FIGURE 12.2 Place the most important information where it receives the most emphasis. See page 180 for a version of this flyer with colour added.

of text into chunks and to label those chunks with **headings**. One method is simply to centre all the headings so the result looks like Figure 12.3.

The problem with the example in Figure 12.3 is that no distinction has been made between what is more and what is less important. You can determine the importance of each heading by making an outline. Look at which headings go with major sections and which with subsections. Then use one style for main headings and another style for subheadings. The style you choose should give the reader visual clues to the importance of the heading. For example, in Figure 12.4 the main heading stands alone on a line and is a larger type size than the subheading.

Useful tools offered by word processing programs, webpage editors, and presentation software include several ways of making lists. Bulleted lists are used to present items in a series, as in the following example:

Title

Lorem ipsum dolor sit amet, consectetaur adipisicing elit, sed do eiusmod tempor incididunt ut labore et dolore magna aliqua. Ut enim ad minim veniam, quis nostrud exercitation ullamco laboris nisi ut aliquip ex ea commodo consequat. Duis aute irure dolor in reprehenderit in voluptate velit esse cillum dolore eu fugiat nulla pariatur.

Heading 1

Lorem ipsum dolor sit amet, consectetaur adipisicing elit, sed do eiusmod tempor incididunt ut labore et dolore magna aliqua. Ut enim ad minim veniam, quis nostrud exercitation ullamco laboris nisi ut aliquip ex ea commodo consequat. Duis aute irure dolor in reprehenderit in voluptate velit esse cillum dolore eu fugiat nulla pariatur.

Heading 2

Lorem ipsum dolor sit amet, consectetaur adipisicing elit, sed do eiusmod tempor incididunt ut labore et dolore magna aliqua. Ut enim ad minim veniam, quis nostrud exercitation ullamco laboris nisi ut aliquip ex ea commodo consequat. Duis aute irure dolor in reprehenderit in voluptate velit esse cillum dolore eu fugiat nulla pariatur.

FIGURE 12.3

Advantages of using a flowchart

- Allows a team to agree on the steps of a process
- Shows problem areas and unnecessary loops
- Helps to identify steps in a process that could be simplified
- Compares the ideal flow to the way things are done now
- Serves as a training aid for new employees

Bulleted lists are frequently used as visual aids in verbal presentations (see Chapter 14). Speakers use them to give an overview of a presentation so listeners know where a particular point fits. Bulleted lists, however, can be ineffective if the items in the list are not similar. Items bulleted in a list should be grammatically parallel (see Section 28d), demonstrating the link through their similar phrasing. By highlighting similarity in your design, you create visual continuity that links related elements.

Title

Lorem ipsum dolor sit amet, consectetaur adipisicing elit, sed do eiusmod tempor incididunt ut labore et dolore magna aliqua. Ut enim ad minim veniam, quis nostrud exercitation ullamco laboris nisi ut aliquip ex ea commodo consequat. Duis aute irure dolor in reprehenderit

Section Heading

Lorem ipsum dolor sit amet, consectetaur adipisicing elit, sed do eiusmod tempor incididunt ut labore et dolore magna aliqua. Ut enim ad minim veniam, quis nostrud exercitation ullamco laboris nisi ut aliquip ex ea commodo consequat. Duis aute irure dolor in reprehenderit in voluptate velit esse cillum dolore eu fugiat nulla pariatur.

Level 2 Heading Lorem ipsum dolor sit amet, consectetaur adipisicing elit, sed do eiusmod tempor incididunt ut labore et dolore magna aliqua. Ut enim ad minim veniam, quis nostrud exercitation ullamco laboris nisi ut aliquip ex ea commodo consequat. Duis aute irure dolor in reprehenderit in voluptate velit esse cillum dolore eu fugiat nulla pariatur.

FIGURE 12.4

12c MAKE DIFFERENT ITEMS LOOK DIFFERENT

Like similarity, another important design principle is to highlight the difference between different elements on a page. We tend to follow the principle of consistency because that's what we've been taught and that's what writing technologies—from typewriters to computers—do for us. The flyer in Figure 12.1 is an example of letting the technology (in this case centring everything) determine the design. But the principle of contrast takes some conscious effort on our part to implement. Take the sample resumé in Figure 12.5 as an example (see also Section 9f). The resumé has consistency, but there is no contrast between what is more important and what is less important. The writer seeks a position with an innovative high tech company, but there is no sign that the writer might be innovative.

The design of a resumé should direct the reader's attention to certain elements and create the right impression of the writer. Use of contrast can emphasize the key features of the resumé and contribute to a much more forceful and dynamic image, as shown in Figure 12.6. Notice that arrangement and consistency are also important to the revised design. Good design requires that all elements be brought into play to produce the desired impression.

Terrence S. Park
937 2nd Ave NW
Calgary, AB T2N 0E7
tspark@yahoo.ca
403-123-4567

SKILLS

Extensive knowledge regarding PC hardware quality, installation, maintenance, etc.

Quick and efficient learner

Self-motivated and able to work well both independently and in groups

High level of experience with Windows 98/2000/XP

Knowledge of Ubuntu Linux

High degree of experience with Microsoft Office, including Excel and Word

Object-oriented C# programming experience and interest

Experience with wireless and local area networking

EDUCATION

2003–2007 B Sc (Applied), Computer Engineering

University of Calgary, Calgary, AB

EXPERIENCE

2004–2007 Help Desk, University of Calgary

Stationed at help desk 10–15 hours a week, solving users' problems as quickly and efficiently as possible.

Also troubleshot issues with LAN, computer classrooms, and public labs.

2002–2003 Wait Staff, Swiss Chalet, Calgary, AB

Waited on tables, some food preparation, cleaning as necessary.

Won "Wait Person of the Year" in 2003.

AWARDS

Senior Prose English Award for non-fiction essay (High school)

Placed seventh in high jump at the 2004 Canadian Junior Track and Field Championships in Saskatoon, SK.

INTERESTS

High jump: dedicated year-round training 3 days a week. Will continue training for the high jump with the goal of representing Canada at the 2012 Olympics Games in London.

Computer hardware: recently built personal computer with heavy emphasis on performance-to-cost ratio, which required extensive research into every hardware component.

Electronics: including radios, televisions, small appliances, wireless devices, modified video game consoles and how they work

Writing: mostly prose essays, with occasional short stories

WORK AUTHORIZATION

Citizenship: Canadian

Other: U.S. Permanent Resident Card holder

FIGURE 12.5 Without contrast, items do not stand out.

Terrence S. Park

937 2nd Ave NW
Calgary, AB T2N 0E7
tspark@yahoo.ca
403-123-4567

SKILLS

Extensive knowledge regarding PC hardware quality, installation, maintenance, etc.
Quick and efficient learner
Self-motivated and able to work well both independently and in groups
High level of experience with Windows 98/2000/XP
Knowledge of Ubuntu Linux
High degree of experience with Microsoft Office, including Excel and Word
Object-oriented C# programming experience and interest
Experience with wireless and local area networking

EDUCATION

2003–2007 B Sc (Applied), Computer Engineering
University of Calgary, Calgary, AB
> **Experience 2004–2007 Help Desk, University of Calgary**
>> Stationed at help desk 10–15 hours a week, solving users' problems as quickly and efficiently as possible.
>> Also troubleshot issues with LAN, computer classrooms, and public labs.
>
> **2002–2003 Wait Staff, Swiss Chalet, Calgary, AB**
>> Waited on tables, some food preparation, cleaning as necessary.
>> Won "Wait Person of the Year" in 2003.

AWARDS

Senior Prose English Award for non-fiction essay (High school)
Placed seventh in high jump at the 2004 Canadian Junior Track and Field Championships in Saskatoon, SK.

INTERESTS

High jump: dedicated year-round training 3 days a week. Will continue training for the high jump with the goal of representing Canada at the 2012 Olympics Games in London.
Computer hardware: recently built personal computer with heavy emphasis on performance-to-cost ratio, which required extensive research into every hardware component.
Electronics: including radios, televisions, small appliances, wireless devices, modified video game consoles and how they work
Writing: mostly prose essays, with occasional short stories

WORK AUTHORIZATION

Citizenship: Canadian
Other: U.S. Permanent Resident Card holder

FIGURE 12.6 The revised resumé emphasizes relevant work experience.

Colour

Another element that can provide contrast is colour. Until the last few years, colour printers were expensive, but ink-jet printers have made colour printing affordable. Colour costs nothing to add to websites; indeed, it's expected.

We're surrounded by so much colour that sometimes the strongest effects are created by using colour in minimal ways. Limited use of warm colours—yellow, orange, and especially red—can make a strong statement. In the figure below, red is used for the title and headings, which both matches and balances the red uniforms in the image.

12d UNDERSTAND TYPE STYLES

Until computers and word processing software came along, most writers had little or no control over type style. Most typewriters used Courier, a fact many typists didn't even know. Furthermore, the typewriter gave the user no choice about type size. Nearly all used 10-point or 12-point type. (A point is a printer's measure; 1 inch equals 72 points.) There was no way to include italics, so the convention was to underline the word or words that the printer would later set in italics. Boldface could be accomplished only by typing the word over again, making it darker.

Use typefaces and fonts effectively

Even if the general public knew little about type styles and other aspects of printing before computers came along, printers had 500 years' experience learning which type styles are easiest to read and what effects different styles produce. When you open the pull-down font menu of your word processing program, you see a small part of that five-century tradition of developing type styles.

A particular style of type is called a **typeface**, such as Times New Roman or Arial. A specific kind of that typeface, such as Verdana bold, is called a **font**. At first, typefaces may all appear similar, but after you get some practice with using various typefaces, you will begin to notice how they differ.

Serif type

Typefaces are divided into two categories, **serif** and **sans serif**. Serif (rhymes with *sheriff*) faces were developed first. Serifs are the little wedge-shaped ends on letter forms, which scribes produced with wedge-tipped pens. Serif typefaces also have thick and thin transitions on the curved strokes. Five of the most common serif typefaces are

Times

Palatino

Bookman

Garamond

New Century Schoolbook

Serif typefaces were designed to be easy to read. They don't call attention to themselves. Thus they are well suited for long stretches of printed text and are used frequently.

Sans serif type

Sans serif (*sans* is French for "without") typefaces don't have the little wedge-shaped ends on letters, and the thickness of the letters does not vary. Popular sans serif typefaces include

Helvetica
Arial
Verdana

Sans serif typefaces work well for headings and short stretches of text. They give a crisp, modern look. Sans serif typefaces are easier to read on a computer screen. Verdana, Helvetica, and Arial are sans serif typefaces that most computers now have installed, which is why they are popular on websites.

Script and decorative type

There are many script and decorative typefaces. These typefaces tend to draw attention to themselves. They are harder to read, but sometimes they can be used for good effects. Script typefaces imitate handwriting or calligraphy, which is why they often appear on diplomas, formal invitations, and similar documents.

Popular script typefaces include Nuptial Script and Engravers LH:

When you want only the very best

Nguyen, Bhathal, and Chiu, Queen's Counsel

Some decorative typefaces, including Lazyvermont and ComicStrip Classic, are informal, almost irreverent:

That's a no brainer.

Totally awesome!

Use a readable type size

It's easy to change the size of type when you compose on a computer. For long stretches of text, use at least 10- or 12-point type. Use larger type for headings. (Note: in commercial printing, the size effect varies with the font.)

Smaller 8- or 9-point type can be readable on the printed page, but it is next to impossible to read on the computer screen because the resolution on a screen is not as fine as type on a printed page. Use larger type if you expect people to read text on a screen. For text that is to be projected during a presentation, the minimum size is 18-point, with headings and titles larger (see page 202).

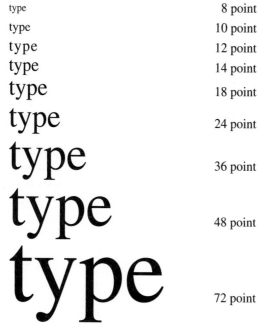

type	8 point
type	10 point
type	12 point
type	14 point
type	18 point
type	24 point
type	36 point
type	48 point
type	72 point

Use other effects as needed

Finally, word processing programs allow you to use type fonts such as **boldface**, *italics*, and underlining. All three are used for emphasis.

CHAPTER *13*

Illustrations, Tables, and Charts

Sophisticated software and hard drives with plenty of memory allow you to create attractive illustrations, tables, and charts. The key is understanding when and how to use graphics for effective communication. Visuals should not be used just for decoration but to clarify points, supply additional information, and provide alternative ways of understanding a subject. Visuals that are well integrated into text can make a presentation more powerful.

13a ILLUSTRATIONS

Drawings

Drawings are useful visual aids you can use to highlight selected details for your reader. Unlike a photograph, which reproduces every detail, a drawing can select and emphasize the key particular details. You can create drawings the old-fashioned way, with pen or pencil, then scan them and import them into computer files. Professionals use Macromedia FreeHand, Adobe Illustrator, CorelDraw, and other complex drawing programs, all of which take time to learn, but you can make simple drawings using the drawing modules on word processing programs and presentation software. You don't have to be an artist to create simple drawings, such as the one shown in Figure 13.1.

FIGURE 13.1

Photographs

Photographs are useful aids because they re-create detailed images. They allow you to convey information clearly and accurately. You can incorporate photographs in text documents if you convert them to a digital format. You can create digital images by taking photographs with a digital camera, by scanning prints, or by using a photo CD service (see Figure 13.2). Once your photographs are in a digital format, you can use an **image editor** to alter them. (See Section 13b.)

FIGURE 13.2

Clip art

Another source of illustrations is clip art. *Clip art* refers to professionally created drawings and illustrations, such as cartoons, symbols, maps, and backgrounds. Clip art is often bundled with software, including word processing programs. You can find public domain clip art on the web or purchase clip art on CDs (see Figure 13.3). Clip art can annoy your readers if you toss it into a document without much regard for its effect, but used thoughtfully, it can indicate content and direct readers.

FIGURE 13.3

Scanners

It's easy to scan drawings and photographs, but unless you drew the picture or snapped the photograph yourself, you need to request permission to scan someone else's sketches or photos. You may also need permission to publish a photograph of someone that you've taken. Computer labs often have scanners, and because scanners have become affordable, many people now own them. Flatbed scanners, which resemble small photocopiers, are the most common type. You place the image face down on the glass, open the image editor on the computer linked to the scanner, select **Import** or a similar command, and select the scanner you are using. You will then see an interactive menu.

All the controls for the scanner are in the software. Because there are many different types of scanners, the software varies a great deal. If you are new to scanning, pay attention to the settings for type of image and resolution.

- **Type of image.** Some scanning software allows you to indicate what you are scanning—a colour photograph, printed matter, or a transparency. Other software will ask you to choose among B/W photo, B/W document, colour RGB, and colour CMYK. All monitors and most ink-jet printers use RGB rather than CMYK; thus you'll likely select RGB for colour images that you scan.
- **Resolution.** Scanning resolution is measured in dots per inch (dpi). Most scanners offer a range from 72 to 1600 dpi. The higher the number, the finer the image, but the file size also becomes larger. Most printers use a resolution from 300 to 600 dpi. Images on the

web or on the screen display at 72 dpi, so resolution higher than 72 is effectively wasted, making the image slower to display without improving the quality.

WRITING IN THE WORLD

Scanning and the law

Images in books, magazines, and on the internet published in the last 75 years are almost always owned by someone. If you copy an image for redistribution of any kind, including putting it on a website, you must find out who holds the copyright and obtain permission to use the image. Always give credit for any image that you copy, even if it is in the public domain.

13b IMAGE EDITORS

Image editors allow you to touch up images, create special effects, and convert image files to the correct format for printing or displaying on a website. Image editors range from extensive software used by professionals, including Macromedia Fireworks and Adobe Photoshop, to shareware programs you can download from the web that allow you to do simple image editing, including Picture Man (for Windows) and GraphicConverter (for Mac). If you own a scanner, you likely have an image editor on your computer. Many computers now come equipped with a photo editor; you can also find free image editors online.

No matter which editor you use, there are a few manipulations that you will need to use frequently. It's always a good idea to copy the image first and work on the copy.

- **Cropping.** Most images can be trimmed to improve visual focus and file size. To crop an image, select the rectangle tool, draw the rectangle over the area you want to keep, and select the **Crop** or **Trim** command (see Figure 13.4). The part of the image outside the rectangle will be discarded. Every pixel you can squeeze out of an image intended for use on the web makes the image display faster on a user's screen.
- **Rotating images.** Often you'll find that you held your camera at a slight angle when taking pictures, especially if your subjects were moving. You can make small adjustments by using the **Rotate Image** command. You can also rotate images 90° to give them a vertical orientation.

FIGURE 13.4 Cropping often improves the image. Smaller images use less memory and thus are able to load faster on the screen.

- **Sizing images.** All photo editing programs will tell you the height and width of an image. You can resize images to fit in a particular area of a webpage or printed page. You can also change the resolution in the dpi window. Increasing the resolution does not improve the image after it has been scanned but does make the file larger.
- **Optimizing images for the web.** Macromedia Fireworks and Adobe Photoshop (versions 5.5 and higher) allow you to optimize images for the web by finding the best mix of colour, compression, and quality. These programs allow you to reduce the size of an image file considerably without a great sacrifice in quality. Optimizing images on webpages makes them load much faster, especially if the user is connecting on a dial-up modem. You will make images for the web quicker to load by dropping the resolution to 72 dpi. Aim for download times for images of fewer than 10 seconds.

- **Adjusting colours.** Often the colours in photographs that you scan appear off when you view the image on a computer monitor. The image may appear too dark or lack contrast. Sometimes the colour balance appears off and you want to correct it. The basic controls for brightness, contrast, and colour saturation are similar to those on your colour TV. Be aware that colours look different on different monitors and what you print may not look like the colours on your screen.
- **Special effects.** Advanced image editors offer a number of different special effects. You can find a list of these effects under the **Filter** menu. The filters allow you to simulate drawings, watercolours, mosaics, and oil paintings, as shown in Figure 13.5 below.

Original image | The effect of a glowing edges filter | The effect of a fresco filter

FIGURE 13.5 Filters can be used to create a variety of special effects.

WRITING SMART

Make a copy of an image before editing it

Always keep a copy of your original scan or digital photo. Once you change an image and save it, you cannot restore what you changed. Use the **Save As** command to make a copy before you start editing an image.

13c FORMATS AND PRINTERS

Native file formats

Native file formats are the ones used by the software that creates the file. When you create an image file in Photoshop, for example, it will be saved as a Photoshop file unless you specify otherwise. Native file formats often give you more possibilities, such as working in layers in a Photoshop file when using Photoshop. You can print image files in native file formats, but you cannot put them on the web. You must use the **Save As** or **Export** command to convert the file to a GIF or JPEG image if you plan to put it on a webpage (see Section 15a).

GIF images

Many images on the web are in **Graphics Interchange Format (GIF)**, which reduces the file size of an image by eliminating redundancies in the data. GIF images have the file ending **.gif**. GIF is the preferred format for images with sharp lines, buttons with text, visual icons, and other small images. The GIF format often makes photographic images splotchy. Thus GIF images are good for icons with sharp lines and solid colours, but not so good for large photographs and complex images.

JPEG images

JPEG is an acronym for Joint Photographic Experts Group, and, as the name suggests, it is the preferred format for photographs on the web. JPEG images have the file ending **.jpeg** or **.jpg**. JPEG compresses the data in a photograph and rearranges it so that it tends to blend the colours and loses some of the detail. For this reason it is not suited for type and sharp-edged graphics.

Printers

Various kinds of printers are well suited for specific tasks. If you lack the printer necessary for a particular job, you can usually find the right one in a campus computer lab or in a retail copy shop.

- **Ink-jet printers**, which have become affordable for most computer users, can produce outstanding colour images, especially on glossy paper. They are also lightweight, making it possible to transport them when necessary. The major disadvantage of ink-jet printers is that they are slow.
- **Laser printers** use a technology similar to photocopying and have the great advantage of speed. Most offices use laser printers because they print documents quickly with crisp text and graphics. Monochrome (black and white) laser printers have become affordable. Colour laser printers, however, remain too expensive for most individuals.
- **Dye-sublimation (dye-sub) printers** produce quality colour prints but do not print text as well as laser printers. Like ink-jet printers, they are slow; like colour laser printers, they are relatively expensive.

13d   TABLES

Extensive statistical data can be dull or cumbersome to communicate in sentences and paragraphs. Readers can more quickly and easily grasp data when they are displayed in a table. For example, a table will allow readers to view an entire set of data at once or to focus only on relevant aspects. Use a table when readers need to know exact numbers.

Tables are easy to create in word processing programs, presentation software, and webpage editors. Usually, the command is **Insert Table** or **Insert** under the **Table** menu. You will then be asked to specify the number of columns and the number of rows. You can use the default width for columns or specify the widths for particular columns. You can also add lines to the table or omit them (see Table 13.1).

Table 13.1 Average Earnings by Highest Level of Schooling in Atlantic Provinces, Age 15 and Older, 2001					
	Canada	**N.L.**	**P.E.I.**	**N.S.**	**N.B.**
			$		
All levels	**31 757**	**24 165**	**22 303**	**26 632**	**24 971**
Less than high school graduation certificate	21 230	15 922	15 058	18 251	17 074
High school graduation certificate and/or some postsecondary	25 477	16 860	18 236	20 553	20 395
Trades certificate or diploma	32 743	26 118	24 090	27 595	27 694
College certificate or diploma	32 736	28 196	25 613	26 930	27 178
University certificate diploma or degree	48 648	41 942	37 063	41 146	40 375

Source: Statistics Canada, *Average Earnings of the Population 15 Years and Over by Highest Level of Schooling, by Province and Territory (2001 Census).* 1 September 2004. 15 June 2006 <http://www40.statcan.ca/l01/cst01/labor50a.htm>.

Using and evaluating tables

When to use tables

- To present a summary of several factors
- To present exact numbers
- To give an orderly arrangement so readers can locate and compare information

Evaluating tables

- Does the table have a clear purpose?
- Does the title indicate the purpose?
- What units do the numbers represent (dollars, people, voters, percentages, and so on)?
- What is the source of the data?
- Is the table clearly organized?
- Is the table clearly labelled?

Name of item	Factor 1	Factor 2	Factor 3
AAA	000	00	0
BBB	00	0	000
CCC	0	000	00

13e CHARTS AND GRAPHS

The terms *chart* and *graph* are often used interchangeably, but there is a distinction between them. Graphs are plotted using coordinates on *x*- and *y*-axes; charts are not. Use charts or graphs when you want to show a relationship between numbers.

You can use spreadsheet applications (Microsoft Excel, Lotus 1-2-3, and others) and presentation software (see Sections 14b and 14c) to create handsome graphs and charts. You can then import these graphs and charts into word processing software or other applications. You need only to type the data into a spreadsheet, then select the kind of chart you want. The program draws the graph or chart for you. You still have to supply the labels for different parts of the chart or graph. You also have to make sure that the chart or graph is legible. If you have too much information to display, you will not have enough space between elements.

Like any graphic, graphs and charts can be used to mislead readers. Small differences can be exaggerated, for example, or relevant data concealed (see Section 6e). You have an ethical responsibility to create accurate graphs and charts.

Bar charts

Bar charts are useful for comparing data. Multiple bars can be set side-by-side, as shown in Figure 13.6, to emphasize comparison, which in this case is between the numbers of men and women employed in different fields.

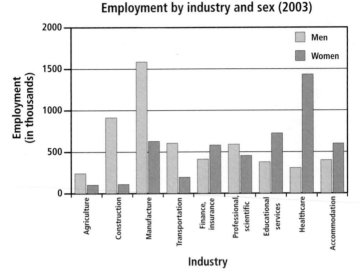

FIGURE 13.6 Bar charts are useful for comparing data.

Source: Statistics Canada. *Employment by Industry and Sex.* 5 Jan. 2006 <http://www40.statcan.ca/l01/cst01/labor10a.htm>.

Line graphs

Line graphs are well suited for displaying changes in data across time. Line graphs can have one line, or two or more sets of data can be displayed on different lines, emphasizing the comparative rates of change (see Figure 13.7).

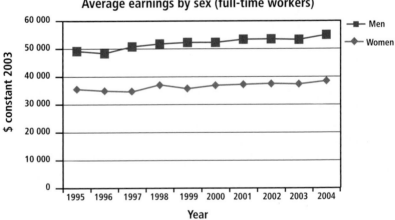

FIGURE 13.7 Line graphs are useful for displaying data across time.

Source: Statistics Canada. *Average Earnings by Sex and Work Pattern (Full-time Workers).* 28 Mar. 2006 <http://www40.statcan.ca/l01/cst01/labor01b.htm>.

Pie charts

Pie charts are commonly used to represent the relationship of parts to a whole. They provide overviews that are quickly understood. For example, Figure 13.8 shows that half the revenue for Newfoundland and Labrador post-secondary education came from government sources. You must have data in percentages to use a pie chart, and the slices of the pie must add up to 100 percent. If the slices are too small, a pie chart becomes confusing. Six or seven slices are about the limit for a pie chart that is easy to interpret.

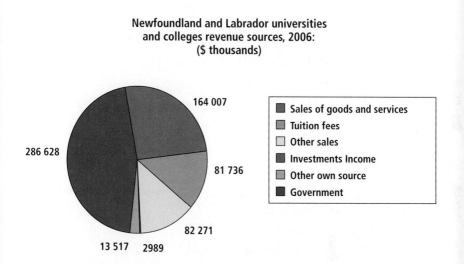

FIGURE 13.8   Pie charts display the relationship of parts to a whole.

Source: Statistics Canada. *Universities and Colleges Revenue and Expenditures, by Province and Territory,* 15 June 2006 <http://www40.statcan.ca/l01/cst01/govt41a. htm?sdi=education%20level>.

Organizational charts and flowcharts

Presentation software and the drawing module in word processing programs allow you to create organizational charts and flowcharts. You can make organizational and flowcharts by selecting shapes and arrows on the drawing module and inserting them. Select the text tool for typing labels on the shapes (see Figure 13.9).

Stage 1: Planning

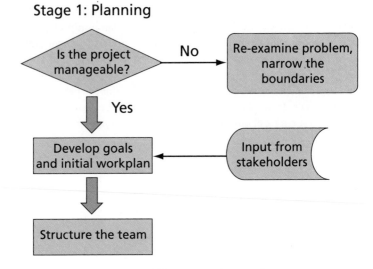

FIGURE 13.9 Flowcharts are useful for representing steps in a process.

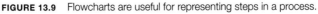

Using and evaluating charts

When to use charts

- To direct readers to what is important
- To give evidence for claims
- To show factual information visually
- To show statistical relationships more clearly than either words or numbers alone permit

Selecting the right chart

	Bar charts	Make comparisons in particular categories
	Line graphs	Show proportional trends over time
	Pie charts	Show the proportion of parts in terms of the whole
	Flowcharts	Show the steps in a process

Evaluating charts
- Does the chart have a clear purpose?
- Does the title indicate the purpose?
- What do the units represent (dollars, people, voters, percentages, and so on)?
- What is the source of the data?
- Is the type of chart appropriate for the information presented?
- Is there any distortion of information (see Section 6e)?

CHAPTER *14*

Verbal and Visual Presentations

New technologies have blurred the line between oral and written presentations. Often a speech later becomes the basis for a written report, or a written report is summarized in a verbal and visual presentation, perhaps even transmitted by teleconferencing. New technologies make producing high-quality visuals to accompany oral presentations easy, but these technologies also offer many choices that place new demands on speakers. The key to success is remembering that your purpose is to communicate effectively. In any medium, your goals, your subject, and your audience should shape your presentation.

14a PLAN A PRESENTATION

Analyze your task

Successful presentations, like writing assignments, require careful planning. First, consider what kind of presentation you are being asked to give. Look closely at your assignment for words such as *argue for, explain, describe, report, summarize,* and *propose*; they indicate what is expected. Some common types of presentations include the following:

- **Informative speeches** explain a concept or analyze a subject (see Chapter 8).
- **How-to presentations** are a subset of informative presentations aimed at providing the audience with the knowledge necessary to perform a task.
- **Persuasive speeches** attempt to change the audience's attitudes and beliefs or to convince them that a particular course of action is best (see Chapter 9).
- **Summaries** give an overview of a report or long document.
- **Group presentations** allow several people to present individual aspects of a subject.

Think about where you will give your presentation

Consider early on where you will be giving the presentation. If you want to use visual elements to support your presentation, make sure the room has the equipment you need. If you know the room is large or has poor acoustics, you may need to arrange for a microphone, amplifier, and speakers. Some rooms have other limitations, such as the inability to darken the room enough for visuals to show up well. Find out in advance what limitations you will face and plan for them.

Select your topic

Choosing and researching a topic for an oral presentation is similar to preparing for a written assignment. If you have a broad choice of topics, make a list of subjects that interest you. Then go through your list and answer these questions:

- Will you enjoy speaking on this topic?
- Will your audience be interested in this topic?
- Does the topic fit the situation for your presentation?
- Do you know enough to speak on this topic?
- If you do not know enough, are you willing to do research to learn more about the topic?

Section 3a describes how to find a topic and Section 3b offers ways of exploring that topic. Remember that your enthusiasm for a topic will be contagious.

Researching a topic for an oral presentation is similar to researching a written assignment. See Chapter 16 for guidelines for planning your research. You should write a working thesis just as you would for a research paper, then modify the thesis as needed. Consult Chapters 17 and 18 for help on finding and evaluating sources in the library and online. You may also wish to conduct interviews, surveys, and observations (see Section 16f). Remember that you may need to develop a bibliography for a presentation just as you would for a research paper, documenting the sources of your information and providing those sources in your talk or in handouts.

Think about the scope of your topic

Length is a critical consideration. How much time you will have to speak determines the depth you can go into. Speakers who ignore this simple principle are often forced to rush toward the end and omit major points, leaving the audience confused about what the speaker had to say.

Consider your audience

Unlike writing for readers you've never seen, when you give a speech, you have your audience directly before you. Your audience will give you concrete feedback during your presentation by smiling or frowning, by paying attention or losing interest, by asking questions or sitting passively.

Think about the general characteristics of your audience—their ages, their occupations, their educational level, their ethnic and cultural background, and the mix of men and women. Think specifically about your audience in relation to your topic.

- Will your audience be interested in your topic?
- Are there ways you can make them more interested?
- What is your audience likely to know or believe about your topic?
- What does your audience probably not know about your topic?
- What key terms will you have to define or explain?
- What assumptions do you hold in common with your audience?
- How is your audience most likely to disagree with you?
- What questions is your audience likely to ask?

Organize your presentation

After you have done your research and analyzed your audience, it's time to organize your presentation. Make a list of key points and consider how best to organize them. Your visuals should clearly indicate your major points. These types of organization are common for presentations:

- **Chronological organization** orders major points according to a time sequence.
- **Topical organization** divides a speech into several connected topics and elaborates on those topics.
- **Problem/solution organization** is often used for proposals, where a problem is identified and a solution proposed (see Chapter 9).

Organize a group presentation

Changing speakers is a distraction for the audience in a group presentation. For the group presentation to be successful, each speaker must have a clearly defined role and the transition from one speaker to the next should be smooth. The first speaker should serve as the host. The host previews the topic and introduces the speakers. The host may also provide the transitions from one speaker to another and offer the conclusion.

- **Determine the roles and the goals.** Each member of the group must understand his or her role in the presentation and the goal of that segment.
- **Coordinate research.** Each speaker should be well informed on the subtopic he or she is to present. The audience will expect answers to in-depth questions.
- **Coordinate visuals.** An advantage of group presentation is that a person not speaking can handle the visuals, allowing the speaker to focus on the delivery. This advantage is gained by practising in advance.
- **Rehearse.** Groups that try to make a presentation on the fly rarely succeed. Timing is critical. Pausing to read notes is a sure way to lose the audience.

Support your presentation

When you have organized your main points, you next need to decide how to support those points. Look at your research notes and think about how best to incorporate the information you found. Consider using one or more of these strategies:

- **Facts.** Speakers who know their facts build credibility.
- **Statistics.** Good use of statistics can give the audience the impression that you have done your homework. Statistics also can indicate that a particular example is representative.
- **Statements by authorities.** Quotations from credible experts can support key points.
- **Narratives.** Narratives are brief stories that illustrate key points. Narratives can hold the attention of the audience—but keep them short or they will become a distraction.
- **Humour.** Humour is one of the primary ways to convince an audience to share your point of view. You have to know the audience well, however, to predict with confidence what they will think is funny.

Think about your medium

Audiences now expect that most informative and persuasive presentations will include visuals. Visual elements range from simple transparencies and handouts to elaborate multimedia presentations. Visual elements that are easy to create include

- Outlines
- Text
- Statistical charts
- Flowcharts
- Photographs
- Models
- Maps

Plan your introduction

The most critical part of a presentation is the introduction. You have to get the audience's attention, introduce your topic, convince the audience that it is important, present your thesis, and give your audience either an overview of your presentation or a sense of your direction. Accomplishing all this in a short time is a tall order, but if you lose your audience in the first two minutes, you won't recover their attention. You might begin with a compelling example or anecdote that both introduces your topic and indicates your stance.

Plan your conclusion

The second most important part of your presentation is your conclusion. You want to end on a strong note. First, you need to signal that you are entering the conclusion. You can announce that you are concluding, or you can give signals in other ways such as turning off the projector. Touching on your main points again will help your audience remember them. But simply summarizing is a dull way to close. Think of an example or an idea that captures the gist of your speech, something that your audience can take away with them.

14b DESIGN EFFECTIVE VISUALS

Advantages and disadvantages of visuals

Visuals offer many advantages in a presentation. They focus the attention of the audience. Visuals can keep your audience oriented throughout your presentation while providing you with memory aids. Charts, pictures, and diagrams can help you emphasize major points and provide information that would be tedious to describe verbally. Visuals also give your audience something to look at besides you, which helps you to relax.

At a minimum, consider putting an outline of your talk on an overhead transparency. Most computer printers can make transparencies using blank transparency sheets inserted into the paper feeder. Charts, maps, photographs, and other graphics in digital format can thus be printed directly onto transparencies. Many photocopiers can also make transparencies. Visuals take time to prepare, so start planning them early.

On the other hand, the unplanned or unpractised use of visuals can be distracting to both you and your audience. If you cannot find the right transparency or you lose track of your slides, your presentation may fall apart. Visuals can be frustrating for the audience if they are too small or don't show up well. Visuals can also tempt you to look at the screen instead of looking at the audience. Keep practising with your visuals until you feel comfortable and get your timing right.

Guidelines for creating and using visuals effectively

The following guidelines will help you create better visuals and use them effectively.

- **Keep the text short.** You don't want your audience straining to read long passages on the screen and neglecting what you have to say. Except for quotations, use short words and phrases on transparencies and slides.
- **Always proofread.** Typos and misspelled words make you look careless and can distract the audience from your point.
- **Use dark text on a white or light-coloured background.** Light text on a dark background is hard to read. If you use it you may have to close every window and turn off all the lights in order for your audience to see the text.
- **Use graphics that reproduce well.** Some graphics do not show up well on the screen, often because there isn't enough contrast.
- **Plan your timing when using visuals.** Usually you can leave a slide on the screen for one to two minutes, which allows your audience time to read the slide and connect its points to what you are saying.

Presentation software

Presentation software allows you to combine text, images, sounds, animations, and even video clips on computer-generated slides, which can be projected onto a large screen. Most presentation software gives you a choice of templates that you can use to format slides, and a variety of backgrounds and colour schemes that make your slides attractive. Once you have created the file, you need do no more than click a mouse to move from one slide to another. You can also prepare paper handouts from the slides to accompany the visual presentation. The most popular software is Microsoft PowerPoint, which is bundled with Microsoft Office, but there are many competing products, often specialized for particular uses.

Presentation software is easy to use. It offers quality visuals produced with no more effort than it takes to use a word processing program. It allows you to import charts and other graphics that you have created in other programs. It gives you several options for presentation, including printed handouts and webpages. Presentation software can be quite portable: you can plug your laptop into a projector to give your presentation or carry the presentation on a CD or other storage device and use an on-site computer.

Give your audience ideas—not fluff

If you use presentation software, make sure its attractive features do not distract you from the meat of your presentation: its content. The software does not do the planning, researching, and thinking about your audience described in Section 14a.

Another drawback of presentation software is that it is easy to get carried away with the special effects, such as fade-ins, fade-outs, and sound effects. Remember that your goal is to communicate information and ideas, not to dazzle your audience with special effects. Presentations heavy on special effects often come off as heavy on style and light on substance. They also can be time-consuming to produce.

COMMON ERRORS

Slides with too much type and too small type

If you have taken many lecture classes that use presentation software, you've probably had at least one professor who put more text on the slides than could be read in a few seconds. It's a common complaint. Limit your information to the essentials. Six lines is generally the maximum, and six words or fewer in a line is desirable. If you want to give your audience long stretches of text, think about providing a handout along with your slide presentation.

Make sure that the audience can read the text from more than three metres away. You may depend on your transparencies and slides to convey important information, but if your audience cannot read the slides, not only will the information be lost but the audience will become frustrated.

Use these type sizes for transparencies and slides.

	Transparencies	**Slides**
Title	36 pt	24 pt
Subtitles	24 pt	18 pt
Other text	18 pt	14 pt

Remember: Preview your transparencies and slides from a distance equal to the rear of the room where you will be speaking. If you cannot read them, increase the type size.

14c DELIVER A PRESENTATION WITH VISUALS

Team Guidelines
From "me" to "we"

Agree on team roles and behavior

◆ Discuss how the team will choose a leader

◆ Determine roles

◆ Recognize the importance of communication

◆ Agree on what is acceptable team behavior

Nervousness

Nervousness is usually invisible. If you make a mistake, remember that your audience will understand. Stage fright is normal, and often you can draw off that energy to make a more forceful presentation. Take a deep breath before you begin, and smile.

Practice

There is no substitute for rehearsing your speech several times.

- You will become more confident.
- You will be able to focus more on your audience and on maintaining eye contact.
- You will be more comfortable using your visuals.
- You will know how long your presentation will take.

Effective techniques

- Practise in advance.
- Talk, don't read.
- Stand, don't sit.
- Make eye contact.
- Signal main points with gestures.
- Speak loudly.
- Use effective visuals.
- Focus on main points.
- Give an overview in the introduction.
- Give a conclusion that ends with a key idea or example.
- Believe in what you say; enthusiasm is contagious.
- Finish on time.

WRITING IN THE WORLD

Home-field advantage

Athletes know that the home-field advantage involves much more than having the crowd behind them. Each field and court has its own special characteristics. In many cases small bits of knowledge acquired from playing on the field (such as a position from which the sun is blinding at a certain time of day) can mean the difference between winning and losing. Visiting teams practise on the opponent's field or court before the game to learn as much as possible.

In post-secondary education many or all presentations will be in your classroom, which can give you your own home-field advantage. You'll know whether acoustics are good, whether it is easy to see visuals from everywhere in the room, and so on. In the workplace, you may be required to give presentations in unfamiliar places, such as a client's site. You will have to work a little harder to ensure success.

Practise your presentation in the room where you will deliver it. Bring a friend who can tell you whether you can be heard in the back of the room and whether your visuals can be read at that distance. Make sure any equipment you need is working.

Have a back-up plan for visuals. If your presentation depends on a projector that stops working unexpectedly, think about what you will do if you suddenly cannot use the visuals you brought. For example, you can write a few main points on a white board or flip chart if necessary.

Remember that the audience is with you. Most people are patient when something goes wrong. They have been in similar situations themselves. If, for example, a projector bulb burns out and another one is available, ask the audience to give you a minute or two.

CHAPTER *15*

Writing for the Web

The World Wide Web first came online at a particle physics laboratory in Switzerland in 1990. The goal of the original web was to allow scientists to pass around reports of research. The web as we know it today did not come into being until the first browser, Mosaic, became available in 1993. For the first time, surfing among pages that contained both words and images was possible. It took a while, however, for writers to adjust to the new medium.

People now expect the content of websites to be shaped for the web, including images and graphics along with words. Web-editing programs such as Macromedia Dreamweaver, Adobe GoLive, and Microsoft FrontPage have made the creation of webpages almost as easy as writing papers using a word processor. As the technical barriers have been lowered, the expectations for high-quality content have been raised. Just as for paper, people respect well-organized and well-written content on the web.

15a PLAN A WEBSITE

The process of creating a website is similar in many ways to other kinds of writing. Thinking about your audience and what you want to accomplish at the beginning will guide you in making decisions as you compose and revise.

What should your website accomplish?

The original purpose of the web was **informative**—it allowed physicists to share scientific papers quickly and easily. After improved browsers made the web easy to use, companies rushed to advertise and later to sell goods and services online. Many organizations advocating particular causes also put up websites. Even though these sites display a wide range of goals, their general purpose is **persuasive**; they want you to buy something, believe something, or take some action. Individuals have also put up many thousands of webpages, some informative, some persuasive, some just for the fun of it—to display artwork, to post a family album, to list personal interests in the hope of meeting like-minded people, to tell a little about themselves. We might classify these sites as **expressive**. Before you begin designing a site, you need to answer these questions.

- What's your main goal?
- What personality do you want your site to project?
- What "look and feel" do you want your site to possess?

Who is your intended audience?

Many times when you write on paper, you have a good sense of who will read your writing. But when you put up a website, even one that fulfills a course requirement, you cannot be sure who will visit it. Many students have received email from people in other countries only hours after putting up a site in a trial version. Think about your larger audience as well as your intended audience.

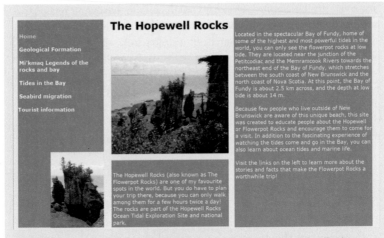

FIGURE 15.1   Homepage of Kaila Maddox's website on the Flowerpot Rocks

Kaila Maddox created *The Hopewell Rocks* website (Figure 15.1) for a course project in multimedia writing. The assignment allowed her to introduce a place that she felt more Canadians should know about and visit. Her goals are both informative and persuasive. She wants visitors to the site to learn more about the geographical formation and perhaps decide to visit the area during a summer vacation. After Maddox has described the beauty of the area and its unique features, she describes how the formations were created both from the perspective of geological science (see Figure 15.2) and from Aboriginal legends and myths about the area. She includes tourist information for viewers who decide to visit the area after exploring her site.

The personality of Maddox's site is friendly. She created images of some of the rocks to pique the viewer's interest. She writes in an informal, sometimes humorous tone.

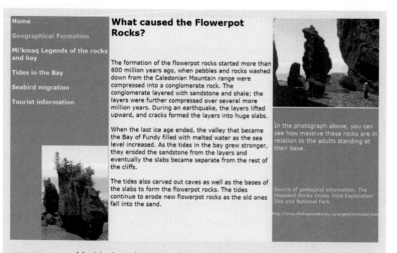

FIGURE 15.2 Maddox's webpage on how the Flowerpot Rocks were formed geologically

Maddox identifies her intended audience as vacationers interested in beautiful and educational natural sites. She assumes they know little about the area or the Bay of Fundy. She includes a series of tidbits that inform readers as well as underscore some of the spectacular aspects of the vacation site. In addition to teaching viewers, she also wants them to be moved to see the tides in action and wander the shores beside the flowerpot rocks.

- Are you aiming your site at a target group of viewers? If so, what are they likely to know about your subject? What attitudes will they likely have toward your subject?
- If you are creating a site for a general audience, what assumptions can you make about that audience? What kinds of general knowledge can you assume they are likely to have?
- Do you want people with relatively slow telephone modem connections to be able to access your site? If so, you will have to make sure that the site loads quickly.
- Will you make your site accessible to people with disabilities?

15b DEFINE SPECIFIC GOALS

To begin to translate a vision of a website into specific goals, think about your own experiences on the web. You might start out by making two lists, such as what you hate about the web and what you like about the web. Your "hate" list might look something like this:

What I hate about the web

1. Sites that take too long to appear
2. Can't find what I'm looking for on a site
3. Pages that are too crowded, hard to read
4. Too many bells and whistles that don't add anything
5. Sites that are hard to navigate
6. Poorly written content with many errors

Some of these might sound like technical issues, but in fact they are all writing issues. Even when a site is visually appealing, it seems sloppy and poorly executed if the organization of the site is jumbled and the text poorly written.

Your list of what you like about the web might look like this:

What I like about the web

1. Sites that load fast, even on a slow modem connection
2. When information I want is easy to find
3. Content that is up to date and interesting
4. Sites that are visually attractive
5. When navigation is easy—there's always a way back to the start and to other major parts of the site
6. Text that is well written

On a well-designed site, the images contribute to the overall effect. Information on the site can be located without difficulty—so if you return to the site later, you don't have the frustrating experience of being unable to find something you have seen before. The best websites show care with small details, including careful attention to the writing. You should include in your goals the characteristics of websites that you find most appealing. You want your website to be handsome, well organized, easy to navigate, informative, and well written.

WRITING IN THE WORLD

Evaluating a website

You can learn a great deal about effective web design by keeping these criteria in mind when you visit websites. Some will be more critical than others, depending on the site. For example, good navigational tools become more important on extensive sites.

1. **Audience and purpose:** How does the site identify its intended audience? How would you characterize its purpose: informative, persuasive, or expressive?
2. **Content:** How informative is the content? Has the site been updated recently? What do you want to know more about? Are there any mechanical, grammatical, or style problems?
3. **Readability:** Is there sufficient contrast between the text and the background to make it legible? Are the margins wide enough? Are there any paragraphs that go on too long and need to be divided? Are headings inserted in the right places, and if headings are used for more than one level, are these levels indicated consistently? Is high-contrast text, including text in boldface and all caps, kept short?
4. **Visual design:** Does the site have a consistent visual theme? Where is the focal point on each page? Do the images contribute to the visual appeal or do they detract from it?
5. **Navigation:** Does the first page indicate what else is on the site? How easy or difficult is it to move from one page to another on the site? Is a consistent navigation scheme used throughout the site? Are there any broken links?

15c DESIGN FOR THE WEB

Keeping a few principles in mind when you design a webpage can lead to much better end results.

Give your site a visual theme

A consistent look and feel makes a website appear unified and supports the content. A website does not need a loud background or flashy animations to achieve a visual theme. Instead, little things such as selecting a simple set of colours for the text, headings, links, and background do more to create a consistent visual theme than an attention-grabbing image. Similar graphics and images should be the same size, and often their placement can be repeated from page to page.

Maddox places small images on her pages to show the beauty of the formations and the park (Figure 15.3). She designed the site with a template so that each page would share a common look and placement of content. The repeated close-up of one rock grouping in the navigational bar on each page provides a visual cue to the site name, no matter what page users are on.

FIGURE 15.3   Through consistent design, Maddox has created a predictable site.

Make the navigational structure visible and consistent

How to move through a website should be evident from the beginning. An overview of your site should be presented in the navigation tools on the first page. The tools should reflect the primary subjects of your site.

The format of the navigation tools should be consistent from one page to another. For example, if your main navigation tool is a row of buttons down the left side of the page, subsequent pages should also have a row of buttons down the left side. Colours used for navigation should also remain consistent.

Maddox's navigation bar is prominent on the left side of all her pages (Figure 15.4). She uses the same links in the same order on each page, so visitors can easily move around on her site. She also greys out the link to the page that users are currently viewing to help them recognize their location on the site.

Home

Geographical Formation

Mi'kmaq Legends of the rocks and bay

Tides in the Bay

Seabird migration

Tourist information

FIGURE 15.4 This navigational bar appears on the left side of each webpage on Maddox's site.

Steve Sanchez designed this menu for a class exercise in multimedia writing. He incorporated visual metaphors into the type, suggesting the content of the pages he was linking to. In addition to bringing interest and humour to what otherwise would have been a dull list, visual metaphors can help viewers to understand concepts and to better remember them.

FIGURE 15.5

Make the text readable

Long stretches of text on the web tend not to get read. Maddox divided the content into six pages so that viewers can move to the geographical formation, the First Nations' legends about the origins of the rocks and bay, or the tides in the Bay of Fundy. She limited the length of each page to what would appear on a viewer's screen. She invites viewers to click on the links rather than forcing them to scroll down to see what else is on the site; Maddox knows that most web users don't like reading long passages of text on the screen.

You can make your text more readable on the web if you do the following:

- **Divide your information into chunks.** If your information runs longer than a page, consider placing it on two webpages.
- **Use shorter paragraphs when possible.** Long paragraphs are harder to read on the screen than in print.
- **Use a sans serif typeface.** You can specify typefaces using the font command on your web-editing software.
- **Control for line width.** Lines of type that run across the entire page often are difficult to read. Divide your page into columns as Kaila does.
- **Use white space to separate elements and to give visual relief.**
- **Avoid dark backgrounds.**

TEXT IN ALL CAPS OR IN A SERIF FONT IS HARD TO READ ON SCREEN AGAINST A BLACK BACKGROUND, *ESPECIALLY IF THE TEXT IS IN ITALICS.*

Use upper and lower case and a sans serif font for maximum legibility.

 For a tutorial on creating and building a website, visit www.pearsoned.ca/faigley/210.

PART FIVE

Researching

- How do I plan and execute a research project? (16a–c)

- What is an *annotated bibliography*? (17f, 19d)

- How can I use library databases to locate and cite articles on my topic? (18a)

- Are all of my print and internet sources trustworthy? How can I tell? (19b-c)

- What's the difference between paraphrasing a source and plagiarism? (20e)

5 RESEARCHING

Research means both investigating existing knowledge and creating new knowledge. When you conduct research in a college or university course, you need to understand the different kinds of research, know how and where to find the types of sources you need, and be able to use sources effectively in your own writing.

Writing in the World Project

Tracing the Family History

Interview members of your extended family to identify some of the family origins. Select one branch and research the geographical area and cultural history from which those ancestors emigrated. If you were to take a trip to that part of the world, who might you visit and what important sites might you see? Write a research paper in which you present the information that you uncover about your family and describe the itinerary for a trip that you could take to visit the area and learn more about your family history and roots.

Visit *The Brief Penguin Handbook* Companion Website at
www.pearsoned.ca/faigley/

MyCanadianCompLab
Where writing and research help is a click away.
MyCanadianCompLab may be packaged with your textbook.
If not, it can be purchased from your college or university's bookstore.
Go to **www.pearsoned.ca/highered/mycanadiancomplab/**
for a tour.

 **C H A P T E R** *16*

Planning Your Research

You do research every day. If you read movie reviews in your newspaper to decide which movie you want to see, or if you visit travel websites to find out where you can get the best deal on airline fares, you are doing research. If you want to settle an argument about who last won an Olympic gold medal for Canada in pairs figure skating, you need to do research. In post-secondary education, research means both **investigating existing knowledge** that is stored on computers and in libraries and **creating new knowledge** through original analysis, surveys, experiments, and theorizing. When you start a research task in a post-secondary course, you need to understand the different kinds of possible research and to plan your strategy in advance.

16a ANALYZE THE RESEARCH TASK

If you have an assignment that requires research, look closely at what you are being asked to do. The assignment may ask you to review, compare, survey, analyze, evaluate, or prove that something is true or untrue. The purpose of your research and a knowledge of your potential audience will help guide your strategies for research.

Determine your purpose

Often the assignment itself will tell you what is expected. Look for keywords:

- An *analysis* or *examination* requires you to look at an issue in detail, explaining how it has evolved, who or what it affects, and what is at stake.
- A *review of scholarship* requires you to summarize what key scholars and researchers have written about the issue.
- A *survey* requires you to gather opinion about a particular issue, either by a questionnaire or by interviews.
- An *evaluation* requires you to make critical judgments.
- An *argument* requires you to assemble evidence in support of a claim you make.

Ask your instructor for guidance if you remain unsure of what is expected.

Identify your potential readers

Think about whom you are writing for.

- How familiar are your readers likely to be with your subject?
- What are they likely to know and not know about your subject?
- What aspects of your subject might interest them the most?
- What background information will you need to supply?
- If your subject is controversial, what opinions or beliefs are your readers likely to have about it?
- Do you want to inform your readers, change their attitudes, or persuade them to take some action?

Assess the project's length and scope

Think about exactly what you are expected to produce.

- What kind of research are you being asked to do? Library research? Survey research? Field observations?
- How long is the paper you are writing or how extensive is the website you are creating?
- How many sources are you expected to include?
- What steps are required by your instructor in advance of the final draft? A topic proposal? A first draft? A working bibliography?

16b   SET A SCHEDULE

The secret to a successful research project is allowing enough time to do the job well. To use the schedule on the next page, fill in the date your final draft is due and work backward to the present. You can use your schedule to make a research log in which you keep track of your progress.

WRITING SMART

Use folders

Writers who make their living doing research rely on both paper and computer folders. Before you begin, get a few paper folders for your handwritten notes, photocopies, and early drafts. Create a folder on your desktop, if you are using a computer, and create subfolders for drafts and sources. Make sure you have a folder labelled something like "old project" and put in it all your early drafts and other material that you decide not to use. You never know when you may want to refer to work you had done earlier but didn't think you would need.

Schedule for research project

Task to complete	Date
Find a topic that interests you (16c)	_____
Ask a question and draft a working thesis (16d)	_____
Decide what kind of research you need to do (16e, 16f)	_____
Begin library or web research (17a, 18a)	_____
Start a working bibliography (17f)	_____
Read and evaluate your sources (19)	_____
Summarize and paraphrase your sources (20)	_____
Review your goals and thesis (21a)	_____
Plan your organization (21b)	_____
Decide what material from your sources to include (21c)	_____
Write the first draft (21d)	_____
Review your draft (21e)	_____
Revise your draft (21f)	_____
Edit and check formatting of your revised draft (21f)	_____
Submit final draft	_____

16c FIND A TOPIC THAT INTERESTS YOU

If you ask meaningful questions, research will be enjoyable. Your courses may give you some ideas about questions to ask, or you may simply want to pursue an interest of your own. One good way to begin is by browsing, either in your library or on the web. Browsing may lead you to topics you hadn't yet considered; it may also show you the breadth of possibilities included in a topic you have already selected. For example, perhaps you're interested in key policy issues that are likely to affect the internet over the next few years. One issue that is certain to be controversial is privacy, but when you start browsing, you realize privacy is a wide-ranging concept involving many concerns, including web security, encryption, spam, and employer surveillance of employees. You will need to narrow your topic—perhaps to the issue of "cookies." (A cookie is a small file placed on your computer by a web server so that it recognizes you the next time you access the site from your browser.)

Browse a web subject directory

A web search engine is a set of programs that sort through millions of items with incredible speed. Several web search sites (Britannica, LookSmart, and Yahoo!) include **subject directories**. Web directories are useful when you want to narrow a topic or learn what subcategories a topic might contain. The most popular subject directory, Yahoo! (www.yahoo.ca or www.yahoo.com), will retrieve both websites indexed by Yahoo! staff members and sites

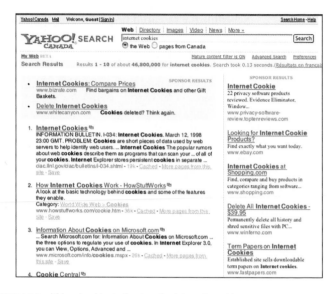

FIGURE 16.1 Yahoo! subject directory for internet cookies

from the entire web using **search engine** technology. (See Figure 16.1.) In addition to the web subject directories, the Library of Congress Virtual Reference Shelf (www.loc.gov/rr/askalib/virtualref.html) may help you identify sites relevant to your topic.

Consult a general encyclopedia

General encyclopedias, which provide basic information about a wide range of topics, are also a good starting point for browsing. Some encyclopedias are now available online without charge; your library reference room will undoubtedly have others. Two of the best known are the *Columbia Encyclopedia* (www.bartleby.com/65) and *Encyclopaedia Britannica* (www.britannica.com).

Consult a specialized encyclopedia

Specialized encyclopedias focus on a single area of knowledge, go into more depth about a subject, and often include bibliographies. Specialized encyclopedias are available for virtually any area that may interest you, from the *Encyclopedia of Accounting Systems* to the *Encyclopedia of Zoroastrianism*. Your library may have handouts for specialized encyclopedias and other specialized reference sources, or you can consult Robert Balay's *Guide to Reference Books*, which should be available at the reference desk.

16d ASK A QUESTION AND DRAFT A WORKING THESIS

Often you'll be surprised by the amount of information your initial browsing uncovers. Your next task will be to identify in that mass of information a question for your research project. This **researchable question**, to which you may want to formulate an initial answer, or **working thesis**, will be the focus of the remainder of your research and ultimately of your research project or paper.

Research profile: Mary Kingsley

Let's say you are interested in learning more about female explorers. During your research you quickly discover that there were many women who travelled in the 1800s to areas unknown to Europeans. One who interests you is Mary Kingsley (1862–1900), a British woman who journeyed alone in remote areas of West Africa between 1893 and 1895. The information you find suggests that Kingsley was incredibly independent and undeterred by danger and hardship. You'd like to write about her, but you do not have a researchable question. You read more and discover that she defended the beliefs and practices of native Africans and had little good to say about missionaries. A question begins to emerge, and so does your working thesis.

Write your topic, research question, and working thesis on a notecard or sheet of paper. Keep your working thesis handy. You may need to revise it several times until the wording is precise.

TOPIC	Mary Kingsley's travels in West Africa
RESEARCH QUESTION	What was Mary Kingsley's attitude toward the people she encountered in West Africa, both native and European?
WORKING THESIS	Mary Kingsley presented a view of West Africa contrary to the one prevailing in her time because she valued the great diversity of native peoples, customs, and beliefs, and attacked European missionaries for doing more harm than good.

Research profile: Casino gambling

Take another example. You want to write about legalizing casino gambling, but that topic turns out to be massive. You find that the debate over allowing casino gambling on First Nations' property goes back to the early 1980s. In order to narrow your topic, you look at arguments for and against expanding casino gambling. An argument that proponents of casino gambling often use is: casinos bring tourist dollars that benefit the entire community. Opponents of casino gambling argue the opposite:

people who go to casinos spend money on gambling that they might spend elsewhere. In your initial research, you discover that studies on this issue show that some businesses are helped but others are hurt. This initial research gives you a working thesis.

TOPIC	Economic impacts of casino gambling
RESEARCH QUESTION	How does the presence of a casino affect the economy of the community where it is located?
WORKING THESIS	The economic impact of casino gambling on the communities in which it is located is mixed, with some businesses benefiting and others suffering.

16e DECIDE WHAT KIND OF RESEARCH YOU NEED TO DO

Once you have formulated a research question, you should begin thinking about what kind of research you will need to do to address the question.

Secondary research

Most people who do research rely partly or exclusively on the work of others as sources of information. Research based on the work of others is called **secondary research**. In the past this information was contained almost exclusively in collections of print materials housed in libraries, but today enormous amounts of information are available on the internet and in various recorded media.

Primary research

Much of the research done at post-secondary institutions creates new information through **primary research**: experiments, data-gathering surveys and interviews, detailed observations, and the examination of historical documents. Although most post-secondary students do not do primary research, sometimes you have to gather the needed information yourself. If you are researching a campus issue such as the problem of inadequate parking for students, you may need to conduct interviews, make observations, and take a survey.

16f PLAN YOUR FIELD RESEARCH

Even though much of the research you do for post-secondary courses will be secondary research conducted at a computer or in the library, some topics do call for primary research, requiring you to gather information on your own by conducting interviews, making observations, or administering surveys. Field research of this kind can be especially important for exploring local issues.

Interviews

Post-secondary institutions are a rich source of experts in many areas, including those on the faculty and in the surrounding community. Interviewing experts on your research topic can help build your knowledge base. You can use interviews to discover what the people most affected by a particular issue are thinking and feeling. Before you contact anyone, think carefully about your goals; knowing what you want to find out through your interviews will help you determine whom you need to interview and what questions you need to ask.

1. Decide what you want or need to know and who best can provide that for you.
2. Schedule each interview in advance, and let the person know why you are conducting the interview and how long it should take.
3. Plan your questions in advance. Write down more questions than you think you'll need and have a few more in mind. Listen carefully so you can follow up on key points.
4. Come prepared with a notebook and pencil. A tape recorder sometimes can intimidate the person you are interviewing. If you want to use a tape recorder, ask for permission in advance.

Observations

Local observation can also be a valuable source of data. For example, if you are researching why a particular office on your campus does not operate efficiently, observe what happens when students enter and how they are handled by the staff.

- Choose a place where you can observe with the least intrusion. The less people wonder about what you are doing, the better.
- Carry a notebook and write extensive field notes. Get down as much information as you can, and worry about analyzing it later.
- Record the date, exactly where you were, exactly when you arrived and left, and important details like the number of people present.
- Write on one side of your notebook so you can use the facing page to note key observations and analyze your data later.

Surveys

Extensive surveys that can be projected to large populations, like the ones used in political polls, require the effort of many people. Small surveys, however, often can provide insight into local issues. You need to decide what exactly you want to know, then design a survey that will provide that information.

- Write a few specific questions. Make sure that they are unambiguous—people will fill out your survey quickly, and if the questions are confusing, the results will be meaningless. To make sure your questions are clear, test them on a few people before you conduct the survey.

- Include one or two open-ended questions, such as "What do you like about X?" "What don't you like about X?" The answers to open-ended questions can be difficult to interpret, but sometimes they turn up information you had not anticipated.
- Decide whom and how many people you will need to survey. For example, if you want to claim that the results of your survey represent the views of your residence-mates, your method of selecting respondents should give all residents an equal chance to be selected. Don't select only your friends.
- Decide how you will contact participants in your survey. If you are going to mail or email your survey, include a statement about what the survey is for.
- Think about how you will interpret your survey. Multiple-choice formats make data easy to tabulate, but often they miss key information. Open-ended questions will require you to figure out a way to group responses.

C H A P T E R   1 7

Finding Print Sources in Libraries

You may have heard people say that you can find any information you want on the web. In fact, most books, films, recordings, scholarly journals, and older copies of newspapers that you can find in a large library are not on the web. The resources in your library have been reviewed by librarians, so the quality is generally high and the materials are logically organized. Furthermore, when you go to the library, you have a librarian to help you if you cannot find what you are looking for.

17a   DETERMINE WHAT KINDS OF SOURCES YOU WILL NEED

Before you begin your library research, you should determine what kinds of sources you will need. Knowing where to start will help you to get more quickly to what you need. Look again at your assignment. Your instructor may specify the kinds of sources and how many sources you are expected to use.

Types of sources

Source	Type of Information	How to Find Them
Scholarly books (see pp. 225–27)	Extensive and in-depth coverage of nearly any subject	Library catalogue
Scholarly journals (see pp. 227–32)	Reports of new knowledge and research findings written by experts	Print indexes and library databases
Trade journals (see pp. 227–32)	Reports of information pertaining to specific fields and products	Print indexes and library databases
Popular magazines (see pp. 227–32)	Reports or summaries of current news, sports, fashion, entertainment subjects	Print indexes and library databases
Newspapers (see pp. 232–33)	Recent and current information; foreign newspapers are useful for international perspectives	Print indexes and library databases
Government publications (see pp. 222–25)	Government collected statistics, studies, and reports; especially good for science and medicine	Library catalogue and municipal, provincial, and federal government websites
Videos, audios, documentaries, maps (see pp. 222–25)	Information varies widely	Library catalogue

Ask these questions before you start.

- How much information do you need?
- Do you need to use particular types of sources?
- How current should the information be? Some assignments require you to find the most up-to-date information you can locate.
- Do you need to consider point of view? Argument assignments sometimes require you to consider opposing viewpoints on an issue.

17b IDENTIFY KEYWORDS

Your library catalogue offers you two primary ways of searching. You can search by exact phrase, called **browse** searching. Or you can search by using **keywords**.

Browse searches

Browse searches allow you to search by author and title. You have to use the exact words.

- For authors: The name is inverted with the last name first. No comma is needed.
    Example: **Shakespeare William**
- For titles: The initial article (*a, an, the*) must be dropped.
    Example: **Merchant of Venice** *not* The Merchant of Venice. You can also search with the initial word or words of a title, e.g., **Merchant**.

Keyword searches

Keyword searches allow you to search all fields in the library's catalogue. Furthermore, keyword searches are the primary way to find information in library databases (see Section 18b) and on the web (see Section 18c).

Begin with your research question and working thesis (see Section 16d).

TOPIC	Religious symbols in public high schools
RESEARCH QUESTION	Does it endanger other students to allow Sikh students to wear ceremonial daggers to school?
WORKING THESIS	While traditional weaponry is properly banned from Canadian high schools due to possible violence, the ceremonial dagger worn by Sikh students poses no threat and should be an exception to the ban.

Underline the key terms in your thesis. Then think of as many synonyms and related terms as you can and make lists.

TRADITIONAL WEAPONRY	CANADIAN HIGH SCHOOLS AND VIOLENCE	BANNED ITEMS	EXCEPTIONS
daggers worn by Sikhs	violent incidents at secondary schools	cell phones	head coverings (scarves, hats, etc.)
knives	stabbings at secondary schools	pagers	ceremonial weapons
guns	beatings at secondary schools	concealed weapons	kirpans
ceremonial weapons	shootings at high schools	gang wear	wristbands
religious weapons	bullying at secondary schools	inappropriate slogans, logos	ceremonial daggers
arms	harassment at high schools		dirks
	kirpan violence		legal restrictions
	legal discussion of kirpans in schools		

When you have your keywords, use them to search your library's catalogue. For example, if you do a keyword search using *ceremonial weapons* as the keywords, you might find these words in the TITLE field (see Figure 17.1).

Narrowing a keyword search

If you start with only one keyword, chances are the search will give you too many items to be useful. If, for example, you type the word *genetics* into the subject search window on your library's online catalogue, you likely will get more than a thousand items, perhaps several thousand. To narrow your search, you can combine search terms with the word AND.

For example, you may have read or heard that attention deficit hyperactivity disorder (ADHD) tends to run in families, so there may be genetic factors involved. You can do additional searches for "attention deficit hyperactivity disorder AND genetics" to narrow the topic. (See Figure 17.2.)

AUTHOR	Bharadia, Seema, 1966–
TITLE	The arts of the Sikh kingdoms : the Canadian collections / Seema Bharadia.
PUBLISHER	Toronto : Royal Ontario Museum, 2000
DESCRIPTION	61 p. ill. 24 cm.
NOTE	Catalogue of Canadian Sikh artifacts added to the exhibition. The arts of the Sikh kingdoms, held at the Royal Ontario Museum. May 22–Aug 20, 2000.
	Includes bibliographical references.
SUBJECT	Sikh art—Exhibitions.
ALTERNATE AU	Royal Ontario Museum.
ISBN	0888544340
NAT.BIB. #	C009317309
NLC #	009317309

FIGURE 17.1   Keywords in the TITLE field of a library record

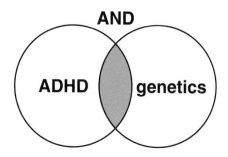

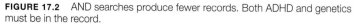

FIGURE 17.2   AND searches produce fewer records. Both ADHD and genetics must be in the record.

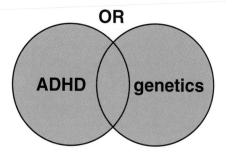

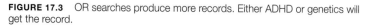

FIGURE 17.3   OR searches produce more records. Either ADHD or genetics will get the record.

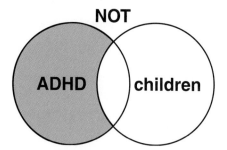

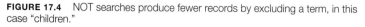

FIGURE 17.4   NOT searches produce fewer records by excluding a term, in this case "children."

Most search tools also allow you to use OR to retrieve items that include either term. Note that replacing AND with OR in the previous search would yield very different results, since using OR would make the search retrieve all items about ADHD and all items about genetics, not just items related to genetic influences on ADHD. (See Figure 17.3.)

Another strategy to limit your search is to specify what you don't want by using NOT. If, for example, you are interested in ADHD only in adults, you could eliminate items that mention children by typing "attention deficit hyperactivity disorder NOT children." (See Figure 17.4)

Using the words AND, BUT, and NOT is called Boolean searching, named after the mathematician George Boole. Many search tools support Boolean searching. In some search engines the AND and NOT is implied by putting a plus or a minus in front of the search term.

+ADHD –children

17c FIND BOOKS

Scholarly books offer you in-depth analyses of many subjects. They also contain bibliographies that can help you find other resources on the particular subject. Libraries have well-developed systems for locating books. Nearly all libraries now shelve books according to the Library of Congress Classification System, which uses a combination of letters and numbers to give you the book's unique location in the library. The Library of Congress call number begins with a letter or letters that represent the broad subject area into which the book is classified.

Subject searches

You can search the extensive Library and Archives Canada online catalogue (www.collectionscanada.ca) to find out how your subject might be indexed, or you can go straight to your own library's catalogue and conduct a subject search. The main Library and Archives Canada site includes a link to the AMICUS webpage. AMICUS is a free web service that lets you search 1300 Canadian libraries to find books, photographs, public records—all the items you would expect to find in a library. You can log directly on to that service from this address: http://amicus.collectionscanada .ca/ aaweb/aalogine.htm (see Figure 17.5).

Locating books in your library

A subject search for "attention deficit hyperactivity disorder" AND "adults" might turn up the following record in your library.

AUTHOR

Wender, Paul H., 1934–

TITLE

ADHD: attention-deficit hyperactivity disorder in children and adults

PUBLISHED

Oxford; New York: Oxford University Press, 2000.

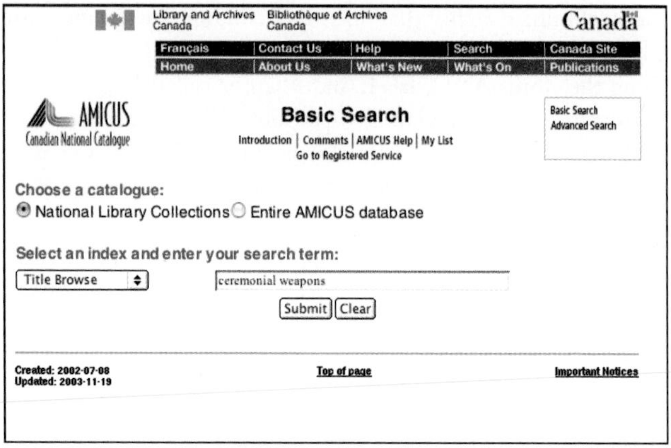

FIGURE 17.5 AMICUS is a free web service that lets you search 1300 Canadian libraries to find books, photographs, and public records.

DESCRIPTION

ix, 277 p.; 22 cm.

NOTES

Includes index.

SUBJECTS

Attention-deficit hyperactivity disorder.
Attention-deficit disordered children.
Attention-deficit disordered adults.

OCLC NUMBER

44118022
Locations
RJ 506 H9 W448 2000 Main Library Stacks

The floors of your library where books are shelved are referred to as the stacks. The call number will enable you to find the item in the stacks. You will need to consult the locations guide for your library. The locations guide will give the level and section.

Finding book reviews

You may want to consult book reviews in your research to learn how others understand particular books and if they find them important. You need to know the author's name, the title of the book, and the date of original publication in order to search for book reviews. Book reviews are included in periodical indexes (see Section 17d). The most comprehensive index dedicated to

The signs in the stacks guide you to the books you are looking for.

book reviews is *Book Review Digest* (1905–), which includes excerpts and some full-text reviews. You can find the printed version in your library's reference collection, and your library may subscribe to the online version, which contains reviews written since 1983.

17d FIND JOURNAL ARTICLES

Like books, scholarly journals provide in-depth examinations of subjects. The articles in scholarly journals are written by experts, and they usually contain lists of references that can guide you to other research on a subject. Articles in trade and popular journals and magazines are typically written by journalists. Popular magazines are useful for gaining general information. Some instructors frown on using popular magazines, but these journals can be valuable for researching current opinion on a particular topic.

Searching for articles in scholarly journals and popular magazines works much the same way as searching for books. Indexes for scholarly journals and magazines are located in the reference area of your library, and many may also be available on your library's website. Online indexes are fully searchable by author, title, subject, or keywords, and they are often referred to as *databases* instead of *indexes* (see Section 18b). Some online indexes even contain the full text of articles, allowing you to copy the contents onto your computer. Others give you a citation, which you then have to find in your library's resources.

Your library has a list of databases and indexes by subject. Find this subject index either on your library's website or in the reference section of your library. Follow these steps to find articles:

1. Select an index appropriate to your subject. (For researching ADHD, you might start with Health Reference Center, MEDLINE, and PsycINFO.)
2. Search the index using relevant subject heading(s). (You could start with ADHD and then combine ADHD with other terms to narrow your search.)
3. Print or copy the complete citation to the article(s).
4. Print or copy the full text if it is available.
5. If the full text is not available, check the periodicals holdings to see if your library has the journal.

General indexes and databases

General indexes include thousands of publications from many fields. They will give you either the full text of a publication or an **abstract**—a short summary of the contents. The names of the vendors are given here in parentheses following the name of the index or database. Your library website may ask you to click on the name of the vendor (EBSCOhost Web) and then select the database (Academic Search Premier). For more on how to use full-text databases, see Section 18b.

- **Academic Search Premier** (EBSCO). Provides full text for over 3000 scholarly publications, including social sciences, humanities, education, computer sciences, engineering, language and linguistics, literature, medical sciences, and ethnic studies journals.
- **ArticleFirst** (FirstSearch). Indexes over 15 000 journals in business, the humanities, medicine, science, and social sciences.
- **Biography and Genealogy Master Index** (Thomson Gale). Indexes biographies, autobiographies, and interviews for over four million people.
- **Canadian Newsstand Major Dailies** (EZProxy). Indexes major Canadian newspapers.

WRITING SMART

Subject headings

Often the key to a successful search is finding the right subject headings. Here are some strategies:

1. **Use subject guides.** Many indexes have subject guides or thesauruses that you can browse.
2. **Find a good article and use its subject headings for your search.** If you have one article that targets your subject precisely, look to see how it is indexed. Then use its subject terms for your search.
3. **Use keywords.** Use the same keyword strategies to find articles that you use to find books. Different periodical indexes offer slightly different options for searching their databases, but almost all will offer a keyword search option. As explained in Section 17b, you can combine keywords with the operators AND, OR, and NOT to focus your online search. Another keyword strategy is to use quotation marks around words, which will make the search engine select only sources with that exact phrase or sequence of words. Using quotation marks is an effective way to narrow the number of search results. For example, a search for *"seasonal migration"* with quotation marks will probably yield a more focused set of sources than *seasonal migration* without quotation marks. However, you may narrow your search too much if you put too many words inside the quotation marks. *"The seasonal migration of whooping cranes"* may eliminate relevant sources that address whooping cranes and seasonal migration but that do not have that exact phrasing in the text.
4. **Ask a reference librarian for help.** Reference librarians often can direct you to the right subject headings. You can find the location of scholarly journals and magazines by using the title search in your library's online catalogue. You may find that some indexes will link directly to the online subscriptions to journals. This feature gets you quickly to a copy of the article.

- **Canadiana: The National Bibliography** (AMICUS). Indexes work by Canadians and work published in Canada.
- **Expanded Academic ASAP** (Thomson Gale). Indexes 2300 periodicals from the arts, humanities, sciences, social sciences, and general news, some with full-text articles available.

- **Factiva** (Dow Jones). Gives full-text access to major newspapers, market research reports, and business journals, including *The Wall Street Journal.*
- **Ingenta.com** (Ingenta). Gives citations to over 20 000 multidisciplinary journals.
- **LexisNexis Academic** (LexisNexis). Provides full text of a wide range of newspapers, magazines, government and legal documents, and company profiles from around the world.
- **WorldCat** (FirstSearch). Contains over 52 million records of books and other materials in libraries throughout the world but very few articles in journals.

Specialized indexes and databases

In addition, many specialized indexes list citations to journal articles in various fields. While some are full-text databases, most will give you abstracts of publications. Some of the more important are the following.

- **Business and Company Resource Center** (Thomson Gale). Provides access to company profiles, investment reports, company histories, and periodicals.
- **Business Source Premier** (EBSCO). Indexes and provides abstracts for articles in scholarly journals in accounting, economics, finance, management, and international business.
- **Canadian Periodicals Index.** Indexes articles from Canadian magazines and newspapers as well as international periodicals that publish articles on Canada.
- **CBCA Reference (ProQuest).** Provides access to many Canadian periodicals, both academic and general interest.
- **CINAHL** (EBSCO, Ovid). The Cumulative Index to Nursing & Allied Health (CINAHL) database lists books and nearly a thousand journals related to nursing and allied health disciplines.
- **ERIC** (EBSCO, FirstSearch). Indexes journal articles, technical reports, curricular materials, and other publications in education.
- **GeoRef** (COS, EBSCO). Indexes books, journal articles, conference papers, maps, dissertations, and other publications related to geology and geoscience.
- **MEDLINE** (EBSCO, FirstSearch, Ovid). Primary index and source for abstracts of publications and journals related to medicine and health care.
- **MLA International Bibliography** (EBSCO, Ovid). Indexes books and articles about literature in English and other languages, folklore, linguistics, drama, and rhetoric and writing.

- **PsychINFO** (EBSCO, Ovid). Covers thoroughly the discipline of psychology, but also has many items from business, education, law, linguistics, medicine, sociology, and other related disciplines.
- **SciFinder Scholar** (ACS). Offers easy-to-use and comprehensive coverage of chemistry from the American Chemical Society. Also accesses MEDLINE.
- **Web of Science** (ISI). Provides web access to all three ISI citation indexes: Arts & Humanities Citation Index, Science Citation Index Expanded, and Social Sciences Citation Index.

Your library will probably have handouts that tell you which specialized index to use for a particular subject. Ask a librarian who works at the reference or information desk to help you. Take advantage of your librarian's experience in searching for information.

Knowing what kinds of articles you want to look for—scholarly, trade, or popular—will help you select the right index. Many indexes include more than one type of journal. Although the difference among journals is not always obvious, you should be able to judge whether a journal is scholarly, trade, or popular by its characteristics.

Scholarly journals

Scholarly journals are shelved in the periodicals section of your library. They are also called "peer-reviewed" or "academic" journals. They

- Contain long articles typically written by scholars in the field, usually affiliated with a university or research centre
- Usually include articles that report original research and have footnotes or a list of works cited at the end
- Assume that readers are other experts in the field
- Display few advertisements or illustrations
- Usually are published quarterly or biannually

Examples of scholarly journals include *Canadian Journal of Physics*; *College English*; *JAMA: Journal of the American Medical Association*; *PMLA: Publication of the Modern Language Association*; and *Psychological Reports*.

Trade journals

Trade journals can be found in libraries and on large newsstands. They

- Publish articles related to particular fields, occupations, and interests
- Often give practical information
- Usually include articles that do not report original research and have few or no footnotes, and no list of works cited at the end
- Contain advertisements aimed at people in specific fields
- Are published weekly, monthly, or quarterly

Examples of trade journals include *Books in Canada, Advertising Age, Byte, PC Computing, Pulp and Paper Canada,* and *Teacher Magazine.*

Popular journals

Popular journals including magazines are found primarily on newsstands. They

- Publish short articles aimed at the general public
- Contain many advertisements and photos
- Seldom include footnotes or the source of information in detail
- Are published weekly or monthly

Examples of popular journals include *Canadian Living, GQ, Rolling Stone, Sports Illustrated,* and *Maclean's.*

17e   FIND NEWSPAPER ARTICLES

Newspaper articles are a valuable resource, especially on local topics that aren't covered by other sources and on very recent topics. You can also read newspaper articles from the past to learn how people understood events as they happened. Newspaper articles can be located in indexes similar to those for journals. For issues more than a few years old, you likely will have to read the newspaper on microfilm. Nearly all libraries have *The New York Times Index*, which indexes by subject articles in the *New York Times* from 1913 to the present. Also, your library probably has *The Wall Street Journal* index, which is the best single source for detailed business news.

Online newspaper collections

For current topics you can now find many newspaper articles online. The best way to begin is to look at the newspaper section on your library's website. You will find links to many individual online newspapers and other online collections. Check your library's webpage to find out if your library subscribes to these important online collections, which give you access to hundreds of newspapers.

- **Canadian Newsstand Major Dailies (Proquest)**. Provides access to articles from major Canadian daily newspapers.
- **Canadian Newspaper Association** (www.cna-acj.ca/client/cna/cna.nsf/web/online). Provides links to Canadian newspapers in both small and larger markets.
- **Factiva** (Dow Jones). Gives full-text access to major newspapers with a business orientation.

- **InfoTrac Newspapers** (Thomson Gale). Offers full-text access to over 100 newspapers.
- **LexisNexis Academic** (LexisNexis). Provides full-text access to international, national, and regional newspapers.
- **Newspaper Source** (EBSCO). Gives full-text access to leading national and international newspapers and over 200 regional newspapers.

Links to newspaper sites

Nearly every major newspaper now allows you to read current articles online. Be aware, however, that what you find one day may not be available without charge when you return to the newspaper's website. You can find links to hundreds of newspapers on these sites.

- **Culture.ca** (www.culture.ca/english.jsp). Provides links to newspapers as well as art and media sites in Canada.
- **News and Newspapers Online** (library.uncg.edu/news). Offers links to U.S. and foreign newspapers.
- **NewsLink** (newslink.org). Gives links to newspapers, magazines, and radio and TV stations in the United States and other countries.
- **News Voyager** (www.newspaperlinks.com). Provides links to U.S. and Canadian newspaper sites, as well as selected links to international newspapers.
- **CollegeNews.com** (www.collegenews.com). Search tool for finding student-run and campus newspapers.

Many newspapers now make some past issues available online for a fee. The most comprehensive directory of online newspaper archives is *U.S. News Archives on the Web* (www.ibiblio.org/slanews/internet/archives. html). Pages of the Past provides past issues of the *Toronto Star* online (thestar.pagesofthepast.ca/).

17f START A WORKING BIBLIOGRAPHY

As you begin to collect your sources, make sure you get full bibliographic information for everything you might want to use in your project: articles, books, websites, and other materials. Decide which documentation style you will use. If your instructor does not tell you which style is appropriate, ask. (The major documentation styles—MLA, APA, Chicago, and CSE—are dealt with in detail in Chapters 22 through 25.)

Necessary bibliographic information

For books you will need, at minimum, the following information, which can typically be found on the front and back of the title page:

- Author's name
- Title of the book
- Place of publication
- Name of publisher
- Date of publication

You will also need the page numbers if you are quoting directly or referring to a specific passage, and the title, author, and page numbers of the individual chapter if your source is an edited book with contributions by several people.

For journals you will need

- Author's name
- Title of the article
- Title of the journal
- Volume and issue of the journal
- Date of the issue
- Page numbers of the article

In general, as you research and develop a working bibliography, the rule of thumb is to write down more information, rather than less. You can always cull unnecessary information when it comes time to format your citations according to your chosen documentation style (APA, MLA, CMS, or CSE), but it is time-consuming to go back to sources to find missing bibliographic information.

Recording bibliographic information

There are many ways to record and organize your sources. You can record each source's bibliographic information on individual index cards; you can save and organize source information in individual computer files; you can even print out or photocopy relevant pages from each source. Whichever way you choose, remember to keep track of sources in a format you can easily alphabetize and that will help you organize and group sources when you begin to construct your argument and compile your bibliography.

Sample index card

An index card for Romeo Dallaire's *Shake Hands with the Devil* would look like this:

> DT
> 450.435D14
> 2005
>
> Dallaire, Romeo. With Brent Beardsley. <u>Shake Hands</u>
>   <u>with the Devil: The Failure of Humanity in Rwanda.</u>
>   Toronto: Vintage Canada, 2005.
>   Dallaire argues that the inadequate and
>   indifferent response by the international
>   community to the civil war that resulted in the
>   Rwandan genocide of 1994 suggests that the
>   developed countries of the world believe that the
>   lives of their own citizens are worth more than
>   the lives of those in developing countries.

The same information should appear in any computer file you are generating to build your bibliography.

If you make notes in a computer file or on an index card, be sure to distinguish your summary from material you quote directly. You will also need to identify by page number any quoted material.

> Dallaire offers evidence that the developed world
> values its own citizens' lives above those of developing
> countries.
>
> p. 522, "An American officer felt no shame as he
> informed me that the lives of 800,000 Rwandans were
> only worth risking the lives of ten American troops;
> the Belgians, after losing ten soldiers, insisted that the
> lives of Rwandans were not work risking another
> single Belgian soldier. The only conclusion I can reach is
> that we are in desperate need of a transfusion of
> humanity."

Alternatives to copying from a source are cutting and pasting into a file (for online sources) or making photocopies (for a print source). Both methods ensure accuracy in copying sources, but in either case make sure you attach full bibliographic information to the file or photocopy. It's easy to get confused about where the material came from. In Chapter 22 you'll find detailed instructions on how to find the information you need for MLA documentation. Chapter 23 gives you instructions for finding the information you need for APA documentation.

C H A P T E R *18*

Finding Sources Online

Information—and knowing how to find it—is power in the digital era. After you graduate you will often need to find information in your career and in your life in the community. The distinction between doing research online and in the library is blurring as more and more library resources go online. Many community colleges and universities have made most of the major resources in their reference rooms available online. Newspapers, scholarly journals, and government documents are increasingly being published and archived in digital form. Knowing how to use library databases gives you access to vast quantities of information delivered to your computer.

18a   DATABASE SOURCES VERSUS WEB SOURCES

When you access sources on the web, they may seem alike, but there is a world of difference between doing a search on library databases through your library's website and doing a general search on the web using Google.

Advantages and disadvantages	Library database sources	Web sources
Speed—find information quickly	✓	✓

Advantages and disadvantages	Library database sources	Web sources
Accessible—available 24/7	✓	✓
Organized—materials are organized for efficient search and retrieval	✓	
High quality—librarians review and select the resources	✓	
Comprehensive—librarians review and select the resources	✓	
Permanent—library materials remain available for many years	✓	
Biased—often the soapbox for organizations		✓
Commercial—often trying to sell you something		✓
Lack permanence—here today, gone tomorrow		✓
Uneven quality—anyone can put up a website		✓

Library databases have the advantages of high quality and no commercial intrusion along with the convenience of web delivery. But when you search a subject on Google, the results often give you a series of commercial sites selling books and products related to the words you typed in.

Most databases are proprietary, which means that your library pays for them. That's why they aren't available to the public. Nonetheless, some important databases, including ERIC, Ingenta.com, and MEDLINE, have many free-of-charge resources available both through library websites and through the web.

18b FIND ARTICLES AND OTHER SOURCES IN LIBRARY DATABASES

Find databases

You must first locate databases in order to use them. Usually you can find them on your library's website. Sometimes you will find a list of databases. Sometimes you select a subject, and then you are directed to databases. Sometimes you select the name of a database vendor such as EBSCO, FirstSearch, or Ovid. The vendor is the company that provides databases to the library. It can be confusing to determine the name of the database and the name of the vendor. LexisNexis, for example, is both the name of the database and the name of the vendor (see Section 17d for a list of frequently used databases).

You can learn how to use databases in your library with the help of a reference librarian. Your library may also have online and printed tutorials on using databases. Once you know how to access the databases you need, you can work from computers in other locations. Many post-secondary institutions allow you to access databases from your home, apartment, or residence room with your student login name and password.

Reference librarians are familiar with the information resources in your library and can help you learn how to use databases. Find them at the reference desk and ask for assistance.

Use databases

To use databases effectively, make a list of keywords in advance (see Section 17b). You will need keywords to search in a database. For example, a search for information about the social effects of online gaming might begin with the terms *social* and *online gaming*. You will also need the most recent information you can find. It's important to know if online gaming is creating new social problems and what effects are being observed.

Your next decision is to choose a database to begin your research. To research social effects of online gaming, you'll need to access newspapers, popular journals, and scholarly journals. You'll need to use a general database such as ProQuest Education Journals, Expanded Academic ASAP, or LexisNexis Academic.

ProQuest Education Journals is a good general database to research current topics. You can find ProQuest Education Journals either on a list of databases or sometimes under EBSCOhost on your library's website. If you wish to get only full-text articles, you can check that option (see Figure 18.1). Full-text documents give you the same text you would find in print. Sometimes the images are not reproduced in the HTML versions, but the PDF versions give you an image of the actual printed copy.

Another major database for researching current issues is LexisNexis Academic, which offers full-text and summary versions of articles from thousands of newspapers and magazines. It also gives you access to company

FIGURE 18.1   Results of a full-text search for *social* AND *online gaming* on ProQuest Education Journals

profiles, financial reports, government documents, and other databases. LexisNexis Academic allows you to limit a search by the kind of publication and by date. For example, the results of a search for *social* and *online gaming* are shown in Figure 18.2. Often you can determine by the title of the article if it is relevant to your topic.

Keep track of database sources

Sometimes you will find exactly what you are looking for by using a database, but then you may become frustrated when you cannot find it again. It's critical to keep track of how you get to particular articles and other material—both to find them again and to cite the items in your list of works cited.

You must document information you get from database sources just as for print sources. The reason you document sources is to allow your readers to view the same sources you looked at. Consequently, when you find a source on a database, you must give the name of the database in addition to the name of the source where it was printed.

LexisNexis.   Figure 18.3 shows an example article from the LexisNexis Academic search for *online gaming social.* From the first two paragraphs you can surmise that this article will be useful to identify some of the problems caused by online gaming.

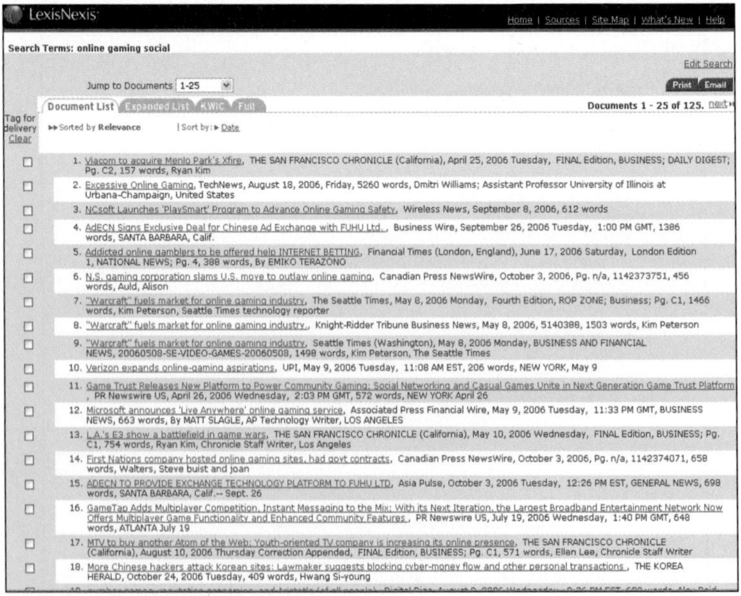

FIGURE 18.2   Results of a search in major newspapers for *online gaming* and *social* on LexisNexis Academic

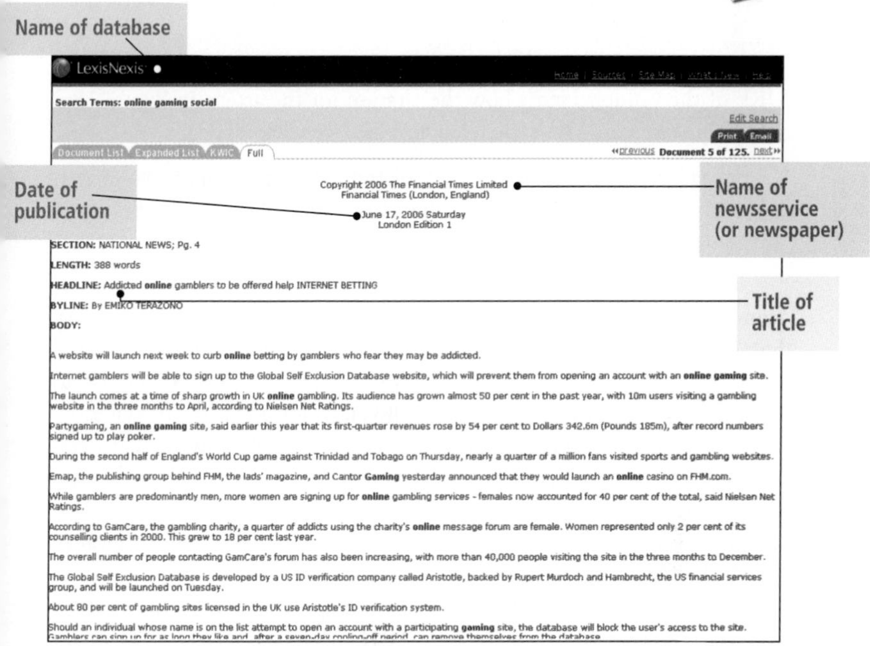

Name of database

FIGURE 18.3 Citing a database article from LexisNexis Academic

To cite this article in both MLA and APA styles, you'll need the following information:

- Author, if any
- Title of article
- Name of periodical or news service
- Date of publication (and edition for newspapers)
- Section and page number, if applicable
- Name of database
- Date of access (the day you found the article in the database)

MLA style also requires you to provide the name of the library where you accessed the database and the URL of the vendor's homepage. In this case, you would give the name of the library you used (D. B. Weldon Library at the University of Western Ontario) and the URL of LexisNexis (www.lexisnexis.com). (The vendor's URL is sometimes on a link of "home" or "terms and conditions.") The citation for the article in Figure 18.3 would appear as follows in an MLA-style list of works cited (see Chapter 22).

Terazono, Emiko. "Addicted Online Gamblers to Be Offered Help Internet Betting." *The Financial Times* 17 June 2006, London ed.: 4. *LexisNexis Academic*. LexisNexis. D. B. Weldon Lib., U of Western Ontario. 24 Oct. 2006 <http://www.lexisnexis.com/>.

APA style does not require that you give the name of the library or the URL of the vendor. Here's how the citation for the article in Figure 18.3 would appear in an APA-style references list (see Chapter 23).

> Terazono, E. (2006, June 17). Addicted online gamblers to be offered help internet betting. *The Financial Times*, p. 4. Retrieved October 24, 2006, from LexisNexis Academic database.

ProQuest Education Journals.   Figure 18.4 shows an example article from a ProQuest Education Journals search for *social* AND *online gaming*. Sometimes it's difficult to distinguish between the database and the vendor. If the vendor's name is more prominent than the database, look closely to locate both pieces of information, which you will need for the full citation. For example, if EBSCO sponsors the database (i.e., sells your library access to the database), sometimes their name appears more prominently than that of the database.

Here's how the citation for the article in Figure 18.4 would appear in an MLA-style list of works cited.

> Kerbs, Robert W. "Social and Ethical Considerations in Virtual Worlds." *The Electronic Library* 23.5 (2005). ProQuest Education Journals. D. B. Weldon Lib., U of Western Ontario. 20 Mar. 2006 <http://proquest.umi.com/>.

Here's how it would appear in an APA-style references list.

> Kerbs, R. W. (2005). Social and ethical considerations in virtual worlds. *The Electronic Library 23*(5). Retrieved March 20, 2006, from ProQuest Education Journals.

For a tutorial on finding and citing information using databases, visit **www.pearsoned.ca/faigley/211.**

FIGURE 18.4   Citing a database article from ProQuest Education Journals

18c FIND INFORMATION ON THE WEB

Because anyone can publish on the web, there is no overall quality control and no system of organization as a library would have. Nevertheless, the web offers you some resources for current topics that would be difficult or impossible to find in a library. The keys to success are knowing where you are most likely to find current and accurate information about the particular question you are researching and knowing how to access that information.

Search engines

Search engines designed for the web work in ways similar to library databases and your library's online catalogue but with one major difference. Databases typically do some screening of the items they list, but search engines potentially take you to everything on the web—millions of pages in all. Consequently, you have to work harder to limit searches on the web or you can be deluged with tens of thousands of items.

Kinds of search engines

A search engine is a set of programs that sort through millions of items at incredible speed. There are four basic kinds of search engines.

1. **Keyword search engines** (e.g., AltaVista, Google, Hotbot, Lycos, Mooter, MSN Search, Teoma). Keyword search engines give different results because they assign different weights to the information they find. Mooter uses algorithms to sort the results.
2. **Web directories** (e.g., Britannica.com, LookSmart, ProFusion, Yahoo!). Web directories classify websites into categories and are the closest equivalent to the cataloguing system used by libraries. On most directories professional editors decide how to index a particular website. Web directories also allow keyword searches.
3. **Metasearch agents** (e.g., Dogpile, Metacrawler, WebCrawler). Metasearch agents allow you to use several search engines simultaneously. While the concept is sound, metasearch agents are limited by the number of hits they can return and their inability to handle advanced searches.
4. **Natural-language search engines** (e.g., Ask.com). Natural- or real-language search engines allow you to search by asking questions such as "Where can I find a recipe for pound cake?" Natural-language search engines are still in their infancy; no doubt they will become much more powerful in the future.

Advanced searches

Search engines often produce too many hits and are therefore not always useful. If you look only at the first few items, you may miss what is most valuable. The alternative is to refine your search. Most search engines offer you the option of an advanced search, which gives you the opportunity to limit numbers.

The advanced searches on Google and Yahoo! give you the options of using a string of words to search for sites that contain (1) all the words, (2) the exact phrase, (3) any of the words, (4) without certain words. They also allow you to specify the language of the site, the date range, the file format, and the domain. For example, you may want to limit a search for ADHD to Canadian government websites such as Health Canada or U.S. government sites like the National Institutes of Health. For U.S. government websites, use the domain **.gov**; for Canadian federal government websites, use the domain **.gc.ca** (see Figure 18.5).

Archives

An archive is traditionally a physical place where historical documents, such as manuscripts and letters, are stored. Recently the term has come to mean any collection of documents, typically preserved for educational purposes. All archives focus on preserving materials for posterity. Given the rapidly changing nature of the web, electronic archives strive to preserve access to their materials.

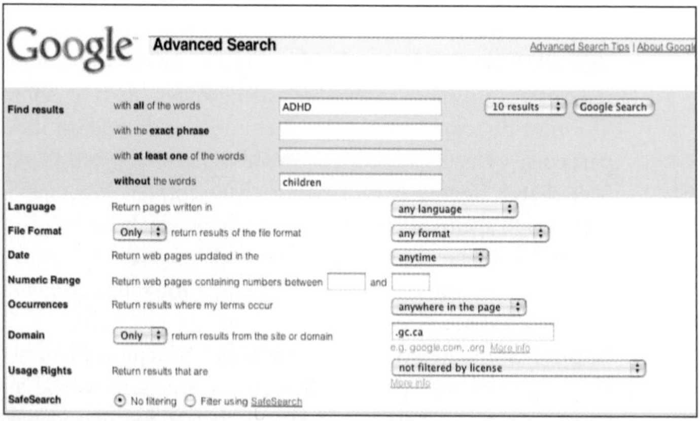

FIGURE 18.5   Google advanced search for *ADHD* excluding *children* and limiting the domain to .gc.ca

WRITING SMART

Tips for web searches

Help! My search turned up too many results.

- Try more specific search terms.
- Combine the words with AND.
- Use a phrase within quotation marks or specify "the exact phrase."
- Specify NOT for terms you are not interested in finding.
- Limit the search by a date range.

Help! My search turned up too few results.

- Check your spelling.
- Try broader search terms.
- Use OR instead of AND, or specify "find any of the words."
- Try another index or search engine.

For example, if you want to do a research project on Pier 21 and the war brides' immigration to Canada, you will need to look at documents written at the time—letters, diaries, newspaper articles, passenger lists, and border entry records. The Pier 21 Press Archives (www.pier21.ca/Press_Archives.348.0.html) is a good place to start research on this topic. Here are three other excellent electronic archive sites where you can find documents, films, photographs, and news clippings from the period.

- **CBC Archives** (archives.cbc.ca). A selection of radio and television clips from more than 60 years of broadcasting by the Canadian Broadcasting Corporation.
- **JSTOR: The Scholarly Journal Archive** (www.jstor.org) Electronic archive of the back issues of over 100 scholarly journals, mainly in the humanities and social sciences fields.
- **National Archives of Canada** (www.collectionscanada.ca/). Huge repository of texts, photographs, and documents related to Canada's cultural, social, and political development. Combines the collections of the National Library of Canada and National Archives of Canada.

Listservs, bulletin boards, and discussion forums

The internet allows you to access other people's opinions on thousands of topics. A listserv is an electronic discussion forum in which members exchange messages via email. Everyone who is subscribed to the list receives email sent to the list. Bulletin boards and newsgroups post messages on a website, often organized in discussion threads. Sometimes you must register to post messages, but you usually can read the messages without registering. Much of the conversation on these sites is undocumented and highly opinionated, but you can still gather important information about people's attitudes and get tips about other sources, which you can verify later.

These websites catalogue online discussion forums:

- Cyberfiber Newsgroups (www.cyberfiber.com)
- Tile.net (tile.net/lists/)

In addition, the Groups section of Google (groups.google.com) has an archive of 700 million messages that can be searched.

Many commercial and non-profit websites also maintain their own discussion or "chat" forums. Depending on your topic, it might be useful to check out these forums. For example, if you wanted to research the psychological support services available for women who have had miscarriages, you might scan the discussion forum on www.womenshealthmatters.ca, a site sponsored by the New Women's College Hospital that offers information and advice on all aspects of pregnancy and childrearing. Or, if you wanted to examine how the negative reports of SUV safety have affected SUV owners, you might look at the discussion forum on www.cartalkcanada.com. Be aware, though, that people who are drawn to participate in the forums on these sites do not represent the general population.

Research profile: Keyword search for Canadian First Nations artists

All too often the obvious keywords turn up too much material in a search. Let's take an example. You have been assigned a paper discussing the cultural importance of a major work of Canadian art. If you use Google to search for *Canadian First Nations artists*, you will get millions of matches. Clearly, this is too general to be an effective search term. Combining *Canadian First Nations Artists* with *sculpture* gets the number down, but still too many hits. In your research you may learn that Norval Morrisseau (one of the first professionally trained First Nations artists in the late twentieth century) is a sculptor as well as a painter. Changing your search slightly to include *Norval Morrisseau, sculpture,* and *cultural importance,* brings the number down to under 500. Google sorts by relevance, so the first 50 hits should yield something useful (see Figure 18.6).

Research profile: A subject search for global warming

Subject indexes offered by web directories like Yahoo! often divide large topics into subcategories. These subcategories can be quite useful in helping you narrow your topic to one that is manageable. To use the subject

FIGURE 18.6 Results of a Google search for *Norval Morrisseau, sculpture,* and *cultural importance*

search, ignore the keyword search box and select one of the subject fields listed below it. You will get a list of narrower topics within the field, from which you can select still narrower subject areas.

When you begin to research a massive topic such as global warming, a subject search is a good way to begin. The Yahoo! subject directory on global warming starts with the most popular sites and gives a short annotation for each, describing the contents and point of view of the site (see Figure 18.7).

Keep track of web research

The internet makes it easy to find many sources in a hurry—often too many. If you click away on the web one day and a day later want to go back to a site you visited, locating it may be almost impossible. When you find a website you think will be worth consulting again, always click on **Add Bookmark** (on Netscape) or **Add Page to Favorites** (on Internet Explorer). That will allow you simply to open up your Bookmarks or Favorites list on your next visit and return to the site immediately. You will need the following information to document sources you find on the web.

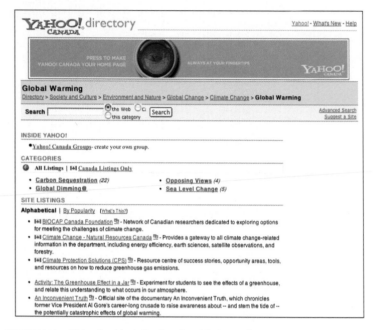

FIGURE 18.7 Yahoo! subject directory for global warming

- Name of the page
- Author if listed
- Sponsoring organization if listed
- Date the site was posted
- Date you visited
- Complete URL

See Section 22f for detailed instructions on how to find the information you need for MLA documentation. See Section 23d for instructions on finding the information you need for APA documentation.

18d FIND VISUAL SOURCES ONLINE

Visual databases and the web give you access to many visual sources that were difficult to locate just a few years ago. Before you search for visuals, have a clear idea of what you are looking for and why a particular visual would be effective in your research paper.

Visual databases

Most of the provinces and territories have large collections of photographs and other visual materials available on their websites. The National Archives

FIGURE 18.8 A 1909 political cartoon comments on women achieving voting rights.

of Canada (www.collectionscanada.ca) allows searches for film, video, and sound related to the history of Canada. The Canadian Council of Archives' website affords access to more than 50 000 descriptions of archival records from all the provinces and territories (see www.cdncouncilarchives.ca/cain. html). For example, if you are researching public attitudes toward women's suffrage at the beginning of the twentieth century, you might want to look at political cartoons. They can be located using the search terms "cartoon women's suffrage" (see Figure 18.8).

Visual sources on the web

Millions of images have been published on the web, and you can search for them using Google and other search engines that allow you to specify searches for images. For example, if you are writing a research paper on the moons of Jupiter, you might want to include an image of Io, one of the moons. In Google, choose **Images** and type *Jupiter moon Io* in the search box. You'll find a selection of images of Io, including Figure 18.9.

Some search engines such as Ditto (www.ditto.com) are designed specifically to find images. Yahoo! Picture Gallery has over 400 000 images that can be searched by subject (gallery.yahoo.com). In addition to images, you can find statistical data represented in charts and graphs on government websites. Especially useful is Statistics Canada for finding charts and graphs of statistics related to Canadian population, resources, economy,

FIGURE 18.9   The *Galileo* spacecraft acquired this image of Io, one of Jupiter's moons, in July 1999. The blemishes on the surface are active volcanoes.

society, and culture (www.statcan.ca/). You can also find thousands of maps on the web. (See www.lib.utexas.edu/maps/map_sites/map_sites.html for a directory of map sites.)

Downloading and inserting images

Images can be downloaded from websites by right-clicking on the image and selecting **Save Picture As** in Windows (on a Mac, hold the mouse button down and select **Save This Image As**). When you have the image file on your desktop, you can use the **Insert** command on your word processing or web editing program; in some programs you can simply drag and drop the image into your text. Often you will need to resize the image after you insert it by clicking on the corners and dragging the mouse to make the image bigger or smaller.

Image copyright

Just because images are easy to download from the web does not mean that every image is available for you to use. Look for the image creator's copyright notice and suggested credit line. This notice will tell you if you can reproduce the image. For example, the Cascades Volcano Observatory makes their images available to all: "The maps, graphics, images, and text found on our website, unless stated otherwise, are within the Public Domain. You may download and use them. Credit back to the USGS/Cascades Volcano Observatory is appreciated." You should acknowledge the source of any image you use. To reproduce any documents or images from Canadian government websites, you must request permission.

In many cases you will find a copyright notice that reads, "Any use or retransmission of text or images in this website without written consent of the copyright owner constitutes copyright infringement and is prohibited." You must write to the creator to ask permission to use an image from a site that is not in the public domain, even if you cannot find a copyright notice.

WRITING SMART

Using visuals in a research paper

Here are a few guidelines to keep in mind for incorporating visual sources into your research papers.

- **Use visuals for examples and supporting evidence, not for decoration.** For example, if the subject of your research is drug-related crime in Vancouver, including a picture of the Lions Gate Bridge is irrelevant and will detract from your paper.
- **Refer to images and other graphics in the body of your research paper.** Explain the significance of any images or graphics in the body of your paper. The relevance of the visual should not be left to the reader to guess.
- **Include captions for images and other graphics.** Describe the content of the image or graphic in the caption.
- **Respect the copyright of visual sources.** You may need to request permission to use a visual from the web. Use public domain material whenever possible.
- **Get complete citation information.** You are required to cite visual sources in your list of works cited just as you are for other sources.

CHAPTER *19*

Evaluating Sources

You may have heard someone say that everything on the web is either advertising or garbage. Certainly a great deal of what's on the web is advertising, and since no one is in charge of what appears on the web, there is also a great deal of misinformation and highly biased information. But the fact that a work is in print doesn't necessarily mean it is accurate or unbiased either. There are many examples of people witnessing the same event and then writing about it in ways so different that it's hard to believe they were in the same place at the same time. Similarly, there are many examples of respected scientists examining the same data and reaching different conclusions. Not everything you find in a library will be true, just as not everything you find on the web is false. Becoming a successful researcher requires that you take a critical view of all sources you find. In short, you need to evaluate potential sources.

19a   DETERMINE THE RELEVANCE OF SOURCES

Whether you use print or online sources, a successful search will turn up many more items than you can expect to use in your final product. You have to make a series of decisions about what is important and relevant. Return to your research question and working thesis (Section 16d). You should be able to use your research question and working thesis to create guidelines for yourself about importance and relevance.

For example, if your research question asks why the Roman Empire declined rapidly at the end of the fourth and beginning of the fifth centuries CE, you may find older sources as valuable as new ones. Edward Gibbon's three-volume history, *The Decline and Fall of the Roman Empire*, remains an important source, even though it was published in 1776 and 1781. But if you ask a research question about contemporary events—for example, to what extent online post-secondary courses have replaced courses held in traditional classrooms—you will need the most current information you can find. You also will want to find information on how many students were enrolled in distance education before the advent of the internet. However, it is easy to be sidetracked: likely you will find both glowing and grim predictions about the future of online education, but if your focus is on what has happened, not on what might happen, then these sources are not relevant.

Use these guidelines to determine the importance and relevance of your sources to your research question.

- Does your research question require you to consult primary or secondary sources?
- Does a source you have found address your question?
- Does a source support or disagree with your working thesis? (You should not throw out work that challenges your views.)
- Does a source add to your content in an important way?
- Is the material you have found persuasive?
- What indications of possible bias do you note in the source?

19b DETERMINE THE RELIABILITY OF PRINT SOURCES

Determining the reliability of sources is not a problem new to the web. Print sources contain their share of biased, inaccurate, and misleading information. But because books are expensive to print and distribute, book publishers generally protect their investment by providing some level of editorial oversight. Print sources in libraries have an additional layer of oversight because someone has decided that a book or journal is worth purchasing and cataloguing. Websites, in contrast, can be put up and changed quickly, so information can be—and often is—posted thoughtlessly. No one filters information that is posted to the web, and virtually anyone who has access to the internet can generate it.

Traditional criteria for evaluating print sources

Over the years librarians have developed a set of criteria for evaluating print sources.

1. **Source.** Who published the book or article? Scholarly books and articles in scholarly journals are reviewed by experts in the field before they are published. They are generally more reliable than popular magazines and books, which tend to emphasize what is sensational or entertaining at the expense of accuracy and comprehensiveness.

2. **Author.** Who wrote the book or article? What are the author's qualifications?

3. **Timeliness.** How current is the source? If you are researching a fast-developing subject such as treating attention deficit hyperactivity disorder (ADHD), then currency is very important. Currency might not be so important for an older subject, but even historical topics are subject to controversy or revision.

4. **Evidence.** Where does the evidence come from—facts, interviews, observations, surveys, or experiments? Is the evidence adequate to support the author's claims?

5. **Biases.** Can you detect particular biases of the author? How do the author's biases affect the interpretation offered?

6. **Advertising.** Is advertising a prominent part of the journal or newspaper? How might the ads affect what gets printed?

19c DETERMINE THE RELIABILITY OF INTERNET SOURCES

All electronic search tools share a common problem: they often give you too many sources. Web search engines not only pull up thousands of hits, but these hits may vary dramatically in quality. No one regulates or checks information put on the web, and it's no surprise that much of what is on the web is highly opinionated or false.

Some websites are put up as jokes. Other websites are deliberately misleading. Many prominent websites draw imitators who want to cash in on the commercial visibility. The websites for the Campaign for Tobacco-Free Kids (www.tobaccofreekids.org), for example, has an imitator (www.smokefreekids.com) that sells software for antismoking education. The .com URL is often a tip-off that a site has a profit motive.

Always approach websites with an eye toward evaluating content. The website of the B.C. Ministry of Education, turned up during an ADHD search, can be verified in several ways, beginning with the URL. Government agencies, for example, will always have gc.ca or .gov in the URLs (see Figure 19.1).

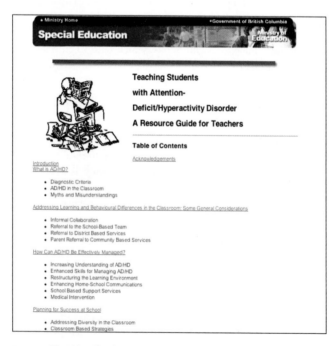

FIGURE 19.1   Teaching Students with Attention Deficit/Hyperactivity Disorder, B.C. Ministry of Education (www.bced.gov.bc.ca/specialed/adhd/)

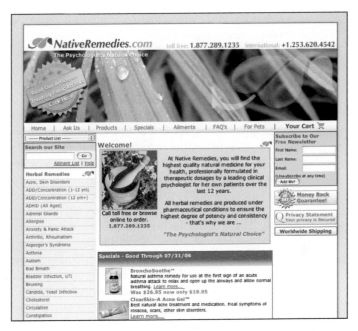

FIGURE 19.2 Native Remedies.com website (www.nativeremedies.com)

Other sites may have equally reliable information, but you should be prepared to look at them closely. For example, the website "Native Remedies.com" (see Figure 19.2) claims that their "natural remedy" for ADHD was created by a clinical psychologist to demonstrate its legitimacy and effectiveness. But an examination of the site reveals that it is designed to sell alternative treatments for the disorder. The URL (www.nativeremedies. com), which has a .com URL rather than .edu, gc.ca, .gov, or .org, tells you that this site is on a free or commercial server, not an institutional site. It could have been put up by anyone.

Extending print criteria for evaluating web sources

The criteria for evaluating print sources can be applied to web sources if the special circumstances of the web are acknowledged. For example, when you find a webpage by using a search engine, often you go deep into a complex site without having any sense of the context for that page. To evaluate the credibility of the site, you would need to examine the homepage, not just the specific page you get to first.

1. **Source.** Websites sponsored by organizations often are as reliable as print sources. For example, major newspapers now make some or all of their reportage available on the web. Look for the

site's ownership in the web address. If a website doesn't indicate ownership, then you have to make judgments about who put it up and why. The suffix can offer clues: .org is used by organizations, including non-profits, .gc.ca by Canadian federal government bodies, .gov by U.S. government bodies, and .edu by U.S. educational institutions, generally colleges and universities.

2. **Author.** Often websites give no information about their authors other than an email address, if that. In such cases it is difficult or impossible to determine the author's qualifications.

3. **Timeliness.** Many webpages do not list when they were last updated; thus you cannot determine their currency. Furthermore, there are thousands of deserted ghost sites on the web—sites that the owners have abandoned but search engines still turn up.

4. **Evidence.** The accuracy of any evidence found on the web is often hard to verify. The most reliable information on the web stands up to the tests of print evaluation, with clear indication of the sponsoring organization. Any factual information should be supported by indicating where the information came from. Reliable websites that offer information will list their sources.

5. **Biases.** Many websites announce their viewpoint on controversial issues, but others conceal their attitude with a reasonable tone and seemingly factual evidence such as statistics. Citations and bibliographies do not ensure that a site is reliable. Look carefully at the links and sources cited.

6. **Advertising.** Many websites (see Figure 19.2) are infomercials aimed at getting you to buy a product or service. While they might contain useful information, they are no more trustworthy than other forms of advertising.

WRITING SMART

What can the URL tell you?

The URL—the web address—often contains clues that help you determine the reliability of a website.

1. What is the domain name?

The domain tells you much about the source.

2. Is the website a personal page?

Many web hosts have a convention for indicating personal pages. For college and university websites, you'll often find a name following a

Domain	Source	Example
.edu	used by American and private Canadian colleges	www.ufl.edu/academics/
.gov	created by a Canadian provincial or territorial or a U.S. government office	www.gov.on.ca/
.gc	created by a Canadian federal government office	canada.gc.ca/
.cfc.forces	created by Canadian armed forces	www.cfc.forces.gc.ca/
.mil	created by the U.S. military	www.army.mil
.com	created in most cases by a company or for-profit organization	www.blackberry.com
.org	created in most cases by an individual or non-profit organization	www.canadahelps.org
.net	origin varies widely from the name of an internet provider to an individual site	www.earthlink.net
.au	created in a country other than Canada—in this case Australia	www.nla.gov.au

tilde (~) to indicate a personal page (publish.uwo.ca/~rgraves3/). Other ways that a personal page is identified on a college or university website are by "personal" or "home": (home.cc.umanitoba.ca/). Many addresses on commercial sites, including Rogers Yahoo! and MSN, are personal pages. Personal pages are not necessarily bad, but anyone can put them up without review. Consequently, the burden is on you to determine the credentials of the author and if the information on the site is accurate.

3. Does the URL match the contents?

Many websites conceal their motives. For example, cool-2b-real .com, sponsored by Cattlemen's Beef Board and the National Cattlemen's Beef Association, aims at getting teenage girls to eat more beef, but you would not recognize this purpose from the URL and the design of the homepage.

Other internet sources

Other internet sources, such as online newsgroups, can give you useful ideas but are generally not considered authoritative. Weblogs or "blogs" can provide first-hand observations and offer opinions on many topics, but they remain the views of one person and are not reviewed by anyone else for accuracy. Email communication from an expert in the field might be considered an authoritative source, but personal emails are generally not considered worthy of inclusion in a research paper. Remember that a key reason to cite sources is so other researchers can read and evaluate the sources you used.

WRITING SMART

A checklist for evaluating web sources

- **What organization sponsors or pays for the website?** If the name of the organization is not given, determine what you can from the URL. Try cutting off the URL from right to left a step at a time.
- **Is the author of the website identified?** Can you get in touch with the author? Be cautious of information on an anonymous site.
- **Are the author's credentials listed on the website?** If the credentials are listed, are they relevant to the subject?
- **Is the information on the website current?** Can you discover when the website was last updated?
- **Are references provided for information given on the site?** References give you one way to check the validity of the information on the site.
- **Are there links to additional information?** Do the links work? Is the linked information reliable?
- **Does the website present balanced information or does it chiefly present one point of view?** Many websites appear to be balanced but neglect other points of view.
- **Is the website an advertisement for a product or service?** Many so-called informative websites are trying to sell you something.

19d CREATE AN ANNOTATED BIBLIOGRAPHY

A working bibliography is an alphabetized list of sources a writer has used to research and write a paper on a specific topic. This list includes the author and title of each source, as well as bibliographic information. An **annotated bibliography** builds on this basic citation by adding a brief summary and/or evaluation of each source. After the initial entry, a writer adds several sentences that comment on the source's content and its relevance to his or her research.

One student is writing an essay on organic models of the brain for her cognitive science course. She uses her annotated bibliography to summarize each source and comment on how it might strengthen her argument:

> Zimmer, Carl. Soul Made Flesh: The Discovery of the Brain—and How It Changed the World. New York: Free Press, 2004. Carl Zimmer documents the dawn of the age of the brain in seventeenth-century England by focusing on how Thomas Willis showed that the brain was the physical seat of intelligence. The final chapter will help me add a neurological perspective that I can compare to artificial intelligence models of brain function.

Annotated bibliographies assist writers in the early stages of research gathering. By taking the time to write a brief summary and evaluation of each source you locate on your topic, you create building materials that you can use when it comes time to narrow your focus and start outlining and drafting.

Sample annotated bibliography

Mandeep Gupta is researching the topic of childhood obesity. As he locates sources, he takes careful notes on each source's main points and on how this information will help him construct his main arguments. The teacher has asked that he turn in an annotated list of five sources that he thinks will be crucial for his thesis. Since this paper is for a health studies course, Gupta uses CSE style for citations (see Chapter 25).

Gupta 1

Mandeep Gupta

Professor Honoré

Health Studies 102: Human Health

14 November 2006

Annotated Bibliography

Belfry J. 1996. Canadian children face activity and fitness
crisis. Interaction. Canadian Child Care Federation.
Available from: Child and Family Canada.
http://www.cfc-efc.ca/docs/cccf/00010_en.htm.
Accessed 2006 Apr 2.

Belfry gives a concise but compelling argument
that Canadian children will be less healthy than
they could be if they got more exercise. This is a
short but useful article that lists facts about
children's need for activity and fitness and the
existing chances they have to get exercise.
When I talk about solutions to the obesity
crisis, this article will provide some positive
solutions.

Mooibroek M., Dozois E. 2005. A framework for community
action. Report by Calgary Community for Prevention
of Obesity Steering Committee. Calgary Health
Region. Available from: http://www.
calgaryhealthregion.ca/childobesity/pdf/
Prevention%20of%20Obesity%20Framework.pdf.
Accessed 2006 Apr 3.

From 1981 to 1996, the prevalence of
overweight children has doubled and obesity
tripled. This means obesity is an increasing
problem in Canadian children. As well as some
useful statistics, this report gives a great
overview of the problem of childhood obesity,
including definitions and causes, that will help
me develop my paper introduction.

Mulligan C. 2006 Mar 24. Baby fat can be dangerous:
    medical consequences of childhood obesity could be
    devastating if problem isn't addressed. Sudbury Star,
    Final Ed. A4. 1 p. Available from: ProQuest Education
    Journals. D. B. Weldon Library, U of Western Ontario.
    Accessed 2006 Apr 4.

> Summarizes Brian McCrindle's guest speech to
> symposium series on consequences of infant
> overweight. Interesting information about
> increasing obesity in China and Japan. I will use
> some of McCrindle's research on adult diseases
> that can affect obese children, such as arterio-
> sclerosis, cardiovascular disease, diabetes, etc.

Robertson HJ. 2004. Doing it daily. Phi Delta Kappan
    Bloomington 85: 411–412.

> Great overview of problems with childhood
> obesity in Canada linked to advertising for
> unhealthy foods. Includes useful statistics.
> There is a great quotation that I will use to help
> reinforce the point that if children are not
> active, they need to eat in moderation.

Schlosser E. 2005. Fast food nation: the dark side of the
    all-American meal. 2 ed. Toronto: HarperCollins
    Canada. 383 p.

> Schlosser makes a persuasive argument that fast
> food and the fast food industry are leading
> causes of America's current childhood obesity
> epidemic. His examples are always surprising
> and sometimes shocking. Since we have some of
> the same fast food restaurants here, I can use
> some of his statistics to get a reader's attention
> in my own paper.

CHAPTER *20*

Avoiding Plagiarism When Using Sources

From a student's point of view, documenting sources can seem like learning Latin—something obscure and complicated that has little use in daily life. You don't see footnotes or lists of works cited in magazines and newspapers, so you may wonder why they are so important in post-secondary writing. Careful documentation of sources, however, is essential to developing knowledge and allows scholars and researchers to build on the work of other scholars and researchers. Large bodies of knowledge that have been accumulated over many years allow a scholar to reinterpret the fall of the Roman Empire or a researcher to advance a new hypothesis about how moving plates shape the surface of the earth.

20a THE PURPOSE OF DOCUMENTING SOURCES

Knowledge building

Knowledge is built through ongoing conversations that take place in writing as well as talking. The practice of citing sources provides a disciplinary map, indicating the conversation in which the writer is participating and how that writer responds to what has been said before. Often knowledge building does not move in a straight line but reflects wrong turns and backtracking. Tracing these movements would be extremely difficult if writers did not acknowledge their sources. Accurate referencing of sources allows you or any reader the opportunity to consult those sources. For example, historians who write about the distant past must rely on different kinds of evidence, including letters, records, public documents, newspaper articles, legal records, and other material from that time; they also take into account the work of contemporary scholars. Other historians working in the same area must be able to find and read these primary sources to assess the accuracy of the interpretation. The system of citing sources requires that summaries and paraphrases be accurate, any strings of words taken from the original be set off in quotation marks, and full information be provided to locate the source.

Fairness

Another basic issue is fairness. If historians draw on the interpretations of other historians, they should give those historians credit. In this respect citing sources builds community with writers of both the present and the past. When you begin to read the published research in an academic discipline, your awareness of that community takes shape. But the issue of fairness also is part of the much larger issues of intellectual property and scholastic honesty—issues that need to be considered carefully when you use sources.

20b INTELLECTUAL PROPERTY AND SCHOLASTIC HONESTY

Intellectual property and copyright

The concepts of intellectual property and copyright date back to the royal patent grants that accompanied the development of printing in the late 1400s, when monarchs sought to control the production of printed books. The modern concept of copyright took shape in the 1700s. In 1710, the Statute of Anne was passed in England, giving authors the rights to what they produced for a limited duration; by the end of the century other countries throughout Europe had passed laws to protect written intellectual property. With the development of new technologies in the twentieth century, these rights have been extended to music, recordings, photographs, films, radio and television broadcasts, computer software, and many other kinds of likenesses.

Plagiarism

Plagiarism is usually associated with writing, but various kinds of work can be lifted and passed off as one's own. **Plagiarism** means claiming credit for someone else's intellectual work no matter whether it's to make money or get a better grade. And it's not strictly a question of intent. Reputable authors have gotten into trouble through carelessness by taking notes from published sources without acknowledging those sources. A number of famous people have had their reputations tarnished by accusations of plagiarism, and several prominent journalists have lost their jobs and careers for copying the work of other writers and passing it off as their own.

The internet likely has increased instances of plagiarism in post-secondary education. Some students view the internet as a big free buffet where they can grab anything, paste it in a file, and submit it as their own work. Cut-and-paste plagiarism is easy to do, but instructors quickly recognize when a student's writing style changes in mid-essay. It's also easy to use the internet to trace sources stolen off the internet.

WRITING IN THE WORLD

The consequences of plagiarism

Most community colleges and universities consider plagiarism a serious form of cheating that deserves severe penalties, including failure of a course for first-time offenders and expulsion for those who are caught cheating more than once. Post-secondary institutions have to take a strong stance against plagiarism. They attempt to make the playing field level for all students; if some get by without doing the required work, it affects every other student. Professional schools and employers look down on graduates of schools that have a reputation for tolerating scholastic dishonesty. Students who blatantly plagiarize often do not realize how much harm they might do to themselves down the road. Employers do not want to hire students who have been caught cheating.

Businesses also have to take a hard line on plagiarism. In many professions, the product is a written document. If that document turns out to be plagiarized, the reputation of the entire company is tarnished.

Copyright, plagiarism, and the web

The issues of intellectual property and copyright concerning the web are far from settled. Copyright law is designed to protect the financial interests of the copyright holder; thus if you use a single image from a site and your motive is not for profit, the copyright owner has to establish that your use of that image caused him or her financial harm (see the Canadian Information Property Offices site, at www.strategis.ic.gc.ca/sc_mrksv/cipo/cp/copy_gd_protect-e.html). It's unlikely that you will be sued for grabbing an image from another site. Nonetheless, whether or not you get caught, taking someone else's work without acknowledgment is plagiarism. It's only fair to give other people credit for the work they have done. Unless a site is clearly labelled for public use, ask permission when you take something from another site, and always give credit to the source.

20c AVOID PLAGIARISM

You know that copying someone else's paper word for word or taking an article off the internet and turning it in as yours is plagiarism. That's plain stealing, and people who take that risk should know that the punishment can be severe. But if plagiarism also means using the ideas, melodies, or images of someone else without acknowledging them, then the concept is much broader and more difficult to define. If you think about it, you might wonder whether it is possible to avoid plagiarizing in the strictest sense when you write. How many phrases and ideas are truly original? And how can you know where every idea comes from?

What you don't have to document

Fortunately, common sense governs issues of academic plagiarism. The standards of documentation are not so strict that the source of every fact you cite must be acknowledged. Suppose you are writing about the causes of maritime disasters and you want to know how many people drowned when the *Titanic* sank on the early morning of April 15, 1912. You check the *Britannica Online* website and find that the death toll was around 1500. Since this fact is available in many reference works, you would not need to cite *Britannica Online* as the source.

But let's say you want to challenge the version of the sinking offered in the 1998 movie *Titanic,* which repeats the usual explanation that the *Titanic* sideswiped an iceberg, ripping a long gash along the hull that caused the ship to go down. Suppose that, in your reading, you discover that a September 1985 exploration of the wreck by an unmanned submersible did not find the long gash previously thought to have sunk the ship. The evidence instead suggested that the force of the collision with the iceberg broke the seams in the hull, allowing water to flood the ship's watertight compartments. You would need to cite the source of your information for this alternative version of the *Titanic*'s demise.

What you do have to document

For facts that are not easily found in general reference works, statements of opinion, and arguable claims, you should cite the source. You should also cite the sources of statistics, research findings, examples, graphs, charts, and illustrations. As a reader you should be skeptical about statistics and research findings when the source is not mentioned. When a writer does not cite the sources of statistics and research findings, there is no way of knowing how reliable the sources are or whether the writer is making them up. From the writer's perspective careful citing of sources lends credibility. If you take your statistics from a generally trusted source, your readers are more likely to trust your conclusions. When in doubt, always document the source.

Be careful when taking notes and copying material online

The best way to avoid unintentional plagiarism is to take care to distinguish source words from your own words. Don't mix words from the source with your own words. If you copy anything from a source when taking notes,

COMMON ERRORS

Plagiarism and writing in post-secondary education

If you find any of the following problems in your academic writing, it is likely you are plagiarizing someone else's work. Because plagiarism is usually inadvertent, it is especially important that you understand what constitutes using sources responsibly.

- **Missing attribution.** The author of a quotation has not been identified. A lead-in or signal phrase that provides attribution to the source is not used, and no author is identified in the citation.
- **Missing quotation marks.** Quotation marks do not appear around material quoted directly from a source.
- **Inadequate citation.** No page number is given to show where in the source the quotation, paraphrase, or summary is drawn from.
- **Paraphrase relies too heavily on the source.** Either the wording or sentence structure of a paraphrase follows the source too closely.
- **Distortion of meaning.** A paraphrase or summary distorts the meaning of the source, or a quotation is taken out of context, resulting in a change of meaning.
- **Missing Works Cited entry.** The Works Cited page does not include all the works cited in the paper.
- **Inadequate citation of images.** A figure or photo appears with no label, number, caption, or citation to indicate the source of the image. If material includes a summary of data from a visual source, no attribution or citation is given for the graph being summarized.

 For guidelines on avoiding plagiarism and exercises in responsible documentation, go to **www.pearsoned.ca/faigley/213.**

you will need to place those words in quotation marks and note the page number(s) where those words appear (see Section 17f). You should also write down all the information you need for a list of works cited or a list of references (see Chapters 22, 23, 24, and 25).

If you copy words from an online source, you need to take special care to note the source. You could easily copy online material and later not be able to find where it came from. Instead of cutting and pasting words straight from an online document, print out the entire source so you can refer to it later. Having photocopies of printed sources also allows you to double-check later that you haven't used words from the source by mistake and that any words you quote are accurate.

20d QUOTE SOURCES WITHOUT PLAGIARIZING

Most people who get into plagiarism trouble lift words from a source and use them without quotation marks. Where the line is drawn is easiest to illustrate with an example. In the following passage, Steven Johnson takes sharp issue with the metaphor of surfing applied to the web:

> The concept of "surfing" does a terrible injustice to what it means to navigate around the Web. . . . What makes the idea of cybersurf so infuriating is the implicit connection drawn to television. Web surfing, after all, is a derivation of channel surfing—the term thrust upon the world by the rise of remote controls and cable panoply in the mid-eighties. . . . Applied to the boob tube, of course, the term was not altogether inappropriate. Surfing at least implied that channel-hopping was more dynamic, more involved, than the old routine of passive consumption. Just as a real-world surfer's enjoyment depended on the waves delivered up by the ocean, the channel surfer was at the mercy of the programmers and network executives. The analogy took off because it worked well in the one-to-many system of cable TV, where your navigational options were limited to the available channels.
>
> But when the term crossed over to the bustling new world of the Web, it lost a great deal of precision. . . . Web surfing and channel surfing are genuinely different pursuits; to imagine them as equivalents is to ignore the defining characteristics of each medium. Or at least that's what happens in theory. In practice, the Web takes on the greater burden. The television imagery casts the online surfer in the random, anaesthetic shadow of TV programming, roaming from site to site like a CD player set on shuffle play. But what makes the online world so revolutionary is the fact that there *are* connections between each stop on a Web itinerant's journey. The links that join those various destinations are links of association, not randomness. A channel surfer hops back and forth between different channels because she's bored. A Web surfer clicks on a link because she's interested.

—Steven Johnson. *Interface Culture: How New Technology Transforms the Way We Create and Communicate.* New York: Harper, 1997. 107–09.

If you were writing a paper or putting up a website that concerned web surfing, you might want to mention the distinction that Johnson makes between channel surfing and surfing on the web. Your options are to paraphrase the source or to quote it directly.

If you quote directly, you must place quotation marks around all words you take from the original:

> One observer marks this contrast: "A channel surfer hops back and forth between different channels because she's bored. A Web surfer clicks on a link because she's interested" (Johnson 109).

Notice that the quotation is introduced and not just dropped in. This example follows Modern Language Association (MLA) style, where the citation goes outside the quotation marks but before the final period. In MLA style, source references are made according to the author's last name, which refers you to the full citation in the works-cited list at the end. Following the author's name is the page number where the quotation can be located. (Notice also that there is no comma after the name.) If you want to cite a newspaper article without a byline or another anonymous source, you use the first important word or two of the title to make the reference. This system allows you to find the reference easily in the list of works cited, since the list is arranged alphabetically by author and title.

If the author's name appears in the sentence, cite only the page number, in parentheses:

> According to Steven Johnson, "A channel surfer hops back and forth between different channels because she's bored. A Web surfer clicks on a link because she's interested" (109).

If you want to quote material that is already quoted in your source, use single quotes for that material:

> Steven Johnson uses the metaphor of a Gothic cathedral to describe a computer interface: " 'The principle of the Gothic architecture,' Coleridge once said, 'is infinity made imaginable.' The same could be said for the modern interface" (42).

20e SUMMARIZE AND PARAPHRASE SOURCES WITHOUT PLAGIARIZING

Summarize

When you summarize, you state the major ideas of an entire source or part of a source in a paragraph or perhaps even a sentence. The key is to put the summary in your own words. If you use words from the source (see page 267), you have to put those words in quotation marks.

PLAGIARIZED

Steven Johnson argues in *Interface Culture* that the concept of "surfing" is misapplied to the internet because channel surfers hop back and forth between different channels because they're bored, but web surfers click on links because they're interested. [Most of the words are lifted directly from the original.]

ACCEPTABLE SUMMARY

Steven Johnson argues in *Interface Culture* that the concept of "surfing" is misapplied to the internet because users of the web consciously choose to link to other sites while television viewers mindlessly flip through the channels until something catches their attention.

Paraphrase

When you paraphrase, you represent the idea of the source in your own words at about the same length as the original. You still need to include the reference to the source of the idea. The following example illustrates what is not an acceptable paraphrase.

PLAGIARIZED

Steven Johnson argues that the concept of "surfing" does a terrible injustice to what it means to navigate around the web. What makes the idea of web surfing infuriating is the association with television. Surfing is not a bad metaphor for channel hopping, but it doesn't fit what people do on the web. Web surfing and channel surfing are truly different activities; to imagine them as the same is to ignore their defining characteristics. A channel surfer skips around because she's bored while a web surfer clicks on a link because she's interested (107–09).

Even though the source is listed, this paraphrase is unacceptable. Too many of the words in the original are used directly here, including much or all of entire sentences. When a string of words is lifted from a source and inserted without quotation marks, the passage is plagiarized. Changing a few words in a sentence is not a paraphrase. Compare these two sentences:

SOURCE

Web surfing and channel surfing are genuinely different pursuits; to imagine them as equivalents is to ignore the defining characteristics of each medium.

UNACCEPTABLE PARAPHRASE

Web surfing and channel surfing are truly different activities; to imagine them as the same is to ignore their defining characteristics.

The paraphrase takes the structure of the original sentence and substitutes a few words. It is much too similar to the original.

A true paraphrase represents an entire rewriting of the idea from the source.

ACCEPTABLE PARAPHRASE

Steven Johnson argues that "surfing" is a misleading term for describing how people navigate on the web. He allows that "surfing" is appropriate for clicking across television channels because the viewer has to interact with what the networks and cable companies provide, just as the surfer has to interact with what the ocean provides. Web surfing, according to Johnson, operates at much greater depth and with much more consciousness of purpose. Web surfers actively follow links to make connections (107–09).

Even though there are a few words from the original in this paraphrase, such as *navigate* and *connections*, these sentences are original in structure and wording while accurately conveying the meaning of the source.

C H A P T E R *21*

Writing the Research Project

Once you've completed the research portion of a research paper, it is time to report on your findings. Research writing may seem formidable at first, but if you've kept your materials organized during the research phase, you can complete the writing phase on schedule with excellent results.

21a REVIEW YOUR GOALS AND THESIS

Before you begin writing your paper, you should review the assignment and your goals (see Chapter 16). Your review of the assignment will remind you of your purpose (analyze, review, survey, evaluate, argue), your potential readers, your stance on your subject, and the length and scope you should aim for.

By now you should have formulated a working thesis, which will be the focus of your paper. You should also have located, read, evaluated, and taken notes on enough source material to write your paper (see Chapters 17, 18, 19, and 20). At this stage in the writing process, your working thesis will probably be somewhat rough and may change as you write your draft, but having a general idea of what you hope to argue will help keep your paper focused.

21b PLAN YOUR ORGANIZATION

After you have drafted a thesis, you should look back over your notes and determine how to group the ideas you researched. Decide what your major points will be, and how those points support your thesis. Group your research findings so that they match up with your major points.

Now it is time to create a working outline. Always include your thesis at the top of your outline as a guiding light. Some writers create formal outlines with roman numerals and the like; others compose the headings for the paragraphs of their paper and use them to guide their draft; still others may start writing and then determine how they will organize their draft when they have a few paragraphs written. Experiment and decide which method works best for you.

21c INCORPORATE QUOTATIONS, SUMMARIES, AND PARAPHRASES EFFECTIVELY

The purpose of using sources is to *support* what you have to say, not to say it for you. Next to plagiarism, the worst mistake you can make with sources is to string together a series of long quotations. This strategy leaves your readers wondering whether you have anything to say. Relying too much on quotations from others also makes for a bumpy read.

When to quote and when to paraphrase

The general rule in deciding when to include direct quotations and when to paraphrase lies in the importance of the original wording. If you want to refer to an idea or fact and the original wording is not critical, make the point in your own words. Save direct quotations for language that is memorable or gives the character of the source.

Suppose you are writing about the effects of the internet on literacy, and you want to acknowledge those who maintain that the effects are largely negative. You find books by Sven Birkerts (*The Gutenberg Elegies: The Fate of Reading in an Electronic Age*), Mark Slouka (*War of the Worlds: Cyberspace and the High-Tech Assault on Reality*), and Clifford Stoll (*Silicon Snake Oil*) that argue the internet is a disorganized wasteland that discourages people from thinking for themselves. You also find a book by Jay David Bolter (*Writing Space: The Computer, Hypertext, and the History of Writing*), someone more sympathetic to digital technologies who also sees them as a threat to the power of prose. You could paraphrase each argument, but you realize that there are common themes that run through these books, so you decide to summarize these sources by making a list of the themes expressed. You want to use a direct quote from Bolter that articulates the themes. You might write:

> The rapid spread of the internet has produced many critics, such as Sven Birkerts, Mark Slouka, and Clifford Stoll, who all complain about how the internet is destroying the foundations of literacy—that critical thinking and reflection, a sense of order, logical relations in

texts, depth of analysis, trails of sources, and the reform mission of public discourse are going to be lost. Even those who take a more balanced view fear the multimedia capability of the web will undermine the power of prose. Jay David Bolter writes,

> The new media . . . threaten to drain contemporary prose of its rhetorical possibilities. Popular prose responds with a desire to emulate computer graphics. Academic and other specialized forms respond by a retreat into jargon or willful anachronism. (270)

The coming of the web, however, does not have to be viewed as a loss to literacy. Images and words have long coexisted on the printed page and in manuscripts, but relatively few people possessed the resources to exploit the rhetorical potential of images combined with words.

You would include all four books in your works-cited list.

Block quotations

As you see in the example above, when a direct quotation is long, it is indented from the margin instead of being placed in quotation marks. In MLA style, a quotation longer than 4 lines should be indented 10 spaces. A quotation of 40 words or longer is indented 5 spaces in APA style. In both MLA and APA styles, long quotations are double-spaced. When you indent a long quotation this way, it is called a **block quotation**. (There is an HTML tag that allows you to make block quotations on a webpage.) You still need to integrate a block quotation into the text of your paper. Block quotations should be introduced by mentioning where they came from. Note three points about form in the block quotation.

- There are no quotation marks around the block quotation.
- Words quoted in the original retain the double quotation marks.
- The page number appears after the period at the end of the block quotation.

It is a good idea to include at least one or two sentences following the quotation to describe its significance to your thesis.

Whether they are long or short, you should double-check all quotations you use to be sure they are accurate and that all words belonging to the original are set off with quotation marks or placed in a block quotation. If you wish to leave out words from a quotation, indicate the omitted words with ellipses (. . .), but make sure you do not alter the meaning of the original quote. If you need to add words of your own to a quotation to make the meaning clear, place your words in square brackets (see Section 44d).

WRITING SMART

Use quotations effectively

Quotations are a frequent problem area in research papers. Review every quotation to ensure that each is used effectively and correctly.

- **Limit the use of long quotations.** If you have more than one block quotation on a page, look closely to see if one or more can be paraphrased or summarized. Use direct quotations only if the original wording is important.
- **Check that each quotation is supporting your major points rather than making major points for you.** If the ideas rather than the original wording are what's important, paraphrase the quotation and cite the source.
- **Check that each quotation is introduced and attributed.** Each quotation should be introduced and the author or title named. Check for verbs that signal a quotation: McDaniel *claims*, Assad *argues*, Arribe *states*.
- **Check that each quotation is properly formatted and punctuated.** Prose quotations longer than 4 lines (MLA) or 40 words (APA) should be indented 10 spaces in MLA style or 5 spaces in APA style. Shorter quotations should be enclosed within quotation marks.
- **Check that you cite the source for each quotation.** You are required to cite the sources of all direct quotations, paraphrases, and summaries.
- **Check the accuracy of each quotation.** It's easy to leave out words or mistype a quotation. Compare what is in your paper to the original source. If you need to add words to make the quotation grammatical, make sure the added words are in brackets. Use ellipses to indicate omitted words.
- **Read your paper aloud to a classmate or a friend.** Each quotation should flow smoothly when you read your paper aloud. Put a check beside rough spots as you read aloud so you can revise later.

Integrate quotations, summaries, and paraphrases

You should also check to see whether all sources are well integrated into the fabric of your paper. Introduce quotations by attributing them in the text:

> Even those who fought for the United States in the U.S.-Mexican War of 1846 were skeptical of American motives: "We were sent to provoke a fight, but it was essential that Mexico should commence it" (Grant 68).

This quotation is used correctly, but it loses the impact of the source. Compare it with the following:

> Many soldiers who fought for the United States in the U.S.-Mexican War of 1846 were skeptical of American motives, including Civil War hero and future president Ulysses S. Grant, who wrote: "We were sent to provoke a fight, but it was essential that Mexico should commence it" (68).

Summaries and paraphrases likewise need introductions. The following paragraph is the summary of a book. The source is noted at the end, but the reader cannot tell exactly which ideas come from the source.

> In 2001 it became as fashionable to say the internet changes nothing as it had been to claim the internet changes everything just two years before. While the profit-making potential of the internet was overrated, the social effects were not. The internet is demolishing old castles of expertise along with many traditional relationships based on that expertise (Lewis).

In contrast, in the following summary signal phrases make it clear which ideas come from the source. The summary also indicates the stance of Lewis and includes a short quotation that gives the flavour of the source.

> In 2001 it became as fashionable to say the internet changes nothing as it had been to claim the internet changes everything just two years before. In the midst of the internet gloom, one prominent contrarian has emerged to defend the internet. Michael Lewis observes in *Next: The Future Just Happened* that it's as if "some crusty old baron who had been blasted out of his castle and was finally having a look at his first cannon had said, 'All it does is speed up balls' " (14). Lewis claims that while the profit-making potential of the internet was overrated, the social effects were not. He sees the internet demolishing old castles of expertise along with many traditional relationships based on that expertise.

21d WRITE YOUR DRAFT

Before you begin writing your first paragraph, organize your notes in the order in which you plan to use them. Some writers prefer to write their introductory paragraphs first; others wait until they have written the body of the paper to decide how they want to introduce their topic. No matter what order you write your paper in, you should announce your thesis in your introductory section.

Verbs that introduce quotations and paraphrases

acknowledge	claim	emphasize	offer
add	comment	explain	point out
admit	compare	express	refute
advise	complain	find	reject
agree	concede	grant	remark
allow	conclude	illustrate	reply
analyze	contend	imply	report
answer	criticize	insist	respond
argue	declare	interpret	show
ask	describe	maintain	state
assert	disagree	note	suggest
believe	discuss	object	think
charge	dispute	observe	write

21e REVIEW YOUR DRAFT

After you've finished your first draft, you'll want to get comments from other writers. A good source of help is fellow students. Your instructor may include a peer review session as part of the assignment. Before going to your peer review session, run one last spell-check, and then print a double-spaced version of your paper for each member of your group.

Reading another student's paper

It is usually best to read through a paper twice, looking at different levels (see Chapter 5). The first time you read through a paper, concentrate on comprehension and overall impressions. See if you can summarize the paper after reading it once. Ask yourself whether the writing is convincing or informative.

On your second reading show the writer where you got confused or highlight parts that were especially good by adding comments in the margins. Consider the following questions when reading a research paper:

- Does the title describe the subject of the paper? Does it create interest in the subject?
- Are the introductory paragraphs effective and relevant to the paper that follows?
- Is the thesis clearly stated in the beginning paragraphs of the paper?
- Does the writer offer support for the thesis from a variety of valid and reliable sources?

- Does the paper go into enough detail to support the thesis, and are the details relevant to the thesis?
- Do the arguments presented in the paper flow logically? Is the paper well organized?
- Is the tone of the paper consistent throughout? Is the word choice varied and appropriate throughout?
- Did you have to read some parts more than once to fully understand them?
- Are quotations properly introduced and integrated into the text?
- Are all facts and quotations that are not common knowledge documented?
- Is the documentation in the correct form?
- Is the paper free of errors of grammar and punctuation?

Once you've read through the paper a second time, write concluding suggestions and comments about how the writer could improve the paper, using the questions as your guide. Be specific. Saying "I liked your paper" or "It's a good first draft" does not help the writer. Comments like "You need to cite more sources," "You might consider switching paragraphs 2 and 4," or "Try to use a more formal tone in your introductory and concluding paragraphs" give the writer specific areas to concentrate on in the revision. It is important to be supportive in the peer editing process, so try to offer comments that are positive and encouraging.

Reading your own paper

If others read and comment on your paper, you cannot expect them to tell you everything you need to do in a revision. You need to be able to read your own draft with the same distance that you have when you read the drafts of others. Sometimes you will not have another person available who can comment on your paper.

Reading your paper aloud to yourself will help you find rough places. Parts that are difficult for you to speak aloud are going to be hard for your readers to get through. Try to imagine yourself as a reader who does not know much about your subject or who holds a viewpoint different from yours. What could you add that would benefit those readers?

21f REVISE, EDIT, AND CHECK FORMATTING

After you've gone through the peer editing process or assessed your own draft, sit down with your paper and consider the changes you need to make. Start from the highest level, reorganizing paragraphs and possibly even cutting large parts of your paper and adding new sections (see Sections 5b and 5c). If you make significant revisions, likely you will want to repeat the overall evaluation of your revised draft when you finish.

When you feel your draft is complete, you should begin the editing phase. Use the guidelines in Section 5d to revise style and grammatical errors. Finally, you should proofread your paper, word by word, checking for mistakes (see Section 5e). After you print out the final paper, check each page for printer or formatting errors. Make sure all the pages were printed and that all are readable.

You can read a student's completed paper in Section 22k.

WRITING SMART

Documenting sources on a website

Websites provide you the opportunity to link directly to other websites. Thus when you make a reference to another website, you can make a link from the author's name or the title of the website that takes you directly to it. By clicking these links, a visitor to your site can immediately consult the source. Format the link so that the other site opens in a new browser window, so that you don't lose visitors to your site.

In addition, it's a good idea to include a works-cited list. One reason is that you don't necessarily want your visitors leaving your site in the middle of what you have to say. If you link off the works-cited list to other websites, the visitor will have at least had a chance to read your text first. It's also a good idea to have all of your references in one place. Third, because websites change so quickly and often disappear, the date you accessed the source you cite is important. That date is included in the works-cited entry.

PART SIX

MLA Documentation

- How do I format in-text citations in MLA documentation style? (22a)

- How do I format the citation for a book with a translator? (22b)

- How do I cite an online source in my works cited? (22f)

6 MLA DOCUMENTATION

The Modern Language Association (MLA) style is used in disciplines in the humanities and fine arts. The beginning of a citation always emphasizes the information that the disciplines consider most important. MLA style uses in-text citations—that is, the reference to the author and page number of the source cited appears in parentheses in the text of the paper. When the citation appears in the text, the writer provides readers with immediate access to the source and location of the quotation. This information allows readers to assess the centrality of the source to the topic being discussed, since they are familiar with the major contributors to scholarship in that area. The full citation to the source then appears in a Works Cited page at the end of the paper.

MLA style highlights the author and title of the work cited (these appear first in each entry—see Langston East's Works Cited in the sample essay). This highlighting indicates that in disciplines in the humanities and fine arts writers value the source of the idea (the author) and the work where it appears (the title of the paper and the volume). Other documentation styles emphasize different aspects of the research.

 Visit *The Brief Penguin Handbook* Companion Website at
www.pearsoned.ca/faigley/

MLA C H A P T E R *22*

MLA Documentation

(continued next page)

The two styles of documentation used most frequently are the American Psychological Association (APA) style and the Modern Language Association (MLA) style. The APA style is followed in the social sciences and education (see Chapter 23), while the MLA style is the norm for the humanities and fine arts disciplines. If you have questions that the examples in this chapter do not address, consult the *MLA Handbook for Writers of Research Papers*, sixth edition (2003), and the *MLA Style Manual and Guide to Scholarly Publishing*, second edition (1998).

In-text citations

Each use of a source in MLA style is indicated by a citation in parentheses. When readers find a parenthetical reference to a source in the body of a paper, they can turn to the works-cited list and find the full publication information.

Describing humans as "innate mind readers," one observer argues that "our skill at imagining other people's mental states ranks up there with our knack for language and our opposable thumbs" (Johnson 196).

Works Cited

Johnson, Steven. *Emergence: The Connected Lives of Ants, Brains, Cities, and Software.* New York: Scribner, 2001.

The writer quotes a passage from page 196 of Johnson's book. The reader can use the information in the works-cited list to locate the book and check whether the writer accurately represents Johnson and how the point quoted fits into Johnson's larger argument. See Section 22a (pages 285–289) for further information on in-text citations.

Entries in the works-cited list

The works-cited list is organized alphabetically by authors' last names. MLA style uses three basic forms for entries in the works-cited list: books, periodicals (scholarly journals, newspapers, magazines), and online sources.

Books

Entries for books have three main elements:

Author's name. *Title of book.* Publication information.

For examples of different types of book entries see Section 22b.

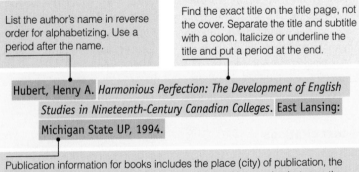

List the author's name in reverse order for alphabetizing. Use a period after the name.

Find the exact title on the title page, not the cover. Separate the title and subtitle with a colon. Italicize or underline the title and put a period at the end.

Hubert, Henry A. *Harmonious Perfection: The Development of English Studies in Nineteenth-Century Canadian Colleges.* East Lansing: Michigan State UP, 1994.

Publication information for books includes the place (city) of publication, the name of the publisher, and the date of publication. Use a colon between the place of publication and the publisher's name (using accepted abbreviations), followed by a comma and then the publication date.

Periodicals

Entries for periodicals have three main elements:

Author's name. "Title of article." Publication information.

For examples of periodical entries see Sections 22c and 22d.

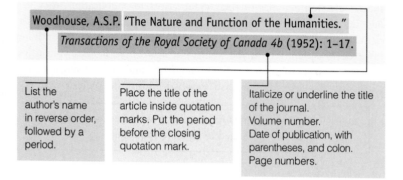

Woodhouse, A.S.P. "The Nature and Function of the Humanities."
Transactions of the Royal Society of Canada 4b (1952): 1–17.

List the author's name in reverse order, followed by a period.	Place the title of the article inside quotation marks. Put the period before the closing quotation mark.	Italicize or underline the title of the journal. Volume number. Date of publication, with parentheses, and colon. Page numbers.

Online sources

Entries for online sources may have five main elements:

Author's name. "Title of document" and/or *Title of Website*. Print publication information. Electronic publication information. Date of access <URL>.

There are many formats for the different kinds of electronic publications, which are described in Sections 22f and 22g. Here is the format of an entry for a professional website.

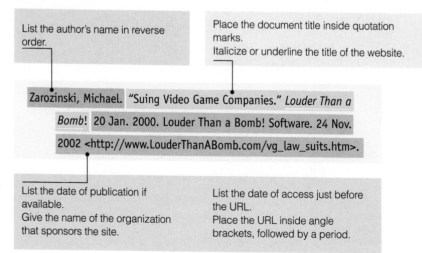

List the author's name in reverse order.	Place the document title inside quotation marks. Italicize or underline the title of the website.

Zarozinski, Michael. "Suing Video Game Companies." *Louder Than a Bomb!* 20 Jan. 2000. Louder Than a Bomb! Software. 24 Nov. 2002 <http://www.LouderThanABomb.com/vg_law_suits.htm>.

List the date of publication if available. Give the name of the organization that sponsors the site.	List the date of access just before the URL. Place the URL inside angle brackets, followed by a period.

Formatting the works-cited list

Type the list of works cited on a separate page at the end of the paper.

Traditionally, MLA style has dictated underlining for titles in a manuscript. When printers typeset the manuscript, they would reformat all underlining as italics in the printed text. With many writers now able to submit electronic copies of their manuscripts for publication, they can italicize titles easily while they write the text, making underlining inefficient. In this section, italics are used for titles, even though MLA continues to advocate underlining. If you want to be up-to-date, italicize your titles. However, if you are in doubt about whether to underline or italicize titles for a particular class, ask your instructor about his or her preference.

> Remember: Entries in your list of works cited should be
> arranged in alphabetical order.

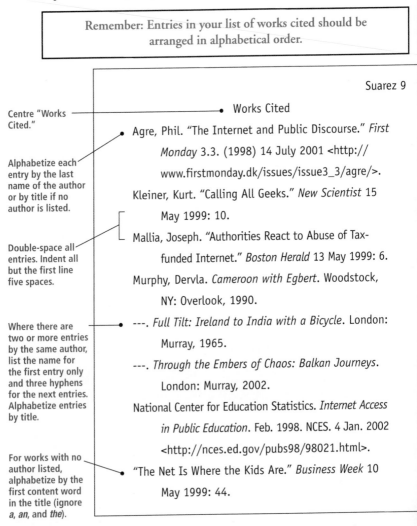

Suarez 9

Centre "Works Cited."

Alphabetize each entry by the last name of the author or by title if no author is listed.

Double-space all entries. Indent all but the first line five spaces.

Where there are two or more entries by the same author, list the name for the first entry only and three hyphens for the next entries. Alphabetize entries by title.

For works with no author listed, alphabetize by the first content word in the title (ignore *a*, *an*, and *the*).

Works Cited

Agre, Phil. "The Internet and Public Discourse." *First Monday* 3.3. (1998) 14 July 2001 <http://www.firstmonday.dk/issues/issue3_3/agre/>.

Kleiner, Kurt. "Calling All Geeks." *New Scientist* 15 May 1999: 10.

Mallia, Joseph. "Authorities React to Abuse of Tax-funded Internet." *Boston Herald* 13 May 1999: 6.

Murphy, Dervla. *Cameroon with Egbert*. Woodstock, NY: Overlook, 1990.

---. *Full Tilt: Ireland to India with a Bicycle*. London: Murray, 1965.

---. *Through the Embers of Chaos: Balkan Journeys*. London: Murray, 2002.

National Center for Education Statistics. *Internet Access in Public Education*. Feb. 1998. NCES. 4 Jan. 2002 <http://nces.ed.gov/pubs98/98021.html>.

"The Net Is Where the Kids Are." *Business Week* 10 May 1999: 44.

22a IN-TEXT CITATIONS IN MLA STYLE

Paraphrase, summary, or short quotation

A short quotation takes four lines or fewer in your paper.

> The computing power of networked technology is growing at an accelerating rate, prompting some visionaries to argue that the internet "may actually become self-aware sometime in the next century" (Johnson 114).

Here, the author's name is provided in the parenthetical reference.

The author of the quotation is clearly named in this sentence, so only a page number is needed in the parenthetical reference.

Note that the period goes *after* the parentheses.

> Science writer and cultural critic Steven Johnson poses the question this way: "Is the Web itself becoming a giant brain?" (114).

Quotations longer than four lines

> Technology writer and cultural commentator Steven Johnson relates how he often responded to questions about whether or not networked computers would ever be able to think or develop awareness:
>
> > For there to be a single, global consciousness, the Web itself would have to be getting smarter, and the Web wasn't a single, unified thing—it was just a vast sum of interlinked data. You could debate whether the Web was making us smarter, but that the Web itself might be slouching toward consciousness seemed ludicrous. (114)
>
> Despite his initial skepticism, however, Johnson slowly began to change his mind about the idea of artificial consciousness or intelligence.

The sentence introducing the quotation names the author, so only the page number needs to appear in the parenthetical reference.

Note that the period appears *before* the parentheses in an indented block quote.

> **When do you provide a page number?**
> - If the source is longer than one page, provide the page number for each quotation, paraphrase, and summary.
> - If an online source includes paragraph numbers rather than page numbers, use *par.* with the number.
>
> (Cello, par. 4)
>
> - If the source does not include page numbers, consider citing the work and the author in the text rather than in the parentheses.
>
> In a hypertext version of James Joyce's *Ulysses*, . . .

Sample in-text citations

1. Author named in your text

Put the author's name in a signal phrase in your sentence.

> Astrobiologist Ranjit Patel argues that Enceladus, one of Saturn's moons, may have "extraterrestrial life" (3).

2. Author not named in your text

> According to Statistics Canada figures, women in 2003 were actually earning "slightly less—2%" than they had compared to men in 1995 (Grisson 254).

3. Work by one author

The author's last name comes first, followed by the page number. There is no comma.

> (Patel 3)

4. Work by two or three authors

The authors' last names follow the order of the title page. If there are two authors, join the names with *and*. If there are three, use commas between the first two names and a comma with *and* before the last name.

> (Francisco, Vaughn, and Lynn 7)

5. Work by four or more authors

You may use the phrase *et al.* (meaning "and others") for all names but the first, or you may write out all the names. Make sure you use the same method for both the in-text citations and the works-cited list.

> (Abrams et al. 1653)

6. Work by no named author

Use a shortened version of the title that includes at least the first important word. Your reader will use the shortened title to find the full title in the works-cited list.

> A review in *The New Yorker* of Ryan Adams's new album focuses on the artist's age ("Pure" 25).

Notice that "Pure" is in quotation marks because it refers to the title of an article. If it were a book, the short title would be italicized or underlined.

7. Work by a group or organization

Treat the group or organization as the author. Try to identify the group author in the text and place only the page number in the parentheses.

> According to the *Irish Free State Handbook*, published by the Ministry for Industry and Finance, the population of Ireland in 1929 was approximately 4 192 000 (23).

8. Quotations longer than four lines

NOTE: When using indented ("block") quotations of longer than four lines, the period appears *before* the parentheses enclosing the page number.

> In her article "Art for Everybody," Susan Orlean attempts to explain the popularity of painter Thomas Kinkade:
>> People like to own things they think are valuable. . . . The high price of limited editions is part of their appeal: it implies that they are choice and exclusive, and that only a certain class of people will be able to afford them. (128)
>
> This same statement could possibly also explain the popularity of phenomena like PBS's *Antiques Road Show*.

If the source is longer than one page, provide the page number for each quotation, paraphrase, and summary.

9. Online sources

If an online source includes paragraph numbers rather than page numbers, use *par.* with the number.

> (Cello, par. 4)

If the source does not include page numbers, consider citing the work and the author in the text rather than in parentheses.

> In a hypertext version of James Joyce's *Ulysses*, . . .

10. Work in an anthology

Cite the name of the author of the work within an anthology, not the name of the editor of the collection. Alphabetize the entry in the list of works cited by the author, not the editor. For example, Xiao-ming Li published the chapter "'Track (Dis)Connecting': Chinese High School and University Writing in a Time of Change," in *Writing and Learning in Cross-National Perspective*, a book edited by David Russell and David Foster.

> In "'Track (Dis)Connecting': Chinese High School and University Writing in a Time of Change," Xiao-ming Li notes that the number of students accepted into Chinese universities increased from 1 080 000 in 1999, to 1 530 000 in 2000, "an increase over 40%" (81).

Note that Li, not Russell and Foster, is named in parenthetical citations.

> (Li 81)

11. Two or more works by the same author

Use the author's last name and then a shortened version of the title of each source.

> The majority of books written about co-authorship focus on partners of the same sex (Laird, *Women* 351).

Note that *Women* is italicized because it is the name of a book.

12. Different authors with the same last name

If your list of works cited contains items by two or more different authors with the same last name, include the initial of the first name in the parenthetical reference. Note that a period follows the initial.

> Web surfing requires more mental involvement than channel surfing (S. Johnson 107).

13. Two or more sources within the same sentence

Place each citation directly after the statement it supports.

> Many sweeping pronouncements were made in the 1990s that the internet is the best opportunity to improve education since the printing press (Ellsworth xxii) or even in the history of the world (Dyrli and Kinnaman 79).

14. Two or more sources within the same citation

If two sources support a single point, separate them with a semicolon.

> (McKibbin 39; Gore 92)

15. Work quoted in another source

When you do not have access to the original source of the material you wish to use and only an indirect source is available, put the abbreviation *qtd. in* (quoted in) before the information about the indirect source.

> National governments have become increasingly what Ulrich Beck, in a 1999 interview, calls "zombie institutions"—institutions which are "dead and still alive" (qtd. in Bauman 6).

16. Work in more than one volume

Give the volume number in the parenthetical reference before the page number, with a colon and a space separating the two.

> Contrary to the legend that Vincent van Gogh succumbed to personal demons before his suicide in 1890, his letters from the last two months describe feelings of calmness and an end to his recurrent nightmares (Walther and Metzger 2: 647).

17. Poems, plays, and classic works

Poems

If you quote all or part of two or three lines of poetry that do not require special emphasis, put the lines in quotation marks and separate the lines using a slash (/) with a space on each side.

> John Donne's "The Legacy" associates the separation of lovers with death: "When I died last, and, Dear, I die / As often as from thee I go" (1-2).

Plays

Give the act, scene, and line numbers when the work has them, the page numbers when it does not. Abbreviate titles of famous works (like *Hamlet*).

> (*Ham.* 3.2.120-21).

Classic Works

To supply a reference to classic works, you sometimes need more than a page number from a specific edition. Readers should be able to locate a quotation in any edition of the book. Give the page number from the edition that you are using, then a semicolon and other identifying information.

> "Marriage is a house" is one of the most memorable lines in *Don Quixote* (546; pt. 2, bk. 3, ch. 19).

22b BOOKS IN MLA-STYLE WORKS CITED

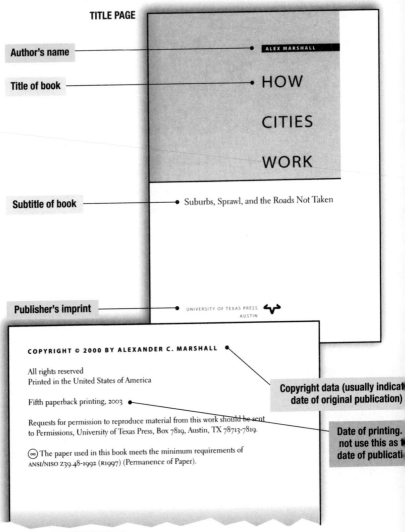

TITLE PAGE

Author's name — ALEX MARSHALL

Title of book — HOW CITIES WORK

Subtitle of book — Suburbs, Sprawl, and the Roads Not Taken

Publisher's imprint — UNIVERSITY OF TEXAS PRESS AUSTIN

COPYRIGHT © 2000 BY ALEXANDER C. MARSHALL

All rights reserved
Printed in the United States of America

Fifth paperback printing, 2003

Requests for permission to reproduce material from this work should be sent to Permissions, University of Texas Press, Box 7819, Austin, TX 78713-7819.

∞ The paper used in this book meets the minimum requirements of ANSI/NISO Z39.48-1992 (R1997) (Permanence of Paper).

Copyright data (usually indicate date of original publication)

Date of printing. not use this as date of publicati

DETAIL OF COPYRIGHT PAGE

Marshall, Alex. *How Cities Work: Suburbs, Sprawl, and the Roads Not Taken*. Austin: U of Texas P, 2000.

AUTHOR'S OR EDITOR'S NAME

The author's last name comes first, followed by a comma and the first name.

For edited books, put the abbreviation *ed.* after the name, preceded by a comma:

MacDonald, Brock, ed.

BOOK TITLE

Use the exact title, as it appears on the title page (not the cover).

Italicize or underline the title.

All nouns, verbs, pronouns, adjectives, adverbs, and subordinating conjunctions, and the first and last word of the title are capitalized. Do not capitalize articles, prepositions, coordinating conjunctions, or *to* infinitives, unless they are the first or last word of the title.

PUBLICATION INFORMATION

Place of publication

If more than one city is given, use the first.

For cities outside Canada that are not well known, add an abbreviation of the province, state, or country.

Publisher

Use a short form of the name:

Omit words such as *Press*, *Publisher*, and *Inc.*

For university presses, use *UP*: Wilfrid Laurier UP.

Shorten the name. For example, shorten *Addison, Wesley, Longman* to Longman; *W. W. Norton & Co.* to *Norton*.

Date of publication

Give the year as it appears on the copyright page.

If no year of publication is given, but can be approximated, put a *c.* ("circa") and the approximate date in brackets: [c. 1999].

Otherwise, put *n.d.* ("no date"): Ottawa: U of Ottawa P, n.d.

Sample works-cited entries for books

18. **Book by one author**

> Blair, Hugh. *An Abridgment of Lectures on Rhetoric*. Richmond, VA:
> Jacob Johnson, 1808.

19. **Two or more books by the same author**

In the entry for the first book, include the author's name. In the second entry, substitute three hyphens and a period for the author's name. List the titles of books by the same author in alphabetical order.

> Harris, Robin S. *A History of Higher Education in Canada, 1663-1960*.
> Toronto: U of Toronto P, 1976.

> ---. *English Studies at Toronto: A History*. Toronto: U of Toronto P, 1988.

20. **Book by two or three authors**

The second and subsequent authors' names appear first name first.

> Miller, Toby, and Alec McHoul. *Popular Culture and Everyday Life*.
> London: Sage, 1998.

21. **Book by four or more authors**

You may use the phrase *et al.* (meaning "and others") for all authors but the first, or you may write out all the names. You need to use the same method in the in-text citation as you do in the works-cited list.

> North, Stephen M., et al. *Refiguring the Ph.D. in English Studies*.
> Urbana: NCTE, 2000.

22. **Book by an unknown author**

Begin the entry with the title.

> *The Canadian Encyclopedia*. 2nd ed. Toronto: McClelland & Stewart, 1988.

23. **Book revised by a second author**

Place the editor's name after the book title.

> Strunk, William. *Elements of Style*. Ed. E. B. White. 4th ed. Boston:
> Allyn, 2000.

24. Book by a group or organization

Treat the group as the author of the work.

United Nations. *The Charter of the United Nations: A Commentary*.
New York: Oxford UP, 2000.

FOREIGN AND EMBEDDED TITLES

25. Title within a title

If the title contains the title of another book or a word normally itali-cized, do not underline that title or word.

Higgins, Brian, and Hershel Parker. *Critical Essays on Herman
Melville's* Moby Dick. New York: Hall, 1992.

26. Title in a foreign language

If the title is in a foreign language, copy it exactly as it appears on the title page.

Fontaine, Jean. *Etudes de Littérature Tunisienne*. Tunis: Dar
Annawras, 1989.

IMPRINTS, REPRINTS, AND UNDATED BOOKS

27. Book published before 1900

You may omit the publisher for books published prior to 1900.

Rodd, Renell. *Rose Leaf and Apple Leaf*. Philadelphia, 1882.

28. Books that include a special imprint of the publisher

In the example below, Flamingo is a special imprint of Harper.

O'Brien, Flann. *The Poor Mouth*. London: Flamingo-Harper, 1993.

29. Book with no publication date

If no year of publication is given, but can be approximated, put a *c.* ("circa") and the approximate date in brackets: [c. 1999]. Otherwise, put *n.d.* ("no date").

O'Sullivan, Colin. *Traditions and Novelties of the Irish Country Folk*.
Dublin [c. 1793].

James, Franklin. *In the Valley of the King*. Cambridge: Harvard UP, n.d.

30. Reprinted works

For works of fiction that have been printed in many different editions or reprints, give the original publication date after the title.

Wilde, Oscar. *The Picture of Dorian Gray*. 1890. New York: Norton, 2001.

PARTS OF BOOKS

31. Introduction, foreword, preface, or afterword

Give the author and then the name of the specific part being cited. Next, name the book. Then, if the author for the whole work is different, put that author's name after the word *By*. Place inclusive page numbers at the end.

Strong-Boag, Veronica. Introduction. *In Times Like These*. By Nellie McClung. 1915. Toronto: U of Toronto P, 1972. vii-xx.

32. Single chapter written by same author as the book

Ardis, Ann. "Mapping the Middlebrow in Edwardian England." *Modernism and Cultural Conflict: 1880-1922*. Cambridge: Cambridge UP, 2002. 114-42.

33. Selection in an anthology or a chapter in an edited collection

Auden, W. H. "1929." *W. H. Auden: Collected Poems*. Ed. Edward Mendelson. New York: Vintage-Random, 1991. 45-49.

34. Article in a reference work

You can omit the names of editors and most publishing information for an article from a familiar reference work. Identify the edition by date. There is no need to give the page numbers when a work is arranged alphabetically. Give the author's name, if known.

"Utilitarianism." *The Columbia Encyclopedia*. 6th ed. 2001.

A full entry is required for less familiar works.

RELIGIOUS TEXTS

35. Religious texts

Holy Bible. King James Text: Modern Phrased Version. New York: Oxford UP, 1980.

Use a period to separate the chapter and verse in the in-text note.

(John 3.16)

EDITIONS AND TRANSLATIONS

36. **Book with an editor—focus on the editor**

    Lewis, Gifford, ed. *The Big House of Inver*. By Edith Somerville and
        Martin Ross. Dublin: Farmar, 2000.

37. **Book with an editor—focus on the author**

    Somerville, Edith, and Martin Ross. *The Big House of Inver*. Ed.
        Gifford Lewis. Dublin: Farmar, 2000.

38. **Book with more than one editor**

    Kaplan, Fred, and Sylvère Monod, eds. *Hard Times*. By Charles
        Dickens. New York: Norton, 2001.

39. **Book with a translator**

    Benjamin, Walter. *The Arcades Project*. Trans. Howard Eiland and
        Kevin McLaughlin. Cambridge: Harvard UP, 1999.

40. **Second or subsequent edition of a book**

    Hawthorn, Jeremy, ed. *A Concise Glossary of Contemporary Literary
        Theory*. 3rd ed. London: Arnold, 2001.

MULTIVOLUME WORKS

41. **One volume of a multivolume work**

    If you cite only one volume of a multivolume work, give the publica-
    tion information for only that volume.

    Samuel, Raphael. *Theatres of Memory*. Vol. 1. London: Verso, 1999.

42. **More than one volume of a multivolume work**

    List the total number of volumes in Works Cited.

    Samuel, Raphael. *Theatres of Memory*. 2 vols. London: Verso, 1999.

    Identify the specific volume in your in-text citations.

    (Samuel 2: 36-37)

43. **Book in a series**

    Give the series name just before the publishing information.

    Watson, James. *William Faulkner: Self-Presentation and Performance*.
        Literary Modernism Series. Austin: U of Texas P, 2000.

22c JOURNALS AND MAGAZINES IN MLA-STYLE WORKS CITED

JOURNAL COVER

CONTENTS PAGE

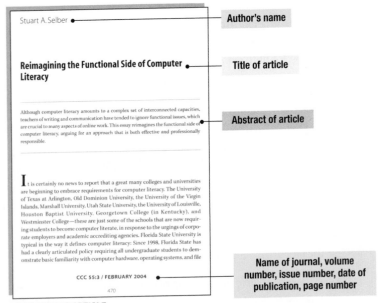

Stuart A. Selber ●———— **Author's name**

Reimagining the Functional Side of Computer ●——— **Title of article**
Literacy

Although computer literacy amounts to a complex set of interconnected capacities, teachers of writing and communication have tended to ignore functional issues, which are crucial to many aspects of online work. This essay reimagines the functional side of computer literacy, arguing for an approach that is both effective and professionally responsible.
●——— **Abstract of article**

It is certainly no news to report that a great many colleges and universities are beginning to embrace requirements for computer literacy. The University of Texas at Arlington, Old Dominion University, the University of the Virgin Islands, Marshall University, Utah State University, the University of Louisville, Houston Baptist University, Georgetown College (in Kentucky), and Westminster College—these are just some of the schools that are now requiring students to become computer literate, in response to the urgings of corporate employers and academic accrediting agencies. Florida State University is typical in the way it defines computer literacy: Since 1998, Florida State has had a clearly articulated policy requiring all undergraduate students to demonstrate basic familiarity with computer hardware, operating systems, and file

CCC 55:3 / FEBRUARY 2004 ●——— **Name of journal, volume number, issue number, date of publication, page number**

470

FIRST PAGE OF ARTICLE

Selber, Stuart A. "Reimagining the Functional Side of Computer
Literacy." *CCC* 55 (2004): 470-503.

AUTHOR'S NAME

The author's last name comes first, followed by a comma and the first name.

For two or more works by the same author, consult the sample Works Cited list on page 284.

TITLE OF ARTICLE

Use the exact title, which appears at the top of the article.

Put the title in quotation marks. If a book title is part of the article's title, italicize or underline the book title. If a title requiring quotation marks is part of the article's title, use single quotation marks.

All nouns, verbs, pronouns, adjectives, adverbs, and subordinating conjunctions, and the first and last word of the title are capitalized. Do not capitalize any article, preposition, coordinating conjunction, or *to* in an infinitive, unless it is the first or last word of the title.

PUBLICATION INFORMATION

Name of journal

Italicize or underline the title of the journal.

Abbreviate the title of the journal if it commonly appears that way (as in this example).

Volume, issue, and page numbers

- For journals paginated separately by issue, list the volume number, a period, and then the issue number before the year and page numbers.

- For continuously paginated journals, include the volume number before the year, but do *not* include the issue number (as in this example).

Date of publication

- For magazines and journals identified by the month or season of publication, use the month (or season) and year in place of the volume.

- For weekly or biweekly magazines, give both the day and month of publication, as listed on the issue. Note that the day precedes the month and no comma is used.

Sample works-cited entries for journals and magazines

JOURNAL AND MAGAZINE ARTICLES

44. Article by one author

> Mallory, Anne. "Burke, Boredom, and the Theater of
> Counterrevolution." *PMLA* 119 (2003): 329-43.

45. Article by two or three authors

The second and subsequent authors' names are printed first name first.

> Kearns, Judith, and Brian Turner. "Negotiated Independence: How a
> Canadian Writing Program Became a Centre." *WPA: Writing
> Program Administration* 21 (1997): 31-43.

Notice that a comma separates the authors' names.

46. Article by four or more authors

You may use the phrase *et al.* (meaning "and others") for all authors but the first, or you may write out all the names. You need to use the same method in the in-text citation as you do in the works-cited list.

> Breece, Katherine E., et al. "Patterns of mtDNA Diversity in
> Northwestern North America." *Human Biology* 76 (2004): 33-54.

47. Article by an unknown author

Begin the entry with the title.

> "Idol Gossip." *People* 12 Apr. 2004: 34-35.

48. Article with a title in a foreign language

Copy the title exactly as it appears on the title page.

> Frostin, Georges. "Les Colons de Saint Dominigue." *Revue Historique*
> 237 (1967): 67-78.

MONTHLY, WEEKLY, AND BIWEEKLY MAGAZINES

49. Monthly or seasonal magazines or journals

For magazines and journals identified by the month or season of publication, use the month (or season) and year in place of the volume. Abbreviate the names of all months except May, June, and July.

> Kahn, Jennifer. "A Nation of Guinea Pigs." *Wired* Mar. 2006: 142-47.

50. Weekly or biweekly magazines

For weekly or biweekly magazines, give both the day and month of publication, as listed on the issue. Note that the day precedes the month and no comma is used.

> George, Lianne. "It's Not Just a Car Anymore . . . It's a Home."
> *Maclean's* 27 Feb. 2006: 20-25.

DIFFERENT TYPES OF PAGINATION

51. Article in a journal paginated by volume

Include the volume number but do not include the issue number.

Lerer, Seth. "Medieval English Literature and the Idea of the
Anthology." *PMLA* 118 (2003): 1251-67.

52. Article in a journal paginated by issue

List the volume number, a period, and then the issue number (here, *2/3*) before the year and page numbers.

Davis, Jim. "Rethinking Globalisation." *Race and Class* 40.2/3
(1999): 37-48.

REVIEWS, EDITORIALS, LETTERS TO THE EDITOR

53. Review

Provide the title, if given, and name the work reviewed. If there is no title, just name the work reviewed.

Steyn, Mark. "What Should I do, Imam?" Rev. of *Prayers for the
Assassin*. By Robert Ferrigno. *Maclean's* 27 Feb. 2006: 54-55.

54. Letter to the editor

Add the word *Letter* after the name of the author.

Patai, Daphne. Letter. *Harper's Magazine* Dec. 2001: 4.

If it is a reply to a previous letter, add *Reply to the letter of [name]* followed by a period.

55. Editorial

If the editorial is unsigned, put the title first. Add the word *Editorial* after the title.

Gunter, Lorne. "Americans Do Pre-emptive strikes well." Editorial.
Edmonton Journal. 19 Mar. 2006: A18.

56. Published interview

Frum, Linda. "Peter Bergen Talks to Linda Frum." *Maclean's* 30 Jan.
2006: 10-11.

57. Article on microfilm

Cite an article on microfilm or microfiche as you would the original.

Bowen, Elizabeth. "The Case for Summer Romance." *Glamour* 43
(1960): 94-95, 180.

22d NEWSPAPERS IN MLA-STYLE WORKS CITED

Date of publication

Name of newspaper

TUESDAY, JULY 11, 2006

SERVING KITCHENER, CAMBRIDGE, WATERLOO AND THE REGION

THE RECORD

MASTHEAD OF THE NEWSPAPER AS IT APPEARS ON THE FRONT PAGE

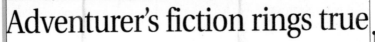

Novelist Jon Evans, a graduate of the University of Waterloo, has just finished another of his adventure novels, tentatively titled Absolute Darkness.

DAVID BEBEE, RECORD STAFF

Adventurer's fiction rings true

By Colin Hunter
Record Staff

Toronto

My heels burned, my knees ached, my back itched, my back felt like an anvil, but I had grown accustomed to my posi-

Those words are fiction, taken from the pages of the thriller Dark Places by novelist Jon Evans.

And the words are also true, inspired by Evans' real-life struggle to endure altitude sickness during a trek through the

sarily stranger than fiction. But it certainly does make for great fiction material.

The 33-year-old Waterloo native lives by the author's mantra: "Write what you know."

his second novel, Blood Price.

Over the past couple of years he has dodged incoming mortars in Iraq and travelled through tumultuous central Africa on public transit. He has filled his mind with story ideas

something that is defining, yet so deeply weird that I couldn't have imagined it on my own," he says between sips of coffee.

On this morning, Evans is relaxing in the comparatively unexciting confines of Java

FIRST PAGE OF ARTICLE (PAGE A1)

Author's name

Title of article

Novel: Getting good reviews

CONTINUED FROM PAGE A1

It's a favourite haunt from his days as a computer programmer at a nearby firm.

He's decompressing, having handed in a manuscript for his next novel (tentatively titled Absolute Darkness) to his publisher just hours earlier.

Gy coincidence, it has been exactly one year since he handed in a draft of Invisible Armies, which was released just over a month ago to positive reviews in North America and over-

one. He read voraciously, immersing himself in four or five sci-fi novels a week.

But writing his own masterpiece, he soon discovered, was much easier in theory than in practice.

"I wrote a very, very, very bad fantasy novel when I was 15," he admits, lowering his shaved-bald head in exaggerated shame.

"I hope no pages of it survive."

Evans didn't give up hope on his writing career but was also realistic

ment.

Book sales have been strong enough lately that Evans hasn't needed to supplement his income with high-tech jobs.

"I haven't had a day job in about three years," he says. "I strongly recommend it. It's very nice."

Sometimes it gets frustrating, though, when story ideas refuse to go from his brain onto the computer the way he'd like. For every book that gets published he has scrapped many more,

CONTINUATION OF ARTICLE (PAGE A2)

Hunter, Colin, "Adventurer's Fiction Rings True."
The Record [Waterloo], 11 July 2006: A1+.

AUTHOR'S NAME

The author's last name comes first, followed by a comma and the first name.

For two or more works by the same author, consult the sample Works Cited list on page 284.

TITLE OF ARTICLE

Use the exact title, which appears at the top of the article.

Put the title in quotation marks. If a book title is part of the article's title, italicize or underline the book title. If a title requiring quotation marks is part of the article's title, use single quotation marks.

All nouns, verbs, pronouns, adjectives, adverbs, and subordinating conjunctions, and the first and last word of the title are capitalized. Do not capitalize any article, preposition, coordinating conjunction, or *to* in an infinitive, unless it is the first or last word of the title.

PUBLICATION INFORMATION

Name of newspaper

Italicize or underline the name.

Omit introductory articles. (*Globe and Mail* not *The Globe and Mail*).

If the city is not mentioned in the name of the paper, add it in square brackets after the name (as in this example).

Section and page numbers

Provide the section label (usually A, B, C, etc.).

Include the page number. If the article continues to a non-consecutive page, add a plus sign after the number of the first page.

Date of publication and edition

Give the complete date for a newspaper— day, month, and year.

Abbreviate the names of all months except May, June, and July.

Do *not* give the volume and issue numbers for a newspaper.

Specify the edition if one is given on the masthead: *natl. ed., final ed., suburban ed.*

Place a colon after the edition if an edition name or number is given. If no edition is listed, place the colon after the date.

Sample works-cited entries for newspapers

NEWSPAPER ARTICLES

58. Article by one author

> Boyd, Robert S. "Solar System Has a Double." *Montreal Gazette* 14
> June 2002, final ed.: A1.

59. Article by two or three authors

The second and subsequent authors' names are printed in regular order, first name first:

> Davis, Howard, June Allstead, and Jane Mavis. "Rice's Testimony to
> 9/11 Commission Leaves Unanswered Questions." *Dallas
> Morning News* 9 Apr. 2004, final ed.: C5.

Notice that a comma separates the authors' names.

60. Article by four or more authors

You may use the phrase *et al.* (meaning "and others") for all authors but the first, or you may write out all the names. You need to use the same method in the in-text citation as you do in the works-cited list.

> Watson, Anne, et al. "Childhood Obesity on the Rise." *Daily
> Missoulian* 7 July 2003: B1.

61. Article by an unknown author

Begin the entry with the title.

> "Balmy Winter Backs Global-Warming Theory." *The Record* 14 Mar.
> 2006: A1+.

62. Article with a title in a foreign language

If the title is in a foreign language, copy it exactly as it appears on the title page, paying special attention to accent marks and capitalization.

> "Iraq, Liberati gli Ostaggi Sudcoreani." *Corriere Della Sera*
> 8 Apr. 2004: A1.

63. Article that continues to a non-consecutive page

Add a plus sign after the number of the first page.

> Saccone, Julie. "Findings May Diffuse Stem-Cell Controversy." *Saskatoon StarPhoenix* 18 Mar. 2006: A10+.

REVIEWS, EDITORIALS, LETTERS TO THE EDITOR

64. Review

> Eisenthal, Bram. "Stephen King Turns Cellphone Users into Zombies." Rev. of *Cell* by Stephen King. *Montreal Gazette* 18 Feb. 2006: H1.

65. Letter to the editor

> Lapointe, Kenneth. "Ojibway Conservation Not 'Twisted Priority.'" *Windsor Star* 18 Mar. 2006: A6.

66. Editorial

Add the word *Editorial* after the title.

> Pei, Minxin. "Don't Believe the China Hype." Editorial. *National Post* 14 Mar. 2006: A16.

67. Unsigned editorial

If the editorial is unsigned, put the title first.

> "Weighty Problem Facing Our Kids." Editorial. *Charlottetown Guardian* 14 Mar. 2006: A6.

68. Article on microfilm

Cite an article on microfilm or microfiche as you would the original.

> "Woman's Sphere is in the Home Says Premier to Women." *Winnipeg Free Press*, 27 Jan. 1914: n.p.

22e GOVERNMENT DOCUMENTS, PAMPHLETS, DISSERTATIONS, AND LETTERS IN MLA-STYLE WORKS CITED

Title

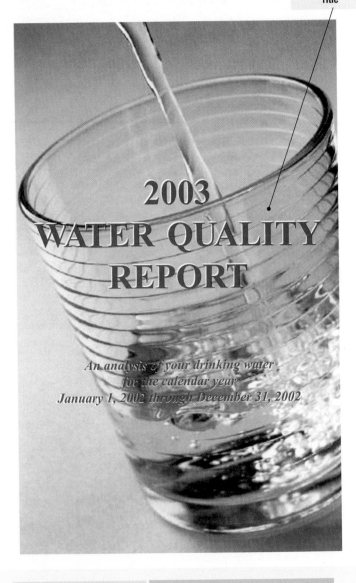

2003

WATER QUALITY

REPORT

*An analysis of your drinking water
for the calendar year
January 1, 2002 through December 31, 2002*

2003 Water Quality Report. Waterloo, ON: City of Waterloo Water
Division, 2003.

GOVERNMENT DOCUMENTS

69. Government documents

If you are citing a government document, be sure to identify the division or department that sponsored the publication, as well as the document number, after the title of the document.

Gu, Wulong, and Garu D. Sawchuk. "How Are Canadian Regions Adjusting to a Larger and More Integrated North American Market?" Economic Analysis Research Paper Series (Online) No. 039. Micro-Economic Analysis Division, Statistics Canada. Gov. doc. CS11-0027/39E-PDF 11F0027MIE, no. 39. June 13, 2006.

Indian and Northern Affairs. *After Marriage Breakdown*. Gov. of Canada no. R2-261/2003. 2003.

Kunz, Jean Lock. *Being Young and Visible*. Gov. of Canada no. RH63-1/581-08-03E. Human Resources Development Canada. 2003.

House of Commons Debates. Cat. no. X3-391/9E. Vol. 141, No. 9. 25 Apr. 2006.

BULLETINS, PAMPHLETS, AND LETTERS

70. Bulletin or pamphlet

Health Insurance for Your Pet. Winnipeg: SecuriCan General Insurance Co., 2005.

71. Published letter

Wilde, Oscar. "To Lord Alfred Douglas." 17 Feb. 1895. In *The Complete Letters of Oscar Wilde*. Ed. Merlin Holland and Rupert Hart-Davis. New York: Holt, 2000. 632-33.

72. Unpublished letter

Welty, Eudora. Letter to Elizabeth Bowen. 1 May 1951. Harry Ransom Humanities Research Center, Austin, TX.

DISSERTATIONS

73. **Published dissertation or thesis**

    Mason, Jennifer. *Civilized Creatures: Animality, Cultural Power, and
    American Literature, 1850–1901*. Diss. U of Texas at Austin,
    2000. Ann Arbor: UMI, 2000. 9992865.

74. **Unpublished dissertation or thesis**

    McMullin, Stan E. *Thomas McCulloch: The Evolution of a Liberal Mind*.
    Diss. Dalhousie U, 1975.

CONFERENCE PROCEEDINGS

75. **Published proceedings of a conference**

    Weir, Lorraine. "The Discourse of 'Civility': Strategies of
    Containment in Literary Histories of English-Canadian
    Literature." *Problems of Literary Reception/Problèmes de
    Reception Littéraire*. Ed. E. D. Blodgett and A. G. Purdy. Proc.
    of conference on Towards a History of the Literary
    Institution in Canada 1/Vers une Histoire de L'institution
    Littéraire au Canada. 16-18 Oct. 1986. Edmonton: U of
    Alberta, 1988. 24-39.

22f ONLINE PUBLICATIONS IN MLA-STYLE WORKS CITED

Name of site

Date of publication

HOMEPAGE

Author's name

Title of article

FIRST PAGE OF THE ARTICLE

Alexander, Kathryn. "Liminal Identities and Institutional Positioning: On Becoming a 'Writing Lady' in the Academy." *Inkshed* 22.3 (Fall 2005). 18 Mar. 2006 <http://www.stthomasu.ca/inkshed/nlettc05/alexander.htm>.

AUTHOR'S NAME

Authorship is sometimes hard to discern for online sources. If you know the author or creator, follow the rules for books and journals.

If the only authority you find is a group or organization, list its name after the date of publication or last revision.

NAME OF SITE AND TITLE OF PAGE OR ARTICLE

- The name of a website will usually be found on its index or homepage. If you cannot find a link back to the homepage on the page you are on, look at the URL for clues. You can work your way back through the URL, deleting sections (separated by slashes) until you come to a home or index page.

- If there is no title for the website, list it by author or creator. If it is a personal homepage, place the words *Homepage* after the name of the owner of the page.

PUBLICATION INFORMATION

Dates

List two dates for each website.

1. List the date the site was produced or last revised (often at the bottom of the page; might also be a copyright date) after the name of the site. This date might be just a year.

2. List the date you accessed the site. Place this second date just before the URL. Notice that there is no period after the date of access.

URLs

Copy the address exactly as it appears in your browser window. You can even copy and paste the address into your text for greater accuracy. Put it in angle brackets followed by a period.

Common questions about citing online sources

Where do I find the title?

Websites are often made up of many separate pages or articles. Each page or article on a website may or may not have a title. If you are citing a page that has a title, treat the title like that of an article in a periodical. Otherwise, treat the name of the website itself as you would a book.

How do I handle very long URLs?

If the URL is excessively long and complicated, give the URL of the site's search page. If the document is from a subscription service, give the URL of the service's homepage or the keyword assigned, preceded by the word *Keyword.* You can also give the sequence of links you followed, preceded by the word *Path.* Place a colon after *Keyword* or *Path.*

Note: Be sure to test your URLs as part of your proofreading process.

Sample works-cited entries for online publications

ONLINE PUBLICATIONS

76. Publication by a known author

Grundy, Isobel, et al. "Dates and ChronStructs: Dynamic Chronology in the Orlando Project." *Literary and Linguistic Computing* 15:3 (2000), 265-289. The Orlando Project. 13 Mar. 2006 <http://www.ualberta.ca/ORLANDO/>.

77. Publication by a group or organization

"Bird Check Lists." Birding in Canada. 2001. 15 Feb. 2005 <http://www.web-nat.com/bic/lists.html>.

78. Publication with an author and a group affiliation

List the name of the organization or institution after the publication date or revision date.

Edwards, Rebecca. "Socialism." *1896*. 2000. Vassar College. 20 Nov. 2001 <http://iberia.vassar.edu/1896/socialism.html#debs>.

79. Publication where the author's name is a pseudonym

If the author's or creator's name is a pseudonym or is unconventional, list it exactly as it appears on the website.

Akma. Akma's Random Thoughts. Weblog. 12 Nov. 2003. 1 Apr. 2004
    <http://akma.disseminary.org>.

ONLINE PERIODICALS

Note: Because most online periodicals do not have page numbers, you should identify the site in your paper. That way, you can avoid awkward parenthetical citations.

80. Article in a scholarly journal

The volume and issue number follow the name of the journal. The date in parentheses is the date of publication.

Caramanica, Laura. "Shared Governance: Hartford Hospital's
    Experience." *Online Journal of Issues in Nursing* 9.1 (2004).
    12 Apr. 2004 <http://www.nursingworld.org/ojin/topic23/
    tpc23_2.htm/>.

81. Article in a newspaper

The first date is the date of publication, the second is the date of access.

Boyer, Suzanne. "Some Youth Are Already Trying to Stay in Motion."
    Moose Jaw Times-Herald 14 Mar. 2006. 18 Mar. 2006
    <http://www.mjtimes.sk.ca/>.

82. Article in a popular magazine

The first date is the date of publication, the second is the date of access.

Cohen, Jesse. "When Harry Met Maggie." *Slate* 16 Nov. 2001.
    21 Nov. 2001 <http://slate.msn.com/?id=2058733>.

ONLINE BOOKS AND SCHOLARLY PROJECTS

83. Online book

Careless, J.M.S. *Canada: A Celebration of Our Heritage.* Surrey, BC:
    Heritage 1997. 20 Mar. 2006 <http://www.canadianheritage
    .org/books/index.htm>.

84. Online scholarly project

If you are citing a page that has a title, treat the title like that of an article in a periodical. Otherwise, treat the name of the website itself as you would a book, as in the following example.

The Orlando Project: A History of Women's Writing in the British Isles.
    Edmonton: U of Alberta. 1 July 2005 <http://www.ualberta
    .ca/ORLANDO/>.

85. Document within a scholarly project

Give the author and title of the work first, as well as its date and place of publication if it is a book. Then give the name of the project or database, its editor, version or revision date, affiliation, and date of access. The address is the address of the document itself.

> Sutherland, Patricia D. "Strands of Culture Contact: Dorset-Norse Inter-
> actions in the Canadian Eastern Arctic." *Identities and Cultural*
> *Contacts in the Arctic: Proceedings from a Conference at the Danish*
> *National Museum, Copenhagen, November 30 to December 2, 1999.*
> Ed. Martin Appelt et al. Copenhagen: The Danish National Museum
> & Danish Polar Center, 2000. Helluland Archaeology Project. 14 Mar.
> 2006 <http://www.civilisations.ca/academ/articles/suth_01e.html>.

LIBRARY DATABASES

86. Work from a library database

Give the print publication information, then the name of the database (underlined or italicized), the name of the vendor, the name of the library or library system, date of access, and the URL.

> Haigh, Susan. "League of Women Voters Pushing for Campaign
> Finance Reform." *Associated Press State & Local Wire.*
> 22 Nov. 2005. *LexisNexis Academic.* LexisNexis. D. B.
> Weldon Lib., U of Western Ontario. 19 Mar. 2006
> <http://web.lexis-nexis.com.proxy2.lib.uwo.ca>.

SUBSCRIPTION SERVICES

87. Work from a personal subscription service

For a personal subscription service that allows you to retrieve material by entering a keyword, write *Keyword* followed by a colon and the word you entered at the end of the entry.

> "Anasazi." *Compton's Encyclopedia Online.* Vers. 2.0. 1997. America
> Online. 12 Dec. 2001. Keyword: Anasazi.

ONLINE GOVERNMENT PUBLICATIONS

88. Online government publication

Begin with the same information you would give for printed government works and conclude with information for the electronic source.

> Canada Revenue Agency. *Fairness and Client Rights.* 12 Jan. 2005.
> 1 Apr. 2006 <http://www.cra-arc.gc.ca/agency/fairness/
> rights-e.html>.

22g   CD-ROM, SOFTWARE, AND UNEDITED ONLINE SOURCES IN MLA-STYLE WORKS CITED

Title

THE NORTON SHAKESPEARE WORKSHOP CD-ROM

EDITED BY
MARK ROSE
University of California,
Santa Barbara

Content Copyright © 1998 W. W. Norton & Company • Software Copyright © CIT/BookWorm
The text of the plays on this CD-ROM has been authorized by the Oxford University Press for world use.

Author/Editor

Publication information

Rose, Mark, Ed. *The Norton Shakespeare Workshop*. CD-ROM. New York:
Norton, 1998.

PUBLICATIONS ON CD-ROM

89. CD-ROM by a known author

When page numbers aren't available, use the author's name in the text to avoid an awkward parenthetical citation.

> Hagen, Edward, and Phillip Walker. *Human Evolution: A Multimedia*
> *Guide to the Fossil Record.* 2002 ed. CD-ROM. New York: Norton,
> 2002.

90. Periodically revised database on CD-ROM

For a CD-ROM database that is often updated (e.g., *ProQuest* or *InfoTrac*), provide the publication dates for the article you are citing as well as for the data disc itself.

> Roper, Jill. "Why Don't We Teach Reading in High School?" *Journal*
> *of Secondary Education* 22 (1999): 423-40. *ProQuest General*
> *Periodicals.* CD-ROM. UMI-ProQuest. June 2000.

91. Multidisc CD-ROM

Follow the publication medium with either the total number of discs or the number of the specific disc you are using. Mentioning the CD-ROM in the text itself is preferable to a parenthetical citation.

> *The Great Books Series I and II.* CBC Audio. CD-ROM. 2 discs.
> Toronto: CBC Broadcasting, 2004.

SOFTWARE

92. Computer software

Provide the author's name (if known), the version number (if any), the manufacturer, and the date. You can also list the operating system, if relevant.

> *Fireworks.* Vers. 8. Macromedia, 2004.

93. Online synchronous communication (MOOs, MUDs)

Provide the speaker and/or site, the title and date of the session, the forum for communication (if specified), the date of access, and the electronic address.

> Sirius, B. Discussion of popularity of *Harry Potter*. 12 Dec. 2000.
>
> LinguaMOO. 24 Nov. 2001 <telnet:lingua.utdallas.edu8090>.

94. Email communication

Give the name of the writer, the subject line, a description of the message, and the date.

> Wilson, Samuel. Email to the author. 18 Sept. 2006.

95. Online newsgroup or listserv posting

Give the author's name (or alias), the subject line, the descriptor *Online posting*, the date of posting, the name of the newsgroup or listserv, the date of access, and the URL of the posting.

> IrishMom. "Re: Spain Will Send Troops to Aid US." Online posting.
>
> 2 Nov. 2001. Ireland List. 21 Nov. 2001
>
> <ireland_list-og@email.rutgers.ed>.

96. Course homepage

Begin with the instructor's name, the name of the course, the words *Course homepage*, the dates of the course, the name of the department, school, date of access, and URL.

> Sundaram, Mark S. English 240Y Old English Language and Literature.
>
> Course syllabus. Sept.-Dec. 2005. Dept. of English. U of
>
> Toronto. 17 Mar. 2006 <http://www.chass.utoronto
>
> .ca/~msundara/eng240/syllabus.htm>.

97. Personal homepage

If there is no title for the website, list it by author or creator. If it is a personal homepage, place the words *Homepage* after the name of the owner of the page.

> Stallman, Richard. Home page. 21 Mar. 2004. 8 Apr. 2004
>
> <http://www.stallman.org/>.

98. Entry in a weblog

Citing a weblog entry is similar to citing other websites. In many cases the author's name will be only a first name, pseudonym, or email address. Often there is no sponsoring organization mentioned as in the example below.

> Wells, Paul. "It's Wide Open for Dan Now." Weblog posting. *Inkless*
>
> *Wells*. 13 Mar. 2006. 15 Mar. 2006 <http://weblogs.macleans
>
> .ca/paulwells/>.

WORKS PUBLISHED IN MULTIPLE FORMATS

99. Work in more than one medium

Specify all of the media that constitute the publication (e.g., book, CD-ROM, diskette) or list only the media you used.

> Scowen, Paul. *21st Century Astronomy*. Book, CD-ROM.
>
> New York: Norton, 2002.

22h VISUAL SOURCES IN MLA-STYLE WORKS CITED

Title

Publication information

The Colorado Plateau. Map. Mancos: Time Traveler Maps, 1999.

VISUAL SOURCES

100. Cartoon

> Chast, Roz. "Are You in Your Goddess Years?" Cartoon. *New Yorker*
> 10 Mar. 2004: 113.

101. Advertisement

> Lancome Paris. Advertisement. *Inside Entertainment* Mar. 2006: 1-2.

102. Map, graph, or chart

> *Western Ontario*. Map. Oshawa: Peter Heiler, 2004.

103. Table reproduced in your text

This is how a table might appear in your text:

In *The Republic*, Plato explains how the three parts of the individual soul should be repeated in the structure of the ideal city-state (see Table 1).

Soul	Reason	Courage	Appetites
State	Elite guardians	Soldiers	Masses

Table 1. Plato's politics, table from Richard Osborne, *Philosophy for Beginners* (New York: Writers and Readers, 1992) 15.

This is how a table appears on your list of works cited.

Work Cited

Plato's Politics. Table. New York: Writers and Readers, 1992. 15.

104. Painting, sculpture, or photograph

Provide the artist's name, the title of the work, the name of the institution or individual who owns the work, and the city.

Reid, Bill. *The Spirit of Haida Gwaii*. 1991. Canadian Embassy, Washington, D.C.

If you are citing a photograph of a work, give the information for the work, followed by the publication information for the source that you got the photograph from. Include the slide, plate, figure, or page number, as relevant. In the text, mentioning the work and the artist in the text itself is preferable to a parenthetical citation.

ONLINE VISUAL SOURCES

105. Online map

Xpeditions Atlas. Map. *National Geographic.com*. 2003. National Geographic Society. 24 Nov. 2004 <http:// www .nationalgeographic.com/xpeditions/atlas/>.

106. Online work of art

Carr, Emily. *Totem Poles, Kitseukla*. 1912. Vancouver Art Gallery. 16 Mar. 2006 <http://www.vanartgallery.bc.ca/permanent_ carr.cfm>.

107. Online cartoon

Doligan, Tim. "Coffin Up Justice." Cartoon. Recent Political Cartoons. 19 Mar. 2006 <http://www.mapleleafweb.com/community/ editorial/cartoons/archive/index.html>.

22i MULTIMEDIA SOURCES IN MLA-STYLE WORKS CITED

108. Musical composition

If you have the sheet music or a score, list the publication information. If not, just provide the composer, the title of the composition, and the year.

Gershwin, George. *Cuban Overture*. 1932.

109. Sound recording

> Barenaked Ladies. "If I Had a Million Dollars." *Gordon*. Sire Records,
>   1992.

110. Online video or sound file

> "Irregular around the Margins." Perf. James Gandolfini and Edie
>   Falco. *The Sopranos*. 2004. HBO. 5 Apr. 2004 <http://www.hbo
>   .com/sopranos/episode/season5/episode57.shtml>.

111. Film

> *C.R.A.Z.Y.* Dir. Jean-Marc Vallée. Perf. Michel Côté, Marc-André
>   Grondin, Danielle Proulx. TVA Films, 2005.

112. Video or DVD

> *The Mikado*. By W. S. Gilbert and Arthur Sullivan. Stratford Festival.
>   8 Feb. 2000.

113. Television or radio program

Provide the title of the episode or segment, followed by the title of the program and series (if any). After the titles, list any performers, narrators, directors, or others who might be pertinent. Then give the name of the network, call numbers and city for any local station, and the broadcast date.

> "The Quality of Mercy." *Da Vinci's Inquest*. Perf. Nicholas Campbell,
>   Ian Tracey, Donnelly Rhodes. CBC. 28 Oct. 1998.

114. Telephone interview

Minnelli, Liza. Telephone interview. 5 Mar. 2003.

115. Broadcast interview

St. John, Lara and Scott. Interview with Jill LaForty. *In Performance.* CBC Radio 2. Toronto. 10 Feb. 1999.

116. Musical, dramatic, dance, or artistic performance

The Lord of the Rings. By J.R.R. Tolkien. Adapted by Shaun McKenna and Matthew Warchus. Dir. Matthew Warchus. Perf. Brent Carver, James Loye, Michael Therriault, Evan Buliung. Princess of Wales Theatre. Toronto. 24 Mar. 2006.

117. Speech, debate, mediated discussion, or public talk

Ignatieff, Michael. "Human Rights and the Rights of States: Are They on a Collision Course?" Hagey Lecture Series. U of Waterloo. Waterloo. 24 Jan. 2001.

22j INFORMATIONAL NOTES

The MLA style is designed to avoid the need for either footnotes or endnotes. Documentation should be handled using in-text citations and a list of works cited. However, two kinds of notes sometimes appear in MLA style. Notes may be placed at the bottom of the page or at the end of the paper.

Content notes supply additional information that would interrupt the flow of the text, yet may be important to provide the context of a source.

Much speculation has blamed electronic media, especially television, for an alleged decline in literacy, following Newton N. Minow's famous 1961 description of television as a "vast wasteland."[1]

The note explains who Minow was and why the remark was newsworthy.

[1]Minow, the newly appointed chairman of the U.S. Federal Communications Commission, told the assembled executives of the National Association of Broadcasters in May 1961 that "[w]hen television is bad, nothing is worse" (Adams). Minow's efforts to upgrade programming were met with cries of censorship from the television industry, and Minow resigned two years later.

You need to include any sources you use in notes in the list of works cited.

Work Cited

Adams, Val. "F.C.C. Head Bids TV Men, Reform 'Vast Wasteland.' " *New York Times* 10 May 1961, late ed.: 1+.

Bibliographic notes give either evaluative comments about sources or additional references.

"Fordism" is a summary term for the system of mass production consolidated by Henry Ford in the early decades of the twentieth century.[1]

The note gives the origin of the term "Fordism."

[1]The term *Fordism* was first used by Italian political theorist Antonio Gramsci in his prison notebooks, written while he was jailed under Mussolini's fascist dictatorship.

Work Cited

Gramsci, Antonio. *Selections from the Prison Notebooks of Antonio Gramsci.* Ed. and trans. Quintin Hoare and Geoffrey Nowell Smith. New York: International, 1971.

22k SAMPLE RESEARCH PAPER WITH MLA DOCUMENTATION

Chapters 16 through 21 discuss how to plan and write a research paper. The sample informative research paper that follows, written by Langston East, is documented and formatted according to MLA guidelines. The paper is annotated to show specific features of MLA style and to show how the works-cited page is organized.

Include your last name and page number as page header, beginning with the first page, 1/2″ from the top.

East 1

Langston East

Early Modern Women 1400–1600

Professor Pelham

April 3, 2006

Centre the title. Do not underline the title, put it inside quotation marks, or type it in all capital letters.

Lady Anne Clifford's Diary as a Means of Resistance and Self-Definition

Spurred on by a Protestant endorsement of self-writing and an emerging interest in personal history, many Englishwomen began journals in the early modern period. These journals represent an important moment in the history of the self. The process of looking inward can be given credit in the formation of the modern idea of personhood; it was an essential component in the creation of an inner life for women. Diary writing contributed immensely to the development of the feminine consciousness. The religiously sanctioned activity of diary writing gave women a chance to consider themselves separate from the complicated web of relationships that defined their daily life. On the pages of her diary, writing under the auspices of spiritual contemplation, a woman could consider herself as a genderless human being and alone in the eyes of God.

East 2

The diary of Lady Anne Clifford is among the earliest surviving examples of self-writing by English women. The record left by this noblewoman invokes the theme of self-fashioning. Although Lady Clifford's diary makes frequent mention of her strong belief in God, the impetus for her writing was less concerned with the divine than with the historical. Engaged in a decades-long legal battle over the right to her ancestral lands, Lady Clifford resisted the will of two husbands and even that of King James. Her diary documents this remarkable perseverance, placing it within the larger context of Lady Clifford's project to write her family's history.

When examining these writings, it is important to consider that their creation was a task, just as needlework and household management were for noblewomen of the day. Reading an early modern woman's diary as an exact account of her daily life and nothing more prevents full understanding and awareness of its value. Lady Anne Clifford's diary is an important historical record, but its foremost value is as a document of feminine self-creation. Rather than straightforward accounts of daily life, these diaries recount a struggle for the word. In recording the world as she saw it, Lady Clifford formed her own sphere of influence. During the misogynistic cultural backlash of the rule of James I, she used her privileged position in society to engage in self-definition. She understood the power and finality of writing and succeeded in her efforts to control the written word to achieve her own ends.

A central issue of Lady Clifford's diary is her affirmation of selfhood, but it was also created for a

Specify 1″ margins all around. Double-space everything. Indent each paragraph five spaces (1/2″ on the ruler in your word processing program).

East's thesis appears here, at the end of her second paragraph. The preceding paragraph establishes a context for her thesis.

specific purpose separate from inward contemplation. With almost legal precision, Lady Clifford's *Knole Diary*, begun in 1616, records the daily events of her life, organized in order of months. This somewhat unusual format indicates that the diary was probably completed from a series of earlier diaries condensed into one book, part of a larger project of condensing and publishing her diaries that Lady Clifford embarked upon in the last part of her life. Highborn and remarkably well educated, Lady Anne Clifford was involved in a struggle lasting nearly 50 years over the ownership of her familial land. She refused under any circumstances to part with ownership of it and was punished by both of her husbands for rejecting various offers of money in exchange for her repudiation of her right to the estate, Westmorland.

Cite publications within the text by the name of the author (or authors).

    Supported by her mother, Lady Margaret Clifford, Lady Clifford saw herself as the sole guardian of her family's ancient land, and cast herself in this role in order to stand steadfast as its protector. Lady Clifford used her diary to establish her historic and familial right to Westmorland, "the lands of my ancient inheritance" (Clifford qtd. in Martin 246), as well as her passionate love of the property: "I told him that I would never part with Westmorland upon any condition whatsoever" (Clifford 265). She writes variants of this sentence in reference to arguments with her husbands and King James. Noting her mother's desire to be interred away from Westmorland, she laments, "I took it as a sign that I should be dispossessed of the inheritance of my forefathers" (Clifford 254).

East 4

By frequently and forcefully reaffirming her right to Westmorland in the text of her journal, Lady Clifford provided a steadying ground against which to brace herself for the trials of everyday life. Embattled on all sides, Lady Clifford weathered not only the disapproval and anger of her first husband, Richard Sackville, Earl of Dorset—who at different times limited her monetary allowance, removed their child from her custody, and essentially abandoned her company—but also of the public at large:

> Presently after dinner Mr Oberton and I had a great deal of talk, he telling me how much I was condemned in the world, and what strange censures most folks made of my courses. So as I kneeled down to my prayers and desired God to send a good end to these troublesome businesses, my trust being wholly in him that has always helped me. (Clifford 262)

Quotations of more than four lines should be indented 1″ or 10 spaces. Do not use quotation marks. Introduce block quotations rather than just dropping them into the text.

Her continued strength in the face of such wide disapproval found its source in Lady Clifford's belief that her position as sole heir of her family was not only a matter of bloodline, but also divine interference. The wording of her description of her relationship with God in the quotation above is important because it recognizes God as helping Lady Clifford, rather than Lady Clifford struggling for God's favour. Assured in her right to Westmorland, Lady Clifford also used her diary to air her daily emotional state. Uniquely candid for a woman of her time period, Lady Clifford openly records episodes of grief and depression; it was a matter of daily occurrence provoked by her situation and indicative of the necessity

East 5

of her victory. Lady Clifford records weeping "bitterly" on several occasions, and describes herself variously as "sorrowful," "troubled," "afflicted," "melancholy," and "fearful." She does not list her miseries to elicit pity from the reader; at the time of the *Knole Diary*'s writing, Lady Clifford could not have been certain anyone would read it. Her sadness is the result of her plight; in her diary, it serves as proof that her suffering is unjust and must be stopped.

Some of Lady Clifford's more elegant turns of phrase have been cited as evidence of a poetic gift. The most famous is "I may truly say, I am like an owl in the desert" (Clifford 252); almost as notable is "I lived in both these my lords' great families as the river of Roan or Rodamus, runs through the lake of Geneva, without mingling any part of its streams with that lake" (qtd. in Martin 246). More than mere purple prose, elaborate pronouncements such as these serve to highlight both Lady Clifford's superior education and independent character. Such were the personality traits of a born leader and the heir to a great tradition. Lady Clifford, recognizing herself as both, writ bold her qualifications as the rightful owner of Westmorland. Similarly, entries that touch upon Lady Clifford's interest in and concern for her tenants are indicative of her efforts to cast herself as the ancestral protector of the realm:

> Upon the 17th I rid into Whinfell park, and there
> I willed the tenants that were carrying of hay at
> Billain Town that they should keep the money in
> their own hands till it were known who had a
> right to it . . . Upon the 29th I sent my folks

East 6

> into the park to make hay, where, they being
> interrupted by my uncle Cumberland's people,
> two of my uncle's people were hurt by Mr
> Kidd . . . complaint was made to the judges at
> Carlisle. (Clifford 256)

Lady Clifford's tumultuous relationship with her first
husband is well documented in her *Diary*. She is frank
about their many conflicts and frequent periods of unrest,
but never condemns him. In a show of verisimilitude
remarkable for any writer of her time, Lady Clifford paints
a portrait of her marriage as complex and unstable:
sometimes tender, others tough. Richard Sackville was an
avid gambler who accrued many debts; his interest in
Westmorland was financially motivated, as the cash
settlement Lady Clifford stood to receive would have
allowed him to become more solvent. The Earl of Dorset
was also a bon vivant, and he had a particularly close
relationship with a manservant named Matthew. Lady
Clifford often contrasts her embattled existence with her
husband's easygoing leisure, but she also notes Sackville's
good qualities. In her *Diary* he is described a good father
and occasionally loving husband. Lady Clifford especially
notes instances of courtesy and respect shown her by
Sackville in public situations: "I was much bound to my
lord, for he was far kinder to me in all these businesses
than I expected and was very unwilling that the King
should do me any public disgrace" (Clifford 260).

The realistic view presented of Lady Clifford's marriage
is integral to the text, for through these descriptions she
makes it clear that her role as the Clifford heir is both

The author's name and page number appear in parentheses after the end of the block quotation. No period is needed after the citation.

East 7

more important and more righteous than her position as Sackville's wife. Her responsibilities as the inheritor and caretaker of Westmorland also take precedence over her position as a mother on a daily scale. This was illustrated when Sackville removed their young daughter, Isabelle, from their home as a sort of punishment in response to Lady Clifford's refusal to release her claim to Westmorland. Her efforts to preserve the estate that her daughter was necessarily heir to, however, indicate not only love and concern for her daughter but an interest in the greater good of the Clifford line. In this way Lady Anne Clifford was acting as a matriarch, protecting Westmorland for her daughter just as her mother, Lady Margaret Clifford, had fought for the estate for her own daughter.

Through the device of her diary, Lady Anne Clifford created the world as she saw it, and she set out to make that world a reality. Placing herself in the typically male role of noble heir allowed her to subvert the expectations of a wife, mother and noblewoman in the interest of a higher purpose—the preservation of her legacy. The Appleby Castle Triptych (see Figure 1), a series of portraits painted first in 1589 and then copied onto a single canvas around 1646, is another important document of Lady Clifford's self-fashioning. The triptych includes two portraits of Lady Clifford, one as a young woman and the other as an aged widow. The portraits flank a central painting of George Clifford, Earl of Cumberland, and Lady Margaret Russell with their two young children: Lady Anne Clifford and her brother Henry, who died young.

East 8

Figure 1. The Appleby Castle Triptych ("The Great Picture") of Lady Anne Clifford <www.open.ac.uk/ Arts/a220/greatpic.htm>

Do not include a page number for items without pagination, such as websites.

Lady Clifford once wrote in her diary that she "made good books and virtuous thoughts" (qtd. in Martin 246) her companions, and both are represented in the triptych. Each painting's background boasts a bookshelf as well as documents related to the heritage of Lady Clifford's family. As a young woman she is posed with a mandolin and a neat assemblage of books arranged on the shelves above her head. As a widow, Lady Clifford wears her preferred black and is accompanied by a greyhound and a small cat; the books behind her are in a state of disarray, which Mary Ellen Lamb proposes may be intended to suggest "mastery embodied in [the books'] continual use" (Lamb 365). Most strikingly, the only images of Lady Clifford's husbands are small portraits within the portraits hanging on the wall behind both the young and old Anne Clifford.

The Appleby Triptych ("The Great Picture") vividly portrays the self that Lady Anne Clifford meticulously constructed through the use of her diary. Lady Clifford's high level of education and erudite knowledge of the intricacies of land ownership prove that she took her role as the Clifford heir seriously—so seriously that this role is the one she chose to define her life. The other details of her existence recede into the background: her vocations as wife and mother are secondary to her divine appointment as protector of Westmorland.

The degree to which Lady Clifford's self-fashioning succeeded is most apparent, however, in her eventual fate: in 1643, her uncle's son Henry, the claimant to her estate, died without an heir. After the end of the Civil War six years later Lady Clifford took control of Westmorland, where for the remaining three decades of her life she ruled the surrounding area as "High Sheriffess of Westmorland and Lady of the Honour of Skipton in Craven" (Martin 245). Lady Clifford's tenacious insistence on her role as her family's rightful heir eventually won her the position that she had cast herself in for the duration of her life.

Lady Clifford's diary allowed her to visit places otherwise closed to women and to envision a life outside the traditional boundaries of masculine domination. The control over the word exercised by this woman was not a unique phenomenon. By the close of the seventeenth century, diary keeping for women, first necessitated by spiritual and historical record keeping, had become an essential instrument of the female self. Elizabeth Bury, writing in the late seventeenth century, concluded, "if it were not for her *Diary,* she would neither know what she *was,* or what she *did,* or what she *had*" (qtd in Botonaki 9).

East 10

Works Cited

Belkamp, Jan van (attr.). *The Great Picture*. 1646. Abbot

Hall Art Gallery, Kendal, Cumbria, UK/Bridgeman Art

Library. 28 June 2006 <www.open.ac.uk/

Arts/a220/greatpic.htm>.

Botonaki, Effie. "Seventeenth Century Englishwomen's

Spiritual Diaries: Self-Examination, Covenanting, and

Account Keeping." *Sixteenth Century Journal* 30.1,

(1999): 3-21.

Clifford, Lady Anne. "From *The Diary of Lady Anne Clifford*

(1616-1619)." *Women Writers in Renaissance

England*. Ed. Randall Martin. Longman Annotated

Texts. London: Longman, 1997. 245-75.

Lamb, Mary Ellen. "The Agency of the Split Subject: Lady

Anne Clifford and the Uses of Reading." *English

Literary Renaissance* 22 (1992): 347-68.

Martin, Randall, ed. "From *The Diary of Lady Anne Clifford*

(1616-1619)." *Women Writers in Renaissance

England*. Longman Annotated Texts. London:

Longman, 1997. 245-75.

Rose, Mary Beth. "Gender, Genre and History: Seventeenth-

Century English Women and the Art of

Autobiography." *Women in the Middle Ages and the

Renaissance, Literary and Historical Perspectives*. Ed.

Mary Beth Rose. Syracuse: Syracuse UP, 1986.

Centre "Works Cited" on a new page.

Italicize or underline the titles of books and periodicals.

Go through your text and make sure all the sources you have used are in the list of works cited.

WRITING SMART

Putting an MLA works-cited list on a website

The convention of putting the URL inside angle brackets creates no difficulties for a works-cited list on paper. Anything in angle brackets on a website, however, will be interpreted by your browser as an HTML tag, and it will not show up on your webpage. To get the angle brackets on a webpage requires using a special name for the opening and closing brackets.

< for <
> for >

You may have to go into the HTML file and type in these special names for the angle brackets if your webpage editor does not do it for you. You will know that the conversion to the special names has not been made if the angle brackets and what is inside them do not show up on your webpage.

APA
Documentation

- Where do I put the date in APA documentation style? (23a)

- How do I cite a brochure in APA style? (23b)

- Do I need to cite the date that I visited a website when citing online sources? (23d)

7 APA DOCUMENTATION

Social science disciplines, including political science, linguistics, psychology, sociology, and education, frequently use the American Psychological Association (APA) documentation style. This style uses in-text citations (that is, the author's last name and initials, date, and page number appear in parentheses following a quotation in the text of the paper). The full citation appears at the end of the text under the heading "References." The reference citation also foregrounds the author and date of the publication by placing them first. By highlighting the author and date of the references, APA style emphasizes not only the originator of the idea but also how recently the source was published. Readers assess the significance of the work in APA disciplines based partly on how up-to-date the writer is on the research in the area. Another notable aspect of APA style is that it obscures the gender of the author by citing only initials.

APA style highlights the author and date of the work cited (these appear first in each entry—see Moshenrose and Braitman's References section, partially reproduced below, in the sample student essay). This highlighting indicates that disciplines that use this style value the source of the idea and how contemporary it is. Other documentation styles emphasize different aspects of the research.

Moshenrose and Braitman 15

References

Akan, G. E., & Grilo, C. M. (1995). Sociocultural influences on eating attitudes and behaviors, body image, and psychological functioning: A comparison of African-American, Asian-American, and Caucasian college women. *International Journal of Eating Disorders, 18,* 181–187.

Altabe, M. N. (1998). Ethnicity and body image: Quantitative and qualitative analysis. *International Journal of Eating Disorders, 23,* 153–159.

Cash, T. F., & Henry, P. E. (1995). Women's body images: The results of a national survey in the U.S.A. *Sex Roles, 33,* 19–28.

Visit *The Brief Penguin Handbook* Companion Website at
www.pearsoned.ca/faigley/

MyCanadianCompLab
Where writing and research help is a click away.
MyCanadianCompLab may be packaged with your textbook.
If not, it can be purchased from your college or university's bookstore.
Go to **www.pearsoned.ca/highered/mycanadiancomplab/**
for a tour.

APA CHAPTER 23

APA Documentation

(continued next page)

Social sciences disciplines, including political science, linguistics, psychology, sociology, and education, frequently use the American Psychological Association (APA) documentation style. The APA style is similar to the MLA style in many ways. Both styles use parenthetical citations in the body of the text, with complete bibliographical citations in the list of references at the end. Both styles avoid using footnotes for references. For a detailed treatment of APA style, consult the *Publication Manual of the American Psychological Association*, fifth edition (2001).

APA style emphasizes the date of publication. When you cite an author's name in the body of your paper, always include the date of publication. Notice too that the APA style includes the abbreviation for page (p.) in front of the page number. A comma separates each element of the citation.

Zukin (2004) observes that teens today begin to shop for themselves at age 13 or 14, "the same age when lower-class children, in the past, became apprentices or went to work in factories" (p. 50).

If the author's name is not mentioned in the sentence, the reference looks like this:

> One sociologist notes that teens today begin to shop for themselves at age 13 or 14, "the same age when lower-class children, in the past, became apprentices or went to work in factories" (Zukin, 2004, p. 50).

The corresponding entry in the references list would be

> Zukin, S. (2004). *Point of purchase: How shopping changed American culture.* New York: Routledge.

23a IN-TEXT CITATIONS IN APA STYLE

Paraphrase, summary, or short quotation

In APA style a short quotation has fewer than 40 words.

> "The appeal of a shopping spree," one sociologist comments, "is not that you'll buy a lot of stuff; the appeal is that, among all the stuff you buy, you'll find what you truly desire" (Zukin, 2004, p. 112).

In this example, the author's name is provided inside the parentheses at the end of the sentence.

The author's name is provided in the parenthetical reference.

Put the author's name in a signal phrase in your sentence, particularly when you want to add an affiliation or title to indicate the authority of your source.

> "The appeal of a shopping spree," noted sociologist Sharon Zukin comments, "is not that you'll buy a lot of stuff; the appeal is that, among all the stuff you buy, you'll find what you truly desire" (2004, p. 112).

Note that the period comes *after* the parentheses.

The author of the quotation is clearly named in the sentence, so only the date and page number are needed in the parenthetical reference.

Quotations 40 words or longer

Orlean (2001) has attempted to explain the popularity of the painter Thomas Kinkade:

> People like to own things they think are valuable. . . . The high price of limited editions is part of their appeal; it implies that they are choice and exclusive, and that only a certain class of people will be able to afford them. (p. 128)

| The sentence introducing the quotation names the author. | The date appears in parentheses immediately following the author's name. | Note that the period appears before the parentheses in an indented "block" quotation. |

Where do you put the date?

You have two choices. You can put the date (1) in your text in parentheses:

Zhang, Liu, and Cao (2001) specify . . .

or (2) between the author's name and the page number in the citation note.

. . . visual languages (Zhang, Liu, & Cao, 2001, p. 192).

For translations, reprints, and later editions, either put *trans.* or *revised* before the date of the source you have, or give the original date, if known.

(O'Brien, trans. 1973) or (O'Brien 1941/1973).

When do you need to give a page number?

- Give the page number for all quotations.
- For electronic sources that do not provide page numbers, give the paragraph number when available. Use the abbreviation *para.* or the symbol ¶.
- If the source does not include page numbers, it is preferable to reference the work and the author in the text.

In Jason Reitman's 2006 film *Thank You for Smoking, . . .*

Sample in-text citations

1. Author named in your text

Astrobiologist Ranjit Patel (2006) argues that Enceladus, one of Saturn's moons, may have "extraterrestrial life" (p. 3).

2. Author not named in your text

According to Statistics Canada figures in 2006, women in 2003 were actually earning "slightly less—2 %" than they had compared to men in 1995 (Grisson, 2006, p. 254).

3. Work by a single author

(Patel, 2006, p. 3)

4. Work by two authors

List both authors' last names, joined with an ampersand.

(Suzuki & Irabu, 2002, p. 404).

If you cite the authors' names in a sentence, use *and* in place of the ampersand.

> Suzuki and Irabu (2002) report . . .

5. Work by three to five authors

The authors' last names follow the order of the title page.

> (Francisco, Vaughn, & Romano, 2001, p. 7).

Subsequent references can use the first name and *et al.*

> (Francisco et al., 2001, p. 17)

6. Work by six or more authors

Use the first author's last name and *et al.* for all in-text references.

> (Swallit et al., 2004, p. 49)

7. Work by a group or organization

Identify the group in text and place the page number in parentheses.

> The National Organization for Women (2001) observed that this "generational shift in attitudes towards marriage and childrearing" will have profound consequences (p. 325).

If you use the name of the group in an in-text citation, the first time you cite the source put its acronym (if there is one) in brackets.

> (National Organization for Women [NOW], 2001)

Use the acronym in subsequent in-text citations.

> (NOW, 2001)

8. Work by an unknown author

Use a shortened version of the title in place of the author's name.

("Derailing the Peace Process," 2003, p. 44)

9. Two works by one author with the same copyright date

Assign the dates letters (a, b, etc.) according to their alphabetical arrangement in the references list.

The majority of books written about co-authorship focus on partners of the same sex (Laird, 2001a, p. 351).

10. Parts of an electronic source

If an online or other electronic source does not provide page numbers, use the paragraph number preceded by either the paragraph symbol ¶ or the abbreviation *para.*

(Robinson, 2004, ¶7)

11. Two or more sources within the same sentence

Place each citation directly after the statement it supports.

"Some surveys report an increase in homelessness rates (Alford, 2004) while others chart a slight decrease (Rice, 2003a) . . ."

If you need to cite two or more works within the same parentheses, list them in the order they appear in the references list.

(Alford, 2004; Rice, 2003a)

12. Work quoted in another source

Saunders and Kellman's study (as cited in Rice, 2003a)

23b BOOKS AND NON-PERIODICAL SOURCES IN THE APA-STYLE REFERENCES LIST

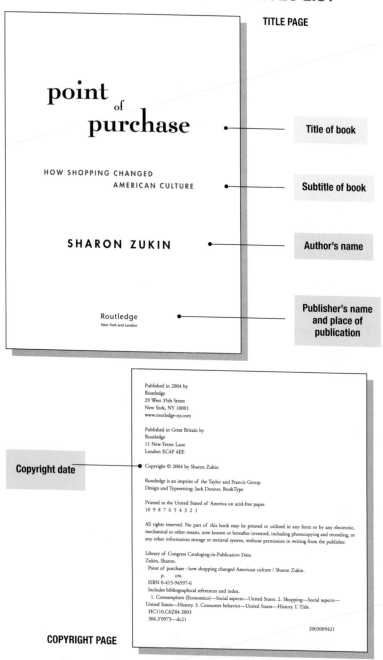

TITLE PAGE

point of purchase — Title of book

HOW SHOPPING CHANGED
AMERICAN CULTURE — Subtitle of book

SHARON ZUKIN — Author's name

Routledge
New York and London — Publisher's name and place of publication

Published in 2004 by
Routledge
29 West 35th Street
New York, NY 10001
www.routledge-ny.com

Published in Great Britain by
Routledge
11 New Fetter Lane
London EC4P 4EE

Copyright date — Copyright © 2004 by Sharon Zukin

Routledge is an imprint of the Taylor and Francis Group.
Design and Typesetting: Jack Donner, BookType

Printed in the United Stated of America on acid-free paper.
10 9 8 7 6 5 4 3 2 1

All rights reserved. No part of this book may be printed or utilized in any form or by any electronic,
mechanical or other means, now known or hereafter invented, including photocopying and recording, or
any other information storage or retrieval system, without permission in writing from the publisher.

Library of Congress Cataloging-in-Publication Data
Zukin, Sharon.
  Point of purchase : how shopping changed American culture / Sharon Zukin.
     p.   cm.
  ISBN 0-415-94597-6
  Includes bibliographical references and index.
   1. Consumption (Economics)—Social aspects—United States. 2. Shopping—Social aspects—
United States—History. 3. Consumer behavior—United States—History. I. Title.
  HC110.C6Z84 2003
  306.3'0973—dc21

                                                                          2003009421

COPYRIGHT PAGE

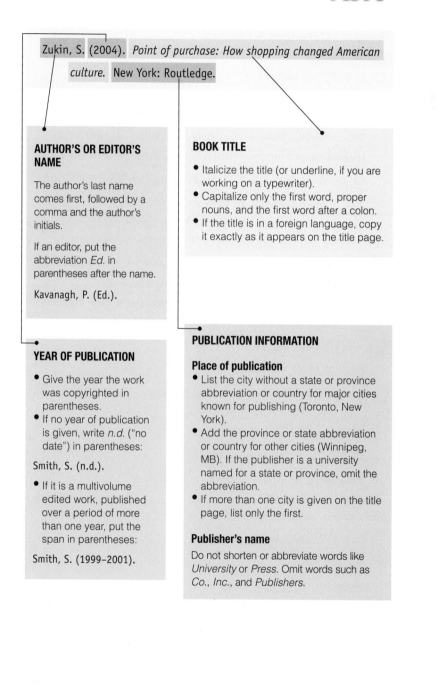

Zukin, S. (2004). *Point of purchase: How shopping changed American culture.* New York: Routledge.

AUTHOR'S OR EDITOR'S NAME

The author's last name comes first, followed by a comma and the author's initials.

If an editor, put the abbreviation *Ed.* in parentheses after the name.

Kavanagh, P. (Ed.).

BOOK TITLE

- Italicize the title (or underline, if you are working on a typewriter).
- Capitalize only the first word, proper nouns, and the first word after a colon.
- If the title is in a foreign language, copy it exactly as it appears on the title page.

YEAR OF PUBLICATION

- Give the year the work was copyrighted in parentheses.
- If no year of publication is given, write *n.d.* ("no date") in parentheses:

Smith, S. (n.d.).

- If it is a multivolume edited work, published over a period of more than one year, put the span in parentheses:

Smith, S. (1999–2001).

PUBLICATION INFORMATION

Place of publication
- List the city without a state or province abbreviation or country for major cities known for publishing (Toronto, New York).
- Add the province or state abbreviation or country for other cities (Winnipeg, MB). If the publisher is a university named for a state or province, omit the abbreviation.
- If more than one city is given on the title page, list only the first.

Publisher's name
Do not shorten or abbreviate words like *University* or *Press*. Omit words such as *Co.*, *Inc.*, and *Publishers*.

Sample references for books

ONE AUTHOR

13. Book by one author

The author's last name comes first, followed by a comma and the first initial of the author's first name and middle initial, if any.

> Ball, E. (2000). *Slaves in the family*. New York: Ballantine Books.

If an editor, put the abbreviation *Ed.* in parentheses after the name.

> Kavanagh, P. (Ed.). (1969). *Lapped furrows*. New York: Hand Press.

14. Two or more books by the same author

Arrange according to the date, with the earliest publication first, or alphabetically according to the names of additional authors.

> Harris, R. S. (1976). *A history of higher education in Canada, 1663–1960*. Toronto: University of Toronto Press.

> Harris, R. S. (1988). *English studies at Toronto: A history*. Toronto: University of Toronto Press.

MULTIPLE AUTHORS

15. Book by two authors

> Hardt, M., & Negri, A. (2000). *Empire*. Cambridge, MA: Harvard University Press.

If editors, use *(Eds.)* after the names.

> McClelland, D., & Eismann, K. (Eds.).

16. Book by three or more authors

Write out all of the authors' names up to six. The seventh and subsequent authors can be abbreviated to *et al.*

> Anders, K., Child, H., Davis, K., Logan, O., Petersen, J., Tymes, J., et al.

17. Authors listed with the word *with*

> Dallaire, R. (with B. Beardsley).

UNKNOWN AND GROUP AUTHORS

18. Book by an unknown author

> *Survey of developing nations*. (2003). New York: Justice for All Press.

19. Book by a group or organization

> Canadian Diabetes Association. (2005). *Living with diabetes*. Toronto: Dorling Kindersley.

TRANSLATIONS, EDITIONS, AND MULTIVOLUME BOOKS

20. Translated book

Voltaire. (1959). *Candide* (R. Aldington, Trans.). Garden City, NY: Hanover. (Original work published 1759)

21. Revised or later edition of a book

Weintraub, A. (2004). *Yoga for depression: A compassionate guide to relieve suffering through Yoga* (2nd ed.). New York: Broadway Books.

22. Multivolume book

Theweleit, K. (1993). *Male fantasies* (Vol. 1). Minneapolis: University of Minnesota Press.

PARTS OF BOOKS

23. Chapter written by the same author as the book

Add the word *In* after the chapter title and before the book title. Include inclusive page numbers for the chapter inside parentheses.

Savage, T. (2004). Challenging mirror modeling in group therapy. In *Collaborative practice in psychology and therapy* (pp. 130–157). New York: Haworth Clinical Practice Press.

24. Chapter in an edited collection

McCracken, J. L. (1995). Northern Ireland, 1921–66. In T. W. Moody & F. X. Martin (Eds.), *The course of Irish history* (pp. 313–323). Niwot, CO: Roberts Rinehart.

25. Chapter in a volume in a series

Jackson, E. (1998). Politics and gender. In F. Garrity (Series Ed.) & M. Halls (Vol. Ed.), *Political library: Vol. 4. Race, gender, and class* (2nd ed., pp. 101–151). New York: Muse.

26. Article in a reference work

Viscosity. (2001). In *The Columbia encyclopedia* (6th ed.). New York: Columbia University Press.

27. Selection reprinted from another source

Thompson, H. S. (1997). The scum also rises. In K. Kerrane & B. Yagoda (Eds.), *The art of fact* (pp. 302–315). New York: Touchstone. (Reprinted from *The great shark hunt*, pp. 299–399, by H. S. Thompson, 1979, New York: Simon & Schuster)

RESEARCH REPORTS, CONFERENCE PROCEEDINGS, AND DISSERTATIONS

28. Technical and research reports

Austin, A., & Baldwin, R. (1991). *Faculty collaboration: Enhancing the quality of scholarship and teaching* (ASCHE-ERIC Higher Education Report 7). Washington, DC: George Washington University.

29. Published conference proceedings

Abarkan, A. (1999). Educative physical planning: Housing and the emergence of suburbia in Sweden. In T. Mann (Ed.), *Power of imagination. Proceedings of the 30th annual conference of the Environmental Design Research Association*. (pp. 23–32). Edmond, OK: Environmental Design Research Association.

30. Unpublished paper presented at a symposium or meeting

Kelly, M. (2004, November). *Communication in virtual terms*. Paper presented at the annual meeting of the National Communication Association, Chicago.

31. Poster session

Wilson, W. (2005, September). *Voting patterns among college students, 1992–2004*. Poster session presented at the annual meeting of the American Political Science Association, Washington, DC.

32. Unpublished dissertation or thesis

Davis, J. (2004). *A quantitive analysis of student activism and the effects of online communication, 1994–2002*. Unpublished doctoral dissertation, New York University.

33. Published dissertation or thesis

If the dissertation you are citing is published by University Microfilms International (UMI), provide the order number as the last item in the entry.

Price, J. J. (1998). Flight maps: Encounters with nature in modern American culture. *Dissertation Abstracts International, 59* (5), 1635. (UMI No. 9835237)

GOVERNMENT AND LEGAL DOCUMENTS

34. Government document

When the author and publisher are identical, use the word *Author* as the name of the publisher.

Health Canada. (2001). *Assessment report of the Canadian Food Inspection Agency activities related to the safety of aquaculture products.* (Cat. H39-577/2001E). Ottawa, ON: Author.

In-text

(Health Canada, 2001).

35. Online government publication

Public Health Agency of Canada. (1998). *Aboriginal Head Start: Urban and northern initiative principles and guidelines.* Retrieved April 6, 2006, from http://www.phac-aspc.gc.ca/dca-dea/publications/pdf/ahs_princguide_e.pdf

In-text

(Public Health Agency of Canada [PHAC], 1998).

RELIGIOUS TEXTS, PAMPHLETS, INTERVIEWS, AND LETTERS

36. Religious or classical texts

Reference entries are not required for major classical works or the Bible, but in the in-text first citation, identify the edition used.

John 3.16 (Modern Phrased Version)

37. Bulletins or pamphlets

SecuriCan General Insurance. (2005.) *Health insurance for your pet.* [Brochure]. Winnipeg, MB: Author.

38. Published interview

Frum, L. (2006, January 30). Peter Bergen talks to Linda Frum. *Maclean's,* 10–11.

39. Unpublished letter

Personal communications are not listed on the references list; they are cited in text only.

(S. Straw, personal communication, April 4, 2006).

23c # PERIODICAL SOURCES IN THE APA-STYLE REFERENCES LIST

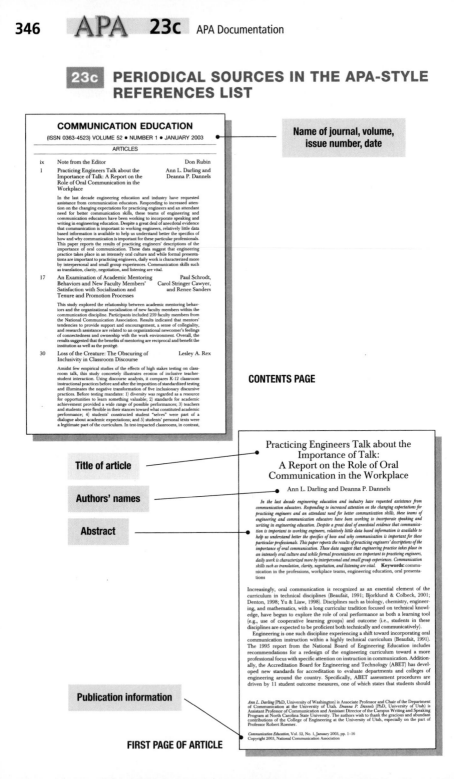

Name of journal, volume, issue number, date

COMMUNICATION EDUCATION

(ISSN 0363-4523) VOLUME 52 ● NUMBER 1 ● JANUARY 2003

ARTICLES

ix   Note from the Editor   Don Rubin

1   Practicing Engineers Talk about the   Ann L. Darling and
     Importance of Talk: A Report on the   Deanna P. Dannels
     Role of Oral Communication in the
     Workplace

     In the last decade engineering education and industry have requested
     assistance from communication educators. Responding to increased atten-
     tion on the changing expectations for practicing engineers and an attendant
     need for better communication skills, these teams of engineering and
     communication educators have been working to incorporate speaking and
     writing in engineering education. Despite a great deal of anecdotal evidence
     that communication is important to working engineers, relatively little data
     based information is available to help us understand better the specifics of
     how and why communication is important for these particular professionals.
     This paper reports the results of practicing engineers' descriptions of the
     importance of oral communication. These data suggest that engineering
     practice takes place in an intensely oral culture and while formal presenta-
     tions are important to practicing engineers, daily work is characterized more
     by interpersonal and small group experiences. Communication skills such
     as translation, clarity, negotiation, and listening are vital.

17   An Examination of Academic Mentoring   Paul Schrodt,
     Behaviors and New Faculty Members'   Carol Stringer Cawyer,
     Satisfaction with Socialization and   and Renee Sanders
     Tenure and Promotion Processes

     This study explored the relationship between academic mentoring behav-
     iors and the organizational socialization of new faculty members within the
     communication discipline. Participants included 259 faculty members from
     the National Communication Association. Results indicated that mentors'
     tendencies to provide support and encouragement, a sense of collegiality,
     and research assistance are related to an organizational newcomer's feelings
     of connectedness and ownership with the work environment. Overall, the
     results suggested that the benefits of mentoring are reciprocal and benefit the
     institution as well as the protégé.

30   Loss of the Creature: The Obscuring of   Lesley A. Rex
     Inclusivity in Classroom Discourse

     Amidst few empirical studies of the effects of high stakes testing on class-
     room talk, this study concretely illustrates erosion of inclusive teacher-
     student interaction. Using discourse analysis, it compares K-12 classroom
     instructional practices before and after the imposition of standardized testing
     and illuminates the negative transformation of five inclusionary discursive
     practices. Before testing mandates: 1) diversity was regarded as a resource
     for opportunities to learn something valuable; 2) standards for academic
     achievement provided a wide range of possible performances; 3) teachers
     and students were flexible in their stances toward what constituted academic
     performance; 4) students' constructed student "selves" were part of a
     dialogue about academic expectations; and 5) students' personal texts were
     a legitimate part of the curriculum. In test-impacted classrooms, in contrast,

CONTENTS PAGE

Practicing Engineers Talk about the Importance of Talk: A Report on the Role of Oral Communication in the Workplace

Title of article

Ann L. Darling and Deanna P. Dannels

Authors' names

In the last decade engineering education and industry have requested assistance from communication educators. Responding to increased attention on the changing expectations for practicing engineers and an attendant need for better communication skills, these teams of engineering and communication educators have been working to incorporate speaking and writing in engineering education. Despite a great deal of anecdotal evidence that communication is important to working engineers, relatively little data based information is available to help us understand better the specifics of how and why communication is important for these particular professionals. This paper reports the results of practicing engineers' descriptions of the importance of oral communication. These data suggest that engineering practice takes place in an intensely oral culture and while formal presentations are important to practicing engineers, daily work is characterized more by interpersonal and small group experiences. Communication skills such as translation, clarity, negotiation, and listening are vital. **Keywords:** communication in the professions, workplace teams, engineering education, oral presentations

Abstract

Increasingly, oral communication is recognized as an essential element of the curriculum in technical disciplines (Beaufait, 1991; Bjorklund & Colbeck, 2001; Denton, 1998; Yu & Liaw, 1998). Disciplines such as biology, chemistry, engineering, and mathematics, with a long curricular tradition focused on technical knowledge, have begun to explore the role of oral performance as both a learning tool (e.g., use of cooperative learning groups) and outcome (i.e., students in these disciplines are expected to be proficient both technically and communicatively).

Engineering is one such discipline experiencing a shift toward incorporating oral communication instruction within a highly technical curriculum (Beaufait, 1991). The 1995 report from the National Board of Engineering Education includes recommendations for a redesign of the engineering curriculum toward a more professional focus with specific attention on instruction in communication. Additionally, the Accreditation Board for Engineering and Technology (ABET) has developed new standards for accreditation to evaluate departments and colleges of engineering around the country. Specifically, ABET assessment procedures are driven by 11 student outcome measures, one of which states that students should

Publication information

Ann L. Darling (PhD, University of Washington) is Associate Professor and Chair of the Department of Communication at the University of Utah. *Deanna P. Dannels* (PhD, University of Utah) is Assistant Professor of Communication and Assistant Director of the Campus Writing and Speaking Program at North Carolina State University. The authors wish to thank the gracious and abundant contributions of the College of Engineering at the University of Utah, especially on the part of Professor Robert Roemer.

Communication Education, Vol. 52, No. 1, January 2003, pp. 1–16

FIRST PAGE OF ARTICLE

Darling, A. L., & Dannels, D. P. (2003). Practicing engineers talk about the importance of talk: A report on the role of oral communication in the workplace. *Communication Education, 52,* 1–16.

AUTHOR'S NAME

The author's last name comes first, followed by the author's initials.

Join two authors' names with a comma and an ampersand.

DATE OF PUBLICATION

Give the year the work was published in parentheses.

Most popular magazines are paginated per issue. These periodicals might have a volume number, but are more often referenced by the season or date of publication.

TITLE OF ARTICLE

- Do not use quotation marks. If there is a book title in the article title, italicize it.
- The first word of the title, the first word of the subtitle, and any proper nouns in the title are capitalized.

PUBLICATION INFORMATION

Name of journal

- Italicize the journal name (or underline if you are working on a typewriter).
- All nouns, verbs, and pronouns, and the first word of the title are capitalized. Do not capitalize any article, preposition, or coordinating conjunction unless it is the first word of the title or subtitle.
- Put a comma after the journal name.
- Italicize the volume number followed by a comma.

Volume, issue, and page numbers

See sample references 46 and 47 for more on different types of pagination.

JOURNAL AND MAGAZINE ARTICLES

40. Article by one author

Kellogg, R. T. (2001). Competition for working memory among writing processes. *American Journal of Psychology, 114*, 175–192.

41. Article by two authors

McClelland, D., & Eismann, K. (1998).

42. Article by three or more authors

The seventh and subsequent authors can be abbreviated to *et al.*

Andis, S., Franks, D., Girardeau, J., Kellog, K., Oppenheimer, G., Zales, D., et al.

43. Authors listed with the word *with*

Dallaire, R. (with B. Beardsley).

44. Article by an unknown author

The green gene revolution. (2004, February). [Editorial]. *Scientific American, 291*, 8.

45. Article by a group or organization

National Organization for Women. (1980). Where to find feminists in Austin. *The NOW guide for Austin women*. Austin, TX: Chapter Press.

46. Article in a journal with continuous pagination

Include only the volume number and the year, not the issue number.

Engen, R., & Steen, S. (2000). The power to punish: Discretion and sentencing reform in the war on drugs. *American Journal of Sociology, 105*, 1357–1395.

47. Article in a journal paginated by issue

List the issue number in parentheses (not italicized) after the volume number.

Davis, J. (1999). Rethinking globalisation. *Race and Class, 40*(2/3), 37–48.

MONTHLY, WEEKLY, AND BIWEEKLY PERIODICALS

48. Weekly or biweekly periodicals

Hurtley, S. (2004, July 16). Limits from leaf litter. *Science, 305*, 311–313.

Toobin, J. (2001, November 5). Crackdown. *The New Yorker*, 56–61.

49. **Monthly publications**

Barlow, J. P. (1998, January). Africa rising: Everything you know about Africa is wrong. *Wired,* 142–158.

ABSTRACTS

50. **Abstract from an original source**

de Watteville, C. (1904). On flame spectra [Abstract]. *Proceedings of the Royal Society of London, 74,* 84.

51. **Abstract from a printed secondary source**

Van Schaik, P. (1999). Involving users in the specification of functionality using scenarios and model-based evaluation. *Behaviour and Information Technology, 18,* 455–466. Abstract obtained from *Communication Abstracts,* 2000, *23,* 416.

52. **Electronic copy of an abstract retrieved from a database**

Putsis, W. P., & Bayus, B. L. (2001). An empirical analysis of firms' product line decisions. *Journal of Marketing Research, 37*(8), 110–118. Abstract obtained from PsychINFO database.

NEWSPAPERS

53. **Newspaper article**

Saccone, J. (2006, March 18). Findings may diffuse stem-cell controversy. *Saskatoon StarPhoenix,* p. A10+.

If an article has no author, list and alphabetize by the first significant word in the title of the article.

Incorrect cancer tests can be costly. (2004, December 16). *USA Today,* p. 8D.

REVIEWS AND LETTERS TO THE EDITOR

54. **Review**

Berger, S. E. (1999). [Review of the book *The evolution of the book*]. *Library Quarterly, 69,* 402.

55. **Letter to the editor or editorial**

Wilkenson, S. E. (2001, December 21). When teaching doesn't count [Letter to the editor]. *The Chronicle of Higher Education,* p. B21.

23d ONLINE SOURCES IN THE APA-STYLE REFERENCES LIST

URL

Auth

Title

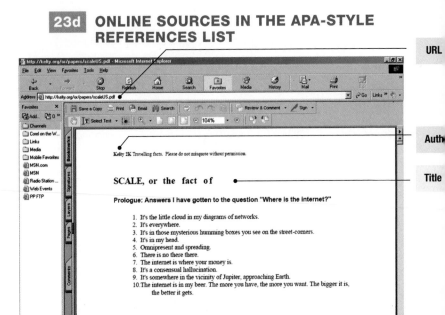

Titles and URLs in APA-style references

Websites are made up of many separate pages or articles. Each page on a website may or may not have a title. If you are citing a page or article that has a title, treat the title like an article in a periodical.

> Heiney, A. (2004). A gathering of space heroes. Retrieved
> April 29, 2004, from the National Aeronautics and Space
> Administration Website: http://www.nasa.gov/missions/
> shuttle/ f_ahofpreview.html

Otherwise, treat the name of the website itself as you would a book.

> American Psychological Association. (2004). *APA Online*. Retrieved
> September 23, 2003, from http://www.apa.org/

If there is no title for the website, list it by author. If it is a personal homepage, write *Homepage* after the name of the author.

> Zhao, H. Homepage. Retrieved April 1, 2004, from http://
> www.geocities.com/ky_jane/

Kelty, C. (2000). *Scale, or the fact of*. Retrieved January 2, 2002,
from http://kelty.org/or/papers/scaleUS.pdf

AUTHOR'S NAME, ASSOCIATED INSTITUTION, OR ORGANIZATION

- Authorship is sometimes hard to discern for online sources. If you do have an author or creator to cite, follow the rules for periodicals and books.

- If the only authority you find is a group or organization, list its name as the author.

- If the author or organization is not identified, begin the reference with the title of the document.

DATES

You need to list two dates for a website.

First, list the date the site was produced or last revised (sometimes the copyright date) after the author. This date might be just a year.

Second, list the date you accessed the site. Place this second date just before the URL.

NAME OF SITE AND TITLE OF PAGE OR ARTICLE

- Websites are often made up of many separate pages or articles. Each page or article on a website may or may not have a title. If you are citing a page or article that has a title, treat the title like an article in a periodical. Otherwise, treat the name of the website itself as you would a book.

- The name of a website will usually be found on its index or homepage. If you cannot find a link back to the homepage, look at the address for clues. You can work your way backward through the URL, deleting sections (separated by slashes) until you come to a home or index page.

- If there is no title for the website, list it by author or creator. If it is a personal homepage, place the words *Homepage* after the name of the owner of the page.

URL

- Copy the address exactly as it appears in your browser window. You can even copy and paste the address into your text for greater accuracy.

- Note that there are no angle brackets around the URL and no period after it.

ONLINE PUBLICATIONS

56. Online publication by a known author

> Alexander, K. 2005. Liminal identities and institutional positioning:
> On becoming a "writing lady" in the academy. *Inkshed, 22.*
> Retrieved April 6, 2006, from http://www.stthomasu.ca/
> inkshed/nlettc05/alexander.htm

57. Online publication by a group or organization

> Girls Incorporated. (2003). Girls' bill of rights. Retrieved April 28,
> 2004, from http://www.girlsinc.org/gc/page.php?id=9

58. Online publication with an author and a group affiliation

Identify the host before giving the URL for the document itself. Precede the URL with a colon.

> Bjork, Olin. (2004, May 5). MOO bots. Retrieved August 5, 2004,
> from CWRL White Papers website: http://www.cwrl.utexas.edu/
> professional/whitepapers/2004/040512-1.pdf

59. Online publication with no known author or group affiliation

Begin the reference with the title of the document.

> *Halloween costumes from my warped mind.* (n.d.). Retrieved November
> 26, 2001, from http://home.att.net/~jgola/hallow01.htm

60. Online publication with no copyright or revision date

If no copyright or revision date is given, use *(n.d.),* as shown in entry 59.

ONLINE PERIODICALS

61. Article online based on a print journal

If you access an article online that is identical to the printed version, note in brackets after the title *Electronic version.*

> Gomez, T. (2001, July). Bungee! Combing DVD with Tivo and Replay TV
> [Electronic version]. *Camcorder and Computer Video, 18,* 40–43.

62. Article in an online scholarly journal

> Brown, B. (2004). The order of service: The practical management of
> customer interaction. *Sociological Research Online, 9*(4).
> Retrieved December 16, 2004, from http://www
> .socresonline.org.uk/9/4/brown.html

63. Article in an online newspaper

Young, M. (2006, April 6). Council rejects boutique rezoning.
Kamloops Daily News. Retrieved April 6, 2006, from
http://www.kamloopsnews.ca/

64. Article in an online magazine

McClure, L. (2003, February 18). The salon interview: Molly Ivins. *Salon*.
Retrieved November 21, 2003, from http://www.salon.com/
opinion/feature/2003/02/18/ivins/index_np.html

ONLINE DATABASES AND ENCYCLOPEDIAS

65. Document from database

APA recommends giving the original publication information and the
date of retrieval from the database.

Holloway, J. D. (2004). Protecting practitioners' autonomy. *Monitor
on Psychology, 35*(1), 30. Retrieved March 15, 2004, from
Expanded Academic ASAP database.

66. Online encyclopedia

Swing. (2002). In *Encyclopaedia Britannica Online*. Retrieved April 29,
2004, from http://www.britannica.com/eb/
article?eu=72497&tocid=0&query=swing&ct=

UNEDITED ONLINE SOURCES

67. Weblog entry

Wells, P. (2005, December 31). Inkless Wells. Macleans.ca. Retrieved
April 6, 2006, from http://weblogs.macleans.ca/paulwells/
archives/week_2005_12_25-2005_12_31.asp

68. Message posted to a newsgroup or electronic mailing list

Only use messages that are archived and accessible by readers.

Fisher, R. (2001, November 11). CFP: The idea of education [Msg. 129100].
Message posted to http://www2.h-net.msu.edu/announce/

69. Email

Email sent from one individual to another should be cited as a personal communication. Personal communication is cited in text but not
included in the reference list.

(R. Hunt, personal communication, August 18, 2005).

23e VISUAL, COMPUTER, AND MULTIMEDIA SOURCES IN THE APA-STYLE REFERENCES LIST

MULTIMEDIA

70. Television program

> Burgess, M., & Green, M. (Writers). (2004). Irregular around the margins [Television series episode]. In D. Chase (Producer), *The sopranos*. New York: HBO.

71. Film, Video, or DVD

> Heyman, D. (Producer), & Columbus, C. (Director). (2001). *Harry Potter and the sorcerer's stone* [Motion picture]. United States: Warner Brothers.

72. Musical recording

> Waits, T. (1980). Ruby's arms. On *Heartattack and vine* [CD]. New York: Elektra Entertainment.

73. Audio recording

> Monahan, V. (2006, February 17). 1,400-year-old moccasin found in Canada. *As it happens*. CBC Radio One, retrieved April 5, 2006, from http://www.radio.cbc.ca/programs/asithappens/ features/2006/oldest_moccasin_20060217.html

74. Graphic, audio, or video files

> Aretha Franklin: A life of soul. (2004, January 23). *NPR Online*. Retrieved April 30, 2004, from http://www.npr.org/features/ feature.php?wfId=1472614

COMPUTER SOFTWARE

75. Computer software

You do not need to cite standard, off-the-shelf software and programming languages. For other software, provide the author's name (if known), the date, the name of the software, and the version number (if any). Also give the place of manufacture (if known) and the manufacturer. You can also list the operating system, if relevant. If you have downloaded the software from the internet, list the URL for the download site.

In-text

Give the proper name of the software and version in the text rather than in a parenthetical citation.

References

> Benjamin, B., Seising, G., & Osborn, A. (1998). Critical Tools [Computer software]. Austin: College of Liberal Arts, University of Texas.

23f SAMPLE PAPER WITH APA DOCUMENTATION

WRITING IN THE WORLD

APA reports of research

Reports of experimental research follow a specific organization in APA style.

- **The abstract** gives a brief summary of the report.
- **The introduction** identifies the problem, reviews previous research, and states the hypothesis that was tested.
- **The methods section** describes how the experiment was conducted and how the participants were selected.
- **The results section** reports the findings of the study. This section often includes tables and figures that provide statistical results and tests of statistical significance. Tests of statistical significance are critical for experimental research because they give the probability that the results could have occurred by chance.
- **The discussion section** interprets the findings and often refers to previous research.

Another common type of paper in APA style is the **review of research**. If you are asked to write a review of research, use the introduction to the sample research report as an example.

Body Objectification 1

Running head: BODY OBJECTIFICATION

Body Objectification: Relationship with
Fashion Magazines and Weight Satisfaction

Michael Moshenrose and Keli A. Braitman

York University

APA style uses a title page.

Include page header and page number, beginning with the title page.

Type the running head (the shortened title) for publication in all caps, flush left.

Centre the title, name of author(s), and name of school.

Body Objectification 2

Abstract

This study examined the relationship between objectified body consciousness and the utilization of fashion magazines for information about fashion and beauty, comparison to models, and weight satisfaction. Participants were 180 female undergraduate students. We hypothesized that highly body-conscious individuals would read more fashion magazines than low body-conscious women and also rate magazine advertisements and articles as important for influencing fashion and beauty ideals. We also hypothesized that highly body-conscious women would compare themselves to models and be less satisfied with their weight as compared to low body-conscious women. A multivariate analysis of variance indicated that significant differences between the groups existed, but that group differences were opposite to hypotheses. Possible explanations for findings are discussed.

Continue to use the running head with the page number in the top right.

The abstract appears on a separate page with the title *Abstract*.

Double-space the abstract.

Do not indent the first line of the abstract.

The abstract must be brief. The limit is 120 words.

Body Objectification 3

Body Objectification: Relationship with Fashion
Magazines and Weight Satisfaction

Introduction

The cultural preoccupation with physical beauty has generated much research regarding how a woman's perception of her body contributes to negative body esteem. Feminist theorists argue that the female body is often treated as an object to be looked at. This objectification causes women to perceive their bodies as

Give the full title at the beginning of the body of the report.

Centre the heading *Introduction*.

Specify 1-inch margins.

Body Objectification 4

detached observers, which means they are attempting to see themselves as others see them. An internalization of the cultural body standards results in women believing that they created these standards and can achieve them. Therefore, objectified body consciousness (OBC) refers to perceiving the body as an object and the beliefs that sustain this perception (McKinley, 1995). McKinley and Hyde (1996) developed the 24-item instrument to assess OBC, and the three scale facets are body surveillance, control beliefs, and body shame. In order to conform to cultural body standards, women engage in self-surveillance to avoid negative evaluations (McKinley & Hyde, 1996). Thus, women are constantly seeing themselves as others see them, and this act of mental disassociation can have negative consequences for women.

The next aspect of OBC is that internalizing cultural body standards can cause women to experience intense shame (McKinley & Hyde, 1996). Because the cultural ideal of a "perfect" body is excessively thin, most women are unable to achieve that standard. Consequently, many women experience a discrepancy between their actual bodies and their ideal bodies (Noll & Fredrickson, 1998). Any comparisons that women make between the ultra-thin standard and their bodies will produce body shame.

The final component of OBC are control beliefs, which assert that women are responsible for their physical characteristics and can alter their appearance to conform to cultural standards (McKinley & Hyde, 1996). However, women must first be convinced that they are responsible for how they look in order to accept attractiveness as a

Include the date in parentheses when you mention authors in the text.

Include authors and date in parentheses when you do not mention authors in the text.

Indent each paragraph five to seven spaces (1/2" on the ruler in the word processing program).

reasonable standard by which to judge themselves. When women perceive the attainment of the cultural body standards as a choice, they are more likely to believe that appearance can be controlled (McKinley & Hyde, 1996).

Related to the concept of self-objectification is exposure to appearance-related information via fashion and beauty magazines. Levine, Smolak, and Hayden (1994), for example, found that fashion magazines were instrumental in providing motivation and guidance for women striving to mirror the thin-ideal. Further, nearly half of the respondents in a sample of middle school girls indicated that they read fashion magazines frequently, and that the magazines were moderately important sources of information about beauty (Levine et al., 1994).

Given that fashion magazines are seen as sources of information about beauty ideals, it seems likely that women scoring high on objectified body consciousness would be more likely to utilize fashion magazines for these purposes. The objective of this study was to examine the relationship between objectified body consciousness and attitudes and behaviours regarding fashion magazines. Specifically, we hypothesized that women scoring high on the OBC scale were more likely to read fashion magazines and to rate both magazine articles and advertisements as important in influencing their fashion and beauty ideas. Further, we hypothesized that highly body-conscious individuals would compare themselves to fashion models and be less satisfied with their bodies in comparison to women who were low on body consciousness.

Body Objectification 6

Methods

Participants

Participants were 180 Caucasian females from undergraduate psychology classes. However, only the data from participants scoring above the median on all three OBC scales or below the median on all OBC scales were analyzed. Thus, data from only 56 participants were analyzed. The mean age of the participants was 19.0 (SD = 1.33). Participants were recruited through general psychology classes and received partial course credit for participation.

Instruments

Instruments were administered to measure (1) the extent to which an individual reads or is exposed to fashion magazines, (2) the importance of magazine *advertisements* in influencing fashion and beauty ideals, (3) the importance of magazine *articles* in influencing fashion and beauty ideals, (4) the extent to which an individual compares herself to fashion magazines on a variety of domains such as happiness and physical appearance, and (5) weight satisfaction.

To measure the magazine-related factors, a media questionnaire was created through a synthesis and modification of Levine et al.'s (1994) Media Questionnaire and Strowman's (1996) Media Exposure and Comparison to Models survey. The first 15 items of the instrument comprised the Exposure subscale. Participants were asked to rate how often they view a variety of listed magazines. Although the focus of the study explored exposure to fashion magazines, non-fashion magazines were also

Body Objectification 7

included in the list to make the focus of the study less apparent. A subscale score indicating exposure to fashion magazines was obtained by summing responses to each fashion magazine item, with a high score indicating higher exposure to fashion magazines.

The next 16 items of the instrument comprised the magazine information subscales. The first 6 of these items assessed the importance of magazine advertisements for providing information about beauty and fashion, and the remaining 10 items assessed the importance of magazine articles for the same purpose. Eight additional items comprised the Comparison to Models subscale, which assessed the extent to which participants compare themselves to models.

To assess weight satisfaction, we employed the Weight Satisfaction subscale of the Body Esteem Scale (Franzoi & Shields, 1984). The entire instrument was administered, but only scores for weight satisfaction were included in the analysis. Subscale scores were obtained by summing items for the weight satisfaction scale.

A demographics survey was included at the end of the questionnaire. This survey contained items assessing such characteristics as age, race, height, weight, and exercise habits. Based on self-reported height and weight, the body mass of each participant was calculated using the following formula: Weight (kg)/Height2 (m2).

Procedure

Participants were solicited from general psychology courses and were tested in small groups ranging in size

Body Objectification 8

from 1 to 10. The participants were provided with a packet marked only with an identification number. They were instructed to remove the informed consent form from the packet and read along with the experimenter as she read the informed consent aloud. The participants were told that the project was examining the effects of marketing on post-secondary school students. Participants agreeing to participate then removed the scantrons and seven-page questionnaire from the packets and began working. Without a time limit being imposed, participants completed the questionnaire and were then presented with a debriefing form describing the true nature of the experiment. Participants were encouraged to contact the researcher if they had any additional questions about the research project.

To identify participants who were either high or low scorers on objectified body consciousness, a median split was conducted for all OBC scales. Participants scoring above the median on all three scales were identified as high on objectified body consciousness, and those scoring below the median on all three OBC scales were identified as low on objectified body consciousness. We then conducted both multivariate and univariate analyses of variance.

Results

Table 1 presents the mean exposure score for each fashion magazine, and Table 2 presents the means, standard deviations, and F-values of the dependent variables for the high and low objectified body consciousness groups.

Table 1

Means and Standard Deviations for Magazines Included in the Media Exposure Scale

Magazine	Mean	SD
Seventeen	2.93	1.35
Cosmopolitan	2.93	1.17
Glamour	2.79	1.17
YM	2.57	1.26
Vogue	2.55	1.06
Mademoiselle	2.45	1.22
Newsweek	2.32	1.25
National Geographic	2.27	1.05
Reader's Digest	2.13	1.13
Marie Claire	1.93	1.25
Self	1.84	1.04
Better Homes and Gardens	1.80	0.88
In Style	1.80	1.00
Elle	1.67	0.97
Redbook	1.64	0.97
Shape	1.63	0.97
Fitness Magazine	1.54	0.97
US News & World Report	1.52	0.83
Model	1.39	0.78
Vanity Fair	1.23	0.66
Playboy	1.18	0.51

Note. 5-point scale: 1 = never look at it; 2 = look through it rarely; 3 = glance through it sometimes; 4 = look through it often; 5 = look through every new issue

Number tables and figures. Give each table and figure a descriptive title. Begin the title flush left and in italics.

Double-space notes to tables.

Table 2

Means and Standard Deviations for the Objectified Body Consciousness Groups

| | Objectified Body Consciousness | | | | |
| | Low (n = 25) | | High (n = 31) | | |
Dependent Variable	M	SD	M	SD	F(1,53)
Fashion Magazines	30.12	15.40	20.65	13.67	5.26
Magazine Advertisements	18.16	4.67	12.84	4.06	19.59***
Magazine Articles	3.24	7.37	21.90	6.14	37.55***
Comparison to Models	21.72	4.84	14.13	5.85	25.82**
Weight Satisfaction	19.36	5.82	26.16	7.65	12.08**

Note. ** $p < .01$, *** $p < .001$.

Asterisks are normally used for notes of statistical probability.

Multivariate analyses of variance indicated that the two groups differed significantly on their mean profiles based on the five fashion magazine and weight satisfaction measures (Wilks' Lambda = .45, F [5, 49] = 12.01, $p < .001$; effect size = .55). Follow-up univariate tests indicated that these groups differed significantly with respect to the importance placed on both magazine advertisements and articles for obtaining information about beauty and fashion, with low objectifiers placing more importance on these items. Low objectifiers were also more likely to compare themselves to fashion models and were less satisfied with their weight than were high objectifiers. Furthermore, low objectifiers also looked at fashion magazines more frequently than did high objectifiers, but this difference was not statistically significant despite the relatively large mean difference between the groups.

Discussion

In contrast to our hypotheses, low objectifiers (1) were more influenced by magazine advertisements and articles than were high objectifiers, (2) were more likely to compare themselves to models, and (3) were less satisfied with their weight. Because our findings counter certain aspects of what the objectification theory predicts, there may be several reasons why this theory was not supported. First, it is assumed that women compare themselves to a cultural beauty ideal when they engage in self-objectification. The question then becomes: How are women exposed to the cultural ideal? In our study, we assumed that women obtain information about the cultural ideal from fashion magazines. The difficulty with this proposition is that the women in our study were not frequently exposed to fashion magazines. Table 1 shows that the highest mean frequency of exposure to any magazine was 2.93, for both *Seventeen* and *Cosmopolitan*. This frequency approached the level of women "glancing through it sometimes." Because of a lack of exposure to fashion magazines, women may not be influenced by the cultural ideals of beauty presented within their pages. Consequently, women may be procuring information regarding cultural standards from alternative media sources, such as television, films, and the internet. Future research may address the influence of these media sources in regard to their impact on women's self-perception.

Another possibility is that women may be making lateral comparisons to members of their peer group as opposed to making upward comparisons to models. According to the social comparison theory, individuals can make upward, lateral, or downward comparisons. It may be that women may accept the fact that they can never achieve the standard of beauty portrayed by the media. Hence, they may decide that the only salient standard for them to achieve is to look as good as their peers. In addition, women may experience intense stress by believing they must conform to a certain standard of appearance; thus, they may make downward social comparisons to regain self-esteem. These women may compare themselves to others whom they consider to be unattractive in order to feel better about themselves.

Although some women may make downward social comparisons, other women who rate highly on body consciousness may decide to invest more resources in their appearance. Because they are concerned with and aware of their appearance, these women may actively engage in activities that help to improve their appearance. According to the preceding logic, high objectifiers would then be more satisfied with their weight than low objectifiers. In support of this idea, Smith, Thompson, Raczynski, and Hilner (1999) found that physical appearance is more important to African-American women and men than to Caucasian women and men, but also that African Americans are more satisfied with their appearance compared to their Caucasian counterparts. Thus, these results support the idea that the more individuals value and invest in their physical characteristics, the more satisfied they will be with their appearance.

The generality of our study is limited by the use of a Caucasian, female, post-secondary school-age sample. However, this sample is appropriate to study because research examining the influence of ethnicity on body satisfaction has found that Caucasian women tend to be less satisfied with their appearance compared to Black and Asian-Canadian women (Akan & Grilo, 1995; Altabe, 1998; Cash & Henry, 1995). In addition to ethnicity, men and women also tend to differ in body image, with women being less satisfied with their appearance than men (Mintz & Betz, 1986; Serdula et al., 1993). Thus, both sex and race differences exist in regard to body image, and these factors should therefore be considered when conducting body-image studies. For this reason, the findings of the present study should be generalized only to Caucasian females. Future studies may explore whether the findings from this study are replicated in samples of individuals of different ethnicity and sex. However, the questions in the instruments may need to be slightly modified to be appropriate with a male sample. For example, the fashion magazines included in the exposure subscale may not be the same magazines that would be appropriate for males. In particular, magazines such as *Seventeen* and *Glamour* may need to be replaced by magazines marketed to men and focusing on the male physique, such as weight-lifting or fitness magazines.

Body Objectification 15
References

Akan, G. E., & Grilo, C. M. (1995). Sociocultural influences on eating attitudes and behaviors, body image, and psychological functioning: A comparison of African-American, Asian-American, and Caucasian college women. *International Journal of Eating Disorders, 18,* 181–187.

Altabe, M. N. (1998). Ethnicity and body image: Quantitative and qualitative analysis. *International Journal of Eating Disorders, 23,* 153–159.

Cash, T. F., & Henry, P. E. (1995). Women's body images: The results of a national survey in the U.S.A. *Sex Roles, 33,* 19–28.

Franzoi, S. L., & Shields, S. A. (1984). The Body Esteem Scale: Multidimensional structure and sex differences in a college population. *Journal of Personality Assessment, 48,* 173–178.

Levine, M. P., Smolak, L., & Hayden, H. (1994). The relation of sociocultural factors to eating attitudes and behaviors among middle school girls. *Journal of Early Adolescence, 14,* 471–490.

McKinley, N. M. (1995). Women and objectified body consciousness: A feminist psychological analysis. *Dissertation Abstracts International, 56,* 05B. (UMI No. 9527111)

McKinley, N. M., & Hyde, J. S. (1996). The Objectified Body Consciousness Scale: Development and validation. *Psychology of Women Quarterly, 20,* 181–216.

Centre "References" heading.

Alphabetize entries by last name of the author.

Double-space all entries.

Indent all but the first line of each entry five spaces.

Go through your text and make sure that everything you have cited, except for personal communication, is in the list of references.

Body Objectification 16

Mintz, L. B., & Betz, N. E. (1986). Sex differences in the nature, realism, and correlates of body image. *Sex Roles, 15*(3/4), 185–195.

Noll, S. M., & Fredrickson, B. L. (1998). A mediational model linking self-objectification, body shame, and disordered eating. *Psychology of Women Quarterly, 22*, 623–636.

Serdula, M. K., Collins, M. E., Williamson, D. F., Anda, R. F., Pamuk, E., & Byers, T. E. (1993). Weight control practices of U.S. adolescents and adults. *Annals of Internal Medicine, 119*, 667–671.

Smith, D. E., Thompson, J. K., Raczynski, J. M., & Hilner, J. (1999). Body image among men and women in a biracial cohort: The CARDIA Study. *International Journal of Eating Disorders, 25*, 71–82.

Strowman, S. R. (1996). *Media exposure survey*. Unpublished manuscript, University of New Hampshire, Durham.

This paper is a shortened and adapted version of a research report by Michael Moshenrose and his faculty advisor, Keli A. Braitman. The original report was published in the online journal *Psych-E*.

 To hear audio commentary on this student paper, visit **www.pearsoned.ca/faigley/218.**

PART EIGHT

CMS and CSE Documentation

- How is CMS documentation different from other citation styles? (24)

- Which Latin abbreviation indicates that a source has been cited in the preceding note? (24a 1.3)

- How do I cite electronic sources in CMS style? (24c)

- What are the two ways I can organize citations using CSE style? (25a)

- Do you use quotation marks, underlining, or italics to indicate book titles in CSE style? (25b)

8 CMS AND CSE DOCUMENTATION

Writers who publish in business, social sciences, fine arts, and humanities outside the discipline of English often use the *Chicago Manual of Style* (CMS) method of documentation. Within the disciplines of natural and applied sciences, the Council of Science Editors (CSE) style is most commonly preferred. Both of these styles emphasize different types of information about the sources being cited.

In CMS style, references to citations appear in footnotes or endnotes, and they include practically the full citation from the Bibliography at the end of the paper. Readers consult the footnotes or endnotes for full bibliographic information, including the page number of the specific quotation. CMS style fully informs readers about cited material, suggesting that they find all aspects of the source information to be relevant as they read. CMS also allows for an author-date citation system that is similar to the APA model described in the previous chapter.

CSE style offers writers two choices for documenting sources: one system that emphasizes the author's name and year, and one system that numbers citations, which correspond to a numbered entry in the References list. The name-year system allows writers to indicate the author and date in parentheses in the text of the paper with the full citation following in the References section. The citation-sequence system numbers quotations with specific information located in the notes. By offering writers a choice, CSE style enables writers to inform readers of the author and date in the text or focus reader attention on their own text without the distraction of source details in the paper. One interesting aspect of this style is that the reference citation also includes the total page-length of the source, suggesting that scholars using this documentation style are interested in the original length of the source cited.

CHAPTER *24*

CMS Documentation

Writers who publish in business, social sciences, fine arts, and humanities outside the discipline of English often use *The Chicago Manual of Style* (CMS) method of documentation. CMS guidelines allow writers a clear way of using footnotes and endnotes (rather than MLA and APA in-text citations) for quotations, summaries, and paraphrases. If you have questions after consulting this chapter, you can consult the full CMS style manual, *The Chicago Manual of Style*, fifteenth edition (Chicago: University of Chicago Press, 2003), or visit the University of Chicago Press website (www.chicagomanualofstyle.org/index.html).

In-text citations

CMS describes two systems of documentation, one similar to APA and the other a style that uses footnotes or endnotes, which is the focus of this chapter. In the footnote style CMS uses a superscript number directly after any quotation, paraphrase, or summary. Notes are numbered consecutively throughout the essay, article, or chapter. This superscript number corresponds to either a footnote, which appears at the bottom of the page, or an endnote, which appears at the end of the text.

In *Canadian Women: A History*, Prentice and colleagues note ironically that the Upper Canada seduction law of 1837 aimed to protect the interests of fathers rather than masters, and it "ignored" rights of the young women involved.[1]

Note

　　1. Alison Prentice and others, *Canadian Women: A History* (Toronto: Harcourt Brace Jovanovich, 1988), 93.

Bibliography

Prentice, Alison, Paula Bourne, Gail Cuthbert Brandt, Beth Light, Wendy Mitchinson, and Naomi Black. *Canadian Women: A History*. Toronto: Harcourt Brace Jovanovich, 1988.

Footnotes and endnotes

Footnotes appear at the bottom of the page on which each citation appears. Begin your footnote four lines from the last line of text on the page. Footnotes are single-spaced, but you should double-space between multiple notes on a single page.

　　Endnotes are compiled at the end of the text on a separate page entitled *Notes*. Centre the title at the top of the page and list your endnotes in the order they appear within the text. The entire endnote section should be double-spaced—both within and between each entry. Even with endnotes it's still possible to include explanatory footnotes, which are indicated by asterisks or other punctuation marks.

CMS Bibliography

Because footnotes and endnotes in CMS format contain complete citation information, a separate list of references is often optional. This list of references can be called the *Bibliography*, or if it only has works referenced directly in your text, *Works Cited, Literature Cited*, or *References*. Generally, CMS bibliographies follow the MLA works-cited format.

24a BOOKS AND NON-PERIODICAL SOURCES IN CMS STYLE

Note

1. Donald A. Norman, *Emotional Design: Why We Love (or Hate) Everyday Things* (New York: Basic Books, 2004), 104.

Bibliography

Norman, Donald A. Emotional Design: *Why We Love (or Hate) Everyday Things.* New York: Basic Books, 2004.

AUTHOR'S OR EDITOR'S NAME

Note: Give the author's name in normal order.

Bibliography: Give the author's name in reverse order. If an editor, put *ed.* after the name.

BOOK TITLE

Use the exact title, as it appears on the title page (not the cover).

Italicize the title.

Capitalize all nouns, verbs, adjectives, adverbs, and pronouns, and the first word of the title and subtitle.

PUBLICATION INFORMATION

In a note, the place of publication, publisher, and year of publication are in parentheses.

Place of publication

• Add the province's or state's postal abbreviation or country when the city is not well known (*Brandon, MB*) or ambiguous (London, ON, or London, UK).
• If more than one city is given on the title page, use the first.

Publisher's name

• You may use acceptable abbreviations (e.g., Co. for Company).
• For works published prior to 1900, the place and date are sufficient.

Year of publication

• If no year of publication is given, write *n.d.* ("no date") in place of the date.
• If it is a multivolume edited work published over a period of more than one year, put the span of time as the year.

Sample citations for books and non-periodical sources

BOOKS

1. Book by one author

In a note the author's name is given in normal order.

1. Elizabeth Bowen, *The Mulberry Tree: Selected Writings* (London: Vintage, 1999), 33–41.

In subsequent references, cite the author's last name only:

2. Bowen, 231.

If the reference is to the same work as the preceding note, you can use the abbreviation *Ibid.*:

3. Ibid., 231.

In the bibliography, give the author's name in reverse order.

Bowen, Elizabeth. *The Mulberry Tree: Selected Writings*. London: Vintage, 1999.

For edited books, put *ed.* after name.

Kavanagh, Patrick, ed. *Lapped Furrows*. New York: Hand Press, 1969.

2. Book by two or three authors

In a note, put all authors' names in normal order. For subsequent references, give only the authors' last names:

4. McClelland and Eismann, 32.

In the bibliography, give second and third names in normal order.

Hauser, Taylor, and June Kashpaw. *January Blues*. Foster City, CA: IDG Books, 2003.

3. Book by four or more authors

In a note, give the name of the first author listed, followed by *and others*.

5. Alison Prentice and others. *Canadian Women: A History*, (Toronto: Harcourt Brace Jovanovich, 1988), 93.

List all of the authors in the bibliography.

Prentice, Alison, Paula Bourne, Gail Cuthbert Brandt, Beth Light, Wendy Mitchinson, and Naomi Black. *Canadian Women: A History*. Toronto: Harcourt Brace Jovanovich, 1988.

4. Book by an unknown author

Begin both the note and the bibliography entries with the title.
Note

6. *Remarks upon the Religion, Trade, Government, Police, Customs, Manners, and Maladys of the City of Corke* (Cork, 1737), 4.

Bibliography

Remarks upon the Religion, Trade, Government, Police, Customs, Manners, and Maladys of the City of Corke. Cork, 1737.

5. Book by a group or organization

Treat the group or organization as the author of the work.

Note

7. World Health Organization. *Advancing Safe Motherhood through Human Rights* (Geneva, Switzerland: World Health Organization, 2001), 18.

Bibliography

World Health Organization. *Advancing Safe Motherhood through Human Rights*. Geneva, Switzerland: World Health Organization, 2001.

PARTS OF BOOKS

6. A single chapter by the same author as the book

Note

1. Ann Ardis, "*The Lost Girl, Tarr*, and the Moment of Modernism," *Modernism and Cultural Conflict, 1880–1922* (New York: Cambridge University Press, 2002), 78–113.

Bibliography

Savage, Gail. "The Ministry of Labour: Accentuating the Negative." Chap. 5 in *The Social Construction of Expertise*. New York: Routledge, 1996.

7. A selection in an anthology or a chapter in an edited collection

Note

2. Lorraine Code, "Who Cares? The Poverty of Objectivism for a Moral Epistemology," in *Rethinking Objectivity*, ed. Alan Megill (Durham: Duke University Press, 1994), 179–195.

Bibliography

Code, Lorraine. "Who Cares? The Poverty of Objectivism for a Moral Epistemology." In *Rethinking Objectivity*, edited by Alan Megill, 179–195. Durham: Duke University Press, 1994.

8. Article in a reference work

Publication information is usually omitted from citations of well-known reference volumes. The edition is listed instead. The abbreviation *s.v.* (*sub verbo* or "under the word") replaces an entry's page number.

4. *Benet's Reader's Encyclopedia,* 1987 ed., s.v. "Lampoon."

9. Introduction, foreword, preface, or afterword

When citing an introduction, foreword, preface, or afterword written by someone other than the book's main author, the other writer's name comes first, and the main author's name follows the title of the book.

Note

5. Edward Larkin, introduction to *Common Sense,* by Thomas Paine (New York: Broadview, 2004).

Bibliography

Larkin, Edward. Introduction to *Common Sense,* by Thomas Paine. New York: Broadview, 2004.

REVISED EDITIONS, VOLUMES, AND SERIES

10. A revised or later edition of a book

Note

1. Jeremy Hawthorn, ed., *A Concise Glossary of Contemporary Literary Theory,* 2nd ed. (London: Arnold, 1994), 30.

Bibliography

Hawthorn, Jeremy, ed. *A Concise Glossary of Contemporary Literary Theory.* 2nd ed. London: Arnold, 1994.

11. Work in more than one volume

Note

1. Oscar Wilde, *The Complete Works of Oscar Wilde,* vol. 3 (New York: Dragon Press, 1998), 1024.

Bibliography

Wilde, Oscar. *The Complete Works of Oscar Wilde.* Vol. 3. New York: Dragon Press, 1998.

EDITIONS AND TRANSLATIONS

12. Book with an editor

Note

1. Thomas Hardy, *Jude the Obscure,* ed. Norman Page (New York: Norton, 1999), 35.

Bibliography

Hardy, Thomas. *Jude the Obscure*, edited by Norman Page. New York: Norton, 1999.

13. Book with a translator

Follow the style shown in entry 12, but substitute "trans." for "ed." in the note and "Translated" for "Edited" in the bibliographic entry.

GOVERNMENT DOCUMENTS

14. Government document

Note

5. Health Canada Food Safety Assessment Program, *Assessment Report of the Canadian Food Inspection Agency Activities Related to the Safety of Aquaculture Products* (Ottawa: Minister of Public Works and Government Services Canada, 2001), 24.

Bibliography

Health Canada Food Safety Assessment Program. *Assessment Report of the Canadian Food Inspection Agency Activities Related to the Safety of Aquaculture Products*. Ottawa: Ministry of Public Works and Government Services, 2001.

RELIGIOUS TEXTS

15. Religious texts

Citations from religious texts appear in the notes, but not in the bibliography. Give the version in parentheses in the first citation only.

Note

4. John 3:16 (King James Version).

LETTERS

16. Published letter

Note

5. Oscar Wilde to Robert Ross, 25 November 1897. *The Complete Letters of Oscar Wilde,* ed. Merlin Holland and Rupert Hart-Davis (New York: Holt, 2000), 992.

Bibliography

Wilde, Oscar. Letter to Robert Ross. 25 November 1897. In *The Complete Letters of Oscar Wilde*, edited by Merlin Holland and Rupert Hart-Davis, 992. New York: Holt, 2000.

17. Personal letter to author

Personal communications are not usually listed in the bibliography because they are not accessible to the public.

Note

7. Ann Williams, letter to author, May 8, 2004.

DISSERTATIONS AND CONFERENCE PROCEEDINGS

18. Unpublished dissertation

Note

7. James Elsworth Kidd, "The Vision of Uncertainty: Elizabethan Windows and the Problem of Sight" (PhD diss., Southern Illinois University, 1998), 236.

Bibliography

Kidd, James Elsworth. "The Vision of Uncertainty: Elizabethan Windows and the Problem of Sight." PhD diss., Southern Illinois University, 1998.

19. Published proceedings of a conference

Note

8. Joyce Marie Jackson, "Barrelhouse Singers and Sanctified Preachers," in *Saints and Sinners: Religion, Blues, and (D)evil in African-American Music and Literature: Proceedings of the Conference held at the Université de Liège,* 14–28 (Liège: Société Liègeoise de Musicologie, 1996).

Bibliography

Jackson, Joyce Marie. "Barrelhouse Singers and Sanctified Preachers." In *Saints and Sinners: Religion, Blues, and (D)evil in African-American Music and Literature: Proceedings of the Conference held at the Université de Liège,* 14–28. Liège: Société Liègeoise de Musicologie, 1996.

24b PERIODICAL SOURCES IN CMS STYLE

Note

1. Antoinette Galotala, "From Bohemianism to Radicalism: The Art of the *Liberator*." *American Studies International* 40 (2002): 2–32.

Bibliography

Galotala, Antoinette. "From Bohemianism to Radicalism: The Art of the *Liberator*," *American Studies International* 40 (2002): 2–32.

AUTHOR'S OR EDITOR'S NAME

Note: Give the author's name in normal order.

Bibliography: Give the author's name in reverse order.

TITLE OF ARTICLE

- Put the title in quotation marks. If there is a title of a book within the title, italicize it.
- Capitalize nouns, verbs, adjectives, adverbs, and pronouns, and the first word of the title and subtitle.

PUBLICATION INFORMATION

Name of journal
- Italicize the name of the journal.
- Journal titles are normally not abbreviated in the arts and humanities unless the title of the journal is an abbreviation (*PMLA, ELH*).

Volume, issue, and page numbers
- Place the volume number after the journal title without intervening punctuation.
- For journals that are paginated from issue to issue within a volume, do not list the issue number.
- When citing an entire article, with no page numbers, place the abbreviation *vol.* before the volume number.

Date
- The date or year of publication is given in parentheses after the volume number, or issue number, if provided.

Sample citations for periodical sources

JOURNAL ARTICLES

20. Article by one author

Note

> 1. Sumit Guha, "Speaking Historically: The Changing Voices of Historical Narration in Western India, 1400–1900." *American Historical Review* 109 (2004): 1084–98.

Bibliography

> Guha, Sumit. "Speaking Historically: The Changing Voices of Historical Narration in Western India, 1400–1900," *American Historical Review* 109 (2004): 1084–98.

In subsequent references, cite the author's last name only:

> 2. Guha, 1088.

If the reference is to the same work as the reference before it, you can use the abbreviation *Ibid.*:

> 3. Ibid., 1089.

21. Article by two or three authors

Note

> 3. Pamela R. Matthews and Mary Ann O'Farrell, "Introduction: Whose Body?" *South Central Review* 18, no. 3–4 (Fall–Winter 2001): 1–5.

All authors' names are printed in normal order. For subsequent references, give both authors' last names.

> 4. Matthews and O'Farrell, 4.

Bibliography

> Matthews, Pamela R., and Mary Ann O'Farrell. "Introduction: Whose Body?" *South Central Review* 18, no. 3–4 (Fall–Winter 2001): 1–5.

22. Article by more than three authors

Note

Give the name of the first listed author, followed by *and others*.

> 5. Thompson and others, 602.

Bibliography
List all of the authors (inverting only the first author's name).

Thompson, Michael J., Jorgen Christensen-Dalsgaard, Mark S. Miesch, and Juri Toomre. "The Internal Rotation of the Sun." *Annual Review of Astronomy and Astrophysics* 41 (2003): 599–643.

23. Article by an unknown author

Note

6. "Japan's Global Claim to Asia," *American Historical Review* 109 (2004): 1196–98.

Bibliography

"Japan's Global Claim to Asia." *American Historical Review* 109 (2004): 1196–98.

DIFFERENT TYPES OF PAGINATION

24. Journals paginated by volume

Note

4. Susan Welsh, "Resistance Theory and Illegitimate Reproduction," *College Composition and Communication* 52 (2001): 553–73.

Bibliography

Welsh, Susan. "Resistance Theory and Illegitimate Reproduction." *College Composition and Communication* 52 (2001): 553–73.

25. Journals paginated by issue

For journals paginated separately by issue, list the issue number after the volume number.

Note

5. Tzvetan Todorov, "The New World Disorder," *South Central Review* 19, no. 2 (2002): 28–32.

Bibliography

Todorov, Tzvetan. "The New World Disorder." *South Central Review* 19, no. 2 (2002): 28–32.

26. Weekly and biweekly magazines

For a weekly or biweekly popular magazine, give both the day and month of publication as listed on the issue.

Note

> 5. Lianne George, "It's Not Just a Car Anymore . . . It's a Home," *Maclean's* February 27, 2006, 22.

Bibliography

> George, Lianne. "It's Not Just a Car Anymore . . . It's a Home." *Maclean's,* February 27, 2006, 20–25.

27. Regular features and departments

Do not put titles of regular features or departments of a magazine in quotation marks.

> 3. This Week Online, *Newsweek*, November 19, 2001, 4.

REVIEWS AND EDITORIALS

28. A review

Provide the title, if given, and name the work reviewed. If there is no title, just name the work reviewed.

Note

> 1. Mark Steyn, "What Should I Do, Imam?" review of *Prayers for the Assassin* by Robert Ferrigno, *Maclean's,* February 27, 2006, 54.

Bibliography

> Steyn, Mark. "What Should I Do, Imam?" Review of *Prayers for the Assassin* by Robert Ferrigno. *Maclean's,* February 27, 2006, 54–55.

29. A letter to the editor or an editorial

Add *letter* or *editorial* after the name of the author (if there is one). If there is no author, start with the descriptor.

Note

> 2. Daphne Patai, letter to the editor, *Harper's Magazine,* December 2001, 4.

Bibliography

> Patai, Daphne. Letter to the Editor. *Harper's Magazine,* December 2001, 4.

NEWSPAPERS

30. Newspaper article

> 1. Julie Saccone, "Findings May Diffuse Stem-Cell Controversy," *Saskatoon StarPhoenix,* March 18, 2006, sec. A.

- The month, day, and year are essential in citations of materials from daily newspapers. Cite them in this order: Month—Day—Year (November 3, 2007).
- For an item in a large city newspaper that has several editions a day, give the edition after the date.
- If the newspaper is published in sections, include the name, number, or letter of the section after the date or the edition (sec. C).
- Page numbers are usually omitted. If you put them in, use *p.* and *col.* (column) to avoid ambiguity.

24c ONLINE AND COMPUTER SOURCES IN CMS STYLE

Citing online sources in CMS style

CMS advocates a style for citing online and electronic sources that is adapted from its style used for citing print sources. Titles of complete works are italicized. Quotation marks and other punctuation in citations for online sources should be used in the same manner as for print sources.

Access dates: CMS does not generally recommend the use of access dates, except in time-sensitive fields such as law or medicine.

Revision dates: Due to the inconsistency in the practice of internet sites stating the date of last revision, CMS also recommends against using revision dates in citations.

URLs: The first letter of a URL is never capitalized in CMS style, even following a period. If a URL has to be broken at the end of a line, the line break should be made after a slash (/) or double slash (//). CMS does not advocate the use of angle brackets to enclose URLs.

For details not covered in this section, consult *The Chicago Manual of Style,* fifteenth edition, sections 17.4–17.15, "The Advent of Electronic Sources."

ONLINE PUBLICATIONS

31. Document or page from a website

To cite original content from within a website, include as many descriptive elements as you can: author of the page, title of the page, title and owner of the website, and the URL. Include the date accessed only if the site is time-sensitive or is frequently updated. If you cannot locate an individual author, the owner of the site can stand in for the author.

Note

11. National Organization for Women, "NOW History," http://www.now.org/history/history.html.

Bibliography

National Organization for Women. "NOW History." http://www.now.org.history/history.html.

32. Online book

Note

12. Angelina Grimké, *Appeal to the Christian Women of the South* (New York: New York Anti-Slavery Society, 1836), http://history.furman.edu/~benson/docs/grimke2.htm.

Bibliography

Grimké, Angelina. *Appeal to the Christian Women of the South*. New York: New York Anti-Slavery Society, 1836. http://history .furman.edu/~benson/docs/grimke2.htm.

33. Online article

Note

13. Phil Agre, "The Internet and Public Discourse," *First Monday* 3, no. 3 (March 1998): http://www.firstmonday.dk/issues/issue3_3/ agre/.

Bibliography

Agre, Phil. "The Internet and Public Discourse." *First Monday* 3, no. 3 (March 1998): http://www.firstmonday.dk/issues/issue3_3/agre/.

OTHER ELECTRONIC SOURCES

34. Posting to a discussion list or group

To cite material from archived internet forums, discussion groups, MOOs, or Gopher sites, include the name of the post author, the name of the list or site, the date of the posting, and the URL. Limit your citation to notes or in-text citations.

16. Theresa Hyland, post to CASLL (Canadian Association for the Study of Language and Literature) listserv, April 12, 2006, https://listserv.unb.ca/.

35. Email

Since personal emails are not available to the public, they are not usually listed in the bibliography.

Note

11. Jamie MacKinnon, "Doyle, Fox, Canadian Sense of Humour," email to author, May 11, 2004.

24d MULTIMEDIA SOURCES IN CMS STYLE

36. Musical recording

Note

8. The Tragically Hip, "Ahead by a Century," *Trouble at the Henhouse*, MCA Music Entertainment compact disc MCAD 81011.

Bibliography

The Tragically Hip. "Ahead by a Century." *Trouble at the Henhouse*. MCA Music Entertainment compact disc MCAD 81011.

37. Film or video

Note

9. *Office Space*, DVD, directed by Mike Judge (Beverly Hills, CA: Twentieth Century Fox, 1999).

Bibliography

Office Space. DVD. Directed by Mike Judge. Beverly Hills, CA, Twentieth Century Fox, 1999.

38. Speech, debate, mediated discussion, or public talk

Note

16. Katherine Tiede, "Using Storyboarding to Engineer Genre" (paper presented at the Conference on College Composition and Communication, Chicago, IL, March 2006).

Bibliography

Tiede, Katherine. "Using Storyboarding to Engineer Genre." Paper presented at the Conference on College Composition and Communication, Chicago, IL, March 2006.

39. Interview

Note

15. Belinda Stronach, "The Dave McGraw Interview: Belinda Stronach, Redux," interview by Dave McGraw, *The Hammer*, May 19, 2005, http://www.thehammer.ca/content/view.php?news=2005-05-19-belinda-stronach-interview-redux.

Bibliography

Stronach, Belinda. "The Dave McGraw Interview: Belinda Stronach, Redux." Interview by Dave McGraw. *The Hammer,* May 19, 2005. http://www.thehammer.ca/content/view.php?news=2005-05-19-belinda-stronach-interview-redux.

40. Illustrations, figures, and tables

When citing figures from sources, use the abbreviation *fig*. However, spell out the word when citing tables, graphs, maps, or plates. The page number on which the figure appears precedes any figure number.

16. Christian Unger, *America's Inner-City Crisis* (New York: Childress, 2003), 134, fig. 3.4.

24e SAMPLE PAGES WITH CMS DOCUMENTATION

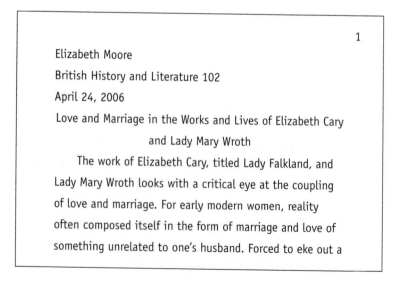

1

Elizabeth Moore

British History and Literature 102

April 24, 2006

Love and Marriage in the Works and Lives of Elizabeth Cary
and Lady Mary Wroth

The work of Elizabeth Cary, titled Lady Falkland, and Lady Mary Wroth looks with a critical eye at the coupling of love and marriage. For early modern women, reality often composed itself in the form of marriage and love of something unrelated to one's husband. Forced to eke out a

2

place in their prescribed roles as wife and mother for their own intellectual expression, Cary and Wroth wrote stories about women who found themselves caught between their own powerful desires and the men who controlled their lives. Their writing is important today not only as literature but as an invaluable record of the thoughts and self-expression of women in a time when their lives were not their own. The protagonists of Cary's and Wroth's work explore the meaning of love and marriage, both topics complex and often dissatisfying in the context of their time. Like their fictional characters, Cary and Wroth navigated the rocky terrain of the heart and the mind. Their biographies both inform and contradict their writing. The dialogue between their realities and their fiction considers what it meant to be woman in the early modern period.

Elizabeth Cary and Mary Wroth were born Elizabeth Tanfield and Mary Sidney, respectively. They were both eminently well educated in childhood. Tanfield, born in 1585, had taught herself "French, Spanish, Italian, Latin, Hebrew and 'Transylvanian'" by the age of 4 and successfully argued for the acquittal of a woman accused of witchcraft at 10.[1] Sidney, born in 1587, was the niece of noted Renaissance poet and literary patron Mary Herbert, countess of Pembroke, for whom she was named. She spent part of her childhood in extended visits with her aunt. She was active in the court of King James I and VI and performed in several masques.[2] Both Sidney and Tanfield were brought up in academically fertile environments. . . .

3

Notes

1. Nancy Cotton Pearse, "Elizabeth Cary, Renaissance Playwright," *Texas Studies in Literature and Language* 18 (1977): 601–608.

2. Josephine Roberts, "The Biographical Problem of *Pamphilia to Amphilanthus*," *Tulsa Studies in Women's Literature* 1, no. 1 (1982): 43–53.

4

Bibliography

Pearse, Nancy Cotton. "Elizabeth Cary, Renaissance Playwright." *Texas Studies in Literature and Language* 18 (1977): 601-608.

Roberts, Josephine. "The Biographical Problem of *Pamphilia* to *Amphilanthus*." *Tulsa Studies in Women's Literature* 1, no. 1 (1982): 43–53.

For a complete sample research paper in CMS style, visit www.pearsoned.ca/faigley/219.

CSE C H A P T E R *25*

CSE Documentation

Within the disciplines of the natural and applied sciences, citation styles are highly specialized. Many disciplines follow the guidelines of particular journals or style manuals within their individual fields. One of these guides, published by the Council of Science Editors (formerly the Council of Biology Editors), is *Scientific Style and Format: The CSE Manual for Authors, Editors, and Publishers*, seventh edition (2006). The *CSE Manual* is influential and widely followed by writers in the sciences.

Name-year and citation-name systems

CSE style now recommends two principal methods for documenting sources: the **name-year** system and the **citation-name** system. (Citation-name appears for the first time in the seventh edition; it differs somewhat from CSE's previous citation-sequence system.) In the CSE name-year system, both the author's last name and the year of publication appear together in parentheses directly following cited material in the text.

> The Red-cockaded Woodpecker (*Picoides borealis*) typically uses a single cavity for nesting (Ligon 1970, Walters et al. 1988).

In the CSE citation-name system, citations in the body of the text are marked by a superscript number placed inside punctuation. For example

> Cold fingers and toes are common circulatory problems found in most heavy cigarette smokers[1].

This number corresponds to a numbered entry on the alphabetized CSE source list, entitled *References*.

The CSE References page lists all sources cited in the paper. To create a CSE References page, follow these guidelines:

1. Title your page "References," and centre this title at the top of the page.
2. Double-space between citations and single-space within citations.
3. For papers using the **citation-name system**, list and number citations in alphabetical order. Begin each citation with its citation number, followed by a period, flush left.
4. For papers using the **name-year system**, list references, unnumbered, in alphabetical order. Begin each citation flush left. Indent any subsequent lines of the citation five spaces.
5. Authors are listed by last name, followed by initials. Capitalize only first words and proper nouns in cited titles. Titles are not underlined, and articles are not placed in quotations. Names of journals should be abbreviated where possible.
6. Cite publication year, and volume or page numbers if applicable.

WRITING IN THE WORLD

The National Library of Medicine

The CSE recommendations for citations and references are based on the *National Library of Medicine Recommended Formats for Bibliographic Citation* (1991). Additionally, the National Library of Medicine (NLM) has an extensive supplement on internet formats available at www.nlm.nih.gov/pubs/formats/internet.pdf.

25a IN-TEXT CITATIONS IN CSE STYLE

Name-year system (N-Y)

In 2006, a Gallup International poll found that 26% of individuals around the world see poverty as humanity's most pressing problem (Vallis, 2006).

PLACEMENT OF AUTHOR'S NAME AND DATE (NAME-YEAR SYSTEM)

You have two choices:

1. As in the example above, place the author's name and the year of publication inside parentheses following the material cited.
2. Put the author's name in a signal phrase right in your sentence. Then, put the year in parentheses right after.

Citation-name system (C-N)

In 2006, a Gallup International poll found that 26% of individuals around the world see poverty as humanity's most pressing problem[1].

The superscript [1] refers to the first entry alphabetically on the References list, where readers will find a complete citation for this source.

What if you need more than one citation in a passage?

N-Y When you cite two or more sources at once, your citation should be arranged chronologically, from the earliest publication to the latest. Each citation is separated by a semicolon.

(Radhost 1969; Barker and others 1972; WHO 2001)

If your sources are published in the same year, arrange these citations alphabetically:

(Earhart and others 1997; Smythe 1997; Matina 1999)

C-N If the numbers are consecutive, separate with a hyphen or en dash. If non-consecutive, use a comma without a space.

The previous work 1,3,5-8,11 . . .

Sample in-text citations (name-year system)

1. Work by a single author

The author's last name comes first, followed by the year of publication:

(Barron 2001)

2. Work by two authors

The authors' last names follow the order of the title page and are joined by *and*.

(Monastersky and Allen 1998)

If the authors have the same surname, add their initials.

(Allen SR and Allen TJ 1997)

3. Work by three or more authors

Use the last name of the first author, followed by *and others*, and the year of publication.

(Barker and others 1972)

4. Work by a group or organization

Treat the group or organization as the author, but abbreviate if possible.

(WHO 2001)

25b BOOKS AND NON-PERIODICAL SOURCES IN CSE-STYLE REFERENCES

Name-Year (N-Y)

Nance JJ. 1991. What goes up: the global assault on our atmosphere. New York: W Morrow. 324 p.

Citation-Name (C-N)

1. Nance JJ. What goes up: the global assault on our atmosphere. New York: W Morrow; 1991. 324 p.

AUTHOR'S OR EDITOR'S NAME

The author's last name comes first, followed by the initials of the author's first name and middle name (if provided). If an editor, put the word *editor* after the name.

The NLM recommends using the full first name for an author. Whichever you choose, be consistent throughout your references.

PUBLICATION INFORMATION

Year of publication
- In **N-Y**, the year comes after the author(s). In **C-N**, the year comes after the other publication information. It follows a semicolon.

- If it is a multivolume edited work, published over a period of more than one year, give the span of years.

Page numbers
- When citing an entire book, give the total number of pages: *324 p.*

- When citing part of a book, give the page range for the selection: *p. 60-90.*

BOOK TITLE

- Do not italicize or underline titles.

- Capitalize only the first word and proper nouns.

Sample references

BOOKS

5. Book by a single author/editor

N-Y   Minger TJ, editor. 1990. Greenhouse glasnost: the crisis of global warming. New York: Ecco. 292 p.

C-N   2. Minger TJ, editor. Greenhouse glasnost: the crisis of global warming. New York: Ecco; 1990. 292 p.

6. Book by two or more authors/editors

N-Y   O'Day DH, Horgen PA, editors. 1981. Sexual interactions in eukaryotic microbes. New York: Academic Press. 407 p.

C-N   3. O'Day DH, Horgen PA, editors. Sexual interactions in eukaryotic microbes. New York: Academic Press; 1981. 407 p.

7. Book by a group or organization

In N-Y, the full name is given, preceded by the abbreviation in brackets.

N-Y   [IAEA] International Atomic Energy Association. 1971. Manual on radiation haematology. Vienna: IAEA. 430 p.

C-N   4. International Atomic Energy Association. IAEA. Manual on radiation haematology. Vienna: IAEA; 1971. 430 p.

8. Two or more books by the same author

In **C-N**, number the references alphabetically by author last name and maintain that numbering for in-text citations. In **N-Y**, arrange them by date, or alphabetically according to names of additional authors. If the date and the additional authors are the same, arrange according to title. To clarify in-text citation, assign a letter (a, b, c) to the repeated dates.

N-Y   Clarke JJ. 1903a. Protozoa and disease. New York: W Wood.
Clarke JJ. 1903b. Rhizopod protozoa. New York: W Wood.

PARTS OF BOOKS

9. A single chapter written by the same author as the book

N-Y Ogle M. 2000. All the modern conveniences: American household plumbing, 1840-1890. Baltimore: Johns Hopkins Univ Pr. Convenience embodied; p. 60-92.

C-N 6. Ogle M. All the modern conveniences: American household plumbing, 1840-1890. Baltimore: Johns Hopkins Univ Pr; 2000. Convenience embodied; p. 60-92.

10. A selection in an anthology or a chapter in an edited collection

N-Y Kraft K, Baines DM. 1997. Computer classrooms and third grade development. In: Green MD, editor. Computers and early development. New York: Academic. p. 168-79.

C-N 7. Kraft K, Baines DM. Computer classrooms and third grade development. In: Green MD, editor. Computers and early development. New York: Academic; 1997. p. 168-79.

REPORTS

11. Technical and research reports

N-Y Austin A, Baldwin R, editors. 1991. Faculty collaboration: enhancing the quality of scholarship and teaching. ASCHE-ERIC Higher Education Report 7. Washington, DC: George Washington University.

C-N 9. Austin A, Baldwin R, editors. Faculty collaboration: enhancing the quality of scholarship and teaching. ASCHE-ERIC Higher Education Report 7. Washington, DC: George Washington University; 1991.

25c PERIODICAL SOURCES IN CSE-STYLE REFERENCES

Name-Year (N-Y)

Board J. 2001. Reduced lodging for soybean in low plant population is related to light quality. Crop Science 41(2):379-87.

Citation-Name (C-N)

1. Board J. Reduced lodging for soybeans in low plant population is related to light quality. Crop Science 2001;41(2):379-87.

AUTHOR'S NAME

The author's last name comes first, followed by the initials of the author's first name and middle name (if provided).

The NLM recommends using the full first name for an author. Whichever you choose, be consistent throughout your references.

TITLE OF ARTICLE

- Do not italicize or underline titles.
- Capitalize only the first word and proper nouns.

PUBLICATION INFORMATION

Name of journal
- Do not abbreviate single-word titles. Abbreviate multiple-word titles according to the National Information Standards Organization (NISO) list of serials.

- Capitalize the journal title, even if abbreviated.

Date of publication, volume, and issue numbers
- For continuously paginated journals, include the year, volume number, and issue number.

JOURNAL ARTICLES

12. Article by one author

N-Y Board J. 2001. Reduced lodging for soybean in low plant population is related to light quality. Crop Science 41(2):379-87.

C-N 1. Board J. Reduced lodging for soybean in low plant population is related to light quality. Crop Science 2001(2);41:379-87.

13. Article by two or more authors/editors

N-Y Simms K, Denison D. 1997. Observed interactions between wild and domesticated mixed-breed canines. J. Mamm 70(78):341-2.

C-N 2. Simms K, Denison D. Observed interactions between wild and domesticated mixed-breed canines. J. Mamm 1997(78); 70:341-2.

14. Article by a group or organization

In **C-N** list the full name only. In **N-Y**, give the abbreviation in brackets, followed by the full name.

N-Y [CSPI] Center for Science in the Public Interest. 2001 Apr 1. Meat labeling: Help! Nutrition Action Health Letter: 2.

15. Article with no identifiable author

In both **N-Y** and **C-N**, begin with the article title.

16. Journals paginated by issue

Use the month or season of publication (and day, if given) for journals that have no volume or issue number.

N-Y Solar-Tuttle R. 2000 Spring-Summer. The invincible ones. Harv AIDS Rev. 19-20.

C-N 8. Solar-Tuttle R. The invincible ones. Harv AIDS Rev. 2000 Spring-Summer: 19-20.

25d ONLINE SOURCES IN CSE-STYLE REFERENCES

Scientific Style and Format: The CSE Manual for Authors, Editors, and Publishers (7th edition, 2006) covers electronic citation, but, for expanded guidelines, see the National Library of Medicine Recommended Formats for Bibliographic Citations supplement on internet formats, available at <www.nlm.nih.gov/pubs/formats/internet.pdf>.

Name-year (N-Y)

Lowe C. 2001. Speech recognition: sci-fi or composition? Currents in Electronic Literacy [Internet]. [Cited 2006 June 10];4. Available from: http://www.cwrl.utexas.edu/currents/archives/spr01/lowe.html

Citation-name (C-N)

1. Lowe C. Speech recognition: sci-fi or composition? Currents in Electronic Literacy [Internet]. 2001 [cited 2006 June 10];4. Available from: http://www.cwrl.utexas.edu/currents/archives/spr01/lowe

Author's name, associated institution, or organization

- Authorship of online sources is sometimes hard to discern. If you have a personal author to cite, follow the rules for periodicals and books.
- An organization or institution can be the author (and, abbreviated if desired, the publisher).

N-Y [WHO] World Health Organization [Internet]. c2006. Washington: WHO/OMS; [cited 2006 Dec 21]. Available from: http://www.who.int/home-page/index.en.shtml

C-N 2. World Health Organization [Internet]. Washington: WHO/OMS; c2006. [Cited 2006 Dec 21]. Available from: http://www.who.int/home-page/index.en.shtml

- If the author is not the publisher, sponsoring organization, or institution, list the name of the organization or institution after the place of publication.
- If there is more than one author, list all, up to ten. If there are more than ten, list the first ten followed by *and others*.
- If no author can be discerned, list by title.

Dates

Include three dates in a website reference: (1) the publication date; if not given, the copyright date: c2002; (2) the most recent revision date, if available; (3) the date you accessed (cited) the site: [revised 2005 Dec; cited 2006 Mar 5].

Name of site and title of page

If a page on a website has a title, treat it like the title of a periodical article. Otherwise, treat the name of the site itself as you would a book title. In either case, put the medium [Internet] in square brackets after the title of the site.

SAMPLE PAGES WITH CSE NAME-YEAR DOCUMENTATION

1

Thuydung Do

BIO 206L Fall 2006

November 13, 2006

The Preference of Home Soil over Foreign Soil in *Pogonomyrmex barbatus*

Abstract

Tests were conducted to see whether or not harvester ants of the species *Pogonomyrmex barbatus* can actually distinguish home soil from foreign soil and neutral soil. These ants were exposed to different types of soils and the time they spent on each soil was recorded. The Wilcoxan Signed Rank test was performed to analyze the collected data. It was observed that *Pogonomyrmex barbatus* does show preference for home soil over foreign soil. There was not enough evidence to see whether or not *P. barbatus* can recognize home soil from neutral soil.

Introduction

Pieces of food are sometimes seen surrounded by hundreds of ants a while after they were dropped on the table or on the ground. There are also trails of ants that line up in an orderly fashion leading from the food to the nests. How do these ants know to follow each other in a line instead of scattering all over? The main method is through releasing pheromones. According to Holldobler and others (2001), "*Pogonomyrmex* workers recruit nestmates to new seed patches by chemical recruitment

2

trails, the pheromone of which originates from the poison gland." Holldobler and his group (2001) also found three alkylpyrazines that are the main composition of the secretions coming out of the poison glands. The pheromones allow the ants to trail after one another, but where will they go? There is certainly more than one nest out there. Will this confuse the ants? Do they actually carry the food back to their own nests, to foreign nests, or to elsewhere? What makes these different ant mounds unique from one another? Based on research done by Diane Wagner and her group (1997), soil biota and soil chemistry of each nest can set themselves apart. It was found that the "Protozoan [such as ciliates, amoebae and flagellates] abundance and biomass were significantly (5-6 fold) greater in ant nest soils than in control soils." Also, "*P. barbatus* nest soils contained significantly higher concentrations of nitrate, ammonium, phosphorus, and potassium than control soils" (Wagner and others 1997). Can the harvester ants detect these differences in the soils at all or are all soils the same to them? In this experiment, the null hypothesis that says harvester ants *Pogonomyrmex barbatus* cannot distinguish home soil from foreign soil and neutral soil was tested in attempt to find the answer to this question.

. . .

3

References

Holldobler B, Morgan ED, Oldham NJ, Liebig J. 2001.
    Recruitment pheromone in the harvester ant
    genus *Pogonomyrmex*. Journal of Insect Physiology
    47(4-5):369-74.

Wagner D, Brown M, Gordon D. 1997. Harvester ant nests,
    soil biota, and soil chemistry. Oecologia 112:232-6.

To see this student paper in its complete form, visit
www.pearsoned.ca/faigley/220.

PART NINE

Effective Style and Language

- What does *passive voice* mean and why should I avoid using it? (26a)

- How can I reduce wordiness in my writing? (27a–c)

- What is parallel structure and how can I use it effectively in my writing? (28c–e)

- How formal should my writing style be? (29b)

- How can I avoid sexist pronouns without using "him or her" all the time? (30b)

26
Write with Power

27
Write Concisely

28
Write with Emphasis

29
Find the Right Words

30
Write to Be Inclusive

31
Write for Diverse Audiences

9 EFFECTIVE STYLE AND LANGUAGE

Make your writing a pleasure to read rather than a confusing slog for your readers. Keeping a few principles in mind can turn a correct but boring style into one that is emphatic, inclusive, and memorable.

MyCanadianCompLab

The MyCanadianCompLab multimedia resource extends the coverage you will find in Common Errors boxes throughout the handbook. Each multimedia module includes a step-by-step explanation of how to fix the problem; corrected examples with complete explanations; and practice on both sentences and paragraphs, with immediate feedback to help you learn. View all the topics at the MyCanadianCompLab website at **www.pearsoned .ca/highered/mycanadiancomplab/**.

Visit *The Brief Penguin Handbook* Companion Website at
www.pearsoned.ca/faigley/

MyCanadianCompLab
Where writing and research help is a click away.
MyCanadianCompLab may be packaged with your textbook.
If not, it can be purchased from your college or university's bookstore.
Go to **www.pearsoned.ca/highered/mycanadiancomplab/**
for a tour.

CHAPTER 26

Write with Power

Keeping a few principles in mind can make your writing a pleasure to read instead of a boring slog.

In visuals

Viewers imagine actions when subjects are captured in motion.

In writing

Readers expect actions to be expressed in verbs: *gallop, canter, trot, run, sprint, dash, bound, thunder, tear away*

In visuals

Viewers interpret the most prominent person or thing as the subject—what the visual is about.

In writing

Readers interpret the first person or thing they meet in a sentence as what the sentence is about (the jockey, the horse). They expect that person or thing to do the action expressed in the verb.

26a   RECOGNIZE ACTIVE AND PASSIVE VOICE

When you were a very young child, you learned an important lesson about language. Perhaps you can remember the day you figured out how to push a chair over to the counter to reach the cookie jar. But the inevitable happened: the jar fell off the counter and smashed on the floor. You knew Mom would be rushing to the kitchen. What would you say? Would you confess and say, "I knocked over the jar"? Probably not. Instead, you might have said, "The jar got broken." This short sentence accomplishes an amazing sleight of hand. Who broke the jar and how the jar was broken remain mysterious. Apparently, it just broke.

"Got" is often used for "was" in informal speech. In written language, the sentence would read, "The jar was broken," which is an example of the passive voice. Passives can be as useful for adults as for children to conceal who is responsible for an action:

> The hard disks containing the top secret files were misplaced.

Who misplaced the hard disks? Who knows?

Sentences with transitive verbs (labelled "TV" below; verbs that need an object; see Section 32c) can be written in the active or passive voice. In the active voice the subject of the sentence is the actor. In the passive voice the subject is being acted upon.

	┌─────── SUBJ ───────┐ ┌──TV──┐
ACTIVE	**Leonardo da Vinci** painted *Mona Lisa* between 1503 and 1506.

	┌── SUBJ ──┐ ┌───── TV─────┐
PASSIVE	*Mona Lisa* **was painted** by Leonardo da Vinci between 1503 and 1506.

The passive is created with a form of *be* and the past participle of the main verb. In a passive voice sentence, you can either name the actor in a *by* phrase following the verb or omit the actor altogether.

PASSIVE	*Mona Lisa* was painted between 1503 and 1506.

Most of the time you are not out to conceal but rather to communicate. To write with power, consider different ways of saying the same thing. The extra effort will bring noticeable results. Listen to the difference:

PASSIVE	The pear tree in the front yard was demolished by the unexpected storm.
ACTIVE	The unexpected storm demolished the pear tree in the front yard.

PASSIVE   A request on your part for special consideration based on
           —————TV—————
           your experience working in the profession will be reviewed
           by the admissions committee.

ACTIVE   If you ask for special consideration because you have
           worked in the profession, the graduate admissions committee
           ——TV——
           will review your request.

WRITING IN THE WORLD

When you need to use passives

Whether you are writing for the world of work or the academic
world, you will find there are times when passives are required.
Passive sentences are used when

- you want to keep the focus on the person or thing being acted upon,
- you don't know the actor, or
- you and your readers know the actor's identity.

1   Our January sales were increased substantially by our deep
    discounts.
2   Analog, digital, and sampled data are simulated together before
    the company commits to the expense of manufacture.
3   The suspect was apprehended within 10 minutes of the conven-
    ience store robbery.

In sentence 1, the focus is on *increased January sales*, not *deep discounts*.
In sentence 2, the process of simulation is the focus, not the unknown
people who actually perform the simulations. In sentence 3, the actors
who do the apprehending are assumed to be the police. The focus is
on the suspect.

26b   USE ACTION VERBS

Where are the "action words"?

A teacher may once have told you that verbs are "action words." Where are
the action words in the following paragraph?

> The 1980 Olympic games were in Moscow. Two months before the start
> of the Olympics was the Soviet invasion of Afghanistan. In response
> to the invasion, it was announced by Prime Minister Joe Clark that
> Canada was to join 61 other countries in not attending those Olympic
> games. There is still bitterness among hundreds of athletes about the
> boycott of the 1980 Olympics.

No action words here! The paragraph describes a series of actions, yet the only verbs are forms of *be* (*is, was, were*). These sentences are not in the passive voice, but they typify writing that uses *be* verbs when better alternatives are available. Think about what the actions are and choose powerful verbs that express those actions.

> Just two months before the start of the Moscow Olympic games in 1980, the Soviet Union **invaded** Afghanistan. Prime Minister Joe Clark denounced the invasion and **declared** a Canadian boycott of the Olympics. Sixty-one other nations also **withdrew** from the Olympics in protest. Today, athletes from those nations who were **denied** the opportunity to participate in the Olympics **remain** bitter about the boycott.

Express actions as verbs

Many sentences contain words that express action, but those words are nouns instead of verbs. Often the nouns can be changed into verbs. For example:

> The arson unit ~~conducted an investigation of~~ **investigated** the mysterious fire.

> The committee ~~had a debate over~~ **debated** how best to spend the surplus funds.

Notice that changing nouns into verbs also eliminates unnecessary words.

26c NAME YOUR AGENTS

The agent is the person or thing that does the action. The most powerful writing usually highlights the agent in a sentence.

Include people

Read the following sentence aloud:

> Mayoral approval of the recommended zoning change for a strip mall on Walnut Street will negatively impact the traffic and noise levels of the Walnut Street residential environment.

It sounds dead, doesn't it? Think about the meaning of the sentence for a minute. It involves people—the mayor and the people who live on Walnut Street. Putting those people in the sentence makes it come alive:

> **WITH PEOPLE**
> If the **mayor** approves the recommended zoning change to allow a strip mall on Walnut Street, **people who live on the street** will have to endure much more noise and traffic.

Here is another example.

WITHOUT PEOPLE

The use of a MIDI keyboard for playing the song will facilitate capturing it in digital form on our laptop for the subsequent purpose of uploading it to our website.

WITH PEOPLE

By playing the song on a MIDI keyboard, **we** can record the digitized sound on our laptop and then upload it to our website.

Including people makes your writing more emphatic. Most readers relate better to people than to abstractions. Putting people in your writing also introduces active verbs because people do things.

COMMON ERRORS

Sentences that begin with infinitive phrases followed by a passive

An infinitive is the verb form that begins with *to: to give, to receive, to play, to drive.* When you begin a sentence with an infinitive phrase, you should not follow it with the passive voice. Instead, name the agent.

INCORRECT   To drive to Prince Edward Island, **the Confederation Bridge** should be used.

CORRECT   To drive to Prince Edward Island, **you** should use the Confederation Bridge.

Remember: Sentences that begin with infinitives followed by a main clause must name the agent after the first comma.

 For step-by-step discussion, examples, and practice of this common error, go to **www.pearsoned.ca/faigley/221**.

If you are not writing about people, keep the focus on the agents. Read this short section of a report written by an engineer who was asked to recommend which of two types of valves an oil company should purchase for one of its refineries.

The refinery now uses two systems for grease lubrication: one made by Farval, the other by Alemite. Although the two systems function similarly, Farval valves have two distinct advantages. First, Farval grease valves include a pin indicator that shows whether the valve is working. Alemite valves must be checked by taking them apart. Second, Farval valves have metal seals, while Alemite valves have rubber

26e PROJECT PERSONALITY

Nobody likes listening to the voice of a robot. Good writing—no matter what the genre—has two unfailing qualities: a human personality that bursts through the page or screen and a warmth that suggests the writer genuinely wishes to engage the readers.

You can project personality in your writing by putting 15 exclamation points in an email message, but that tactic quickly becomes tiresome when you write at length. In fact, personality often is reflected in the lack of gimmicks.

> From age eleven to age sixteen I lived a spartan life without the usual adolescent uncertainty. I wanted to be the best swimmer in the world, and there was nothing else.
> —Diana Nyad

> You don't choose your family. They are God's gift to you, as you are to them.
> —Desmond Tutu

> I have battled an insane and irresponsible government. Perhaps I am a prophet. I have suffered enough.
> —Louis Riel

Sentences like these convince your readers that you are genuinely interested in reaching out to them.

CHAPTER *27*

Write Concisely

Clutter creeps into our lives every day. Clutter also creeps into writing through unnecessary words, inflated constructions, and excessive jargon.

> **In regards to** the website, the content is **pretty** successful **in consideration of** the topic. The site is **fairly** good **writing-wise** and is **very** unique in telling you how to adjust the rear derailleur one step at a time.

The words in **red** are clutter. Get rid of the clutter. You can say the same thing with half the words and gain more impact as a result.

> The well-written website on bicycle repair provides step-by-step instructions on adjusting your rear derailleur.

27a ELIMINATE UNNECESSARY WORDS

Empty words resemble the foods that add calories without nutrition. Put your writing on a diet.

Redundancy

Some words act as modifiers, but when you look closely at them, they repeat the meaning of the word they pretend to modify. These unnecessary words are *redundant*. Have you heard someone refer to a *personal friend*? Aren't all friends personal? Likewise, you may have heard expressions such as *red in colour, small in size, round in shape, several in number, past history, attractive in appearance, visible to the eye*, or *honest truth*. Imagine *red* not referring to colour or *round* not referring to shape. Similarly, if you watch sports, you no doubt have heard an announcer say something like "The 350-pound tackle is big size-wise," or "The sprinter is fast speed-wise." Nearly all modifiers that end in *-wise*, one of the ugliest constructions in English, say the same thing twice.

Legalese

Legal language often attempts to remove ambiguity through repetition and redundancy. Think about what a flight attendant says when your plane arrives:

> Please remain seated, with your seatbelt fastened, until the airplane has come to a full and complete stop; when you deplane from the airplane, be sure to take with you all your personal belongings.

Is there a difference between a *full* stop and a *complete* stop? Can you *deplane* from anything but an airplane? Would you have any *non-personal* belongings?

Some speech situations may require redundancy to ensure that listeners understand, but in writing, say it once.

Empty intensifiers

Intensifiers modify verbs, adjectives, and other adverbs, and they often are overused. One of the most overused intensifiers is *very*. Take the following sentence as an example:

> The new copper roof was **very bright** on a sunny day.

A new copper roof reflects almost all light. *Very bright* isn't an accurate description. Thus another adjective would be more accurate:

> The new copper roof was **blinding** on a sunny day.

Very and *totally* are but two of a list of empty intensifiers that usually can be eliminated with no loss of meaning. Other empty intensifiers include *absolutely, awfully, definitely, incredibly, particularly,* and *really*.

Remember: When you use *very*, *totally*, or another intensifier before an adjective or adverb, always ask yourself whether there is a more accurate adjective or adverb you could use to express the same thought.

 For step-by-step discussion, examples, and practice of this common error, go to **www.pearsoned.ca/faigley/222**.

27b REDUCE WORDY PHRASES

We acquire bad habits because we read and hear so much wordy language. Many inexperienced writers use phrases like "It is my opinion that" or "I think that" to begin sentences. These phrases are deadly to read. If you find them in your prose, cut them. Unless a writer is citing a source, we assume that the ideas are the writer's. (See "When to use *I*" on page 422.)

Coaches are among the worst at using many words for what could be said in a few:

> After much deliberation about Chevalier's future in hockey with regard to possible permanent head injuries, I came to the conclusion that it would be in his best interest not to continue his pursuit of playing hockey again.

The coach might have said simply:

> Because Chevalier risks permanent injury if he plays hockey again, I decided to release him from the team.

Perhaps the coach wanted to sound impressive, authoritative, or thoughtful. But the result is the opposite. Speakers and writers who impress us are those who use words efficiently.

WRITING IN THE WORLD

Wordy phrases

Certain stock phrases plague writing in the workplace, in the media, and in academia. Many wordy phrases can be replaced by one or two words with no loss in meaning.

Wordy	Concise
at this point in time	now
at that point in time	then
due to the fact that	because
for the purpose of	for
have the ability to	can
in order to	to
in spite of the fact that	although
in the event that	if
in the modern world of today	today
in the neighbourhood of	about
it is possible that there might be	possibly
make an attempt	try
met with her approval	she approved

27c SIMPLIFY TANGLED SENTENCES

Long sentences can be graceful and forceful. Such sentences, however, often require several revisions before they achieve elegance. Too often long sentences reflect wandering thoughts that the writer did not bother to go back and sort out. Two of the most important strategies for untangling long sentences are described in Chapter 26: using active verbs (Section 26b) and naming your agents (Section 26c). Here are some other strategies.

Revise expletives

Expletives are empty words that can occupy the subject position in a sentence. The most frequently used expletives are *there is*, *there are*, and *it is*.

> WORDY   There is another banking option that gives you free chequing.

To simplify the sentence, find the agent and make it the subject.

> REVISED   Another banking option gives you free chequing.

> WORDY   There were several important differences between their respective positions raised by the candidates in the debate.

REVISED	The **candidates** raised several important differences between their respective positions in the debate.
WORDY	**It is** always important to read and follow directions when applying pesticides.
REVISED	**Always read and follow directions** when applying pesticides.

Here the agent is implied, not stated: you.

A few kinds of sentences—for example, *It is raining*—do require you to use an expletive. In most cases, however, expletives add unnecessary words, and sentences usually read better without them.

Use positive constructions

Sentences become wordy and hard to read if they include two or more negatives such as the words *no*, *not*, and *nor*, and the prefixes *un-* and *mis-*. For example:

DIFFICULT	A **not un**common complaint among employers of new post-secondary graduates is that they can**not** communicate effectively in writing.
REVISED	Employers frequently complain that new post-secondary graduates cannot write effectively.
EVEN SIMPLER	Employers value the rare post-secondary graduate who can write well.

Phrasing sentences positively usually makes them more economical. Moreover, it makes your style more forceful and direct.

Simplify sentence structure

Long sentences can be hard to read, not because they are long but because they are convoluted and hide the relationships among ideas. Take the following sentence as an example.

When the cessation of eight years of hostility in the Iran-Iraq war occurred in 1988, it was not the result of one side defeating the other but the exhaustion of both after losing thousands of people and much of their military capability.

This sentence is hard to read. To rewrite sentences like this one, find the main ideas, then determine the relationships among them.

After examining the sentence, you decide there are two key ideas:

1. Iran and Iraq stopped fighting in 1988 after eight years.
2. Both sides were exhausted from losing people and equipment.

Next ask what the relationship is between the two ideas. When you identify the key ideas, the relationship is often obvious; in this case (2) is the cause of (1). Thus the word you want to connect the two ideas is *because*.

Iran and Iraq stopped fighting after eight years of an indecisive war because both sides had lost thousands of people and most of their equipment.

The revised sentence is both clearer and more concise, reducing the number of words from 43 to 25. Notice too that the revision replaces nominalizations (*cessation, hostility, exhaustion*) with active verbs.

Write with Emphasis

Photographs and writing gain energy when key ideas are emphasized.

In visuals

Photographers create emphasis by composing the image to direct the attention of the viewer. Putting people and objects in the foreground and making them stand out against the background gives them emphasis.

In writing

Writers have many tools for creating emphasis. Writers can design a page to gain emphasis by using headings, white space, type size, colour, and boldfacing. Just as important, learning the craft of structuring sentences will empower you to give your writing emphasis.

28a MANAGE EMPHASIS WITHIN SENTENCES

Put your main ideas in main clauses

Chapter 32 discusses a grammatical hierarchy that runs from word to sentence. Within a sentence the clauses that can stand by themselves—the main or independent clauses—are more important than those that must be attached to another clause—the subordinate clauses and phrases.

Main Clause

Subordinate Clause   **Phrase**

Placing more important information in main clauses and less important information in subordinate clauses emphasizes what is important.

In the following paragraph all the sentences are main clauses:

> More Canadians are taking herbal remedies. They think that natural herbs must be safe. The remedies can cause bad reactions. They can blunt the effectiveness of prescription drugs. They can also interact with other health products.

This paragraph is grammatically correct, but it does not help the reader understand which pieces of information the author wants to emphasize. Combining the simple sentences into main and subordinate clauses and phrases can improve the paragraph. First, identify the main ideas:

> More Canadians are taking herbal remedies. They think that natural herbs are safe.

These ideas can be combined into one sentence:

> More Canadians are taking herbal remedies because they think they are safe.

Now think about the relationship of the three remaining sentences to the main ideas. Those sentences explain the contrasting view; thus the relationship is *but*.

> More Canadians are taking herbal remedies because they think that natural herbs are safe, **but** herbal remedies can cause bad reactions when they blunt prescription drugs or interact with other health products.

Put key ideas at the beginning and end of sentences

Read these sentences aloud:

> **1**   *Rain Man* and *Born on the Fourth of July*, films marking the actor's transition from teen idol to adult actor, starred **Tom Cruise**.

2   Films such as *Rain Man* and *Born on the Fourth of July*, both featuring **Tom Cruise**, helped the actor make the difficult transition from teen idol to adult actor.

3   **Tom Cruise** made the difficult transition from teen idol to adult actor, starring in films such as *Rain Man* and *Born on the Fourth of July*.

Probably your voice became a little louder when you read the elements at the end: Tom Cruise in sentence 1, teen idol to adult actor in sentence 2, and *Rain Man* and *Born on the Fourth of July* in sentence 3. Two elements of a clause receive the most emphasis: the beginning and the end. Typically a little more weight is given to the end because that's where we expect to find the point of the clause.

Most often what is at the front of a clause is what is known: the topic. What is at the end is the new information about the topic. What is in the middle is subordinate information. If a paragraph is about Tom Cruise, we would not expect the writer to choose sentence 2 over 1 or 3. In sentence 2 Cruise is buried in the middle of the clause.

28b   FORGE LINKS ACROSS SENTENCES

When your writing maintains a focus of attention across sentences, the reader can distinguish the important ideas and how they relate to each other. To achieve this coherence, you need to control which ideas occupy the positions of greatest emphasis. The words you repeat from sentence to sentence act as links.

Link sentences from front to front

In front-to-front linkage, the subject of the sentence remains the focus from one sentence to the next. In the following sequence, sentences 1 through 5 are all about Tom Cruise. The subject of each sentence refers to the first sentence with the pronouns *he* and *his*.

1   **Tom Cruise** was born Thomas Cruise Mapother IV on July 3, 1962.

2   **He** struggled through school, suffering from untreated dyslexia.

3   After a high school knee injury ended his wrestling career, **his** attentions turned to acting.

4   **He** started his motion picture career in films such as *Taps* and *The Outsiders*.

5   **His** career really took off in 1983 with his iconic air guitar performance in *Risky Business*.

Each sentence adds more information about the repeated topic, Tom Cruise.

Link sentences from back to front

In back-to-front linkage, the new information at the end of the sentence is used as the topic of the next sentence. Back-to-front linkage allows new material to be introduced and commented on.

1   Tom Cruise's career really took off in 1983 with his iconic air guitar performance in *Risky Business*.

2   **The film** simultaneously popularized Cruise and **Ray Ban Wayfarer sunglasses**.

3   **Ray Ban Wayfarers** would skyrocket in popularity, with Bausch & Lomb selling 360 000 pairs in 1983 alone.

Back-to-front linkage is useful when ideas need to be advanced quickly, as when you are telling stories. Rarely, however, will you use either front-to-front linkage or back-to-front linkage for long. You will mix them, using front-to-front linkage to add more information and back-to-front linkage to move the topic along.

Check the links between your sentences to find any gaps that will cause your readers to stumble. Where in the following paragraph is your attention disrupted?

> In February 1888, Vincent van Gogh left cloudy Paris for Arles in the sunny south of France. Later that year he persuaded fellow painter Paul Gauguin to join him. Gauguin, who had travelled in the tropics, did not find Arles colourful and exotic. Critics hail this period as the most productive in van Gogh's brilliant but short career.

The last sentence connects distantly with what has come before by mentioning art and van Gogh, but it jars you when you read it because new information, "critics," comes where we expect to find old information. Adding a clause provides a bridge between the old and new information:

> In February 1888, Vincent van Gogh left cloudy Paris for Arles in the sunny south of France. Later that year he persuaded fellow painter Paul Gauguin to join him. Gauguin, who had travelled in the tropics, did not find Arles colourful and exotic. **Although van Gogh and Gauguin argued and soon parted company,** critics hail this period as the most productive in van Gogh's brilliant but short career.

28c   USE PARALLEL STRUCTURE WITH PARALLEL IDEAS

What if Nellie McClung had said, "Don't bother taking back your point, apologizing, or explaining, but get the work finished and ignore their howling"? Would we remember those words today? Many of us do remember the words she did write: "Never retract, never apologize, never explain— get the thing done and let them howl." Writers who use parallel structure often create memorable sentences:

Let us be French, let us be English, but most importantly let us be Canadian.

—John A. Macdonald

Behind every successful man is a surprised woman.

—Maryon Pearson

Until all of us have made it, none of us have made it.

—Rosemary Brown

Man can now fly in the air like a bird, swim under the ocean like a fish, he can burrow into the ground like a mole. Now if only he could walk the earth like a man, this would be paradise.

—Tommy Douglas

Parallel structure in images also creates emphasis. Notice how the horse and the groom have a parallel stance—both tense, both with knees bent, both looking away—connected only by the hand on the rein.

Use parallelism with coordinating conjunctions

When you join elements at the same level with coordinating conjunctions, including *and, or, nor, yet, so, but,* and *for,* normally you should use parallel grammatical structure for these elements.

AWKWARD

In today's global economy, **the method of production and where factories are located** have become relatively unimportant compared to **the creation of new concepts and marketing those concepts.**

PARALLEL

In today's global economy, **how goods are made and where they are produced** have become relatively unimportant compared to **creating new concepts and marketing those concepts.**

Use parallelism with correlative conjunctions

Make identical in structure the parts of sentences linked by correlative conjunctions: *either . . . or, neither . . . nor, not only . . . but also, whether . . . or.*

AWKWARD

Purchasing the undeveloped land **not only** gives us a new park **but also** is something that our children will benefit from in the future.

PARALLEL

Purchasing the undeveloped land **not only** will give our city a new park **but also** will leave our children a lasting inheritance.

The more structural elements you match, the stronger the effect the parallelism will achieve.

CORRECT

Either **we find** a way to recruit new members or **we settle** for the current number of sailboats.

IMPROVED

Either **we find a way to recruit new members** or we drop the plan to increase our fleet.

The first sentence is correct but still a bit clunky. The parallelism is limited to *we find/we settle*. The second sentence delivers more punch by extending the parallelism: *we find a way to recruit new members/we drop the plan to increase our fleet*. Matching structural elements exactly—verb for verb, article for article, adjective for adjective, object for object—provides the strongest parallelism.

COMMON ERRORS

Faulty parallel structure

When writers neglect to use parallel structure, the result can be jarring. Reading your writing aloud will help you catch problems in parallelism. Read this sentence aloud:

> At our club meeting we identified problems in **finding** new members, **publicizing** our activities, and **maintenance** of our website.

The end of the sentence does not sound right because the parallel structure is broken. We expect to find another verb + *-ing* following *finding* and *publicizing*. Instead, we run into *maintenance*, a noun. The problem is easy to fix: change the noun to the *-ing* verb form.

> At our club meeting we identified problems in finding new members, publicizing our activities, and **maintaining** our website.

Remember: Use parallel structure for parallel ideas.

 For step-by-step discussion, examples, and practice of this common error, go to **www.pearsoned.ca/faigley/223**.

28d USE PARALLEL STRUCTURE WITH LISTS

Lists are an effective way of presenting a series of items at the same level of importance. Lists are frequently used in visual aids for oral presentations and in announcements, brochures, instructions, and other kinds of short texts. The effectiveness of a bulleted list is lost, however, if the items are not in parallel form. For example, in a list of action items, such as a list of goals, beginning each item with a verb emphasizes the action.

Sailing Club goals

- Increase the membership by 50% this year
- Compete in all local regattas
- Offer beginning and advanced classes
- Purchase eight new Flying Juniors
- Organize spring banquet
- Publicize all major events

Another common type of list contains instructions. Again, using parallel structure consistently makes the instructions easy to understand.

Creating an animation with GIF Construction Set

1. Select New from the File menu.
2. Click on Insert and select Loop.
3. Click on Insert again and select Control block. Set the delay to 1/100th of a second.
4. Click on Insert again and add the first animation frame.
5. Repeat steps 3 and 4 until all frames are added.

28e USE PARALLEL STRUCTURE IN PARAGRAPHS

Use parallelism to create rhythm

Parallel structure does not have to be used in rigid, mechanical ways. Repeating elements of structure can build a rhythm that gives your prose a distinctive voice.

> Our links to the past, our bonds with the present, our path to a civilized tomorrow are all maintained by libraries.
>
> —Adrienne Clarkson

Use parallel structure to pair ideas

Parallel structure is also useful to pair ideas. The closer the similarity in structure, the more emphasis you will achieve.

> Being a grown-up means assuming responsibility for yourself, for your children, and—here's the big curve—for your parents. In other words, you do get to stay up later, but you want to go to sleep sooner.
>
> —Wendy Wasserstein, from *Bachelor Girls*

CHAPTER *29*

Find the Right Words

Suppose you want to email a friend about a new song you heard on the radio. You might be impressed by the words, which you praise to your friend. Now imagine in your English class you are asked to find an example of common poetry, such as song lyrics or an advertising jingle, and to describe that poetry. You realize the song you like will fulfill the assignment and you write about the lyrics. The language you use in each case will likely be very different.

In the email to your friend, you might use contractions and slang to describe the music. In the school assignment, and in most workplace writing, you will probably use what writers call standard edited Canadian English.

29a RECOGNIZE VARIETIES OF ENGLISH

In its negative definition, **standard edited Canadian English** is what remains after you rid the language of its slang, jargon, regional expressions, and colloquialisms—some of the language's most colourful and striking features. While that definition is certainly true, it doesn't tell the whole story. As a general concept, standard edited English is a dialect that is used in most academic, business, and public contexts. We use this dialect when we wish to be understood by the widest possible audience. That goal requires that we eliminate, or at least explain, words that have particular meanings for particular groups, and especially words that are used only by certain groups. You will write most of your post-secondary assignments in standard edited Canadian, the variety of English that is best suited for a broad post-secondary audience in Canada.

English is the primary language for written communication in many countries, but what is considered standard written English varies a great deal across English-speaking countries. Within countries, what is considered

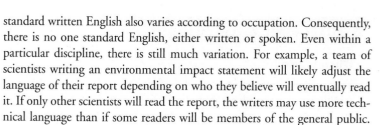

standard written English also varies according to occupation. Consequently, there is no one standard English, either written or spoken. Even within a particular discipline, there is still much variation. For example, a team of scientists writing an environmental impact statement will likely adjust the language of their report depending on who they believe will eventually read it. If only other scientists will read the report, the writers may use more technical language than if some readers will be members of the general public.

29b BE AWARE OF LEVELS OF FORMALITY

Colloquialisms

Colloquialisms are words or expressions that are used informally, often in conversation but less often in writing.

> I'm not happy with my marks, but that's **the way the cookie crumbles**.

> I've **had it up to here** with all of Tom's complaining.

> Liz is always **running on at the mouth** about something.

Aside from carrying meanings that aren't always obvious to your reader, colloquialisms usually indicate a lack of seriousness that runs counter to what you'll be trying to accomplish in most academic and professional writing. Colloquialisms can suggest a flippant attitude, carelessness, or even thoughtlessness.

Using edited Canadian English does not mean, however, that you should try to use big words when small ones will do as well, or that you should use 10 words instead of 2. Formality does not mean being pretentious or wordy.

> WORDY   In this writer's opinion, one could argue that the party scene in Montreal is far superior in every particular to its counterpart in Toronto.

> BETTER   I think Montreal's party scene is better in every way than that of Toronto.

Slang

The most conspicuous kind of language that is usually avoided in edited Canadian English is slang. The next time a friend talks to you, listen closely to the words he or she uses. Chances are you will notice several words that you probably would not use in a college or university writing assignment. Slang words are created by and for a particular group—even if that group is just you and your friend.

Aside from being a fun way to play with language, slang asserts a sense of belonging. The issue is not whether slang is good or bad, but under what circumstances a primarily oral form of language used within a group becomes effective for writing to people outside that group. If the main purpose is to express the identity of the group, slang is often effective.

WRITING IN THE WORLD

When to use *I*

You may have been taught to avoid the first person (*I, we*) in academic and professional writing. Though some instructors and workplace conventions still require that all first-person references be eliminated or rewritten (*I believe* would become *this author believes*), this rule is less commonly enforced than it used to be.

Some instructors feel that first-person references reflect self-indulgence that is inappropriate outside of autobiography. Sentences beginning with *I* refer to the author and make him or her the subject, or at least a fellow subject. In a sentence such as *I think Montreal's party scene is better in every way than that of Toronto*, the reader's attention is divided between the party scenes and the person evaluating the party scenes.

Another reason some instructors prohibit use of the first person is the tendency of writers to overuse it. Some writers feel that nothing can be invalidated as long as each potentially arguable assertion starts with *I think* or *I feel*. *I* becomes a shield, which the writer uses to escape the work of building an argument.

Occasionally, the use of *I* is redundant. In the following sentence, the nature of the assertion clearly indicates that it's the writer's opinion:

Redundant *I*   I think "Rock the Casbah" is a great song!

Here you can safely drop *I think* without changing the sentence's meaning. Sometimes, however, you will want to indicate plainly that an assertion is tentative. *I* is critical to the meaning of this sentence:

Tentative *I*   I thought that the dim, distant light was a planet.

If you're unsure whether or not first-person references are permissible, ask your instructor.

Sometimes slang can be incorporated into more formal writing if the goal is to convey a sense of a particular group. But if the goal is to write about a matter of broad interest for a broad audience, slang often gets in the way.

29c   BE AWARE OF DENOTATION AND CONNOTATION

When you see a Jeep covered with mud, you know the driver has probably been off the pavement. Of course car manufacturers take advantage of these associations. While some advertisements show shiny new cars, ads for Jeeps and similar vehicles show them caked with mud, emphasizing their ruggedness.

Words likewise carry associations from the places they have been. Words have both literal meanings, called **denotations**, and associated meanings, called **connotations**. The contrast is evident in words that mean roughly the same thing but have different connotations. For example, some people are set in their opinions, a quality that can be described positively as *persistent*, *firm*, and *steadfast* or negatively as *stubborn*, *bull-headed*, and *close-minded*.

In post-secondary and professional writing, writers are expected not to rely on the connotations of words to make important points. For example, the statement *It's only common sense to fund education adequately* carries high positive connotations. Most people believe in common sense, and most people want good education systems. What is common sense for one person, however, is not common sense for another; how *adequately* is defined varies greatly. Except for common function words such as *and*, *to*, and *the*, all words carry connotative meanings. Consequently, you cannot write in an entirely neutral language, but you can be forthright about any value judgments you make. You have the obligation in post-secondary writing to support any judgment with evidence.

29d USE SPECIFIC LANGUAGE

Be precise

Effective writing conveys information clearly and precisely. Words such as *situation*, *sort*, *thing*, *aspect*, and *kind* often signal undeveloped or even lazy thinking.

> VAGUE   The violence aspect determines how video games are rated.
>
> BETTER   The level of violence determines how video games are rated.

When citing numbers or quantities, be as exact as possible. A precise number, if known, is always better than slippery words like *several* or *many*, which some writers use to cloak the fact that they don't know the quantity in question. If you know an approximate quantity, indicate the quantity but qualify it: *about 25* tells readers much more than *many*.

Use a dictionary

There is no greater tool for writers than the dictionary. When you write always have a dictionary handy—either a book or an online version—and get into the habit of using it. In addition to checking spelling, you can find additional meanings of a word that perhaps you had not considered, and you can find the etymology—the origins of a word. In many cases knowing the etymology of a word can help you use it to better effect. For example, if you want to argue that universities and colleges as institutions have succeeded because they bring people together in contexts that prepare them for their lives after post-secondary education, you might point out the etymology of *university*. *University* can be traced back to the late Latin word *universitas*, which means "society or guild," thus emphasizing the idea of a community of learning.

COMMON ERRORS

Words often confused

Words with different meanings that are pronounced in the same way are called **homonyms**. Be particularly careful that you select the correct one. These pairs can cause confusion.

bare—unadorned
bear—(1) an animal; (2) to carry

cite—(1) to make mention of; (2) to quote as an example
sight—something seen
site—place, location

coarse—rough
course—plotted-out site or matter

complement—to go with, as in *That tie complements that suit.*
compliment—to flatter

counsel—(1) advice; (2) lawyer; (3) to advise
council—a deliberative body

fair—(1) just; (2) carnival
fare—(1) ticket price; (2) to get along

hear—to listen to
here—location

passed—went by
past—time before the present

patience—the state of calmly waiting
patients—people receiving medical care

peace—serenity
piece—a part of

plain—(1) simple; (2) level land
plane—(1) short for *airplane*; (2) level surface; (3) carpenter's tool

practice—used as a noun
practise—used as a verb

principal—(1) head of an organization; (2) a sum of money; (3) main
principle—a basic law or guideline

wear—(1) to don clothes; (2) to erode
where—location

weather—climatic condition
whether—if

Other words do not sound exactly alike, only similar. The words in the following pairs are frequently confused:

accept—to receive
except (as preposition)—excluding

adverse—difficult
averse—against

advice—a suggestion
advise—to suggest

affect—to act upon or to have an effect on something or somebody
effect—a change caused by an action

allude—to make reference to
elude—to evade

allusion—an indirect reference
illusion—a false impression

censor—to suppress controversial material
censure—to reprimand

conscience—moral compass
conscious—aware

continually—(1) consistently; (2) regularly
continuously—without stopping

desert—(1) geographical feature; (2) to abandon
dessert—sweet snack

elicit—to bring out
illicit—unlawful

loose—not tight
lose—(1) to misplace; (2) to fail to win a game

personal—(1) individual; (2) private
personnel—staff

presence—opposite of absence
presents—(1) gifts; (2) introduces

respectfully—demonstrating respect
respectively—in the given order

Remember: Use a dictionary to check that you are using the right word.

For step-by-step discussion, examples, and practice of this common error, go to **www.pearsoned.ca/faigley/224**.

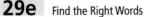

29e USE EFFECTIVE FIGURATIVE LANGUAGE

Figurative language—figures of speech that help readers get a more vivid sense of an object or idea—is what you use when literal descriptions seem insufficient.

LITERAL   The prosecutor presented a much stronger legal case than did the defence.

FIGURATIVE   The prosecutor took the defence lawyer apart like a cheap watch.

The two most common figures of speech are the simile and the metaphor. A **simile** usually begins with *as* or *like*, and makes an explicit comparison between two unlike objects.

A tie in soccer is **like** kissing your dog.

Metaphor is from a Greek term that means "carry over," which describes what happens when you encounter a metaphor: you carry over the meaning from one word to another. Metaphor makes a comparison without using *like* or *as*.

She reached the **pinnacle** of her profession.

[highest point ⟶ best]

Two other forms of figurative language are **synecdoche**, in which the part is used to represent the whole (a hood ornament that represents a car) and **metonymy**, in which something related stands in for the thing itself (*Parliament* for the governing body; *brass* for military officers). The purpose of all figurative language is to suggest, or sometimes to create, a resemblance or link between two otherwise distinct objects and to convey a larger, more complex idea than a simple presentation of the unadorned facts could impart.

If not used imaginatively, figurative language merely dresses up a literal description in fancy clothes without adding to the reader's understanding of the object or idea. The purpose of figurative language is to convey information vividly to help the reader grasp your meaning.

You'll also want to avoid **clichés**, which are relics of figurative language, phrases used so often that they have become tired and stripped of meaning. Among countless others, the following expressions have hardened into clichés.

better late than never	out like a light
blind as a bat	playing with fire
easier said than done	pride and joy
hard as a rock	thin as a rail
ladder of success	water under the bridge
nutty as a fruitcake	wise as an owl

You might find yourself resorting to clichés when you're low on inspiration or energy. Read your drafts aloud to yourself to identify clichés, listening for the phrases that you've used or heard before. Make a note of them and either change the clichés to literal description or, better still, create fresh new phrases to convey what you were trying to say with the cliché.

CHAPTER 30

Write to Be Inclusive

Except for comedians and angry people, few writers want to insult their readers. When readers are offended by a writer's language, most of the time the writer did not intend this result. Instead, the writer likely expressed assumptions that readers rejected as biased. If you want to reach all your potential readers, you should avoid biased language.

Writers who use inclusive language will also be more accurate. Writing *man* to refer to *men and women* only conveys half of what you mean. And perhaps the best reason to strive for inclusiveness is that your writing shapes public discourse, even in the classroom. Exclusionary language perpetuates biases. Writing does not only reflect reality; it shapes reality.

This chapter explains current conventions for avoiding bias in your writing toward specific groups of people. While the conventions of inclusiveness change continually, three guidelines for inclusive language toward all groups remain constant:

- Do not point out people's differences unless those differences are relevant to your argument.
- Call people whatever they prefer to be called.
- When given a choice of terms, choose the more accurate one.

30a BE AWARE OF STEREOTYPES

Reject stereotypes

A **stereotype** makes an assumption about a group of people by applying a characteristic to all of them based on the knowledge of only a few of them. The idea that Asian women are submissive, for instance, is a stereotype; it tries to apply one personality trait to many individuals whose only shared characteristics are their gender and ethnicity. Such a stereotype is just as ridiculous as a belief that all inhabitants of Saskatchewan are wheat farmers. Since individuals in any group are different, stereotypes present a reductive picture of the group being described.

Of course you want to avoid obviously harmful, not to mention inaccurate, stereotypes, such as *People on welfare are lazy*, *gays are effeminate*, or *NASCAR fans are rednecks*. More subtle stereotypes, however, may be harder to identify and eliminate from your writing. If you want to offer an engineer as an example, will you make the engineer a man? If you want your reader to envision clients of a homeless shelter, will you describe them as mentally ill? Instead of using these examples that perpetuate stereotypes, try to choose cases that go against them.

Avoid using stereotypes even if they seem flattering, such as *Asians are smart*, *Blacks dance well*, and *women are nurturing*. Flattering stereotypes are just as inaccurate as unflattering ones, and they can be just as harmful. For instance, the stereotype that women are nurturing has been used to argue that women's only natural role is to raise children, that women aren't suited to work outside the home. By extension, the argument goes, fathers don't have the same responsibility to care for their children because fathers aren't as naturally nurturing. The stereotype that women are nurturing could ultimately offend both women and men.

Watch for assumptions about what's "normal"

Assumptions about what's "normal" or "regular" can create bias. Calling one person or group "normal" implies that others are abnormal. The following problematic statements can be revised to be more inclusive.

PROBLEMATIC NORM

While normal people learn about the Civil War in school, hard-core re-enactors don musty uniforms, grab slabs of old bacon, and live the war during weekend battles.

BETTER

Not satisfied with learning about the Civil War through books, hard-core re-enactors don musty uniforms, grab slabs of old bacon, and live the war during weekend battles.

PROBLEMATIC NORM

Gloria Nuñez isn't like regular sprinters at the Commonwealth Games; while other runners gingerly settle their feet into the blocks, Nuñez plants her prosthetic foot in the block and waits for the starting gun.

BETTER

Gloria Nuñez is one sprinter at the Commonwealth Games who might surprise you; while other runners gingerly settle their feet into the blocks, Nuñez plants her prosthetic foot in the block and waits for the starting gun.

Stereotypical images

Subtle stereotyping comes through the media. Based on images in the news media, many people think that the majority of Muslims live in the Middle East when, in fact, 80 percent live elsewhere, with the highest population in Indonesia, followed by Pakistan. People also think that Muslim women who wear the hijab (a veil or head scarf) do so because their husbands or fathers make them; however, many women choose to wear a veil or head scarf as a way to demonstrate their modesty and piety. Another common misconception about Islamic women's attire is that the burka is dictated by the Koran, when in fact, wearing the burka is a cultural tradition, not a religious requirement. The majority of men in Islamic countries do not have long beards. Again, the issue is accuracy. Some people in Holland still wear wooden shoes, but wooden shoes do not represent everyday Dutch footwear.

30b BE INCLUSIVE ABOUT GENDER

Gender is a term that refers to the social designations of men, women, and their sexual orientations.

Avoid exclusive nouns and pronouns

Don't use masculine nouns and pronouns to refer to both men and women. *He, his, him, man,* and *mankind* are outmoded and inaccurate terms for both genders. Eliminate gender bias by using the following tips:

- Don't say *boy* when you mean *child.*
- Use *men and women* or *people* instead of *man.*
- Use *humanity* or *humankind* in place of *mankind.*

Eliminating *he, his,* and *him* when referring to both men and women is more complicated. Many readers consider *he/she* to be an awkward alternative. Try one of the following instead:

- Make the noun and its corresponding pronoun plural. The pronoun will change from *he, him,* or *his* to *they, them,* or *theirs.*

uniqueness of each nation within the region. *Asian* is currently preferred over *Oriental*; however, terms like *Vietnamese* and *Japanese* are even more specific. Also, *English* and *British* are different. The people who live in England are English, but people from elsewhere in Great Britain—Scotland, Wales, Northern Ireland—will be quick to tell you that they are not English. Again, be specific. Call people from Wales *Welsh* and those from Scotland *Scots*.

30d   BE INCLUSIVE ABOUT OTHER DIFFERENCES

Writing about people with disabilities

The *Publication Manual of the American Psychological Association* (5th ed.) offers some good advice: "Put people first, not their disability" (75). Write *people who are deaf* instead of *the deaf* and *a student who is quadriplegic* instead of *a quadriplegic student*. Discuss *a man who has depression*, not a *depressive*, and *a woman who uses a wheelchair*, not *a wheelchair-bound woman*. Avoid naming someone as a victim; *a person with cancer* is better than *a cancer victim*. *Disability* is the term preferred over *handicap*. The word *handicap* derives from hand-in-cap, a term referring to begging that carries negative connotations.

Writing about people of different ages

Avoid bias by choosing accurate terms to describe age. If possible, use the person's age rather than an adjective, like *elderly* or *older*, which might offend. *Eighty-two-year-old Adele Schumacher* is better than *elderly Adele Schumacher* or *Adele Schumacher, an older resident*.

Writing about people of different financial statuses

When writing about financial status, be careful not to make assumptions (*People who live in trailer parks are uneducated*) or value judgments (*Dishwashing is a less respectable job than managing a restaurant*). While *upper class* and *middle class* are acceptable terms, *lower class* implies a bias. Instead use *working class*. Also, use the word *homeless* as an adjective, not a noun. Instead of writing *the homeless*, write *a homeless person* or, better yet, *a person who is homeless*. Be aware that words like *upper crust* and *white trash* imply value judgments based on a person's financial means.

Writing about people of different religions

Avoid making assumptions about someone's beliefs or practices based on religious affiliation. Even though the Vatican opposes capital punishment, many Roman Catholics support it. Likewise, not all Jewish men wear yarmulkes. The tremendous variation within religions and among individual practitioners makes generalizations questionable.

C H A P T E R *31*

Write for Diverse Audiences

There are more than 2700 different languages spoken in the world. Mandarin and English vie for the position of most-spoken language, with more than one billion speakers each. Hindustani has the third most speakers, and Spanish finishes a close fourth. French is the tenth most widely spoken language in the world, behind languages such as Russian, Arabic, and Bengali. Although English may be widely spoken throughout the world, people in different parts of the world speak different versions of English. These can differ not only in pronunciation but also in structure, usage, and cultural significance.

Given the number of people around the world who speak languages other than English, many writers will find themselves addressing non-native speakers of English in post-secondary education and beyond. To communicate effectively across different varieties of English, writers need to understand how culture and language shape readers' expectations.

31a UNDERSTAND ENGLISH AS A GLOBAL LANGUAGE

English has been adopted as the language of international air traffic and of mariners, and many international agencies such as the United Nations use English as one of the primary languages for their meetings and documents. The growing popularity of the internet has also contributed to the rapid increase in the international use of English. English today comes in various shapes and forms.

PART TEN

Understanding Grammar

- How can I recognize comma splices in my sentences? (33c)

- What's the best way to make sure my subjects and verbs agree? (34a–f)

- What are some examples of irregular verbs? (35b)

- When do I use *whom* instead of *who*? (36a)

- How can I recognize and avoid dangling modifiers? (37e)

32
Grammar Basics

33
Fragments, Run-ons, and Comma Splices

34
Subject-Verb Agreement

35
Verbs

36
Pronouns

37
Modifiers

10 UNDERSTANDING GRAMMAR

Many people think of grammar as a set of mysterious rules that they are constantly in danger of violating. In fact, people know intuitively the grammar of their native language or else they couldn't speak it. If you understand a few concepts of grammar, you can become more confident about many aspects of your writing.

MyCanadianCompLab Multimedia Resources

MyCanadianCompLab multimedia resources extends the coverage you will find in the Common Errors boxes throughout the handbook. Each module includes a step-by-step explanation of how to fix the problem; corrected examples with complete explanations; and practice on both sentences and paragraphs with immediate feedback to help you learn. View all the topics in MyCanadianCompLab at **www.pearsoned.ca/highered/ mycanadiancomplab/**.

 Visit *The Brief Penguin Handbook* Companion Website at
www.pearsoned.ca/faigley/

MyCanadianCompLab
Where writing and research help is a click away.
MyCanadianCompLab may be packaged with your textbook.
If not, it can be purchased from your college or university's bookstore.
Go to **www.pearsoned.ca/highered/mycanadiancomplab/**
for a tour.

CHAPTER *32*

Grammar Basics

Many people feel uncomfortable when they hear the word *grammar.* They think of grammar as a set of mysterious rules that they are constantly in danger of violating. In fact, people know intuitively the grammar of their native language or else they couldn't speak it. What they often don't know is how grammar works. Just as you can enjoy a delicious meal without knowing much about cooking, you can also write without knowing much about the concepts of grammar. But if you know a little about how ingredients work together, you can judge whether or not a recipe or meal choice will appeal to you. Similarly, if you understand a few concepts of grammar, you can be more confident about many aspects of writing.

32a SENTENCE BASICS

Sentences are the basic units in writing. Many people think of a sentence as a group of words that begins with a capital letter and ends with a period, but that definition includes grammatically incomplete sentences called **fragments** (see Section 33a).

Subjects and predicates

Regular sentences must have a subject and a predicate that includes a main verb. Typically the subject announces what the sentence is about, and the predicate says something about that subject or conveys the action of the subject.

SUBJECT	PREDICATE
I	**want** a new monitor.
Your website	**loads** quickly.
Seventy-three percent of Canadians	**prefer to** watch movies at home rather than in a movie theatre.

The exception to this rule is a class of sentences called **imperatives**, in which the subject is usually implied. In these sentences, we know that the subject is *you* without stating it.

Watch this film with me.

Help me carry in the groceries.

Sentence patterns

Sentences can be classified into four major patterns according to function.

- **Declaratives.** Declarative sentences make statements.

  Critics blamed the reduced attendance on the poor movie selection in 2005.

- **Interrogatives.** Interrogatives are usually referred to as questions.

  Who will be the first to volunteer?

- **Imperatives.** Imperatives request or demand some action.

  Stop complaining.

- **Exclamations.** Exclamations are used to express strong emotion.

  What an incredible performance you gave!

Sentences can be classified as either **positive** or **negative**. A sentence can be made negative by inserting a negative word, usually *not* or a contracted form of *not* (*can't*, *isn't*).

POSITIVE   Josette has worked here for a year.

NEGATIVE   Josette has **not** worked here for a year.

Sentences with transitive verbs (see Section 32c) can be considered as **active** or **passive** (see Section 26a). Sentences can be made passive by changing the word order.

ACTIVE   In 1935 a Liberal victory entitled William Lyon Mackenzie King to an unprecedented third term as prime minister.

PASSIVE   In 1935 William Lyon Mackenzie King **was entitled** by a Liberal victory to an unprecedented third term as prime minister.

32b WORD CLASSES

Like players in a team sport who are assigned to different positions, words are classified into parts of speech. The different positions on a team have different functions. The forwards in soccer and hockey do most of the scoring; goalies are responsible for preventing scoring. The parts of speech also serve different functions in sentences. And just as individuals can play more than one position on a team, so too can individual words belong to more than one part of speech. *Try* is a noun in *The third try was successful*, but a verb in *I would not try it*.

Nouns

A noun is the name of a person, place, thing, concept, or action. Names of particular persons, places, organizations, companies, titles, religions, languages, nationalities, ethnicities, months, and days are called **proper nouns** and are almost always capitalized. More general nouns are called **common nouns** and are seldom capitalized unless they begin a sentence (see Section 46a). Most common nouns can be made plural, and most are preceded by articles (*a, an, the*). Nouns have several functions:

- **Subject:** The **cat** scratched the chesterfield.
- **Object:** Please feed the **cat**.
- **Subject complement:** This is my **cat**.
- **Object of a preposition:** This is for the **cat**.
- **Modifier of other nouns:** She moved on **cat** feet.
- **Appositive of other nouns:** My best friend, my **cat**, shares my pillow.
- **Possessive noun:** The **cat's** mouse is under the sofa.

Pronouns

Pronouns are a subclass of nouns and are generally used as substitutes for nouns. Pronouns themselves are divided into several subclasses.

- **Personal pronouns:** *I, you, he, she, it, we, they, me, him, her, us, them*

  I gave my old racquet to **her. She** gave **me** a CD in return.

- **Possessive pronouns:** *my, mine, his, hers, its, our, ours, your, yours, their, theirs*

  My old racquet is now **hers**.

- **Demonstrative pronouns:** *this, that, these, those*

  Those are the shoes I want.

- **Indefinite pronouns:** *all, any, anyone, anybody, anything, both, each, either, everyone, everything, many, neither, no one, none, nothing, one, some, someone, somebody, something*

  Everyone was relieved that the driver's injuries were minor.

- **Relative pronouns:** *that, which, what, who, whom, whose, whatever, whoever, whomever, whichever*

  The house, **which** hung off a steep ridge, had a stunning view of the bay.

- **Interrogative pronouns:** *who, which, what, where*

  What would you like with your sandwich?

- **Reflexive pronouns:** *myself, ourselves, yourself, yourselves, himself, herself, itself, themselves*

  The twins behaved **themselves** around their grandfather.

- **Reciprocal pronouns:** *each other, one another*

  The brothers didn't like **each other**.

See Chapter 36 for more on pronouns.

Verbs

Verbs indicate actions, states of mind, occurrences, and states of being. Verbs are divided into two primary categories: **main verbs** and **auxiliaries**. A main verb must be present in the predicate. The main verb may be the only word in the predicate.

She **slept**.

When he heard the starting gun, Vijay **sprinted**.

Auxiliaries (often called *helping verbs*) include forms of *be, have,* and *do*. A subset of auxiliaries are **modals**: *can, could, may, might, must, shall, should, will, would*.

You **will be** satisfied when you see how well they painted your car.

She **might have been** selected for the lead role in the ballet if her strained muscle **had** healed.

See Chapters 34 and 35 for more on verbs.

Verbals

Verbals are forms of verbs that function as nouns, adjectives, and adverbs. The three kinds of verbals are infinitives, participles, and gerunds.

- **Infinitives:** An infinitive is the base or *to* form of the verb. Infinitives can be used in place of nouns, adjectives, or adverbs.

  ┌NOUN┐
  To fly has been a centuries-old dream of people around the world.

  ┌ADJECTIVE┐
  Keeping your goals in mind is a good way **to succeed**.

- **Participles:** Participles are either present (*biting*) or past (*defeated*). They always function as adjectives.

  The **biting** insects are annoying.

  Napoleon's **defeated** army faced a long march back to France.

- **Gerunds:** Gerunds have the same form as present participles, but they always function as nouns.

  Writing was all that she wanted to do in life.

Adjectives

Adjectives modify nouns and pronouns. Some adjectives are used frequently: *good, bad, small, tall, handsome, green, short.* Many others are recognizable by their suffixes: *-able* (*dependable*), *-al* (*cultural*), *-ful* (*hopeful*), *-ic* (*frenetic*), *-ive* (*decisive*), *-ish* (*foolish*), *-less* (*hopeless*), *-ous* (*erroneous*).

  The forgetful manager was always backed up by her dependable assistant.

Adjectives often follow linking verbs.

  That drumbeat is relentless.

Numbers are considered adjectives.

  Only 10 team members showed up for practice.

See Chapter 37 for more about adjectives and adverbs.

Adverbs

Adverbs modify verbs, other adverbs, adjectives, and entire clauses. The usual suffix for adverbs is *-ly*. Many adverbs do not have suffixes (*then, here*) and others have the same form as adjectives (*fast, hard, long, well*).

  That drummer plays well. [modifies the verb *plays*]

  That drummer plays very well. [modifies the adverb *well*]

  That answer is partly correct. [modifies the adjective *correct*]

  Frankly, I do not care. [modifies the clause *I do not care*]

  Conjunctive adverbs often modify entire clauses and sentences. Like coordinating conjunctions, they indicate the relationship between two clauses or two sentences. Commonly used conjunctive adverbs include *also, consequently, furthermore, hence, however, indeed, instead, likewise, moreover, nevertheless, otherwise, similarly, therefore, thus.*

  Many of the movies released recently look derivative or violent; consequently I have started reading more.

Prepositions

Prepositions indicate the relationship of nouns or pronouns to other parts of a sentence. Prepositions come before nouns and pronouns, and in this sense prepositions are "prepositioned." The noun(s) or pronoun(s) that follow are called the objects of prepositions.

PREP   OBJ   PREP ⎡——OBJ——⎤
She took the job **of web designer for an art gallery.**

Here are some common prepositions.

about	behind	from	than
above	below	in	through
across	beside	inside	to
after	between	into	toward
against	but	off	under
among	by	on	until
around	despite	out	up
as	down	over	upon
at	during	past	with
before	for	since	without

Some prepositions are compounds.

according to	due to	in front of	next to
as well as	except for	in spite of	out of
because of	in addition to	instead of	with regard to

Conjunctions

Conjunctions indicate the relationship between words or groups of words. The two classes of conjunctions are **coordinate**, indicating units of equal status, and **subordinate**, indicating that one unit is more important than the other.

- **Coordinating conjunctions:** The seven coordinating conjunctions are *and, but, or, yet, for, so,* and *nor.*

Do you want pie **or** ice cream?

I finished my preliminary sketch early, **so** I decided to mix the colours to paint the background.

- **Subordinating conjunctions:** Subordinating conjunctions introduce subordinate clauses. Common subordinating conjunctions are *after, although, as, because, before, if, since, that, unless, until, when, where, while.*

Although Jess had landed the triple flip perfectly, she decided to skate her long program one more time to build her confidence.

Articles

There are two classes of articles:

- **Definite article:** *the*
- **Indefinite article:** *a, an*

Interjections

Interjections are words like *oops, ouch, ugh,* and *ah*. They are usually punctuated separately, and they do not relate grammatically to other words.

Ouch! That pair of stilettos looks painful.

32c CLAUSES

Clauses are the grammatical structures that underlie sentences. Each clause has a subject and a predicate, but not all clauses are sentences. The variety of clauses is nearly infinite because phrases and other clauses can be embedded within them in a multitude of ways. Nevertheless, a few basic patterns are central to English clause structure.

Subject-verb-object

On the predicate side of a clause, you always find a main verb and often a direct object that is affected by the action of the verb.

> ⌐S⌐ ⌐V⌐ ⌐DO⌐
> Ahmad **walked the dog**.

This basic pattern, called **subject-verb-object** or **S-V-O**, is one of the most common in English. Verbs that take objects (*walk, revise*) are called **transitive verbs**. Some transitive verbs can take two objects: a **direct object** that completes the sentence and an **indirect object**, usually a person, indirectly affected by the action.

> ⌐S⌐ ⌐V⌐ ⌐IO⌐ ⌐DO⌐
> Mehmet **gave the dog a biscuit**.

Clauses without objects

Not all clauses have objects.

> ⌐S⌐ ⌐V⌐
> Patrice **yawned**.

> ⌐S⌐ ⌐V⌐
> The bobsled run **looks** fast. [*Fast* is an adverb, not an object.]

> ⌐S⌐ ⌐V⌐
> The staff **cannot work** on weekends. [*On weekends* is a prepositional phrase.]

This clause pattern is **subject-verb** or **S-V**. Verbs that do not require objects are called **intransitive verbs**. Many verbs can be both transitive and intransitive.

INTRANSITIVE	Mario **sings** quietly.
TRANSITIVE	Mario **sings** the hymn.

For more on the verbs *lay/lie* and *raise/rise*, see Section 35c.

Linking-verb clauses

A third major pattern links the subject to a noun or adjective following the verb that restates or describes the subject. The most commonly used verbs for this pattern are forms of *be*.

Michaëlle Jean was Governor General of Canada in 2006.

Yasmin Dabousseh is the assistant manager.

The results of the MRI **were negative.**

What follows the verb is the subject complement, either a noun or noun phrase (*Governor General, assistant manager*) or a predicate adjective describing the subject (*negative*).

Other linking verbs besides *be* are *appear, become, feel, look, remain,* and *seem*. These linking verbs often refer to people's perceptions or senses.

Reinhart felt nervous when he accepted the award.

Main versus subordinate clauses

All the examples of clauses we have looked at up to now can stand by themselves as sentences. These clauses are called **main** or **independent clauses**. Other clauses have the necessary ingredients to count as clauses—a subject and a main verb—yet they are incomplete as sentences.

Where you choose to live

Which was the first to be considered

As fast as my legs could carry me

These clauses are examples of **subordinate** or **dependent clauses**. They do not stand by themselves, but must be attached to another clause:

I ran from the explosion **as fast as my legs could carry me.**

Subordinate clauses serve three main functions.

- **Noun clauses:** Noun clauses serve all the functions that nouns perform, including subjects, objects, complements, and appositives. They usually are formed with either a relative pronoun (*that, which, what, who, whom, whose, whatever, whoever, whichever*) or with *when, where, why,* or *how.*

As SUBJECT	That the entry fee included all the food made the price reasonable.
As DIRECT OBJECT	I could not **find** where it was located.
As SUBJECT COMPLEMENT	**The newest version** is what she wants.
As APPOSITIVE	**The reason** that I am here today is obvious.
As OBJECT OF PREPOSITION	He listened **to** what she had to say.

- **Adjective clauses:** Adjective clauses modify nouns and pronouns. They are also called **relative clauses** and usually begin with a relative pronoun.

  Steroids that are used to increase muscle density have many harmful side effects.

  The site where the fort once stood was destroyed by an avalanche.

- **Adverb clauses:** Adverb clauses function as adverbs, modifying verbs, other adverbs, adjectives, and entire clauses. They begin with a subordinating conjunction such as *after, although, as, because, before, if, since, that, unless, until, when, where, while.*

MODIFIES VERB	We **cannot leave** until 4:30 p.m. unless José arrives early with the car.
MODIFIES ADVERB	Jeff laughed **nervously** whenever the boss came around.
MODIFIES ADJECTIVE	The cornfields were not as **tall** as they should have been in late August.
MODIFIES CLAUSE	If the daggers come out, **you should end the discussion.**

32d PHRASES

Along with clauses, phrases add to sentences groups of words that modify or develop parts of the sentence. Some phrases can be confused with clauses, but phrases lack either a subject or a main verb.

Prepositional phrases

Prepositional phrases consist of a preposition and its object, including modifiers of the object. They can modify nouns, verbs, or adjectives.

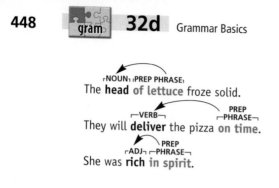

The head of lettuce froze solid.

They will deliver the pizza on time.

She was rich in spirit.

Verbal phrases

Each of the three kinds of verbals—infinitives, participles, and gerunds—can be used to create phrases.

- **Infinitive phrases:** Infinitive phrases can function as nouns, adverbs, and adjectives. As nouns they can be subjects, objects, or complements.

  SUBJECT

  To succeed where others had failed was her goal.

- **Participial phrases:** Participial phrases are formed with either present participles (*flying*) or past participles (*defeated*); they function as adjectives.

  The freighter, **listing noticeably to the port side**, left the harbour without balancing the load.

- **Gerund phrases:** Gerund phrases formed from the present participle (-*ing*) function as nouns.

  SUBJECT

  Feeding stray cats led my next-door neighbour to become a vet.

Appositives

Appositive phrases modify nouns and are often set off by a pair of commas. They usually follow the noun they modify. They are quite useful as identifying tags for nouns.

Andy, **my childhood guitar teacher**, became a rock star with the band *AudioStorm*.

Absolutes

Absolute phrases are nearly clauses because they include a noun or pronoun and a verb; however, the verb is a participle ending in -*ing* or -*ed* and not a main verb. Absolute phrases can appear anywhere in a sentence and are set off by commas.

He struggled at the beginning of the eulogy, **his voice trembling**.

32e SENTENCE TYPES

Simple sentences

A simple sentence consists of one main clause and no subordinate clauses. Simple sentences can be quite short.

    ┌─SUBJ─┐ ┌VERB┐
 The two toy **figures spun** together.

Simple sentences can become quite long if phrases are added.

 ┌──────────MAIN CLAUSE──────────┐
 The two toy figures spun together, standing on top of their round metal pedestal, teetering back and forth in a jerky, clockwise motion, slowing gradually.

Compound sentences

Compound sentences have two or more main clauses and no subordinate clauses. The main clauses are connected in one of three ways: (1) by a semicolon, (2) by a comma and coordinating conjunction (*and, but, or, for, so, nor, yet*), or (3) by punctuation and a conjunctive adverb (*furthermore, however, indeed, nevertheless, therefore*).

 ┌──────────MAIN CLAUSE──────────┐ ┌──────────MAIN CLAUSE──────────┐
 A hawk swooped between the houses, **but** it narrowly missed the dove at the bird feeder.

 ┌──────────MAIN CLAUSE──────────┐ ┌──────── MAIN CLAUSE ───────┐
 The theatre enjoyed record attendance; **however,** rising costs took all the profits.

Complex sentences

Complex sentences have one main clause and one or more subordinate clauses.

 ┌──────MAIN CLAUSE──────┐ ┌──────SUBORDINATE CLAUSE──────┐
 Mike walked to his car **when** he got out of class.

Compound-complex sentences

Compound-complex sentences have at least two main clauses and at least one subordinate clause.

 ┌────── MAIN CLAUSE ──────┐ ┌── SUBORDINATE CLAUSE ──┐ ┌── MAIN CLAUSE ──┐
 Mike walked to his car when he got out of class, **but** he had to go back to hand in his assignment.

C H A P T E R 33

Fragments, Run-ons, and Comma Splices

The most common sources of sentence errors are fragments, run-ons, and comma splices.

33a FRAGMENTS

Fragments in speech and writing

Fragments are incomplete sentences. They are punctuated to look like sentences, but they lack a key element—often a subject or a verb—or else are a subordinate clause or phrase. In spoken language we usually pay little attention to fragments.

MISSING SUBJECT; MISSING VERB	**Nothing like a hot shower when you're cold and wet.**
MISSING SUBJECT	I was completely hooked on the game. **And played it constantly.**
MISSING VERB	**You too?**
SUBORDINATE CLAUSE	**If you think so.**

In writing, however, fragments usually interrupt the reader. Consider another example of a full sentence followed by a fragment:

The school's enrolment rose unexpectedly during the fall semester. Because the percentage of students who accepted offers of admission was much higher than previous years and fewer students than usual dropped out or transferred.

Such fragments compel a reader to stop and reread. When a sentence starts with *because*, we expect to find a main clause later. But here, the *because* clause refers back to the previous sentence. The writer no doubt knew that the fragment gave reasons why enrolment rose, but a reader must stop to determine the connection.

In formal writing you should avoid fragments. Readers expect words punctuated as a sentence to be a complete sentence. They expect writers to complete their thoughts rather than force readers to guess the missing element.

COMMON ERRORS

Recognizing fragments

If you can spot fragments, you can fix them. Grammar checkers can find some of them, but they miss many fragments and identify other sentences wrongly as fragments. Ask these questions when you are checking for sentence fragments.

- **Does the sentence have a subject?** Except for commands, sentences need subjects:

  Jana spent eight hours a day at her job. Then came home and worked all evening too.

- **Does the sentence have a complete verb?** Sentences require complete verbs. Verbs that end in *-ing* must have an auxiliary verb to be complete.

  Raoul keeps changing majors. He trying to figure out what he really wants to do when he graduates.

- If the sentence begins with a subordinate clause, is there a main clause in the same sentence?

  Even though Vancouver is cloudy much of the year, no Canadian city is more beautiful when the sun shines. Which is one reason people continue to move there.

Remember:

1. **A sentence must have a subject and complete verb.**
2. **A subordinate clause cannot stand alone as a sentence.**

 For step-by-step discussion, examples, and practice of this common error, go to **www.pearsoned.ca/faigley/225**.

Basic strategies for turning fragments into sentences

Incorporate the fragment into an adjoining sentence. In many cases you can incorporate the fragment into an adjoining sentence.

She saw him coming. And looked away.
a

I was hooked on the game. Playing day and night.
game, playing

Add the missing element. If you cannot incorporate a fragment into another sentence, add the missing element.

He studying more this term.
(is inserted above "studying")

When aiming for the highest returns, ~~and~~ also ~~thinking~~ about the possible losses.
(investors should think written above)

Watch for these fragments

1. Pay close attention to sentences that begin with transitional words, coordinating conjunctions, and subordinating conjunctions. Among the most common are fragments that begin with a transitional word (*also, therefore, however, consequently*), a coordinating conjunction (*and, but, or*), or a word indicating a subordinate clause (*although, because, if, since*). Prepositional or verbal phrase fragments are also common.

Transitional words and phrases such as *also, however,* and *therefore* mark movement from one idea to another, such as introducing another example, a change in direction, or a conclusion. Writers often produce fragments when trying to separate these shifts with a period.

Naomi found ways to avoid working during her shift.~~T,~~ therefore making more work for the rest of the employees.

Compound predicates are linked by a coordinating conjunction such as *and, but,* or *or*. Because compound predicates share the same subject, the solution for a coordinating conjunction fragment is to incorporate it into the sentence with the subject.

Heroin use among urban professionals is on the rise in the United States.~~A~~ and also in Europe, after several decades during which cocaine was the preferred drug among this group.

2. Look for subordinate clause fragments. Subordinate clauses resemble sentences because they contain subjects and verbs. But subordinate clauses cannot stand alone as sentences because their meaning is dependent on another clause. Subordinate clauses begin with words such as *although, after, before, despite, if, though, unless, whether, while, when, who,* and *that*. Subordinate clause fragments often follow the sentence to which they actually belong. You can fix the subordinate clause fragment by incorporating it into the preceding sentence.

The movie *Gladiator* is fiction, but it is based on extensive research with much of the plot inspired by actual people and historical events.~~W,~~ which explains why it seems more realistic than earlier movies about Rome such as *Spartacus*.

Or you can fix the subordinate clause fragment by turning it into a sentence.

> The movie *Gladiator* is fiction, but it is based on extensive research with much of the plot inspired by actual people and historical events. This attention to historical detail, if not historical accuracy, explains why *Gladiator* seems more realistic than earlier movies about Rome such as *Spartacus*.

3. Look for phrase fragments. Phrases also cannot stand alone as sentences because they lack either a subject, a verb, or both. There are many different kinds of phrase fragments. Prepositional phrase fragments are easy to spot and fix.

> As Sohela looked over the notes for her autobiography, she mused about how much her life had changed. ~~I,~~ *i*n ways she could not have predicted.

> Andrew accepted the Nobel Peace prize. ~~W,~~ *w*ith great dignity and humility.

Appositive phrases, which rename or describe a noun, are often fragments.

> For his advanced history course, Professor Hibbard assigned J.J. Scarisbrick's *Henry VIII.* ~~A,~~ *a*n older text historians still regard as essential when studying sixteenth-century English history and politics.

Verbal phrase fragments are sometimes difficult to spot because verbals look like verbs. But remember: they function as adjectives, nouns, or adverbs.

> On their last trip to Halifax, Greta went to the Maritime Museum, but Georg didn't go. ~~Georg,~~ having visited that museum twice already.

4. Watch for list fragments. Do not isolate a list from the sentence that introduces it. Words or phrases such as *for example, for instance, namely,* and *such as* often introduce lists or examples. Make sure these lists are attached to a sentence with a subject and verb.

> Several Ben and Jerry's ice cream flavours are puns. ~~S,~~ *s*uch as Cherry Garcia, Phish Food, and The Full VerMonty.

33b RUN-ON SENTENCES

Run-on sentences are the opposite of sentence fragments. While fragments are incomplete sentences, run-ons jam together two or more sentences, failing to separate them with appropriate punctuation. And while fragments are sometimes acceptable, especially in informal writing, run-on sentences are never acceptable.

COMMON ERRORS

Recognizing run-on sentences

When you read this sentence, you realize something is wrong.

> I do not recall what kind of printer it was all I remember is that it could sort, staple, and print a packet at the same time.

The problem is that the two main clauses are not separated by punctuation. The reader must look carefully to determine where one main clause stops and the next one begins.

> I do not recall what kind of printer it was | all I remember is that it could sort, staple, and print a packet at the same time.

A period should be placed after *was*, and the next sentence should begin with a capital letter:

> I do not recall what kind of printer it was. All I remember is that it could sort, staple, and print a packet at the same time.

Run-on sentences are major errors.

Remember: Two main clauses must be separated by correct punctuation.

 For step-by-step discussion, examples, and practice of this common error, go to **www.pearsoned.ca/faigley/226**.

Fixing run-on sentences

Take three steps to fix run-on sentences: (1) identify the problem, (2) determine where the run-on sentence needs to be divided, and (3) choose the punctuation that indicates the relationship between the main clauses.

1. Identify the problem. When you read your writing aloud, run-on sentences will often trip you up, just as they confuse readers. You can also search for subject and verb pairs to check for run-ons. If you find two main clauses with no punctuation separating them, you have a run-on sentence.

    ———SUBJ——— ——VERB——
Internet businesses **are** not **bound** to specific locations or old ways
       —S—⌐V⌐
of running a business **they** **are** more flexible in allowing employees to telecommute and to determine the hours they work.

2. Determine where the run-on sentence needs to be divided.

Internet businesses are not bound to specific locations or old ways of running a business | they are more flexible in allowing employees to telecommute and to determine the hours they work.

3. Determine the relationship between the main clauses. You will revise a run-on more effectively if you determine the relationship between the main clauses and understand the effect or point you are trying to make. There are several punctuation strategies for fixing run-ons.

- **Insert a period.** This is the simplest way to fix a run-on sentence.

  Internet businesses are not bound to specific locations or old ways of running a business. They are more flexible in allowing employees to telecommute and to determine the hours they work.

  However, if you want to indicate the relationship between the two main clauses more clearly, you may want to choose one of these strategies:

- **Insert a semicolon (and possibly a transitional word indicating the relationship between the two main clauses):**

  Internet businesses are not bound to specific locations or old ways of running a business; therefore, they are more flexible in allowing employees to telecommute and to determine the hours they work.

- **Insert a comma and a coordinating conjunction (and, but, or, nor, for, so, yet):**

  Internet businesses are not bound to specific locations or old ways of running a business, so they are more flexible in allowing employees to telecommute and to determine the hours they work.

- **Make one of the clauses subordinate.**

  Since internet businesses are not bound to specific locations or old ways of running a business, they are more flexible in allowing employees to telecommute and to determine the hours they work.

33c COMMA SPLICES

Comma splices are a kind of run-on sentence. They do include a punctuation mark—a comma—but it is not a strong enough punctuation mark to separate two main clauses. Comma splices often do not cause the same problems for readers as run-ons. The following sentence can be read aloud with no problem.

Most of us were taking the same classes, if someone had a question, we would all help out.

On the page such sentences may cause confusion because commas are used to distinguish between elements within sentences, not to mark the boundary between sentences. Most readers see comma splices as errors, which is why you should avoid them.

COMMON ERRORS

Recognizing comma splices

When you edit your writing, look carefully at sentences that contain commas. Does the sentence contain two main clauses? If so, are the main clauses joined by a comma and coordinating conjunction *(and, but, for, or, not, so, yet)*?

INCORRECT
    ⎡—SUBJ—⎤   ⎡—VERB—⎤
The **concept** of "nature" **depends** on the concept of
    ⎡—SUBJ—⎤ ⎡V⎤
human "culture," the **problem** **is** that "culture" is itself shaped by "nature." [Two main clauses joined by only a comma]

CORRECT
Even though the concept of "nature" depends on the concept of human "culture," "culture" is itself shaped by "nature." [Subordinate clause plus a main clause]

CORRECT
The concept of "nature" depends on the concept of human "culture," but "culture" is itself shaped by "nature." [Two main clauses joined by a comma and coordinating conjunction]

Treating the word *however* as a coordinating conjunction produces some of the most common comma splice errors. *However* is a conjunctive adverb that does not function grammatically like the coordinating conjunctions *and, but, or, nor, yet, so,* and *for* (see Section 32b).

INCORRECT
Commercials that depict women as sex objects to sell products are obviously demeaning to women, however the always-present man, off-screen, who represents the viewers' gaze is equally demeaning to men.

CORRECT
Commercials that depict women as sex objects to sell products are obviously demeaning to women; however, the always-present man, off-screen, who represents the viewers' gaze is equally demeaning to men. [Two main clauses joined by a semicolon]

Remember: Do not use a comma as a period.

For step-by-step discussion, examples, and practice of this common error, go to **www.pearsoned.ca/faigley/227**.

Fixing comma splices

You have several options for fixing comma splices. Select the one that best fits where the sentence is located and the effect you are trying to achieve.

1. Change the comma to a period. Most comma splices can be fixed by changing the comma to a period.

> It didn't matter that I worked in a windowless room for 40 hours a
> week. On
> ~~week, on~~ the web I was exploring and learning more about distant
> people and places than I ever had before.

2. Change the comma to a semicolon. A semicolon indicates the close connection between the two main clauses.

> It didn't matter that I worked in a windowless room for 40 hours a
> week;
> ~~week,~~ On the web I was exploring and learning more about distant
> people and places than I ever had before.

3. Insert a coordinating conjunction. Other comma splices can be repaired by inserting a coordinating conjunction (*and, but, or, nor, so, yet*) to indicate the relationship of the two main clauses. The coordinating conjunction must be preceded by a comma.

> Digital technologies have intensified a global culture that affects
> us daily in large and small ways, **yet** their impact remains poorly
> understood.

4. Make one of the main clauses a subordinate clause. If a comma splice includes one main clause that is subordinate to the other, rewrite the sentence using a subordinating conjunction.

> *Because community*
> ~~Community~~ is the vision of a great society trimmed down to the size
> of a small town, it is a powerful metaphor for real estate developers
> who sell a mini-utopia along with a house or condo.

5. Make one of the main clauses a phrase. You can also rewrite one of the main clauses as a phrase.

> Community—**the vision of a great society trimmed down to the
> size of a small town**—is a powerful metaphor for real estate developers
> who sell a mini-utopia along with a house or condo.

CHAPTER 34

Subject-Verb Agreement

A verb must match its subject. If the subject is singular (*I, he, she,* or *it*), the verb must take a singular form. If the subject is plural (*we, you, they*), the verb must take a plural form. Therefore, verbs are said to *agree in number* with their subjects. This single rule determines subject-verb agreement.

34a AGREEMENT IN THE PRESENT TENSE

When your verb is in the present tense, agreement in number is straightforward: the subject takes the base form of the verb in all but the third person singular. For example, the verb *walk* in the present tense agrees in number with most subjects in its base form:

FIRST PERSON SINGULAR	I walk
SECOND PERSON SINGULAR	You walk
FIRST PERSON PLURAL	We walk
SECOND PERSON PLURAL	You walk
THIRD PERSON PLURAL	They walk

Third person singular subjects are the exception to this rule. When your subject is in the third person singular (*he, it, Fido, Svetlana, Mr. Jones*) you need to add an *s* or *es* to the base form of the verb.

THIRD PERSON SINGULAR (ADD *S*)	He walks. It talks. Fido barks.
THIRD PERSON SINGULAR (ADD *ES*)	Svetlana goes. Mr. Jones arrives.

34b SINGULAR AND PLURAL SUBJECTS

Sometimes it will be difficult to determine whether your subject is singular or plural, especially when subjects joined by *and* refer to the same thing or idea (*toast and jam, peace and quiet*) or when subjects are linked by *either . . . or* or *neither . . . nor*. Follow these rules when you have trouble determining whether to use a singular or plural verb form.

Subjects joined by *and*

When two subjects are joined by *and*, treat them as a compound (plural) subject.

Etta and Marja are leaving for Winnipeg in the morning.

The teacher and the lawyer have decided to walk from Saskatoon to Regina to raise money for a homeless shelter.

Some compound subjects are treated as singular. These kinds of compounds generally work together as a single noun. Although they appear to be compound and therefore plural, these subjects take the singular form of the verb:

Cookies and cream is my favourite ice cream flavour.

Rock and roll thrives in the twenty-first century.

Also, when two nouns linked by *and* are modified by *every* or *each*, these two nouns are likewise treated as one singular subject:

Every hill and valley is aglow with light.

Each night and day brings no new news of you.

An exception to this rule arises when the word *each* follows a compound subject. In these cases, usage varies depending on the number of the direct object.

The provincial and the federal court systems each have their own judges and prosecutors.

The owl and the pussycat each has a personal claim to fame.

Subjects joined by *or, either . . . or,* or *neither . . . nor*

If a subject is joined by *or, either . . . or,* or *neither . . . nor*, make sure the verb agrees with the subject closest to the verb.

— SING — ┌——PLURAL——┐ ┌ PL ┐
Is it **the drain or the pipes** that are leaking?
┌—PLURAL—┐ — SING — ┌—SING—┐
Is it **the pipes or the drain** that needs unclogging?
┌— SING ——┐ ┌—PLURAL—┐ ┌—PL—┐
Neither my neighbour nor his dogs make a sound at night.
┌—— PLURAL ——┐ ┌——SING——┐ ┌SING┐
Either two butter tarts or one piece of pie is your choice for dessert.

Subjects along with another noun

Verbs agree with the subject of a sentence, even when a subject is linked to another noun with a phrase like *as well as, along with,* or *alongside*. These modifying phrases are usually set off from the main subject with commas.

┌————————— IGNORE THIS PHRASE —————————┐
Chicken, alongside various steamed vegetables, is my favourite meal.
┌— IGNORE THIS PHRASE —┐
Besides David Bowie, **the Beatles** are my favourite band of all time.

COMMON ERRORS

Subjects separated from verbs

The most common agreement errors occur when words come between the subject and verb. These intervening words do not affect subject-verb agreement. To ensure that you use the correct verb form, identify the subject and the verb. Ignore any phrases that come between them.

— IGNORE THIS PHRASE —

INCORRECT **Students** who live in residence **doesn't** have to cook or clean.

CORRECT **Students** who live in residence **don't** have to cook or clean.

Students is plural and *don't* is plural; subject and verb agree.

INCORRECT **The whale shark,** the largest of all sharks, **feed** on plankton.

CORRECT **The whale shark,** the largest of all sharks, **feeds** on plankton.

The plural noun *sharks* that appears between the subject *the whale shark* and the verb *feeds* does not change the number of the subject. The subject is singular and the verb is singular. Subject and verb agree.

Remember: When you check for subject-verb agreement, identify the subject and verb. Ignore any words that come between them.

 For step-by-step discussion, examples, and practice of this common error, go to **www.pearsoned.ca/faigley/228.**

34c INDEFINITE PRONOUNS AS SUBJECTS

The choice of a singular or plural pronoun is determined by the **antecedent**—the noun that a pronoun refers to. For instance, the sentence *My friend likes soup* might be followed by another sentence, *She makes a new kind daily*. The pronoun must be singular because *she* refers to the singular noun *friend*.

Indefinite pronouns, such as *some, few, all, someone, everyone,* and *each,* often do not refer to identifiable subjects; hence they have no antecedents. Most indefinite pronouns are singular and agree with the singular forms of verbs. Some, like *both* and *many,* are always plural and agree with the plural forms of verbs. Other indefinite pronouns are variable and can agree with either singular or plural verb forms, depending on the context of the sentence.

COMMON ERRORS

Agreement errors using *each*

The indefinite pronoun *each* is a frequent source of subject-verb agreement errors. If a pronoun is singular, its verb must be singular. This rule holds true even when the subject is modified by a phrase that includes a plural noun.

A common stumbling block to this rule is the pronoun *each*. *Each* is always treated as a singular pronoun in post-secondary writing. When *each* stands alone, the choice is easy to make:

INCORRECT   **Each are** an outstanding student.
CORRECT   **Each is** an outstanding student.

But when *each* is modified by a phrase that includes a plural noun, the choice of a singular verb form becomes less obvious:

INCORRECT   **Each** of the girls **are** fit.
CORRECT   **Each** of the girls **is** fit.

INCORRECT   **Each** of our dogs **get** a present.
CORRECT   **Each** of our dogs **gets** a present.

Remember: *Each* is always singular.

 For step-by-step discussion, examples, and practice of this common error, go to **www.pearsoned.ca/faigley/229**.

34d COLLECTIVE NOUNS AS SUBJECTS

Collective nouns refer to groups (*administration, audience, class, committee, crew, crowd, faculty, family, fleet, gang, government, group, herd, jury, mob, public, team*). When members of a group are considered as a unit, use singular verbs and singular pronouns.

The **audience was** patient with the novice performer.

The **crowd is** unusually quiet at the moment, but **it** will get noisy soon.

The **fleet leaves** port on June 29, and **it** will not return until next year.

When members of a group are considered as individuals, use plural verbs and plural pronouns.

The **brigade are** in **their** positions on both flanks.

The **faculty have their** differing opinions on how to address the problems caused by reducing funding.

Sometimes collective nouns can be singular in one context and plural in another. Writers must decide which verb form to use based on sentence context.

> The **number** of people who live downtown **is** increasing.

> A **number** of people **are** moving downtown from the suburbs.

> **Sports is** one of the four main buttons on the newspaper's website.

> **Sports are** a central part of many children's lives.

34e INVERTED WORD ORDER

In English a sentence's subject usually comes before the verb: *The nights are tender*. Sometimes, however, you will come across a sentence with inverted word order: *Tender are the nights*. Here the subject of the sentence, *nights*, comes after the verb, *are*. Writers use inverted word order most often in forming questions. The statement *Your cat is friendly* becomes a question when you invert the subject and the verb: *Is your cat friendly?* Writers also use inverted word order for added emphasis or for style considerations.

Do not be confused by inverted word order. Locate the subject of your sentence, then make sure your verb agrees with that subject.

34f AMOUNTS, NUMBERS, AND PAIRS

Subjects that describe amounts of money, time, distance, or measurement are singular and require singular verbs.

> **Three days is** never long enough to unwind.

> **Two hundred dollars stands** as the asking price.

Some subjects, such as courses of study, academic specializations, illnesses, and even some nations, are treated as singular subjects even though their names end in *-s* or *-es*. For example, *economics, news, ethics, measles,* and *the United States* all end in *-s* but are all singular subjects.

> **Economics is** a rich field of study.

> **News keeps** getting more and more commercial.

> **The United States is** a global power.

Other subjects require a plural verb form even though they refer to single items such as *jeans, slacks, glasses, scissors,* and *tweezers*. These items are all pairs.

> Your **jeans look** terrific.

> My **glasses are** scratched.

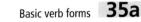

C H A P T E R 35

Verbs

As a reader you've had the experience of stumbling over a sentence, reading it three or four times before it makes sense. Often the cause of the confusion is a verb problem. Problems with verbs, fortunately, are easy to spot and fix if you know what to look for.

35a BASIC VERB FORMS

Almost all verbs in English have five possible forms. The exception is the verb *be*. Regular verbs follow this basic pattern:

Base form	Third person singular	Past tense	Past participle	Present participle
jump	jumps	jumped	jumped	jumping
like	likes	liked	liked	liking
talk	talks	talked	talked	talking
wish	wishes	wished	wished	wishing

Irregular verbs do not follow this basic pattern. See Section 35b for the forms of irregular verbs.

Base form

The base form of the verb is the one you find listed in the dictionary. This form indicates an action or condition in the present.

> I **like** Quebec City in June.

> We **talk** often on weekends.

Third person singular

The base form of the verb changes when used with third person singular subjects. Third person singular subjects include *he, she, it,* and the nouns they replace, as well as other pronouns, including *someone, anybody,* and

everything. (See Section 34c.) Present tense verbs in the third person singular end with an *s* or an *es*.

> Ms. Nessan **speaks** in riddles.

> He **watches** too much television.

Past tense

The past tense describes an action or condition that occurred in the past. For most verbs, the past tense is formed by adding *d* or *ed* to the base form of the verb.

> I **called** at nine, but no one **answered**.

> She **inhaled** the night air.

Many verbs, however, have irregular past tense forms. (See Section 35b.)

COMMON ERRORS

Missing verb endings

Verb endings are not always pronounced in speech, especially in some dialects of English. It's also easy to omit these endings when you are writing quickly. Spelling checkers will not mark these errors, so you have to find them while proofreading.

INCORRECT	Jeremy **feel** as if he's catching a cold.
CORRECT	Jeremy **feels** as if he's catching a cold.

INCORRECT	Sheila **hope** she would get the day off.
CORRECT	Sheila **hoped** she would get the day off.

Remember: Check verbs carefully for missing *s* or *es* endings in the present tense and missing *d* or *ed* endings in the past tense.

 For step-by-step discussion, examples, and practice of this common error, go to **www.pearsoned.ca/faigley/230**.

Past participle

The past participle is used with *have* to form verbs in the perfect tense, with *be* to form verbs in the passive voice (see Section 26a), and to form adjectives derived from verbs.

PAST PERFECT	They **had returned** home unexpectedly.
PASSIVE	The book **was written** 30 years before it was published.
ADJECTIVE	In the 1980s, **teased** hair was all the rage.

Present participle

The present participle functions in one of three ways. Used with an auxiliary verb, it can describe a continuing action. The present participle can also function as a noun, known as a **gerund**, or as an adjective. The present participle is formed by adding *ing* to the base form of a verb.

PRESENT PARTICIPLE	Elks **are competing** for limited food resources.
GERUND	**Sailing** around the Cape of Good Hope is rumoured to bring good luck.
ADJECTIVE	We looked for shells in the **ebbing** tide.

35b IRREGULAR VERBS

A verb is **regular** when its past and past participle forms are created by adding *ed* or *d* to the base form. If this rule does not apply, the verb is considered an **irregular** verb. Here are some common irregular verbs and their basic conjugations.

Common irregular verbs

Base form	Past tense	Past participle
arise	arose	arisen
be (is, am, are)	was, were	been
bear	bore	borne or born
beat	beat	beaten
become	became	become
begin	began	begun
bend	bent	bent
break	broke	broken
bring	brought	brought
buy	bought	bought
choose	chose	chosen
cling	clung	clung
come	came	come
cost	cost	cost
creep	crept	crept
deal	dealt	dealt
dig	dug	dug
dive	dived or dove	dived
do	did	done

(continued next page)

Base form	Past tense	Past participle
draw	drew	drawn
drink	drank	drunk
drive	drove	driven
eat	ate	eaten
fall	fell	fallen
feed	fed	fed
feel	felt	felt
fight	fought	fought
fling	flung	flung
fly	flew	flown
forbid	forbade or forbad	forbidden
forget	forgot	forgotten or forgot
forgive	forgave	forgiven
freeze	froze	frozen
get	got	got or gotten
give	gave	given
go	went	gone
grow	grew	grown
hang	hung	hung
have	had	had
know	knew	known
lay	laid	laid
lend	lent	lent
lie	lay	lain
make	made	made
read	read	read
run	ran	run
say	said	said
see	saw	seen
send	sent	sent
shine	shone	shone
show	showed	shown or showed
sit	sat	sat
sleep	slept	slept
speak	spoke	spoken
spring	sprang or sprung	sprung
swim	swam	swum
take	took	taken
teach	taught	taught
tell	told	told
think	thought	thought
understand	understood	understood
wear	wore	worn
write	wrote	written

COMMON ERRORS

Confusing the past tense and past participle forms of irregular verbs

The past tense and past participle forms of irregular verbs are often confused. The most frequent error is using a past tense form instead of the past participle with *had*.

	PAST TENSE
INCORRECT	She had never **rode** a horse before.
	PAST PARTICIPLE
CORRECT	She had never **ridden** a horse before.

	PAST TENSE
INCORRECT	He had **saw** many white pelicans in Saskatoon.
	PAST PARTICIPLE
CORRECT	He had **seen** many white pelicans in Saskatoon.

Remember: Change any past tense verbs preceded by *had* to past participles.

 For step-by-step discussion, examples, and practice of this common error, go to **www.pearsoned.ca/faigley/231**.

35c TRANSITIVE AND INTRANSITIVE VERBS

Lay/lie and *raise/rise*

Do you know whether you raise or rise from bed in the morning? Do your house keys lay or lie on the kitchen table? *Raise/rise and lay/lie* are transitive and intransitive verbs that writers frequently confuse. Transitive verbs take direct objects, nouns that receive the action of the verb. Intransitive verbs act in sentences that lack direct objects.

The following charts list the trickiest pairs of transitive and intransitive verbs and the correct forms for each verb tense. Pay special attention to *lay* and *lie*, which are irregular.

	lay (put something down)	lie (recline)
Present	lay, lays	lie, lies
Present participle	laying	lying
Past	laid	lay
Past participle	laid	lain

TRANSITIVE	Once you complete your test, please **lay** your pencil (direct object, the thing being laid down) on the desk.
INTRANSITIVE	After working a double shift, I **lie** on the couch for hours, too exhausted to move.

	raise (elevate something)	rise (get up)
Present	raise, raises	rise, rises
Present participle	raising	rising
Past	raised	rose
Past participle	raised	risen

TRANSITIVE   We **raise** our glasses (direct object, the things being raised) to toast Uncle Han.

INTRANSITIVE   The sun **rises** over the bay.

35d   SHIFTS IN TENSE

Appropriate shifts in verb tense

Changes in verb tense are sometimes necessary to indicate a shift in time.

PRESENT TO PAST   [PRESENT TENSE] I never **shop** online anymore because I **heard** [PAST TENSE] that [PRESENT PERFECT TENSE] hackers **have stolen** thousands of credit card numbers used in internet transactions.

PAST TO FUTURE   Because Oda **won** [PAST TENSE] the lottery, she **will quit** [FUTURE TENSE] her job at the hospital as soon as her supervisor **finds** [PRESENT TENSE] a qualified replacement.

Inappropriate shifts in verb tense

Be careful to avoid confusing your reader with unnecessary shifts in verb tense. Once you reach the proofreading stage of your writing, dedicate one careful reading of your text to finding inappropriate tense changes.

INCORRECT   While Brazil **looks** [PRESENT TENSE] to ecotourism to fund rainforest preservation, other South American nations **relied** [PAST TENSE] on foreign aid and conservation efforts.

The shift from present tense (*looks*) to past tense (*relied*) is confusing. The sentence attempts to compare Brazil with other South American countries, but the shift in tenses muddles the comparison. Correct the mistake by putting both verbs in the present tense.

CORRECT   While Brazil **looks** [PRESENT TENSE] to ecotourism to fund rainforest preservation, other South American nations **rely** [PRESENT TENSE] on foreign aid and conservation efforts.

COMMON ERRORS

Unnecessary tense shift

Notice the tense shift in the following example.

INCORRECT   In May of 2000 the "I Love You" virus **crippled** [PAST TENSE] the computer systems of major North American companies and **irritated** [PAST TENSE] millions of private computer users. As the virus **generates** [PRESENT TENSE] millions of emails and **erases** [PRESENT TENSE] millions of computer files, companies such as Ford and the Royal Bank **are** [PRESENT TENSE] forced to shut down their clogged email systems.

The second sentence shifts unnecessarily to the present tense, confusing the reader. Did the "I Love You" virus have its heyday several years ago, or is it still wreaking havoc now? Changing the verbs in the second sentence to the past tense eliminates the confusion.

CORRECT   In May of 2000 the "I Love You" virus **crippled** [PAST TENSE] the computer systems of major North American companies and **irritated** [PAST TENSE] millions of private computer users. As the virus **generated** [PAST TENSE] millions of emails and **erased** [PAST TENSE] millions of computer files, companies such as Ford and the Royal Bank **were** [PAST TENSE] forced to shut down their clogged email systems.

Remember: Shift verb tense only when you are referring to different time periods.

 For step-by-step discussion, examples, and practice of this common error, go to **www.pearsoned.ca/faigley/232**.

35e SHIFTS IN MOOD

Indicative, imperative, and subjunctive verbs

Verbs can be categorized into three moods—indicative, imperative, and subjunctive—defined by the functions they serve.

Indicative verbs state facts, opinions, and questions.

FACT	The human genome project **seeks** to map out human DNA.
OPINION	The scientific advances spurred by the human genome project, including cloning and designer genes, **will allow** normal people to play God.
QUESTION	How long **does** it **take** to map out the entire human genome?

Imperative verbs make commands, give advice, and make requests.

COMMAND	**Research** the technology being used to carry out the human genome project.
ADVICE	**Try** to join a high-profile research project like the human genome project if you want to make a name for yourself in the scientific community.
REQUEST	**Could** you please **explain** the role you played in the human genome project?

Subjunctive verbs express wishes, unlikely or untrue situations, hypothetical situations, requests with *that* clauses, and suggestions.

WISH	We **wish** that unlocking the secrets of our DNA **were** a guaranteed way to cure genetic diseases.
UNLIKELY OR UNTRUE SITUATION	If the genome project **were** as simple as the news media made it out to be, scientists could complete it over a long weekend.
HYPOTHETICAL SITUATION	If the genome project **were** to lose government funding, the scientists working on it would not be able to afford the equipment they need to complete it.

The subjunctive in past and present tenses

Subjunctive verbs are usually the trickiest to handle. In the present tense subjunctive clauses call for the base form of the verb (*be, have, see, jump*).

It is essential that children **be** immunized before they enter kindergarten.

In the past tense they call for the standard past tense of the verb (*had, saw, jumped*), with one exception. In counterfactual sentences the *to be* verb always becomes *were*, even for subjects that take *was* under normal circumstances.

INDICATIVE	I was surprised at some of the choices she made.
SUBJUNCTIVE	If I were in her position, I'd do things differently.
INDICATIVE	The young athletes found that gaining muscle was not easy.
SUBJUNCTIVE	If being muscular were easy, everyone would look like Arnold Schwarzenegger.

pron CHAPTER *36*

Pronouns

Pronouns are little words like *he, she, it, we, our, who,* and *mine* that stand for nouns and other pronouns. They are among the most frequently used words in English, but they also are a frequent source of problems in writing.

36a PRONOUN CASE

Pronoun case refers to the forms pronouns take to indicate their function in a sentence. Pronouns that function as the subjects of sentences are in the **subjective case**. Pronouns that function as direct or indirect objects are in the **objective case**. Pronouns that indicate ownership are in the **possessive case**.

Subjective pronouns	Objective pronouns	Possessive pronouns
I	me	my, mine
we	us	our, ours
you	you	your, yours
he	him	his
she	her	her, hers
it	it	its
they	them	their, theirs
who	whom	whose

People who use English regularly usually make these distinctions among pronouns without thinking about them.

^S   ^O   ^P   ^S   ^O   ^O   ^S   ^O

I let him use my laptop, but he lent it to her, and I haven't seen it since.

Nonetheless, choosing the correct pronoun case sometimes can be difficult.

Pronouns in compound phrases

Picking the right pronoun sometimes can be confusing when the pronoun appears in a compound phrase.

> If we work together, you and **me** can get the job done quickly.

> If we work together, you and **I** can get the job done quickly.

Which is correct—*me* or *I*? Removing the other pronoun usually makes the choice clear.

> **INCORRECT**   Me can get the job done quickly.
>
> **CORRECT**   I can get the job done quickly.

Similarly, when compound pronouns appear as objects of prepositions, sometimes the correct choice isn't obvious until you remove the other pronoun.

> When you finish your comments, give them to Isidora or **I**.

> When you finish your comments, give them to Isidora or **me**.

Again, the choice is easy when the pronoun stands alone:

> **INCORRECT**   Give them to **I**.
>
> **CORRECT**   Give them to **me**.

We and *us* before nouns

Another pair of pronouns that can cause difficulty is *we* and *us* before nouns.

> **Us** friends must stick together.

> **We** friends must stick together.

Which is correct—*us* or *we*? Removing the noun indicates the correct choice.

> **INCORRECT**   Us must stick together.
>
> **CORRECT**   We must stick together.

Who versus whom

Choosing between *who* and *whom* is often difficult, even for experienced writers. When you answer the phone, which do you say?

1. To **whom** do you wish to speak?

2. **Who** do you want to talk to?

Probably you chose 2. *To whom do you wish to speak?* may sound stuffy, but technically it is correct. The reason it sounds stuffy is that the distinction between *who* and *whom* is disappearing from spoken language. *Who* is more often used in spoken language, even when *whom* is correct.

COMMON ERRORS

Who or whom

In writing, the distinction between *who* and *whom* is still often observed. *Who* and *whom* follow the same rules as other pronouns: *who* is the subject pronoun; *whom* is the object pronoun. If you are dealing with an object, *whom* is the correct choice.

INCORRECT	Who did you send the letter to?
	Who did you give the present to?
CORRECT	To whom did you send the letter?
	Whom did you give the present to?

Who is always the right choice for subject pronoun.

CORRECT	Who gave you the present?
	Who brought the cookies?

If you are uncertain of which one to use, try substituting *she* and *her* or *he* and *him*.

INCORRECT	You sent the letter to she [who]?
CORRECT	You sent the letter to her [whom]?

INCORRECT	Him [Whom] gave you the present?
CORRECT	He [Who] gave you the present?

Remember: *Who* = subject
Whom = object

 For step-by-step discussion, examples, and practice of this common error; go to **www.pearsoned.ca/faigley/233**.

Whoever versus *whomever*

With the same rule in mind, you can distinguish between *whoever* and *whomever*. Which is correct?

> Her warmth touched **whoever** she met.
>
> Her warmth touched **whomever** she met.

In this sentence the pronoun functions as a direct object: her warmth touched everyone she met, not someone touched her. Thus *whomever* is the correct choice.

Pronouns in comparisons

When you write a sentence using a comparison that includes *than* or *as* followed by a pronoun, usually you will have to think about which pronoun is correct. Which of the following is correct?

> Vimala is a faster swimmer than **him**.
>
> Vimala is a faster swimmer than **he**.

The test that will give you the correct answer is to add the verb that finishes the sentence—in this case, *is*.

> **INCORRECT**   Vimala is a faster swimmer than him is.
>
> **CORRECT**   Vimala is a faster swimmer than he is.

Adding the verb makes the correct choice evident.

In some cases the choice of pronoun changes the meaning. Consider these examples:

> She likes ice cream more than me. [A bowl of ice cream is better than hanging out with me.]
>
> She likes ice cream more than I. [I would rather have frozen yogourt.]

In such cases it is better to complete the comparison:

> She likes ice cream more than I do.

Possessive pronouns

Possessive pronouns at times are confusing because possessive nouns are formed with apostrophes, but possessive pronouns do not require apostrophes. Pronouns that use apostrophes are always **contractions**.

> It's   = It is
> Who's = Who is
> They're = They are

The test for whether to use an apostrophe is to determine whether the pronoun is possessive or a contraction. The most confusing pair is *its* and *it's*.

| INCORRECT | Its a sure thing she will be elected. [Contraction] |
| CORRECT | It's a sure thing she will be elected. [**It is** a sure thing.] |

| INCORRECT | The dog lost it's collar. [Possessive] |
| CORRECT | The dog lost its collar. |

Whose versus *who's* follows the same pattern.

| INCORRECT | Who's bicycle has the flat tire? [Possessive] |
| CORRECT | Whose bicycle has the flat tire? |

| INCORRECT | Whose on first? [Contraction] |
| CORRECT | Who's on first? [**Who is** on first?] |

Possessive pronouns before *-ing* verbs

Pronouns that modify an *-ing* verb (called a *gerund*) or an *-ing* verb phrase (*gerund phrase*) should appear in the possessive.

| INCORRECT | The odds of **you** making the team are excellent. |
| CORRECT | The odds of **your** making the team are excellent. |

36b PRONOUN AGREEMENT

Because pronouns usually replace or refer to other nouns, they must match those nouns in number and gender. The noun that the pronoun replaces is called its **antecedent**. If pronoun and antecedent match, they are in **agreement**. When a pronoun is close to the antecedent, usually there is no problem.

Maria forgot **her** coat.

The orchestra members collected **their** instruments.

When pronouns and the nouns they replace are separated by several words, sometimes the agreement in number is lost.

When the World Wrestling Federation (WWF) used wrestlers [PLURAL] to represent nations, there was no problem identifying the villains [SING]. He was the enemy if he [SING] came from Russia. But after the Cold War, wrestlers [PLURAL] can switch from good guys to bad guys. We don't immediately know how he [SING] has been scripted—good or bad.

Careful writers make sure that pronouns match their antecedents.

Collective nouns

Collective nouns (such as *audience, class, committee, crowd, family, herd, jury, team*) can be singular or plural depending on whether the emphasis is on the group or on the particular individuals.

CORRECT   The **committee** was unanimous in **its** decision.

CORRECT   The **committee** put **their** opinions ahead of the goals of the unit.

COMMON ERRORS

Indefinite pronouns

Indefinite pronouns (such as *anybody, anything, each, either, everybody, everything, neither, none, somebody, something*) refer to unspecified people or things. Most take singular pronouns.

INCORRECT   **Everybody** can choose **their** roommates.

CORRECT   **Everybody** can choose **his or her** roommate.

CORRECT
ALTERNATIVE   **All students** can choose **their** roommates.

A few indefinite pronouns (*all, any, either, more, most, neither, none, some*) can take either singular or plural pronouns.

CORRECT   **Some** of the shipment was damaged when **it** became overheated.

CORRECT   **All** thought **they** should have a good seat at the concert.

A few are always plural (*few, many, several*).

CORRECT   **Several** want refunds.

Remember: Words that begin with *any*, *some*, and *every* are usually singular.

For step-by-step discussion, examples, and practice of this common error, go to **www.pearsoned.ca/faigley/234**.

Often a plural antecedent is added if the sense of the collective noun is plural.

CORRECT   The individual committee **members** put **their** opinions ahead of the goals of the unit.

COMMON ERRORS

Pronoun agreement with compound antecedents

Antecedents joined by *and* take plural pronouns.

CORRECT   **Huddah and Ioan** practised **their** speeches.

Exception: When compound antecedents are preceded by *each* or *every,* use a singular pronoun.

CORRECT   **Every male cardinal and warbler** arrives before the female to define **its** territory.

When compound antecedents are connected by *or* or *nor,* the pronoun agrees with the antecedent closer to it.

INCORRECT   **Either the Ross twins or Angela** should bring **their** CDs.
CORRECT   **Either the Ross twins or Angela** should bring **her** CDs.
BETTER   **Either Angela or the Ross twins** should bring **their** CDs.

When you put the plural *twins* last, the correct choice becomes the plural pronoun *their.*

Remember:

1. **Use plural pronouns for antecedents joined by and.**
2. **Use singular pronouns for antecedents preceded by each or every.**
3. **Use a pronoun that agrees with the nearest antecedent when compound antecedents are joined by or or nor.**

 For step-by-step discussion, examples, and practice of this common error, go to **www.pearsoned.ca/faigley/235**.

36c PROBLEMS WITH PRONOUNS AND GENDER

English does not have a neutral singular pronoun for a group of mixed genders or a person of unknown gender. Many people find it unacceptable to refer to a group of mixed genders using male pronouns. Unless the school in the following example is all male, many readers would object to the use of *his*.

SEXIST   **Each student** must select **his** courses using the online registration system.

Some writers attempt to avoid sexist usage by substituting a plural pronoun. This strategy, however, produces a grammatically incorrect sentence that also risks putting off some readers.

INCORRECT **Each student** must select **their** courses using the online registration system.

One strategy is to use *his or her* instead of *his*.

> CORRECT   **Each student** must select **his or her** courses using the
> online registration system.

Often you can avoid using *his or her* by changing the noun to the plural form.

> BETTER   **All students** must select **their** courses using the online
> registration system.

In some cases, using *his or her* may be necessary. Use this construction sparingly.

COMMON ERRORS

Problems created by the pronoun *one* used as a subject

Some writers use *one* as a subject in an attempt to sound more formal. At best this strategy produces writing that sounds stilted, and at worst it produces annoying errors.

> SEXIST   **One** can use **his** brains instead of a calculator to do
> simple addition.

> INCORRECT   **One** can use **their** brains instead of a calculator to do
> simple addition. (Agreement error: *their* does not agree
> with *one*.)

> INCORRECT   When **one** runs a 10K race for the first time, **you** often start
> out too fast. (Pronoun shift error: *one* changes to *you*.)

> CORRECT   **One** can use **his or her** brains instead of a calculator to
> do simple addition.

> CORRECT   **One** can use **one's** brains instead of a calculator to do
> simple addition.

You're better off generally avoiding using *one* as the subject of sentences.

> BETTER   **Use your brain** instead of a calculator for simple addition.

Remember: Avoid using the pronoun *one* as a subject.

 For step-by-step discussion, examples, and practice of this common error, go to **www.pearsoned.ca/faigley/236**.

36d VAGUE REFERENCE

Pronouns can sometimes refer to more than one noun, thus confusing readers.

> The **coach** rushed past the injured **player** to yell at the **referee**. **She**
> was hit in the face by a stray elbow.

You have to guess which person *she* refers to—the coach, the player, or the referee. Sometimes you cannot even guess the antecedent of a pronoun.

> The new subdivision destroyed the last remaining habitat for wildlife within the city limits. **They** have ruined our city with their unchecked greed.

Whom does *they* refer to? The mayor and city council? The developers? The people who live in the subdivision? Or all of the above?

Pronouns should never leave the reader guessing about antecedents. If different nouns can be confused as the antecedent, then the ambiguity should be clarified.

COMMON ERRORS

Vague use of *this*

Always use a noun immediately after *this, that, these, those,* and *some.*

VAGUE	Enrique asked Meg to remove the viruses on his computer. **This** was a bad idea.

Was it a bad idea for Enrique to ask Meg because she was insulted? Because she didn't know how? Because removing viruses would destroy some of Enrique's files?

BETTER	Enrique asked Meg to remove the viruses on his computer. **This imposition** on Meg's time made her resentful.

Remember: Ask yourself "*this* what?" and add the noun that *this* refers to.

 For step-by-step discussion, examples, and practice of this common error, go to **www.pearsoned.ca/faigley/237**.

VAGUE	Mafalda's pet boa constrictor crawled across Tonya's foot. **She** was mortified.
BETTER	When Mafalda's pet boa constrictor crawled across Tonya's foot, **Mafalda** was mortified.

If the antecedent is missing, then it should be supplied.

VAGUE	Mafalda wasn't thinking when she brought her boa constrictor into the crowded writing centre. **They** got up and left the room in the middle of consultations.
BETTER	Mafalda wasn't thinking when she brought her boa constrictor into the crowded writing centre. **A few students** got up and left the room in the middle of consultations.

WRITING IN THE WORLD

Pronouns in legal writing

Legal writing is often difficult to read, in part because lawyers often don't use many pronouns. The following paragraph is typical.

LEGALESE

Cancellations by participants received within 30 days of departure are subject to loss of the deposit paid in advance by participant plus cancellation costs for services rendered by the travel agency unless a substitute participant is found by the participant or the letter of cancellation from the participant is accompanied by a letter from a physician stating that the participant is not able to travel due to medical reasons, in which case the participant will not pay cancellation costs.

Legal writing does not have to be this difficult to understand. Some attorneys and others who write legal language wrongly believe that they can avoid any possible misunderstanding by not using pronouns. In fact, many jurisdictions now require consumer contracts to be written in plain English. Using pronouns makes the contract readable.

PLAIN ENGLISH

If you cancel within 30 days of departure, you will lose your deposit and you must pay for any services we have provided unless (1) you find a substitute, or (2) you send a letter from a physician stating that you cannot travel for medical reasons, in which case you lose only the deposit.

CHAPTER 37

Modifiers

Modifiers can limit or elaborate on your words. They make your eggs *scrambled* and your shower *hot*; they allow you to sleep *soundly* and laugh *loudly*. But if you're not careful they can also create unintentionally funny sentences.

Mired in the swampy muck, the alligator swam toward the fisherman.

Who's mired in the muck, the fisherman or the alligator?

Jason returned the new car his parents purchased **after denting a fender.**

The sentence has the parents purchasing a new car after denting the fender. Modifiers are effective when they are both carefully selected and carefully placed.

Modifiers come in two varieties: adjectives and adverbs. The same words can function as adjectives or adverbs, depending on what they modify.

ADJECTIVES MODIFY

nouns—*iced* tea, *first* violin

pronouns—He is *brash*.

ADVERBS MODIFY

verbs—*barely* reach, drive *carefully*

adjectives—*truly* brave activist, *shockingly* red lipstick

other adverbs—*not* soon forget, *very* well

clauses—*Honestly*, I find ballet boring.

Adjectives answer the questions *Which one? How many?* and *What kind?* Adverbs answer the questions *How often? To what extent? When? Where? How?* and *Why?*

37a CHOOSE THE CORRECT MODIFIER

Use the correct forms of comparatives and superlatives

As kids, we used comparative and superlative modifiers to argue that the X-Men were *more powerful* than the Ninja turtles and phys-ed was the *coolest* part of the day. Comparatives and superlatives are formed differently; all you need to know to determine which to use is the number of items you are comparing.

Comparative modifiers weigh one thing against another. They either end in *er* or are preceded by *more*.

Road bikes are **faster** on pavement than mountain bikes.

The **more courageous** juggler tossed flaming torches.

Superlative modifiers compare three or more items. They either end in *est* or are preceded by *most*.

April is the **hottest** month in New Delhi.

Wounded animals are the **most ferocious**.

When should you add a suffix instead of *more* or *most*? The following guidelines work in most cases:

ADJECTIVES

- For adjectives of one or two syllables, add *er* or *est*.

  redder, heaviest

- For adjectives of three or more syllables, use *more* or *most*.

  more viable, most powerful

ADVERBS

- For adverbs of one syllable, use *er* or *est*.

  nearer, slowest

- For adverbs with two or more syllables, use *more* or *most*.

  more convincingly, most humbly

Some frequently used comparatives and superlatives are irregular. The following list can help you become familiar with them.

Adjective	Comparative	Superlative
good	better	best
bad	worse	worst
little (amount)	less	least
many, much	more	most

Adverb	Comparative	Superlative
well	better	best
badly	worse	worst

Do not use both a suffix (*er* or *est*) and *more* or *most*.

INCORRECT	The service at Siam Palace is **more slower** than the service at The Lotus Garden.
CORRECT	The service at Siam Palace is **slower** than the service at The Lotus Garden.

Be sure to name the elements being compared if they are not clear from the context.

UNCLEAR COMPARATIVE	Mice are **cuter**.
CLEAR	Mice are **cuter than rats**.
UNCLEAR SUPERLATIVE	Nutria are the **creepiest**.
CLEAR	Nutria are the **creepiest rodents**.

Absolute modifiers cannot be comparative or superlative

Absolute modifiers are words that represent an unvarying condition and thus aren't subject to the degrees that comparative and superlative constructions convey. How many times have you heard something called *very unique* or *totally unique*? *Unique* means "one of a kind." There's nothing else like it. Thus something cannot be *very unique* or *totally unique*. It is either unique or it isn't. The United States Constitution makes a classic absolute modifier blunder when it begins, "We the People of the United States, in Order to form a more perfect Union. . . ." What is a *more perfect Union*? What's more perfect than perfect itself? The construction is nonsensical.

Absolute modifiers should not be modified by comparatives (*more* + modifier or modifier + *er*) or superlatives (*most* + modifier or modifier + *est*). Note the following list of common absolute modifiers.

absolute	impossible	unanimous
adequate	infinite	unavoidable
complete	main	uniform
entire	minor	unique
false	perfect	universal
fatal	principal	whole
final	stationary	
ideal	sufficient	

Double negatives

In English, as in mathematics, two negatives equal a positive. Avoid using two negative words in one sentence, or you'll end up saying the opposite of what you mean. The following are negative words that you should avoid doubling up:

barely	nobody	nothing
hardly	none	scarcely
neither	no one	

INCORRECT, DOUBLE NEGATIVE	**Barely no one** noticed that the pop star lip-synched during the whole performance.
CORRECT, SINGLE NEGATIVE	**Barely anyone** noticed that the pop star lip-synched during the whole performance.
INCORRECT, DOUBLE NEGATIVE	When the pastor asked if anyone had objections to the marriage, **nobody** said **nothing**.
CORRECT, SINGLE NEGATIVE	When the pastor asked if anyone had objections to the marriage, **nobody** said **anything**.

COMMON ERRORS

Irregular adjectives and adverbs

Switch on a baseball interview and you will likely hear numerous modifier mistakes.

Manager: We didn't play **bad** tonight. Martinez hit the ball **real good**, and I was glad to see Adamski pitch **farther** into the game than he did in his last start. His fastball was on, and he walked **less** hitters.

(continued next page)

While this manager has his sports clichés down pat, he makes errors with five of the trickiest modifier pairs. In three cases he uses an adjective where an adverb would be correct.

Adjectives	Adverbs
bad	badly
good	well
real	really

Bad, an adjective modifying the noun *call*: The umpire made a **bad** call at the plate.

Badly, an adverb modifying the verb *play*: We didn't play **badly**.

Good, an adjective modifying the noun *catch*: Starke made a **good** catch.

Well, an adverb modifying the verb *hit*: Martinez hit the ball **well**.

Exception: *Well* acts as an adjective when it describes someone's health: Injured players must stay on the disabled list until they feel **well** enough to play everyday.

Real, an adjective modifying the noun *wood*: While college players hit with aluminum bats, the professionals still use **real** wood.

Really, an adverb modifying the adverb *well*: Martinez hit the ball **really** well.

The coach also confused the comparative adjectives *less* and *fewer*, and the comparative adverbs *farther* and *further*.

ADJECTIVES

less—a smaller, uncountable amount
fewer—a smaller number of things

LESS   Baseball stadiums with pricey luxury suites cater **less** to families and more to business people with expense accounts.

FEWER   He walked **fewer** hitters.

ADVERBS

farther—a greater distance
further—to a greater extent, a longer time, or a greater number

FARTHER   Some players argue that today's baseballs go **farther** than baseballs made just a few years ago.

FURTHER   The commissioner of baseball curtly denied that today's baseballs are juiced, refusing to discuss the matter **further**.

Remember: *Bad, good, real, less* (for uncountables), and *fewer* (for countables) are adjectives. *Badly, well, really, farther* (for distance), and *further* (for extent, time, or number) are adverbs. *Well* is an adjective when it describes health.

 For step-by-step discussion, examples, and practice of this common error, go to **www.pearsoned.ca/faigley/238**.

37b PLACE ADJECTIVES CAREFULLY

As a general rule, the closer you place a modifier to the word it modifies, the less the chance you will confuse your reader. This section and the next elaborate on this maxim, giving you the details you need to put it into practice. Most native speakers have an ear for many of the guidelines presented here, with the notable exception of the placement of limiting modifiers, which is explained in Section 37c.

Place adjective phrases and clauses carefully

Adjective clauses frequently begin with *when, where,* or a relative pronoun like *that, which, who, whom,* or *whose.* An adjective clause usually follows the noun or pronoun it modifies.

> **Adjective clause modifying *salon:* The salon where I get my hair styled** is raising its prices.

> **Adjective clause modifying *stylist:* I need to find a stylist who charges less.**

Adjective phrases and clauses can also come before the person or thing they modify.

> **Adjective phrase modifying *girl:* Proud of her accomplishment, the little girl showed her trophy to her grandmother.**

Adjective phrases or clauses can be confusing if they are separated from the word they modify.

> CONFUSING   Watching from the ground below, the kettle of turkey vultures circled high above the observers.

Is the kettle of vultures watching from the ground below? You can fix the problem by putting the modified subject immediately after the modifier or placing the modifier next to the modified subject.

> BETTER   The kettle of turkey vultures circled high above the **observers who were watching from the ground below.**

> BETTER   Watching from the ground below, the **observers** saw a kettle of turkey vultures circle high above them.

See dangling modifiers in Section 37e.

Place one-word adjectives before the modified word(s)

One-word adjectives almost always precede the word or words they modify.

> Pass the **hot** sauce, please.

When one-word adjectives are not next to the word or words being modified, they can create misunderstandings.

> UNCLEAR Before his owner withdrew him from competition, the **fiercest** rodeo's bull injured three riders.

Readers may think *fiercest* modifies *rodeo's* instead of *bull*. Placing the adjective before *bull* will clarify the meaning.

> BETTER Before his owner withdrew him from competition, the rodeo's **fiercest** bull injured three riders.

Exception: predicate adjectives follow linking verbs

Predicate adjectives are the most common exception to the norm of single-word adjectives preceding words they modify. Predicate adjectives follow linking verbs such as *is, are, was, were, seem, feel, smell, taste,* and *look.* Don't be fooled into thinking they are adverbs. If the word following a linking verb modifies the subject, use a predicate adjective. If it modifies an action verb, use an adverb. Can you identify the word being modified in the following sentence?

> I feel **odd**.

Odd modifies the subject *I*, not the verb *feel*. Thus, *odd* is a predicate adjective that implies the speaker feels ill. If it were an adverb, the sentence would read *I feel oddly*. The adverb *oddly* modifying *feel* would imply the speaker senses things in unconventional ways. Try the next one:

> The bruise looked **bad**.

Since *bad* modifies *bruise, bad* is a predicate adjective implying a serious injury. *Looked* is the linking verb that connects the two. If we made the modifier an adverb, the sentence would read *The bruise looked badly*, conjuring the creepy notion that the bruise had eyes but couldn't see well. You can avoid such bizarre constructions if you know when to use predicate adjectives with linking verbs.

Put subjective adjectives before objective adjectives

When you have a series of adjectives expressing both opinion and more objective description, put the subjective adjectives before the objective ones. For example, in

> the sultry cabaret singer

sultry is subjective and *cabaret* is objective.

Put determiners before other adjectives

Determiners are a group of adjectives that include possessive nouns (such as *woman's* prerogative and *Pedro's* violin), possessive pronouns (such as *my, your,* and *his*), demonstrative pronouns (*this, that, these, those*), and indefinite pronouns (such as *all, both, each, either, few,* and *many*). When you are using a series of adjectives, put the determiners first.

our finest hour

Tara's favourite old blue jeans

those crazy kids

When you are using a numerical determiner with another determiner, put the numerical determiner first.

both those tattoos

all these people

37c PLACE ADVERBS CAREFULLY

For the most part, the guidelines for adverb placement are not as complex as the guidelines for adjective placement.

Place adverbs before or after the words they modify

Single-word adverbs and adverbial clauses and phrases can usually sit comfortably either before or after the words they modify.

Dimitri **quietly walked** down the hall.

Dimitri **walked** quietly down the hall.

Conjunctive adverbs—*also, however, instead, likewise, then, therefore, thus,* and others—are adverbs that show how ideas relate to one another. They prepare a reader for contrasts, exceptions, additions, conclusions, and other shifts in an argument. Conjunctive adverbs can usually fit well into more than one place in the sentence. In the following example, *however* could fit in three different places.

BETWEEN TWO MAIN CLAUSES

Professional football players earn exorbitant salaries; however, they pay for their wealth with lifetimes of chronic pain and debilitating injuries.

WITHIN SECOND MAIN CLAUSE

Professional football players earn exorbitant salaries; they pay for their wealth, however, with lifetimes of chronic pain and debilitating injuries.

AT END OF SECOND MAIN CLAUSE

Professional football players earn exorbitant salaries; they pay for their wealth with lifetimes of chronic pain and debilitating injuries however.

Subordinating conjunctions—words such as *after, although, because, if, since, than, that, though, when,* and *where*—often begin **adverbial clauses**. Notice that we can place adverbial clauses with subordinating conjunctions either before or after the word(s) being modified:

After some thought, he **stepped** back from the door of the airplane.

He **stepped** back from the door of the airplane **after some thought**.

While you have some leeway with adverb placement, follow the advice in Section 37d: avoid distracting interruptions between the subject and verb, the verb and the object, or within the verb phrase. A long adverbial clause is usually best placed at the beginning or end of a sentence.

COMMON ERRORS

Placement of limiting modifiers

Words such as *almost, even, hardly, just, merely, nearly, not, only,* and *simply* are called limiting modifiers. Although people often play fast and loose with their placement in everyday speech, limiting modifiers should always go immediately before the word or words they modify in your writing. Many writers have difficulty with the placement of *only*. Like other limiting modifiers, *only* should be placed immediately before the word it modifies.

INCORRECT	The gross domestic product **only** gives one indicator of economic growth.
CORRECT	The gross domestic product gives **only** one indicator of economic growth.

Remember: Place limiting modifiers immediately before the word(s) they modify.

 For step-by-step discussion, examples, and practice of this common error, go to **www.pearsoned.ca/faigley/239.**

37d REVISE DISRUPTIVE MODIFIERS

The fundamental way readers make sense of sentences is to identify the subject, verb, and object. Modifiers can sink a sentence if they interfere with the reader's ability to connect the three. Usually, single-word modifiers do not significantly disrupt a sentence. However, avoid placing modifying clauses and phrases between a subject and a verb, between a verb and an object, and within a verb phrase.

DISRUPTIVE	The forest fire, **no longer held in check by the exhausted firefighters**, jumped the firebreak. [Separates the subject from the verb]
BETTER	**No longer held in check by the exhausted firefighters**, the forest fire jumped the firebreak. [Puts the modifier before the subject]
DISRUPTIVE	The fire's heat seemed to melt, **at a temperature hot enough to liquefy metal**, the saplings in its path. [Separates the verb from the object]
BETTER	**At a temperature hot enough to liquefy metal**, the fire's heat seemed to melt the saplings in its path. [Puts the modifier before the subject]

WRITING IN THE WORLD

Split infinitives

An infinitive is *to* plus the base form of a verb. A split infinitive occurs when an adverb separates *to* from the base verb form.

INFINITIVE = *To* + BASE VERB FORM

Examples: **to feel, to speak, to borrow**

SPLIT INFINITIVE = *To* + MODIFIER + BASE VERB FORM

Examples: **to strongly feel, to barely speak, to liberally borrow**

The most famous split infinitive in recent history occurs in the opening credits of *Star Trek* episodes: "to boldly go where no one has gone before." The alternative without the split infinitive is "to go boldly where no one has gone before." The writers in *Star Trek* no doubt were aware they were splitting an infinitive, but they chose *to boldly go* because they wanted the emphasis on *boldly*, not *go*.

Nevertheless, many split infinitives are considered awkward for good reason.

AWKWARD	You have to get away from the city lights **to better appreciate** the stars in the night sky.
BETTER	You have to get away from the city **to appreciate** the stars in the night sky **better**.
AWKWARD	**To, as planned, stay** in Venice, we need to reserve a hotel room now.
BETTER	**To stay** in Venice **as planned**, we need to reserve a hotel room now.

(continued next page)

When a sentence would sound strange without the adverb splitting the infinitive, you can either retain the split or, better yet, revise the sentence to avoid the problem altogether.

ACCEPTABLE   When found by the search party, the survivors were able **to barely whisper** their names.

ALTERNATIVE   When found by the search party, the survivors **could barely whisper** their names.

37e REVISE DANGLING MODIFIERS

Some modifiers are ambiguous because they could apply to more than one word or clause. Dangling modifiers are ambiguous for the opposite reason; they don't have a word to modify. In such cases the modifier is usually an introductory clause or phrase. What is being modified should immediately follow the phrase, but in the following sentence it is absent.

After bowling a perfect game, TwinPin Lanes hung Marco's photo on the wall.

Neither the subject of the sentence, *TwinPin Lanes*, nor the direct object, *Marco's photo*, is capable of bowling a perfect game. Since a missing noun or pronoun causes a dangling modifier, simply rearranging the sentence will not resolve the problem. You can eliminate a dangling modifier in two ways:

1. Insert the noun or pronoun being modified immediately after the introductory modifying phrase.

   After bowling a perfect game, **Marco** was honoured by having his photo hung on the wall at TwinPin Lanes.

2. Rewrite the introductory phrase as an introductory clause to include the noun or pronoun.

   After **Marco** bowled a perfect game, TwinPin Lanes hung his photo on the wall.

PART ELEVEN

Understanding Punctuation and Mechanics

- How do I avoid unnecessary commas? (38i)

- How can I tell when to use a colon and when to use a semicolon? (39)

- When should I use dashes or parentheses instead of commas? (41)

- When should I use quotation marks when incorporating sources in my paper? (43)

- What's wrong with just using a spell-checker on my paper? (45a)

11 UNDERSTANDING PUNCTUATION AND MECHANICS

Punctuation gives readers vital clues about how to read a sentence. Understanding how punctuation and the mechanics of writing (spelling, capitalization, abbreviations) work is essential in making your writing connect with your readers.

MyCanadianCompLab Multimedia Resources

The MyCanadianCompLab multimedia resources extend the coverage you will find in Common Errors boxes throughout the handbook. Each workbook module includes a step-by-step explanation of how to fix the problem, corrected examples with complete explanations, and practice on both sentences and paragraphs with immediate feedback to help you learn. View all the topics at the MyCanadianCompLab website at www .pearsoned.ca/highered/mycanadiancomplab/.

Punctuation Personality Quiz

Are you an exclamation point? Do you like to ask questions? Or do you prefer closure, like a period? Take the quiz to learn more about yourself and to discover the personality punctuation can bring to your writing at www.pearsoned.ca/faigley/273.

 Visit *The Brief Penguin Handbook* Companion Website at
www.pearsoned.ca/faigley/

MyCanadianCompLab
Where writing and research help is a click away.
MyCanadianCompLab may be packaged with your textbook.
If not, it can be purchased from your college or university's bookstore.
Go to www.pearsoned.ca/highered/mycanadiancomplab/
for a tour.

CHAPTER 38

Commas

Commas give readers vital clues about how to read a sentence. They tell readers when to pause, and they indicate how the writer's ideas relate to one another.

38a COMMAS WITH INTRODUCTORY ELEMENTS

Introductory elements like conjunctive adverbs and introductory phrases usually should be set off by commas. Introductory words or phrases signal a shift in ideas or a particular arrangement of ideas; they help direct the reader's attention to the writer's most important points. Commas force the reader to pause and take notice of these pivotal elements.

Common introductory elements

Conjunctive adverbs	Introductory phrases
however	of course
therefore	above all
nonetheless	for example
also	in other words
otherwise	as a result
finally	on the other hand
instead	in conclusion
thus	in addition

When a conjunctive adverb or introductory phrase begins a sentence, the comma follows.

Therefore, the suspect could not have been at the scene of the crime.

Above all, look for an apartment where the heat and utilities are included in the monthly rental price.

When a conjunctive adverb comes in the middle of a sentence, set it off with commas preceding and following.

If you really want to reduce your living expenses, **however,** you should sell your car and take public transit wherever you need to go.

Conjunctive adverbs and phrases that do not require commas

Occasionally the conjunctive adverb or phrase blends into a sentence so smoothly that a pause would sound awkward.

AWKWARD   Of course, we'll come.

BETTER   Of course we'll come.

AWKWARD   Even if you adhere to a strict budget, you may find the cost of renting your own apartment exceeds what you would spend living in residence, **nevertheless**.

BETTER   Even if you adhere to a strict budget, you may find the cost of renting your own apartment exceeds what you would spend living in residence **nevertheless**.

Sometimes the presence or absence of a comma can affect the meaning. For example:

Of course, we'll come. [Be reassured that we will come.]

Of course we'll come. [There is no doubt we will come.]

COMMON ERRORS

Commas with long introductory modifiers

Long subordinate clauses or phrases that begin sentences should be followed by a comma. The following sentence lacks the needed comma.

INCORRECT   Because cell phones now have organizers and email Palm Pilots may soon become another technology of the past.

When you read this sentence, you likely had to go back to sort it out. The words *organizers and email Palm Pilots* tend to run together. When the comma is added, the sentence is easier to understand because the reader knows where the subordinate clause ends and where the main clause begins:

CORRECT   Because cell phones now have organizers and email, Palm Pilots may soon become another technology of the past.

How long is a long introductory modifier? Short introductory adverbial phrases and clauses of five words or fewer can get by without the comma if the omission does not mislead the reader. Using the comma is still correct after short introductory adverbial phrases and clauses:

CORRECT   In the short term taking public transit to school will always be cheaper than owning your own car.

CORRECT   In the short term, taking public transit to school will always be cheaper than owning your own car.

Remember: Put commas after long introductory modifiers.

 For step-by-step discussion, examples, and practice of this common error, go to **www.pearsoned.ca/faigley/240**.

38b COMMAS WITH COMPOUND CLAUSES

Two main clauses joined by a coordinating conjunction (*and, or, so, yet, but, nor, for*) form a compound sentence (see Section 32e). Writers sometimes get confused about when to insert a comma before a coordinating conjunction.

Use a comma to separate main clauses

Main clauses carry enough grammatical weight to be punctuated as sentences. When two main clauses are joined by a coordinating conjunction, place a comma before the coordinating conjunction in order to distinguish them.

Sandy borrowed two boxes full of CDs on Tuesday, **and** she returned them on Friday.

Very short main clauses joined by a coordinating conjunction do not need commas.

She called **and** she called, but no one answered.

Do not use a comma to separate two verbs with the same subject

INCORRECT   Sandy borrowed two boxes full of CDs on Tuesday, **and** returned them on Friday.

Sandy is the subject of both *borrowed* and *returned*. This sentence has only one main clause; it should not be punctuated as a compound sentence.

CORRECT   Sandy borrowed two boxes full of CDs on Tuesday **and** returned them on Friday.

Exceptions to this rule occur when there is a lapse of time or after *said*.

> He did not study, and failed.

> "That's fine," he said, and went on reading.

COMMON ERRORS

Identifying compound sentences that require commas

The easiest way to distinguish between compound sentences and sentences with phrases that follow the main clause is to isolate the part that comes after the conjunction. If the part that follows the conjunction can stand on its own as a complete sentence, insert a comma. If it cannot, omit the comma.

> MAIN CLAUSE PLUS PHRASES
>
> Mario thinks he lost his passport while riding the bus or by absentmindedly leaving it on the counter when he checked in to the hostel.

Look at what comes after the coordinating conjunction *or*:

> by absentmindedly leaving it on the counter when he checked into the hostel

This group of words is not a main clause and cannot stand on its own as a complete sentence. Do not set it off with a comma.

> MAIN CLAUSES JOINED WITH A CONJUNCTION
>
> On Saturday Mario went to the Canadian consulate to get a new passport, but the officer told him that replacement passports could not be issued on weekends.

Read the clause after the coordinating conjunction *but*:

> the officer told him that replacement passports could not be issued on weekends

This group of words can stand on its own as a complete sentence. Thus, it is a main clause; place a comma before *but*.

Remember:

1. Place a comma before the coordinating conjunction (*and, but, for, or, nor, so, yet*) if there are two main clauses.
2. Do not use a comma before the coordinating conjunction if there is only one main clause.

 For step-by-step discussion, examples, and practice of this common error, go to **www.pearsoned.ca/faigley/241**.

Do not use a comma to separate a main clause from a restrictive clause or phrase

When clauses and phrases that follow the main clause are essential to the meaning of a sentence, they should not be set off with a comma.

INCORRECT   Sandy plans to borrow Felicia's DVD collection, while Felicia is on vacation.

CORRECT   Sandy plans to borrow Felicia's DVD collection while Felicia is on vacation.

INCORRECT   Sandy plans to borrow Felicia's records while Felicia is on vacation, in order to convert them to CDs.

CORRECT   Sandy plans to borrow Felicia's records while Felicia is on vacation in order to convert them to CDs.

COMMON ERRORS

Do not use a comma to set off a *because* clause that follows a main clause

Writers frequently place unnecessary commas before *because* and similar subordinate conjunctions that follow a main clause. *Because* is not a coordinating conjunction; thus it should not be set off by a comma unless the comma improves readability.

INCORRECT   I struggled to complete my term papers last year, because I worked too many shifts at the restaurant.

CORRECT   I struggled to complete my term papers last year because I worked too many shifts at the restaurant.

But do use a comma after an introductory *because* clause.

INCORRECT   Because she left her sheet music at home Arianna had to share her stand partner's music.

CORRECT   Because she left her sheet music at home, Arianna had to share her stand partner's music.

Remember: Use a comma after a *because* clause that begins a sentence. Do not use a comma to set off a *because* clause that follows a main clause.

 For step-by-step discussion, examples, and practice of this common error, go to **www.pearsoned.ca/faigley/242**.

38c COMMAS WITH NON-RESTRICTIVE MODIFIERS

Imagine that you are sending a friend a group photo that includes your aunt. Which sentence is correct?

The woman in the back row wearing the pink hat is my aunt.

The woman, in the back row, wearing the pink hat, is my aunt.

Both sentences can be correct depending on what is in the photo. If there are three women standing in the back row and only one is wearing a pink hat, this piece of information is necessary for identifying your aunt. In this case the sentence without commas is correct because it identifies your aunt as the woman wearing the pink hat. Such necessary modifiers are **restrictive** and do not require commas.

If only one woman is standing in the back row, *wearing the pink hat* is extra information and not necessary to identify your aunt. The modifier in this case is **non-restrictive** and is set off by commas.

Distinguish restrictive and non-restrictive modifiers

You can distinguish restrictive and non-restrictive modifiers by deleting the modifier and then deciding whether the remaining sentence is changed. For example, delete the modifier *still stained by its bloody Tiananmen Square crackdown* from the following sentence:

Some members of the Olympic Site Selection Committee wanted to prevent China, **still stained by its bloody Tiananmen Square crackdown,** from hosting the 2008 games.

The result leaves the meaning of the main clause unchanged.

Some members of the Olympic Site Selection Committee wanted to prevent China from hosting the 2008 games.

The modifier is non-restrictive and should be set off by commas.

In contrast, deleting *who left work early* does change the meaning of this sentence:

The employees **who left work early** avoided driving home in the blizzard.

Without the modifier the sentence reads:

The employees avoided driving home in the blizzard.

Now it sounds as if all the employees avoided driving home in the blizzard instead of just the ones who left early. The modifier is clearly restrictive and does not require commas.

Recognize types and placement of non-restrictive modifiers

Non-restrictive modifiers are used frequently to add details. You can add several kinds of non-restrictive modifiers to a short, simple sentence (see Sections 32c and 32d).

The student ran across campus,

which left him panting when he got to class. [adjective clause]
his backpack swaying back and forth. [absolute phrase]
weaving his way down the crowded sidewalks. [participial phrase]

Non-restrictive modifiers can be placed at the beginning of sentences.

When he realized his watch had stopped, [adverb clause]
With his thoughts on the intramural championship later that afternoon, [prepositional phrase]
Rushing to get to class, [participial phrase]

the student ran across campus.

They also can be placed in the middle of sentences.

The student,

who had woken up only 15 minutes before class, [adjective clause]
my old roommate, [appositive]
wearing a ripped black trench coat, [participial phrase]
with one arm in a cast and the other clutching a stack of books, [prepositional phrase]

ran across campus.

Pay special attention to appositives

Clauses and phrases can be restrictive or non-restrictive, depending on the context. Often the difference is obvious, but some modifiers require close consideration, especially appositives. An **appositive** is a noun or noun phrase that identifies or adds information to the noun preceding it.

Consider the following pair.

1 The most popular reading week destination Miami Florida is also one of the most affordable.

2 The most popular reading week destination, Miami, Florida, is also one of the most affordable.

Which is correct? The appositive *Miami, Florida,* is not essential to the meaning of the sentence and offers additional information. Thus, it is a non-restrictive appositive and should be set off with commas. Sentence 2 is correct.

Here's another pair.

1 The disgruntled slave Marie-Joseph Angelique was executed for starting a devastating fire in Montreal on April 10, 1734.

2 The disgruntled slave, Marie-Joseph Angelique, was executed for starting a devastating fire in Montreal on April 10, 1734.

The name *Marie-Joseph Angelique* is essential to identifying which of the slaves kept in Montreal in the early eighteenth century is under discussion. Thus, it is a restrictive appositive and should not be set off with commas. Sentence 1 is correct.

Use commas around non-restrictive clauses within a *that* clause

Restrictive clauses beginning with *that* sometimes have a non-restrictive clause embedded within them.

| INCORRECT | I want you to know that despite all the arguments we have had over the past few months I still value your advice. |
| CORRECT | I want you to know that, despite all the arguments we have had over the past few months, I still value your advice. |

Use commas to mark off parenthetical expressions

A **parenthetical expression** provides information or commentary that usually is not essential to the sentence's meaning.

| INCORRECT | My mother much to my surprise didn't say anything when she saw my pierced nose. |
| CORRECT | My mother, much to my surprise, didn't say anything when she saw my pierced nose. |

Some parenthetical expressions are essential to the point of the sentence, especially ones that make contrasts, but they too are set off by commas.

| INCORRECT | The candidate's conversational skills not her resumé landed her the job. |
| CORRECT | The candidate's conversational skills, not her resumé, landed her the job. |

However, do not use a comma if the parenthetical expression is one word and its function is not obviously parenthetical.

| INCORRECT | The first-year writing course is, fundamentally, an introduction to writing arguments. |
| CORRECT | The first-year writing course is fundamentally an introduction to writing arguments. |

COMMON ERRORS

Commas with *that* and *which* clauses

Writers often confuse when to use commas to set off modifying phrases beginning with *that* and *which*. *That* clauses follow a hard and fast rule: they are used only as restrictive modifiers.

A *THAT* CLAUSE IS A RESTRICTIVE MODIFIER: OMIT COMMAS

Two other women were wearing the same dress **that Sherice bought specifically to wear to the awards banquet**.

Which clauses are usually used as non-restrictive modifiers. While *which* clauses can also function as restrictive modifiers, careful writers observe the difference and change *which* to *that* if the clause is restrictive.

A *WHICH* CLAUSE IS A NON-RESTRICTIVE MODIFIER: USE COMMAS

Jina had to leave her cat with her parents this term because her new apartment, **which is much closer to campus**, prohibits pets of any kind.

WHEN A *WHICH* CLAUSE ACTS AS A RESTRICTIVE MODIFIER, CHANGE *WHICH* TO *THAT*

INCORRECT   The uncertainty which surrounded the selection of the new coach was created by the sudden and unexpected resignation of her predecessor.

CORRECT   The uncertainty that surrounded the selection of the new coach was created by the sudden and unexpected resignation of her predecessor.

Remember:

1. *That* clauses are restrictive modifiers and do not take commas.

2. *Which* clauses can be either restrictive or non-restrictive, but careful writers use them as non-restrictive modifiers and set them off with commas.

 For step-by-step discussion, examples, and practice of this common error, go to **www.pearsoned.ca/faigley/243**.

Use commas to mark off absolute phrases

An **absolute phrase** contains at least one noun or pronoun and at least one participle (see Section 32d). Absolutes can modify a noun or a whole sentence.

INCORRECT   Her project completed Marianne decided to splurge on a beach vacation.

CORRECT   Her project completed, Marianne decided to splurge on a beach vacation.

INCORRECT   Their car having run out of gas Claude and François trudged down the highway in search of a service station.

CORRECT   Their car having run out of gas, Claude and François trudged down the highway in search of a service station.

38d   COMMAS WITH ITEMS IN A SERIES

In a series of three or more items, place a comma after each item but the last one. The comma between the last two items goes before the coordinating conjunction (*and, or, nor, but, so, for, yet*).

Health officials in Burlington, Hamilton, and Oakville have all reported new cases of the West Nile virus.

WRITING IN THE WORLD

Commas between the last two items in a series

Whether you should insert a comma between the last two items in a series depends on what kind of writing you're doing. In newspapers and magazines, the comma is typically omitted; however, academic, business, and professional writing includes a comma before the last series item. Omitting the comma sometimes causes confusion.

JOURNALISTIC CONVENTION   I thank my parents, Robert Pirsig and Harley-Davidson for my outlook on life.

ACADEMIC CONVENTION   I thank my parents, Robert Pirsig, and Harley-Davidson for my outlook on life.

38e COMMAS WITH COORDINATE ADJECTIVES

Coordinate adjectives are two or more adjectives that independently modify the same noun. Coordinate adjectives that are not linked by *and* must be separated by a comma.

> After the NASDAQ bubble burst in 2000 and 2001, the internet technology companies that remain are no longer the **fresh-faced, giddy** kids of Wall Street.

Distinguish coordinate adjectives

You can recognize coordinate adjectives by reversing their order; if their meaning remains the same, the adjectives are coordinate and must be linked by *and* or separated by a comma. In the following example when the order of the adjectives changes, the description of *lifestyles* retains the same meaning:

> Because border collies are bred to herd sheep, their energetic temperaments may not suit city dwellers' more **sedentary, staid** lifestyles.

> Because border collies are bred to herd sheep, their energetic temperaments may not suit city dwellers' more **staid, sedentary** lifestyles.

Do not use commas to link cumulative adjectives

Commas are not used between cumulative adjectives. Cumulative adjectives are two or more adjectives that work together to modify a noun: *deep blue sea, inexpensive mountain bike*. If reversing their order changes the description of the noun (or violates the order of English, such as *mountain inexpensive bike*), the adjectives are cumulative and should not be separated by a comma.

The following example doesn't require a comma in the cumulative adjective series *massive Corinthian*.

> Visitors to Rome's Pantheon pass between the **massive Corinthian** columns flanking the front door.

We know they are cumulative because reversing their order to read *Corinthian massive* would alter the way they modify *columns*—in this case, so much so that they no longer make sense.

38f COMMAS WITH QUOTATIONS

Properly punctuating quotations with commas can be tricky unless you know a few rules about when and where to use commas.

When to use commas with quotations

Commas set off phrases that attribute quotations to a speaker or writer, such as *he argues, they said,* and *she writes.*

> "When you come to a fork in the road, " said Yogi Berra, "take it!"

If the attribution follows a quotation that is a complete sentence, replace the period that normally would come at the end of the quotation with a comma.

> **INCORRECT** "I believe in good omens. I don't believe in the bad ones." notes Silken Laumann.
>
> **CORRECT** "I believe in good omens. I don't believe in the bad ones," notes Silken Laumann.

When an attribution is placed in the middle of a quotation, put the comma preceding the attribution within the quotation mark just before the phrase.

> **INCORRECT** "You have not seen Canada", argued Pierre Elliot Trudeau, "until you have seen the north."
>
> **CORRECT** "You have not seen Canada," argued Pierre Elliot Trudeau, "until you have seen the north."

When not to use commas with quotations

Do not replace a question mark or exclamation point with a comma.

> **INCORRECT** "Bart, stop pestering Satan," said Marge Simpson.
>
> **CORRECT** "Bart, stop pestering Satan!" said Marge Simpson.

Not all phrases that mention the author's name are attributions. When quoting a term or using a quotation within a subordinate clause, do not set off the quotation with commas.

> "Stonewall " Jackson gained his nickname at the First Battle of Bull Run when General Barnard Bee shouted to his men that "Jackson is standing like a stone wall."

Even a quotation that is a complete sentence can be used in a subordinate clause. Such quotations should not be set off with commas. Pay special attention to quotations preceded by *that, which,* and *because*; these words are the most common indicators of a subordinate clause.

> About immigration in Canada, Peter Stoffer has noted that if "[y]ou look at the history—the aboriginal people welcomed the first settlers here with open arms, fed us and took care of us . . . that continues today, we welcome people from all nations to come in and share."

38g COMMAS WITH DATES, NUMBERS, TITLES, AND ADDRESSES

Some of the easiest comma rules to remember are the ones we use every day in dates, numbers, personal titles, place names, direct address, and brief interjections.

Commas with dates

Use commas to separate the day of the week from the month and to set off a year from the rest of the sentence.

> July 1, 1967
>
> Monday, November 18, 2002
>
> On July 27, 2007, the opening ceremony of the World Scout Jamboree will be televised.

Do not use a comma when the month immediately precedes the year.

> 12 June 1988
>
> April 2008

Commas with numbers

In the imperial system, commas mark off thousands, millions, billions, and so on. However, in the International System of Units (i.e., metric), commas are not used. For thousands, put the four numbers together without spaces: 5831. For millions, billions, and so on, leave spaces between the groups of numbers as in this example:

> 16 500 000

Do not use commas in street addresses or page numbers.

> page 1542
>
> 7602 Yonge Street

Commas with personal titles

When a title follows a person's name, set the title off with commas.

> Frederick Banting, MD
>
> Jackie Hart, Vice President for Operations, reported that her company's earnings were far ahead of projections.

Commas with place names

Place a comma between street addresses, city names, province or state names, and countries.

> Fredericton, New Brunswick
>
> Lima, Peru
>
> The prime minister lives at 24 Sussex Drive, Ottawa, Ontario.

Commas in direct address

When addressing someone directly, set off that person's name in commas.

> I was happy to get your letter yesterday, Jamie.
>
> Yes, Virginia, there is a Santa Claus.

Commas with brief interjections

Use commas to set off brief interjections like *yes* and *no*, as well as short questions that fall at the ends of sentences.

> The director said that, no, the understudy would not have to stand in for the lead tonight.
>
> Have another piece of pie, won't you?

38h COMMAS TO AVOID CONFUSION

Certain sentences can confuse readers if you do not indicate where they should pause within the sentence. Use a comma to guide a reader through these usually compact constructions.

> UNCLEAR   With supplies low prices of gasoline and fuel oil will increase.

This sentence could be read as meaning *With supplies, low prices will increase.*

> CLEAR   With supplies low, prices of gasoline and fuel oil will increase.

38i UNNECESSARY COMMAS

Do not place a comma between a subject and a predicate

> INCORRECT   Not all Canadian children of immigrant parents, speak their parents' native language.
>
> CORRECT   Not all Canadian children of immigrant parents speak their parents' native language.

However, you do use commas to set off modifying phrases that separate subjects from verbs.

INCORRECT   Steven Pinker author of *The Language Instinct* argues that the ability to speak and understand language is an evolutionary adaptive trait.

CORRECT   Steven Pinker, author of *The Language Instinct,* argues that the ability to speak and understand language is an evolutionary adaptive trait.

Do not use a comma with a coordinating conjunction unless it joins two main clauses

INCORRECT   Susana thought finishing her first novel was hard, but soon learned that getting a publisher to buy it was much harder.

CORRECT   Susana thought finishing her first novel was hard but soon learned that getting a publisher to buy it was much harder.

CORRECT   Susana thought finishing her first novel was hard, but she soon learned that getting a publisher to buy it was much harder.

Do not use a comma after a subordinating conjunction such as *although, despite,* or *while*

INCORRECT   Although, soccer is gaining popularity in Canada, it will never be as popular as hockey.

CORRECT   Although soccer is gaining popularity in Canada, it will never be as popular as hockey.

Do not use a comma before *than*

Some writers mistakenly use a comma with *than* to try to heighten the contrast in a comparison.

INCORRECT   Any teacher will tell you that acquiring critical thinking skills is more important, than simply memorizing information.

CORRECT   Any teacher will tell you that acquiring critical thinking skills is more important than simply memorizing information.

Do not use a comma before a list

A common mistake is to place a comma after *such as* or *like* before introducing a list.

> INCORRECT   Many hourly workers, such as, waiters, dishwashers, and cashiers, have difficulty earning enough money to support themselves.
>
> CORRECT   Many hourly workers, such as waiters, dishwashers, and cashiers, have difficulty earning enough money to support themselves.

CHAPTER *39*

Semicolons and Colons

Semicolons and colons are punctuation marks that link closely related ideas. They allow writers to emphasize the relationships between elements of a sentence, often using dramatic pauses to direct readers' attention to the most important ideas. Notice how semicolons and colons direct our attention in the following examples:

> "My life has been incredible; I don't believe a word of it," wrote Katherine Anne Porter.

> An ancient Aboriginal proverb provides a new perspective: "Treat the Earth well: it was not given to you by your parents, it was loaned to you by your children. We do not inherit the Earth from our Ancestors; we borrow it from our Children."

39a SEMICOLONS WITH CLOSELY RELATED MAIN CLAUSES

Why use semicolons? Sometimes we want to join two main clauses to form a complete sentence in order to indicate their close relationship. We can connect them with a comma and a coordinating conjunction like *or*, *but*, or *and*. However, using those constructions too often can make your writing cumbersome. Instead you can omit the comma and coordinating conjunction, and insert a semicolon between the two clauses.

Semicolons can join only clauses that are grammatically equal. In other words, they join main clauses only to other main clauses, not to phrases or subordinate clauses. Look at the following examples:

INCORRECT

—————————————MAIN CLAUSE—————————————
Gloria's new weightlifting program will help her recover
——————————————— ┌—————————PARTICIPIAL PHRASE—————————
from knee surgery; doing a series of squats and presses
—————————————
with a physical therapist.

INCORRECT

—————————————MAIN CLAUSE—————————————
Gloria's new weightlifting program will help her regain
——————————————— ┌—————————SUBORDINATE CLAUSE—————————
strength in her knee; which required surgery after she
—————————————
injured it skiing.

CORRECT

—————————————MAIN CLAUSE—————————————
Gloria's new weightlifting program will help her recover
——————————————— ┌—————————MAIN CLAUSE—————————
from knee surgery; a physical therapist leads her
—————————————
through a series of squats and presses.

COMMON ERRORS

Main clauses connected with conjunctive adverbs and transitional phrases

Closely related main clauses sometimes use a conjunctive adverb (such as *however, therefore, moreover, furthermore, thus, meanwhile, nonetheless, otherwise*; see the list in Section 38a) or a transition (*in fact, for example, that is, for instance, in addition, in other words, on the other hand, even so*) to indicate the relationship between them. When the second clause begins with a conjunctive adverb or a transition, a semicolon is needed to join the two clauses. This sentence pattern is frequently used; therefore, it pays to learn how to punctuate it correctly.

INCORRECT
(COMMA SPLICE)

The police and city officials want to crack down on drug use at raves, however, their efforts have been unsuccessful so far.

CORRECT

The police and city officials want to crack down on drug use at raves; however, their efforts have been unsuccessful so far.

The semicolon separates the second main clause from the first. Note that a comma is also needed to separate *however* from the rest of the second clause.

(continued next page)

INCORRECT (COMMA SPLICE)	The poster design left much to be desired, for example, the title was printed in garish red, orange, and green.
CORRECT	The poster design left much to be desired; for example, the title was printed in garish red, orange, and green.

Note that in addition to the semicolon, a comma separates *for example* from the rest of the second clause.

Remember: Main clauses that use a conjunctive adverb or a transitional phrase require a semicolon to join the clauses.

 For step-by-step discussion, examples, and practice of this common error, go to **www.pearsoned.ca/faigley/244**.

Do not use a semicolon to introduce quotations

Use a comma or a colon instead.

INCORRECT	Pauline Johnson's poem "Canadian Born" opens with these lines; "We first saw light in Canada, the land beloved of God / We are the pulse of Canada, its marrow and its blood."
CORRECT	Pauline Johnson's poem "Canadian Born" opens with these lines: "We first saw light in Canada, the land beloved of God / We are the pulse of Canada, its marrow and its blood."

Do not use a semicolon to introduce lists

INCORRECT	William Shakespeare wrote four romance plays at the end of his career; *The Tempest, The Winter's Tale, Cymbeline,* and *Pericles.*
CORRECT	William Shakespeare wrote four romance plays at the end of his career: *The Tempest, The Winter's Tale, Cymbeline,* and *Pericles.*

39b SEMICOLONS TOGETHER WITH COMMAS

When an item in a series already includes a comma, adding more commas to separate it from the other items will only confuse the reader. Use semicolons instead of commas between items in a series that have internal punctuation.

CONFUSING	The church's design competition drew entries from as far away as Gothenburg, Sweden, Caracas, Venezuela, and Athens, Greece.
CLEARER	The church's design competition drew entries from as far away as Gothenburg, Sweden; Caracas, Venezuela; and Athens, Greece.

39c COLONS IN SENTENCES

Like semicolons, colons can join two closely related main clauses (complete sentences). Colons indicate that what follows will explain or expand on what comes before the colon. Use a colon in cases where the second main clause interprets or sums up the first.

Internet retailers have a limited customer base: Only those who have internet access can become e-shoppers.

You may choose to capitalize the first word of the main clause following the colon or leave it lowercase. Either is correct as long as you are consistent throughout your text.

Colons linking main clauses with appositives

A colon calls attention to an appositive, a noun, or a noun phrase that renames the noun preceding it. If you're not certain whether a colon would be appropriate, put *namely* in its place. If *namely* makes sense when you read the main clause followed by the appositive, you probably need to insert a colon instead of a comma. Remember, the clause that precedes the colon must be a complete sentence.

I know the perfect person for the job, **namely** me.

The sentence makes sense with *namely* placed before the appositive. Thus, a colon is appropriate.

I know the perfect person for the job: me.

Never capitalize a word following a colon unless the word starts a complete sentence or is normally capitalized (see Chapter 46).

Colons joining main clauses with quotations

Use a colon to link a main clause and a quotation that interprets or sums up the clause. Be careful not to use a colon to link a phrase with a quotation.

INCORRECT: NOUN PHRASE–COLON–QUOTATION

Jacques Cartier's first encounter with the land that would be Canada: "I am rather inclined," he confessed, "to believe that this is the land God gave to Cain."

CORRECT: MAIN CLAUSE–COLON–QUOTATION

Jacques Cartier's first encounter with the land that would be Canada was not promising: "I am rather inclined," he confessed, "to believe that this is the land God gave to Cain."

Also, a colon is often used after a main clause to introduce an indented block quotation (see Section 21c).

WRITING SMART

Punctuation following quotations

Writing often requires quoting someone else's words. Use the correct sequence of punctuation marks when sharing a quotation with readers.

Place semicolons and colons outside quotation marks

Commas and periods that come after a quotation sit inside the quotation marks. The rule is different, however, for semicolons and colons: they sit outside the quotation marks. Because commas and periods always appear inside the quotation marks, semicolons and colons may seem incorrectly placed if you don't know that they follow a different rule.

PUT COMMAS AND PERIODS INSIDE THE QUOTATION MARKS

"The length of a film," said Alfred Hitchcock, "should be directly related to the endurance of the human bladder."

PUT SEMICOLONS OUTSIDE QUOTATION MARKS

June Callwood wrote, "The beaver, which has come to represent Canada as the eagle does the United States and the lion Britain, is a flat-tailed, slow-witted, toothy rodent known to bite off its own testicles or to stand under its own falling trees"; her point underscores the irony in our choice of national symbol.

PUT COLONS OUTSIDE QUOTATION MARKS

"I believe, absolutely, that if you do not break out in that sweat of fear when you write, then you have not gone far enough": Dorothy Allison reassures would-be writers that they can begin on guts alone.

Remember: Little dogs (commas, periods) sleep in the house. Big dogs (semicolons, colons) sleep outside.

For more on using quotation marks correctly, see Chapter 43.

39d COLONS WITH LISTS

Use a colon to join a main clause to a list. The main clauses in these cases sometimes include the phrases *the following* or *as follows*. Remember that a colon cannot join a phrase or an incomplete clause to a list.

INCORRECT: NOUN PHRASE–COLON–LIST

Three posters decorating Juan's apartment: an Our Lady Peace concert poster, a view of Grouse Mountain, and a Diego Rivera mural.

CORRECT: MAIN CLAUSE–COLON–LIST

Juan bought three posters to decorate his apartment: an Our Lady Peace concert poster, a view of Grouse Mountain, and a Diego Rivera mural.

INCORRECT: INCOMPLETE CLAUSE–COLON–LIST

Volunteers aid biologists in: erosion control, trail maintenance, tree planting, and clean-up.

CORRECT: MAIN CLAUSE WITHOUT A COLON

Volunteers aid biologists in erosion control, trail maintenance, tree planting, and clean-up.

COMMON ERRORS

Colons misused with lists

Some writers think that anytime they introduce a list, they should insert a colon. Colons are used correctly only when a complete sentence precedes the colon.

INCORRECT   Jessica's entire wardrobe for her trip to Cancun included: two swimsuits, one pair of shorts, two T-shirts, a party dress, and a pair of sandals.

CORRECT   Jessica's entire wardrobe for her trip to Cancun included two swimsuits, one pair of shorts, two T-shirts, a party dress, and a pair of sandals.

CORRECT   Jessica jotted down what she would need for her trip: two swimsuits, one pair of shorts, two T-shirts, a party dress, and a pair of sandals.

Remember: A colon should be placed only after a clause that can stand by itself as a sentence.

 For step-by-step discussion, examples, and practice of this common error, go to **www.pearsoned.ca/faigley/245.**

CHAPTER *40*

Hyphens

Hyphens are handy punctuation marks when you want to link words or parts of words. They often give the reader clues about the meaning of a word or sentence. See how a hyphen would clarify the meaning of the word *coop* in the following example.

> This afternoon I'm going to the **coop** to get some eggs.

Is the speaker going to a *chicken coop* or a *grocery co-op* (short for co-operative)? A hyphen indicates a trip to the grocery store:

> This afternoon I'm going to the **co-op** to get some eggs.

Hyphens (-) are frequently confused with dashes (—), which are similar but longer. Dashes are used to separate phrases. Hyphens are used to join words.

40a   HYPHENS WITH COMPOUND MODIFIERS

When to hyphenate
Hyphenate a compound modifier that precedes a noun.

When a compound modifier precedes a noun, you should usually hyphenate the modifier. A compound modifier consists of words that join together as a unit to modify a noun. Since the first word modifies the second, compound modifiers will not make sense if the word order is reversed.

middle-class values	self-fulfilling prophecy
best-selling novel	soft-hearted friend
well-known musician	ill-mannered child

Hyphenate a phrase when it is used as a modifier that precedes a noun.

out-of-body experience	step-by-step instructions
all-you-can-eat buffet	all-or-nothing payoff
devil-may-care attitude	over-the-counter drug

Hyphenate the prefixes *pro-, anti-, post-, pre-, neo-,* and *mid-* before proper nouns.

pro-Catholic sentiment	mid-Atlantic states
neo-Nazi racism	anti-NAFTA protests
pre-Columbian art	post-Freudian theory

Hyphenate a compound modifier with a number when it precedes a noun.

eighteenth-century drama   one-way street
tenth-grade class   47-minute swim

When not to hyphenate

Do not hyphenate a compound modifier that follows a noun.

Avoid using hyphens in compound modifiers when they come after the noun.

The instructor's approach is student centred.

Among country music fans Lyle Lovett is well known.

Do not hyphenate compound modifiers when the first word is *very* or ends in *ly*.

newly recorded data   very cold day
freshly painted bench   very jolly baby

Do not hyphenate chemical terms.

calcium chloride base   hydrochloric acid solution

Do not hyphenate foreign terms used as adjectives.

a priori decision   *post hoc* fallacy

40b HYPHENS WITH COMPOUND NOUNS

A compound noun is made up of two or more words that work together to form one noun. You cannot change the order of words in a compound noun or remove a word without altering the noun's meaning. No universal rule guides the use of hyphens with compound nouns; the best way to determine whether a compound noun is hyphenated is to check the dictionary.

SOME HYPHENATED COMPOUND NOUNS

T-shirt   one-bagger   time-out
sister-in-law   heart-to-heart   baby-sitter
play-by-play   speed-reading   run-through

SOME COMPOUND NOUNS THAT ARE NOT HYPHENATED

picture window   oneself   time zone
hedgehog   heartland   baby boom
open house   speed of light playbook

While there's no set rule for all cases of compound nouns, some prefixes and suffixes that commonly require hyphens are *ex-*, *all-*, and *self-* and *-elect*.

All-American   president-elect
self-conscious   ex-employee

COMMON ERRORS

Hyphens with numbers

Whole numbers between twenty-one and ninety-nine are hyphenated when they are written as words.

| INCORRECT | twentysix |
| CORRECT | twenty-six |

| INCORRECT | sixteen-hundred |
| CORRECT | sixteen hundred |

| INCORRECT | fiftytwo |
| CORRECT | fifty-two |

Also, hyphens connect the numerators and denominators in most fractions.

The glass is one-half full.

A few fractions used as nouns, especially fractions of time, distance, and area, do not take hyphens.

A half century passed before the mistake was uncovered.

Remember: Numbers between twenty-one and ninety-nine and most fractions are hyphenated when written as words.

 For step-by-step discussion, examples, and practice of this common error, go to **www.pearsoned.ca/faigley/246**.

40c HYPHENS THAT DIVIDE WORDS AT THE ENDS OF LINES

A hyphen can show that a word is completed on the next line. Hyphens divide words only between syllables.

The Jackson family waited out the ice storm, grateful for their emergency supplies.

Unless you have a special reason for dividing words at the ends of lines, you should avoid doing it. One special situation might be the need to fit as much text as possible on each line of the narrow columns in a newsletter format. Another might be the need to fit text inside the cells of a table.

Automatic hyphenation

Word processing programs, including Microsoft Word, allow automatic hyphenation of your document. Hyphenations that break words at the ends of lines are common in newspaper and magazine articles that are printed in narrow columns. However, this use of hyphens is rarely necessary in academic papers. Unless you are creating a brochure or other document with narrow columns, leave the automatic hyphenation turned off.

40d HYPHENS FOR CLARITY

Certain words, often ones with the prefixes *anti-*, *re-*, and *pre-*, can be confusing without hyphens. Adding hyphens to such words will show the reader where to pause to pronounce them correctly.

The courts are in much need of **repair**.

The doubles final will **re-pair** the sister team of Venus and Serena Williams.

Reform in court procedure is necessary to bring cases quickly to trial.

The thunderclouds **re-formed** after the hard rain, threatening another deluge.

C H A P T E R *41*

Dashes and Parentheses

Dashes and parentheses can be excellent tools for setting off and calling attention to information that comments on your ideas. They serve as visual cues to the reader of a sudden break in thought or change in sentence structure. Both should be used sparingly. Too-numerous parentheses and dashes indicate that the writer needs to work harder to integrate ideas.

41a DASHES AND PARENTHESES VERSUS COMMAS

Like commas, parentheses and dashes enclose material that adds, explains, or digresses. However, the three punctuation marks are not interchangeable. The mark you choose depends on how much emphasis you want to place on the material. Dashes indicate the most emphasis. Parentheses offer somewhat less, and commas offer less still.

COMMAS INDICATE A MODERATE LEVEL OF EMPHASIS

Bill covered the new tattoo on his bicep, a pouncing tiger, because he thought it might upset our mother.

PARENTHESES LEND A GREATER LEVEL OF EMPHASIS

I'm afraid to go bungee jumping (though my brother tells me it's less frightening than a roller coaster).

DASHES INDICATE THE HIGHEST LEVEL OF EMPHASIS, AND SOMETIMES, SURPRISE AND DRAMA

Christina felt as though she had been punched in the gut; she could hardly believe the stranger at her door was really who he claimed to be—the brother she hadn't seen in 20 years.

41b DASHES AND PARENTHESES TO SET OFF INFORMATION

Dashes and parentheses call attention to groups of words. In effect, they tell the reader that a group of words is not part of the main clause and should be given extra attention. Compare the following sentences.

When Shanele's former roommate, Traci, picked her up at the airport in a new car, a Porsche Carrera GT convertible, she knew that Traci's finances had changed for the better.

When Shanele's former roommate, Traci, picked her up at the airport in a new car (a Porsche Carrera GT convertible), she knew that Traci's finances had changed for the better.

When Shanele's former roommate, Traci, picked her up at the airport in a new car—a Porsche Carrera GT convertible—she knew that Traci's finances had changed for the better.

The Porsche Carrera GT convertible is weighted differently in these three sentences because of punctuation. In the first, it is the name of the car. But in the third, it's as if an exclamation point were added—a Porsche Carrera GT convertible!

The lesson here is simple enough. If you want to make an element stand out, especially in the middle of a sentence, use parentheses or dashes instead of commas.

Dashes with final elements

A dash is often used to set off an element at the end of a sentence that offers significant comments about the main clause. This construction is a favourite of newscasters, who typically pause for a long moment where the dash would be inserted in writing.

> The *Titanic* sank just before midnight on April 14, 1912, at a cost of over 1500 lives—a tragedy that could have been prevented easily by reducing speed in dangerous waters, providing adequate lifeboat space, and maintaining a full-time radio watch.

Dashes can also anticipate a shift in tone at the end of a sentence.

> A full-sized SUV can take you wherever you want to go in style—if your idea of style is a gas-guzzling tank.

Parentheses with additional information

Parentheses are more often used for identifying information, afterthoughts or asides, examples, and clarifications. You can place full sentences, fragments, or brief terms within parentheses.

> Some argue that SUVs (the bestselling vehicles on the market for three years running) are the primary cause of recent gas shortages.

COMMON ERRORS

Do not use dashes as periods

Do not use dashes to separate two main clauses (clauses that can stand as complete sentences). Use dashes to separate main clauses from subordinate clauses and phrases when you want to emphasize the subordinate clause or phrase.

INCORRECT: MAIN CLAUSE–DASH–MAIN CLAUSE

I was one of the few women in my computer science classes—most of the students majoring in computer science at that time were men.

CORRECT: MAIN CLAUSE–DASH–PHRASE

I was one of the few women in computer science—a field then dominated by men.

Remember: Dashes are not periods and should not be used as periods.

 For step-by-step discussion, examples, and practice of this common error, go to **www.pearsoned.ca/faigley/247**.

41c OTHER PUNCTUATION WITH PARENTHESES

Parentheses with numbers or letters that order items in a series

Parentheses around letters or numbers that order a series within a sentence make the list easier to read.

> Angela Creider's recipe for becoming a great novelist is to (1) set aside an hour during the morning to write, (2) read what you've written out loud, (3) revise your prose, and (4) repeat every morning for the next 30 years.

Parentheses with abbreviations

Abbreviations made from the first letters of words are often used in place of the unwieldy names of institutions, departments, organizations, or terms. In order to show the reader what the abbreviation stands for, the first time it appears in a text the writer must state the complete name, followed by the abbreviation in parentheses.

> The University of California, Santa Cruz (UCSC) supports its mascot, the banana slug, with pride and a sense of humour. And although it sounds strange to outsiders, UCSC students are even referred to as "the banana slugs."

Parentheses with in-text citations

The various documentation styles require that information quoted, paraphrased, or summarized from an outside source be indicated with a research citation. In several of the styles, including MLA (see Chapter 22) and APA (see Chapter 23), the citation is enclosed in parentheses.

> E. B. White's advice on writing style is to use your natural voice (Strunk and White 70).

COMMON ERRORS

Using periods, commas, colons, and semicolons with parentheses

When an entire sentence is enclosed in parentheses, place the period before the closing parenthesis.

INCORRECT   Our fear of sharks, heightened by movies like *Jaws,* is vastly out of proportion with the minor threat sharks actually pose. (Dying from a dog attack, in fact, is much more likely than dying from a shark attack).

CORRECT	Our fear of sharks, heightened by movies like *Jaws,* is vastly out of proportion with the minor threat sharks actually pose. (Dying from a dog attack, in fact, is much more likely than dying from a shark attack.)

When the material in parentheses is part of the sentence and the parentheses fall at the end of the sentence, place the period outside the closing parenthesis.

INCORRECT	Reports of sharks attacking people are rare (much rarer than dog attacks.)
CORRECT	Reports of sharks attacking people are rare (much rarer than dog attacks).

Place commas, colons, and semicolons after the closing parenthesis.

INCORRECT	Although newspaper editors generally prize concise letters to the editor, (the shorter the better) they will occasionally print longer letters that are unusually eloquent.
CORRECT	Although newspaper editors generally prize concise letters to the editor (the shorter the better), they will occasionally print longer letters that are unusually eloquent.

Remember: When an entire sentence is enclosed in parentheses, place the period inside the closing parenthesis; otherwise, put the punctuation outside the closing parenthesis.

 For step-by-step discussion, examples, and practice of this common error, go to **www.pearsoned.ca/faigley/248**.

41d OTHER PUNCTUATION WITH DASHES

Dashes with a series of items

Dashes can set off a series. They are especially appropriate when the series comes in the middle of a sentence or when the series simply elaborates on what comes before it without changing the essential meaning of the sentence. Normally commas enclose non-essential clauses; however, placing commas around items separated by commas would confuse readers about where the list begins and ends.

Baseball journeyman Glenallen Hill pulled off the highlight of his career when he hit for the cycle—a single, a double, a triple, and a home run—in last night's game against the White Sox.

Dashes with interrupted speech

Dashes also indicate that a speaker has broken off in the middle of a statement.

> "Why did everybody get so quiet all of a——"; Silvia stopped in her tracks when she noticed that the customer had a pistol pointed at the clerk.

COMMON ERRORS

The art of typing a dash

Although dashes and hyphens look similar, they are actually different marks. The distinction is small but important because dashes and hyphens serve different purposes. A dash is a line twice as long as a hyphen. Most word processing programs will create a dash automatically when you type two hyphens together. Or you can type a special character to make a dash. Your manual will tell you which keys to press to make a dash.

Do not put any spaces between a dash or a hyphen and the words that come before and after them. Likewise, if you are using two hyphens to indicate a dash, do not put any spaces between the hyphens.

INCORRECT   A well - timed effort at conserving water may prevent long - term damage to drought - stricken farms -- if it's not already too late.

CORRECT   A well-timed effort at conserving water may prevent long-term damage to drought-stricken farms—if it's not already too late.

Remember: Do not put spaces before or after hyphens and dashes.

 For step-by-step discussion, examples, and practice of this common error, go to **www.pearsoned.ca/faigley/249**.

 CHAPTER 42

Apostrophes

Apostrophes have three basic functions: to indicate possession, to mark contractions and omitted letters, and to form certain plurals.

42a POSSESSIVES

Nouns and indefinite pronouns (e.g., *everyone, anyone*) that indicate possession or ownership are in the **possessive case**. The possessive case is marked by attaching an apostrophe and an *-s* or an apostrophe only to the end of the word.

Singular nouns and indefinite pronouns

For singular nouns and indefinite pronouns, add an apostrophe plus *-s: -'s.* Even singular nouns that end in *-s* usually follow this principle.

Iris's coat

everyone's favourite

a woman's choice

today's news

the team's equipment

There are a few exceptions to adding *-'s* for singular nouns:

- **Awkward pronunciations** *Herodotus' travels, Jesus' sermons*
- **Official names of certain places, institutions, companies** *Zellers, Loblaws, Staples, KidsAbility-Centre for Child Development.* Note, however, that many companies do include the apostrophe: *Denny's Restaurant, Shopper's Drug Mart, McDonald's, Wendy's Old Fashioned Hamburgers.*

Plural nouns

For plural nouns that do not end in *-s*, add an apostrophe plus *-s: -'s.*

women's rights

media's responsibility

children's section

For plural nouns that end in *-s*, add only an apostrophe at the end.

dancers' costumes

attorneys' briefs

the Trudeaus' legacy

Compound nouns

For compound nouns, add an apostrophe plus *-s* to the last word: *-'s.*

my mother-in-law's house

premier of Nova Scotia's speech

Two or more nouns

For joint possession, add an apostrophe plus -s to the final noun: -'s.

> mother and dad's yard
>
> Lakes, Trails, and Travel's spring sale

When people possess or own things separately, add an apostrophe plus -s to each noun: -'s.

> Roberto's and Edward's views are totally opposed.
>
> Dominique's, Sally's, and Vinatha's cars all need new tires.

COMMON ERRORS

Possessive forms of personal pronouns never take the apostrophe

INCORRECT   *her's, it's, our's, your's, their's*

The bird sang in **it's** cage.

CORRECT   *hers, its, ours, yours, theirs*

The bird sang in **its** cage.

Remember: It's = It is

 For step-by-step discussion, examples, and practice of this common error, go to **www.pearsoned.ca/faigley/250**.

42b CONTRACTIONS AND OMITTED LETTERS

In speech we often leave out sounds and syllables of familiar words. These omissions are noted with apostrophes.

Contractions

Contractions combine two words into one, using the apostrophe to mark what is left out.

I am	⟶ I'm		we are	⟶ we're
I would	⟶ I'd		they are	⟶ they're
you are	⟶ you're		cannot	⟶ can't
you will	⟶ you'll		do not	⟶ don't
he is	⟶ he's		does not	⟶ doesn't
she is	⟶ she's		will not	⟶ won't

Omissions

Using apostrophes to signal omitted letters is a way of approximating speech in writing. They can make your writing look informal and slangy, but overuse can become annoying in a hurry.

rock and roll ⟶ rock'n'roll

the 1960s ⟶ the '60s

neighbourhood ⟶ 'hood

42c PLURALS OF LETTERS, SYMBOLS, AND WORDS REFERRED TO AS WORDS

When to use apostrophes to make plurals

The trend is away from using apostrophes to form plurals of letters, symbols, and words referred to as words. In a few cases adding the apostrophe and *s* is still used, as in this old saying.

Mind your p's and q's.

Words used as words are italicized and their plural is formed by adding an *s* not in italics, not an apostrophe and *s*.

Take a few of the *and*s out of your writing.

Words in quotation marks, however, typically use apostrophe and *s*.

She had too many "probably's" in her letter for me to be confident that the remodelling will be finished on schedule.

WRITING IN THE WORLD

Apostrophes are not used with the plurals of numbers and acronyms

The style manuals of the Modern Language Association (MLA) and the American Psychological Association (APA) do not use apostrophes for indicating plurals of numbers and acronyms. They add only -*s*.

1890s	four CEOs	several VCRs
eights	these URLs	the images are all JPEGs

When not to use apostrophes to make plurals

Do not use an apostrophe to make family names plural.

INCORRECT You've heard of keeping up with the Jones's.

CORRECT You've heard of keeping up with the Joneses.

COMMON ERRORS

Do not use an apostrophe to make a noun plural

INCORRECT The two government's agreed to meet.

CORRECT The two governments agreed to meet.

INCORRECT The video game console's of the past were one-dimensional.

CORRECT The video game consoles of the past were one-dimensional.

Remember: Add only *-s* = plural
Add apostrophe plus *-s* = possessive

For step-by-step discussion, examples, and practice of this common error, go to **www.pearsoned.ca/faigley/251**.

 C H A P T E R **43**

Quotation Marks

Quotation marks, of course, set off quotations from surrounding text. But they also do other jobs that lend clarity to writing, like indicating certain kinds of titles, noting the novel use of a word, and showing that a word is being used as a word. Quotation marks are among the most commonly used and misused marks of punctuation.

43a DIRECT QUOTATIONS

Use quotation marks to enclose direct quotations

Enclose direct quotations—someone else's words repeated verbatim—in quotation marks.

> Anne Lamont advises writers to look at everything with compassion, even something as seemingly inconsequential as a chipmunk: "I don't want to sound too Cosmica Rama here, but in those moments, you see that you and the chipmunk are alike, are part of a whole" (98).

Even brief direct quotations, such as the repetition of someone else's original term or turn of phrase, require quotation marks.

> Though she fears appearing overly "Cosmica Rama," Anne Lamont argues that with compassion, writers' observations can be spiritually transcendent (98).

Do not use quotation marks with indirect quotations

Do not enclose an indirect quotation—a paraphrase of someone else's words—in quotation marks. However, do remember that you need to cite your source not only when you quote directly but also when you paraphrase or borrow ideas.

> Anne Lamont encourages writers to become compassionate observers who ultimately see themselves as equals to everything else, even something as seemingly inconsequential as a chipmunk (98).

Do not use quotation marks with block quotations

When a quotation is long enough to be set off as a block quotation, do not use quotation marks. MLA style defines long quotations as four or more lines of prose or poetry. APA style defines a long quotation as one of more than 40 words. In the following example, notice that the long quotation is indented and quotation marks are omitted. Also notice that the parenthetical citation for a long quotation comes after the period.

> Complaints about maintenance in residence have been on the rise ever since the physical plant reorganized its crews into teams in August. One student's experience is typical:
>> When our ceiling started dripping, my roommate and I went to our floor don right away to file an emergency maintenance request. Apparently the physical plant felt that "emergency" meant they could get around to it in a week or two. By the fourth day without any word from a maintenance person, the ceiling tiles began to fall and puddles began to pool on our carpet. (Albertson)
> The physical plant could have avoided expensive ceiling tile and carpet repairs if it had responded to the student's request promptly.

Set off quotations in dialogue

Dialogue is traditionally enclosed within quotation marks. Begin a new paragraph with each change of speaker.

> Before Jim and Lester walk 50 metres on a faint animal trail, they hear the brush rattle in front of them and the unmistakable snorting of a rhino. Jim crouches and looks through the brush.

Lester watches Jim, wondering why he isn't retreating, then scrambles up a nearby tree. "Come on back," he yells to Jim, who is now out of sight.

    After a few minutes Jim reappears. "I got right next to it but I never did get a good look. I was so close I could even smell it."

    "The other one is still out there in the grass. And I heard a third one behind us toward the river."

    "We better get out of here before it gets dark. Are you going to spend the night in the tree?"

    "I'm thinking about it."

43b   TITLES OF SHORT WORKS

While the titles of longer works such as books, magazines, and newspapers are italicized or underlined, titles of shorter works should be set off with quotation marks. Use quotation marks with the following kinds of titles:

SHORT STORIES	"Boys and Girls," by Alice Munro
MAGAZINE ARTICLES	"Born Again in Syria," by Michael Petrou
NEWSPAPER ARTICLES	"Stamp Auction Revives Canada's Postal Scandal," by Randy Boswell
SHORT POEMS	"We Real Cool," by Gwendolyn Brooks
ESSAYS	"Self-Reliance," by Ralph Waldo Emerson
SONGS	"Sk8er Boi," by Avril Lavigne
SPEECHES, LECTURES, AND SERMONS	"Zero to Web Page in Sixty Minutes," by Jean Lavre
CHAPTERS	"Cigs," *Souvenir of Canada*, by Douglas Coupland
SHORT FILMS	"Bed Head," by Robert Rodriguez
EPISODES OF TELEVISION SHOWS	"Treehouse of Horror," an episode of *The Simpsons*
EPISODES OF RADIO SHOWS	"Building a Bladder," an episode of *Quirks and Quarks*

    The exception. Don't put the title of your own paper in quotation marks. If the title of another short work appears within the title of your paper, retain the quotation marks around the short work. The title of a paper about Alice Munro, for instance, might read as follows:

Gender Roles in Alice Munro's "Boys and Girls"

43c OTHER USES OF QUOTATION MARKS

Quotation marks to indicate the novel use of a word

Quotation marks around a term can indicate that the writer is using the term in a novel way, often with skepticism, irony, or sarcasm. The quotation marks indicate that the writer is questioning the term's conventional definition. Notice the way quotation marks indicate skepticism about the conventional definition of *savages* in the following passage:

> In the early days of England's empire building, it wasn't unusual to hear English anthropologists say that conquered native people were savages. Yet if we measure civilization by peacefulness and compassion for fellow humans, those "savages" were really much more civilized than the British.

Quotation marks to indicate that a word is being used as a word

Italics are usually used to indicate that a word is being used as a word, rather than standing for its conventional meaning. However, quotation marks are correct in these cases as well.

> Beginning writers sometimes confuse "their," "they're," and "there."

43d MISUSES OF QUOTATION MARKS

Do not use quotation marks for emphasis

It's becoming more and more common to see quotation marks used to emphasize a word or phrase. Resist the temptation in your own writing; it's an incorrect usage. In fact, because quotation marks indicate that a writer is using a term with skepticism or irony, adding quotation marks for emphasis will highlight unintended connotations of the term.

INCORRECT   "fresh" seafood

By using quotation marks here, the writer seems to call into question whether the seafood is fresh at all.

CORRECT   fresh seafood

INCORRECT   Enjoy our "live" music every Saturday night.

Again, the quotation marks unintentionally indicate that the writer is skeptical that the music is live.

CORRECT   Enjoy our live music every Saturday night.

You have better ways of creating emphasis using your word processing program: **boldfacing**, <u>underlining</u>, *italicizing*, and using colour.

Do not use quotation marks around indirect quotations or paraphrases (also see Section 43a)

INCORRECT	The airport security guard announced that "all bags will be searched and then apologized for the inconvenience to the passengers."
CORRECT	The airport security guard announced, "All bags will be searched. I apologize for the inconvenience." [direct quotation]
CORRECT	The airport security guard announced that all bags would be searched and then apologized for the inconvenience to the passengers. [indirect quotation]

Avoid using quotation marks to acknowledge the use of a cliché

You may have seen other writers enclose clichés in quotation marks. Avoid doing this; in fact, avoid using clichés at all. Clichés are worn-out phrases; fresh words engage readers more.

INCORRECT	To avoid "letting the cat out of the bag" about forthcoming products, most large companies employ security experts trained in preventing commercial espionage.
CORRECT BUT STALE	To avoid letting the cat out of the bag about forthcoming products, most large companies employ security experts trained in preventing commercial espionage.
CORRECT AND EFFECTIVE	To prevent their savvy competitors from peeking at forthcoming products, most large companies employ security experts trained in preventing commercial espionage.

43e OTHER PUNCTUATION WITH QUOTATION MARKS

The rules for placing punctuation with quotation marks fall into three general categories.

Periods and commas with quotation marks

Place periods and commas inside closing quotation marks.

INCORRECT	"The smartest people", Dr. Geisler pointed out, "tell themselves the most convincing rationalizations".
CORRECT	"The smartest people," Dr. Geisler pointed out, "tell themselves the most convincing rationalizations."

Exceptions occur when a parenthetical citation follows a short quotation. In MLA and APA documentation styles, the period follows the closing parentheses.

INCORRECT "The smartest people," Dr. Geisler pointed out, "tell themselves the most convincing rationalizations." (52)

CORRECT "The smartest people," Dr. Geisler pointed out, "tell themselves the most convincing rationalizations" (52).

Colons and semicolons with quotation marks

Place colons and semicolons outside closing quotation marks.

INCORRECT "From Stettin in the Baltic to Trieste in the Adriatic, an iron curtain has descended across the Continent;" Churchill's statement rang through Cold War politics for the next 50 years.

CORRECT "From Stettin in the Baltic to Trieste in the Adriatic, an iron curtain has descended across the Continent"; Churchill's statement rang through Cold War politics for the next 50 years.

Exclamation points, question marks, and dashes with quotation marks

When an exclamation point, question mark, or dash belongs to the original quotation, place it inside the closing quotation mark. When it applies to the entire sentence, place it outside the closing quotation mark.

IN THE ORIGINAL QUOTATION

"Are we there yet?" came the whine from the back seat.

APPLIED TO THE ENTIRE SENTENCE

Did the driver in the front seat respond, "Not even close"?

COMMON ERRORS

Quotations within quotations

Single quotation marks are used to indicate a quotation within a quotation. In the following example single quotation marks clarify who is speaking. The rules for placing punctuation with single quotation marks are the same as the rules for placing punctuation with double quotation marks.

(continued next page)

INCORRECT	When he showed the report to Paul Probius, Michener reported that Probius "took vigorous exception to the sentence "He wanted to close down the university," insisting that we add the clarifying phrase "as it then existed"" (Michener 145).
CORRECT	When he showed the report to Paul Probius, Michener reported that Probius "took vigorous exception to the sentence 'He wanted to close down the university,' insisting that we add the clarifying phrase 'as it then existed'" (Michener 145).

Remember: Single quotation marks are used for quotations within quotations.

 For step-by-step discussion, examples, and practice of this common error, go to **www.pearsoned.ca/faigley/252**.

 CHAPTER 44

Other Punctuation Marks

Periods, question marks, and exclamation points indicate the conclusion of a sentence and tell the reader how to read it. Brackets, ellipses, and slashes occur much less often, but they also have important uses.

44a PERIODS

Periods at the ends of sentences

Place a period at the end of a complete sentence if it is not a direct question or an exclamatory statement. As the term suggests, a direct question asks a question outright. Indirect questions, on the other hand, report the asking of a question.

DIRECT QUESTION	Hunters who participate in the annual seal hunt wonder, "Why do animal rights activists value the welfare of baby seals over the welfare of my children?"

INDIRECT QUESTION   Hunters who participate in the annual seal hunt wonder why animal activists value the welfare of baby seals over the welfare of their children.

Periods with quotation marks and parentheses

When a quotation falls at the end of a sentence, place the period inside the closing quotation marks.

> Although he devoted decades to a wide range of artistic and political projects, Allen Ginsberg is best known as the author of the poem "Howl."

When a parenthetical phrase falls at the end of a sentence, place the period outside the closing parenthesis.

> Mrs. Chen, a grandmother in Kelowna, B.C., is training for her first 10K race (a fundraiser for the local food bank).

When parentheses enclose a whole sentence, place the period inside the closing parenthesis.

> True to their quirky success, ABBA found a receptive audience in Australia before Canadians embraced them. (Australia, in fact, carries the distinction of being the first country to place ABBA at the top of its music charts.)

Periods with abbreviations

Many abbreviations require periods; however, there are few set rules. Use the dictionary to check how to punctuate abbreviations on a case-by-case basis.

Sir John A. MacDonald	Mr.	misc.	Wed.
a.m.	p.m.	a.s.a.p.	etc.

The rules for punctuating two types of abbreviations do remain consistent: postal abbreviations for provinces and states and most abbreviations for organizations do not require periods.

ON for Ontario	CMHA for the Canadian Mental Health Association
CA for California	JTF-2 for Joint Task Force 2

When an abbreviation with a period falls at the end of a sentence, do not add a second period to conclude the sentence.

INCORRECT   Her flight arrives at 6:22 p.m..

CORRECT   Her flight arrives at 6:22 p.m.

Periods in citations of poetry and plays

Use a period to separate the components of the following kinds of literary citations.

A POEM DIVIDED INTO SECTIONS SUCH AS BOOKS OR CANTOS

book.lines   *The Inferno 27.79-84*

A PROSE PLAY

act.scene   *Beyond Therapy 1.4*

A VERSE PLAY

act.scene.lines   *Twelfth Night 3.4.194-98*

Periods as decimal points

Decimal points are periods that separate integers from tenths, hundredths, and so on.

99.98% pure silver   98.6° Fahrenheit
on sale for $399.97   2.6 litre engine

Since large numbers with long strings of zeros can be difficult to read accurately, writers sometimes shorten them using decimal points. Notice how the decimal points make the second sentence easier to read than the first.

A letter to the editor pointed out that while the Canadian government had contributed **US$160 000 000** toward building the U.S. Joint Strike Fighter, Canadian companies had received only **$130 000 000** in contracts, leaving Canadian taxpayers to make up the shortfall.

A letter to the editor pointed out that while the Canadian government had contributed **US$1.6 million** toward building the U.S. Joint Strike Fighter, Canadian companies had received only **$1.3 million** in contracts, leaving Canadian taxpayers to make up the shortfall.

44b QUESTION MARKS

Question marks with direct questions

Place a question mark at the end of a direct question. A direct question is one that the questioner puts to someone outright. In contrast, an indirect question merely reports the asking of a question. Question marks give readers a cue to read the end of the sentence with rising inflection. Read the following sentences aloud. Hear how your inflection rises in the second sentence to convey the direct question.

INDIRECT QUESTION

Desirée asked whether Dan rode his bicycle without a helmet.

DIRECT QUESTION

Desirée asked, "Does Dan ride his bicycle without a helmet?"

Question marks with quotations

When a quotation falls at the end of a direct question, place the question mark outside the closing quotation mark.

Did Brian Mulroney really say, "My father dreamed of a better life for his family. I dream of a better life for my country"?

Place the question mark inside the closing quotation mark when only the quoted material is a direct question.

Slowly scientists are beginning to answer the question, "Is cancer a genetic disease?"

When quoting a direct question in the middle of a sentence, place a question mark inside the closing quotation mark and place a period at the end of the sentence.

Market researchers estimate that asking Burger World's customers "Do you want fries with that?" is responsible for a 15% boost in their french fries sales.

Question marks to indicate uncertainty about dates or numbers

Place a question mark in parentheses after a date or number whose accuracy is in question.

After his escape from slavery, Frederick Douglass (1817?-95) went on to become a great orator and statesman.

44c EXCLAMATION POINTS

Exclamation points to convey strong emotion

Exclamation points conclude sentences and, like question marks, tell the reader how a sentence should sound. They indicate strong emotion. As with any display of strong emotion, occasional doses can be invigorating, but too many exclamation points quickly become grating. Instead of relying on exclamation points to convey heightened emotion, use strong words and careful phrasing. Use exclamation points sparingly in formal writing; they are rarely appropriate in academic and professional prose.

Exclamation points with emphatic interjections

Exclamation points can convey a sense of urgency with brief interjections. Interjections can be incorporated into sentences or stand on their own.

> Run! They're about to close the doors to the jetway.

Use commas to set off interjections that are not emphatic.

> One study has found that, yes, humans can contract a strain of mad cow disease.

Exclamation points with quotation marks

In quotations, exclamation points follow the same rules as question marks. If a quotation falls at the end of an exclamatory statement, place the exclamation point outside the closing quotation mark.

> The singer forgot the words of "O Canada"!

When quoting an exclamatory statement at the end of a sentence that is not itself exclamatory, place the exclamation point inside the closing quotation mark.

> Jerry thought his car would be washed away in the flood, but Anna jumped into action, declaring, "Not if I can help it!"

When the quotation of an exclamatory statement does not fall at the end of a sentence, place the exclamation point inside the closing quotation mark and place a period at the end of the sentence.

> Someone yelled "Loser!" when the candidate walked on stage.

44d BRACKETS

While brackets (sometimes called *square brackets*) look quite similar to parentheses, the two perform different functions. Brackets have a narrow set of uses.

Brackets to provide clarification within quotation marks

Quoted material sometimes requires clarification because it is removed from its context. Adding clarifying material in brackets can allow you to make the quotation clear while still accurately repeating the exact words of your source. In the following example the writer quotes a sentence with the pronoun *they*, which refers to a noun in a previous, unquoted sentence. The material in brackets clarifies to whom the pronoun refers.

> A quick comparison shows that "In the last three years, they [Pauline Johnson Senior Public School students] collected three times as many donations for the local homeless shelter as their peers at Father Bréboeuf."

Brackets within parentheses

Since parentheses within parentheses might confuse readers, use brackets to enclose parenthetical information within a parenthetical phrase.

> My mother drove off (taking her purse [which contained one set of house keys] and her jacket [which contained the other]), leaving me a virtual prisoner, unable to lock the doors and thereby leave the house.

WRITING IN THE WORLD

Using quotations that contain errors

In scholarly writing you should copy quotations exactly as they appear in your source, but you must also produce a paper free of grammatical and mechanical errors. So how should you handle a source that contains an error? One way is to rephrase the quotation in your own words, crediting your source for the idea. However, if the quotation is so eloquent or effective that you decide to include it despite the error, use *[sic]* (an abbreviation of the Latin "sicut," meaning *thus*) to indicate that the original source is responsible for the mistake.

SPELLING ERROR IN ORIGINAL SOURCE (*TO* INSTEAD OF *TOO*)

"One taste tester reported that the Carb Charge energy bar was to dry; she said it had the consistency of sawdust" (Cisco 22).

REPHRASED

One of the participants in the taste test likened the Carb Charge energy bar to sawdust because it had so little moisture (Cisco 22).

QUOTE USING [SIC]

"One taste tester reported that the Carb Charge energy bar was to [sic] dry; she said it had the consistency of sawdust" (Cisco 22).

44e ELLIPSES

Ellipses let a reader know that a portion of a passage is missing. You can use ellipses to keep quotations concise and direct readers' attention to what is important to the point you are making. An ellipsis is a string of three periods with spaces separating the periods. MLA style formerly required square brackets around the three periods. Your instructor may prefer that you use brackets surrounding ellipses when you delete words from quotations.

Ellipses to indicate an omission from a prose quotation

When you quote only a phrase or short clause from a sentence, you usually do not need to use ellipses.

> Mao Zedong first used "let a hundred flowers blossom" in a Peking speech in 1957.

Except at the beginning of a quotation, indicate omitted words with an ellipsis.

Type a space between each ellipsis and between the ellipses and the words preceding and following them.

THE ORIGINAL SOURCE

"The female praying mantis, so named for the way it holds its front legs together as if in prayer, tears off her male partner's head during mating. Remarkably, the headless male will continue the act of mating. This brutal dance is a stark example of the innate evolutionary drive to pass genes onto offspring; the male praying mantis seems to live and die only for this moment."

AN ELLIPSIS INDICATES OMITTED WORDS

"The female praying mantis . . . tears off her male partner's head during mating."

Note: Retain any punctuation mark falling before the omitted passage that clarifies the sentence. In this case the comma before the omitted passage would not make the sentence any clearer, so it was not retained.

Ellipses to indicate the omission of a whole line or lines of poetry

Using more than three periods is appropriate in just one instance: to signal the omission of a full line or lines of poetry in the middle of a poetry quotation. In such instances, use an entire line of spaced periods.

ORIGINAL

My Shakespeare, rise; I will not lodge thee by
Chaucer or Spenser, or bid Beaumont lie
A little further, to make thee a room;
Thou art a monument, without a tomb,
And art alive still, while thy book doth live,
And we have wits to read, and praise to give.

—Ben Jonson, "To the Memory of My Beloved,
the Author, Mr. William Shakespeare" (1623)

Omitted lines of poetry
My Shakespeare, rise;
. . . .
Thou art a monument, without a tomb,
And art alive still, while thy book doth live,
And we have wits to read, and praise to give.

Ellipses to indicate a pause or an interrupted sentence

Ellipses can provide a visual cue that a speaker is taking a long pause or that a speaker has been interrupted.

"And the winner is ... David Goldstein."

"That ball is going, going, ... gone!"

"Be careful that you don't spill ..."

44f SLASHES

Slashes to indicate alternative words

Slashes between two words indicate that a choice between them is to be made. When using slashes for this purpose, do not put a space between the slash and words.

INCORRECT	Maya was such an energetic baby that her exhausted parents wished she had come with an on / off switch.
CORRECT	Maya was such an energetic baby that her exhausted parents wished she had come with an on/off switch.

The following are common instances of the slash used to indicate alternative words:

either/or	he/she or s/he	player/coach
and/or	actor/director	pass/fail
on/off	win/lose	

Slashes to indicate line breaks in short quotations of verse

Line breaks—where the lines of a poem end—are artistic choices that affect how we understand a poem. Thus it is important to reproduce them accurately when quoting poetry. The task is not difficult in MLA style when the quotation is four or more lines long: simply indent the quoted lines 10 spaces and mimic the line breaks of the original verse. When you quote three or fewer lines of poetry, however, and must integrate the quotation into the paragraph rather than setting it off in a block, use slashes to indicate line breaks. Type a space on either side of the slash.

The concluding lines of T. S. Eliot's "Animula" offer a surprising revision of a common prayer. He writes, "Pray for Floret, by the boarhound slain between the yew trees / Pray for us now and at the hour of our birth." Replacing "death," the final word in the prayer, with "birth" at the end of this dark poem connotes an uneasy sense that we find ourselves adrift in a new and unfamiliar world.

WRITING IN THE WORLD

Should you use *he/she* or *s/he*?

Using *he* as an indefinite pronoun (a pronoun that refers to a person in general rather than to a specific individual) can seem sexist because it omits women. Some writers use *he/she* or the even shorter *s/he* instead. These solutions are unacceptable to many readers, who consider them ugly. Likewise, many readers consider *he or she* annoying. The best solution is to avoid the *he/she* and *he or she* constructions altogether.

SEXIST	Despite popular lore, a hiker bitten by a snake should never suck out the poison. Instead, he should tie a tourniquet above the wound to prevent the poison from circulating to vital organs.
INCLUSIVE BUT CUMBERSOME	Despite popular lore, a hiker bitten by a snake should never suck out the poison. Instead, s/he should tie a tourniquet above the wound to prevent the poison from circulating to vital organs.
INCLUSIVE BUT CUMBERSOME	Despite popular lore, a hiker bitten by a snake should never suck out the poison. Instead, he or she should tie a tourniquet above the wound to prevent the poison from circulating to vital organs.
BETTER	Despite popular lore, a hiker bitten by a snake should never suck out the poison. Instead, tying a tourniquet above the wound will prevent the poison from circulating to vital organs.

Chapter 30 offers more tips for avoiding sexist language and awkward indefinite pronouns.

Slashes with fractions

Place a slash between the numerator and the denominator in a fraction. Do not put any spaces around the slash.

INCORRECT	3 / 4
CORRECT	3/4

Slashes with dates

In informal writing, slashes divide the month, day, and year in a date. A longer format is appropriate for formal academic and professional writing. Omit the slashes, spell out the month, and place a comma after the day.

INFORMAL   Javy, save **1/14/07** on your calendar; I reserved two tickets for the Tragically Hip.

FORMAL   It was a pleasure to meet you during my December 14 interview for SportSystems Unlimited's marketing position. As we discussed, I will not be available for full-time employment until my graduation on **April 29, 2007**. However, I am hopeful that we can work out the part-time arrangement you suggested until that date.

CHAPTER

Write with Accurate Spelling

A few misspelled words can ruin a reader's impression of an otherwise well-written paper. Reserve time near the end of your writing process to check for spelling mistakes. Computer spelling checkers are a good tool for identifying certain kinds of spelling errors, but they do not eliminate the need for careful proofreading. Some writers find it helpful to read both forward and backward. First, read your text from beginning to end, looking for mistakes with homonyms. Then read the text backward, from the last word to the first. Errors often jump out when you aren't caught up in reading sentences for content.

45a KNOW THE LIMITATIONS OF SPELLING CHECKERS

Spelling checkers can actually help you to become a better speller. But spelling checkers are also quite limited and miss many errors. If you type *ferry tail* for *fairy tale*, your spelling checker will not catch the errors.

WRITING SMART

Electronic dictionaries

A number of reputable dictionaries now maintain searchable electronic versions on CD or on the internet. If you don't own a dictionary, these websites offer a convenient, inexpensive alternative.

General dictionaries

American Heritage Dictionary	bartleby.com/61/
Merriam-Webster Dictionary	www.m-w.com/
Oxford English Dictionary	Most research libraries offer access to an online version free to people with borrowing privileges.

Links to dictionaries

- *Yahoo Reference Dictionary:* ca.dir.yahoo.com/Reference/Dictionaries/
- *Canadian Authors Association:* www.canauthors.org/links/dicts.html
- *yourDictionary.com:* www.yourdictionary.com/diction4.html lists specialized electronic dictionaries from a variety of disciplines.

45b   DISTINGUISH HOMONYMS

Homonyms are pairs (*your, you're*) and trios (*their, there, they're*) of words that sound alike but have different spellings and meanings. They are tricky words to spell because we don't learn to distinguish them in spoken language, and spelling checkers don't flag them as errors because they correctly spell other words in their databases. It's easy to type *there* for *their* or *web sight* for *web site* and not catch the error when you proofread.

COMMON ERRORS

Commonly misspelled words

Is *accommodate* spelled with one *m* or two? Is *harass* spelled with one *r* or two? You'll find a list of words commonly misspelled at the URL below.

Remember: Always check a dictionary when you are unsure of how a word is spelled.

 For help with commonly misspelled words and additional spelling exercises, go to **www.pearsoned.ca/faigley/253**.

Capitalization and Italics

Of course you know you should capitalize the first word of a sentence, but you may not be as familiar with the other functions capital letters perform. Capital letters and italics assist readers by indicating certain kinds and uses of words. Learning a few guidelines will help you to become confident when to use each.

46a CAPITAL LETTERS

Capitalize the initial letters of proper nouns and proper adjectives

Capitalize the initial letters of proper nouns (nouns that name particular people, places, and things), including the following:

NAMES	Pierre Elliot Trudeau	Michaëlle Jean
TITLES PRECEDING NAMES	Sir Frederick Banting	Queen Elizabeth the Second
PLACE NAMES	Bay of Fundy	Northwest Territories
INSTITUTION NAMES	Ministry of Labour	St. Xavier University
ORGANIZATION NAMES	World Health Organization	Canadian Cancer Society
COMPANY NAMES	Research in Motion	JoJo's Café and Bakery
RELIGIONS	Protestantism	Islam
LANGUAGES	Chinese	Swahili
MONTHS	November	March
DAYS OF THE WEEK	Monday	Friday
NATIONALITIES	Italian	Puerto Rican
HOLIDAYS	Passover	Thanksgiving
DEPARTMENTS	Chemistry Department	Department of English
HISTORICAL ERAS	Enlightenment	Middle Ages
REGIONS	the Atlantic	Southwestern Ontario

COURSE NAMES	Eastern Religions	Microbiology
JOB TITLE WHEN USED WITH A PROPER NOUN		President Benjamin Ladner

Capitalize the initial letters of proper adjectives (adjectives based on the names of people, places, and things).

Afro-Caribbean bookstore	Avogadro's number	Irish music

Avoid unnecessary capitalization

Do not capitalize the names of seasons, academic disciplines (unless they are languages), or job titles used without a proper noun.

SEASONS	fall, winter, spring, summer
ACADEMIC DISCIPLINES (EXCEPT LANGUAGES)	chemistry, computer science, psychology, English, French, Japanese
JOB TITLES USED WITHOUT A PROPER NOUN	The vice president is on maternity leave.

WRITING SMART

Capitalization in email

some people never press the shift key when typing email. while there are no rules for informal email, long stretches of text with no capitalization are tiresome to read, even in email sent between close friends.

SIMILARLY, SOME PEOPLE TYPE EMAIL IN ALL CAPS, WHICH LIKEWISE IS ANNOYING TO READ OVER LONG STRETCHES. ALSO, SOME PEOPLE FEEL READING ALL CAPS IS LIKE BEING SHOUTED AT.

Capitalization conventions are familiar to readers and thus help make messages easy to read. Using both uppercase and lowercase letters, even in the most informal writing, is a friendly act.

Capitalize titles of publications

In MLA and CMS styles, when capitalizing titles, capitalize the initial letters of all first and last words and all other words except articles, prepositions, and coordinating conjunctions. Capitalize the initial letter of the first word in the subtitle following a colon.

James and the Giant Peach

The Penelopiad

The Writing on the Wall: An Anthology of Graffiti Art

COMMON ERRORS

Capitalizing with colons, parentheses, and quotations

Capitalizing with colons

Except when a colon follows a heading, do not capitalize the first letter after a colon unless the colon links two main clauses (which can stand as complete sentences). If the material following the colon is a quotation, a formal statement, or consists of more than one sentence, capitalize the first letter. In other cases capitalization is optional.

INCORRECT	We are all being integrated into a global economy that never sleeps: An economy determining our personal lives and our relationships with others.
CORRECT	We are all being integrated into a global economy that never sleeps: We can work, shop, bank, and be entertained 24 hours a day.

Capitalizing with parentheses

Capitalize the first word of material enclosed in parentheses if the words stand on their own as a complete sentence.

> Beginning with Rachel Carson's *Silent Spring* in 1962, we stopped worrying so much about what nature was doing to us and began to worry about what we were doing to nature. (Science and technology that had been viewed as the solution to problems suddenly became viewed as their cause.)

If the material enclosed in parentheses is part of a larger sentence, do not capitalize the first letter enclosed in the parentheses.

> Beginning with Rachel Carson's *Silent Spring* (first published in 1962), we stopped worrying so much about what nature was doing to us and began to worry about what we were doing to nature.

Capitalizing with quotations

If the quotation of part of a sentence is smoothly integrated into a sentence, do not capitalize the first word. Smoothly integrated quotations do not require a comma to separate the sentence from the rest of the quotation.

> It's no wonder the *Gazette* wrote that Armand's poutine was "the best in Montreal, bar none"; he spends whole days in his kitchen experimenting over bubbling pots.

(continued next page)

But if the sentence contains an attribution and the quotation can stand as a complete sentence, capitalize the first word. In such sentences a comma should separate the attribution from the quotation.

> According to Andrée of the *Gazette,* "The poutine Armand fusses over for hours in his kitchen is the best in Montreal, bar none."

Remember: For elements following colons or within parentheses or quotation marks, capitalize the first letter only if the group of words can stand as a complete sentence.

 For step-by-step discussion, examples, and practice of this common error, go to **www.pearsoned.ca/faigley/254**.

46b ITALICS

The titles of entire works (books, magazines, newspapers, films) are italicized in print. The titles of parts of entire works are placed within quotation marks. When italicizing is difficult because you are using a typewriter or writing by hand, underline the titles of entire works instead; in papers in MLA style, always italicize or underline them.

BOOKS	*Souvenir of Canada*
MAGAZINES	*Rolling Stone*
JOURNALS	*Canadian Journal of Physics*
NEWSPAPERS	*The Whitehorse Star*
FEATURE-LENGTH FILMS	*Barbarians*
LONG POEMS	*The Divine Comedy*
PLAYS, OPERAS, AND BALLETS	*The Lord of the Rings*
TELEVISION SHOWS	*Falcon Beach*
RADIO SHOWS AND AUDIO RECORDINGS	*As It Happens*
PAINTINGS, SCULPTURES, AND OTHER VISUAL WORKS OF ART	*Starry Night*
PAMPHLETS AND BULLETINS	*Lactose Intolerance or Milk Allergy?*

Also italicize or underline the names of ships and aircraft.

Spirit of St. Louis	*Challenger*
Titanic	*Pequod*

The exceptions. Do not italicize or underline the names of sacred texts.

The text for our Comparative Religions course, *Sacred Texts from around the World,* contains excerpts from the New English Bible, the Quran, the Talmud, the Upanishads, and the Bhagavad-Gita.

WRITING IN THE WORLD

Italicizing for emphasis

Italicizing a word can show the reader where to place the emphasis, but not all readers find italics appropriate. Use them sparingly. If you often find yourself italicizing words to indicate stresses, try to find stronger words that will do the same work.

NOT EFFECTIVE

"You don't *have* to let me win at chess *just because I'm younger,* Lynne."

"I'm not trying to let you win. *I'm just a bad chess player.*"

EFFECTIVE

"You don't have to let me win at chess just because I'm younger, Lynne."

"I'm *not* trying to let you win. I'm just a bad chess player."

---

abbr., number CHAPTER 47

Abbreviations, Acronyms, and Numbers

Abbreviations and acronyms are used much less often in writing for general audiences than in scientific and technical writing. The use of numbers also varies considerably from technical to general writing.

47a ABBREVIATIONS

Abbreviations are shortened forms of words. Because abbreviations vary widely, you will need to look in the dictionary to determine how to abbreviate words on a case-by-case basis. Nonetheless, there are a few patterns that abbreviations follow.

Abbreviate titles before and degrees after full names

Ms. Rita McNeil	**Dr.** Suzanne Smith	David Suzuki, **PhD**
Prof. Vijay Aggarwal	San-qi Li, **MD**	Marissa Limon, **LLD**

Write out the professional title when it is used with only a last name.

Professor Chin   **Doctor** Rodriguez   **Reverend** Ames

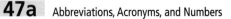

Conventions for using abbreviations with years and times

BCE (before the common era) and CE (common era) are now preferred for indicating years, replacing BC (before Christ) and AD (*anno Domini* ["the year of our Lord"]). Note that all are now used without periods.

> 479 **BCE** (or BC)
> 1610 **CE** (or AD, but AD is placed before the number)

The preferred written conventions for times are a.m. (*ante meridiem*) and p.m. (*post meridiem*).

> 9:03 **a.m.**
> 3:30 **p.m.**

An alternative is military time:

> The morning meal is served from **0600** to **0815**; the evening meal is served from **1730** to **1945**.

Conventions for using abbreviations in post-secondary writing

Most abbreviations are inappropriate in formal writing except when the reader would be more familiar with the abbreviation than with the words it represents. When your reader is unlikely to be familiar with an abbreviation, spell out the term, followed by the abbreviation in parentheses, the first time you use it in a paper. The reader will then understand what the abbreviation refers to, and you may use the abbreviation in subsequent sentences.

> The **World Health Organization (WHO)** has warned that a mutation of the H5N1 from birds to humans could spark a worldwide flu pandemic. The **WHO** has been monitoring outbreaks of the virus in countries around the world.

COMMON ERRORS

Making abbreviations and acronyms plural

Plurals of abbreviations and acronyms are formed by adding *s*, not *'s*.

> Technology is changing so rapidly these days that **PCs** become obsolete husks of circuits and plastic in only a few years.

Use an *'s* only to show possession.

> The **CEO's** sole criterion for selecting VPs was that they play golf well.

Remember: When making abbreviations and acronyms plural, add s, not 's.

 For step-by-step discussion, examples, and practice of this common error, go to **www.pearsoned.ca/faigley/255**.

47b ACRONYMS

Acronyms are abbreviations formed by capitalizing the first letter in each word. Unlike abbreviations, acronyms are pronounced as words.

AIDS for Acquired Immunodeficiency Syndrome
NASA for National Air and Space Administration
NATO for North Atlantic Treaty Organization
WAC for writing across the curriculum

A subset of acronyms are initial-letter abbreviations that have become so common that we know the organization or thing by its initials.

OPP for Ontario Provincial Police
HIV for human immunodeficiency virus
MLA for Modern Language Association
rpm for revolutions per minute
NHL for National Hockey League
MP for Member of Parliament

Familiar acronyms and initial-letter abbreviations such as CBC, CIBC, FBI, IQ, and UN are rarely spelled out. In a few cases, such as *radar* (*ra*dio *d*etecting *a*nd *r*anging) and *laser* (*l*ight *a*mplification by *s*timulated *e*mission of *r*adiation), the terms used to create the acronym have been forgotten by almost all who use them.

Unfamiliar acronyms and abbreviations should always be spelled out. Acronyms and abbreviations frequent in particular fields should be spelled out on first use. For example, MMPI (Minnesota Multiphasic Personality Inventory) is a familiar abbreviation in psychology but is unfamiliar to those outside that discipline. Even when acronyms are generally familiar, few readers will object to your giving the terms from which an acronym derives on the first use.

The **Canadian Association of Retired Persons (CARP)** is Canada's largest advocacy group for people over 50. **CARP** started in 1984 with 10 friends sitting around a kitchen table and now numbers more than 400 000 members.

COMMON ERRORS

Punctuation of abbreviations and acronyms

The trend now is away from using periods after many abbreviations. In formal writing you can still use periods, with certain exceptions.

Do not use periods with

1. **Acronyms and initial-letter abbreviations:**
   CPP, MPP, HMO, NAFTA, NFL, OPEC   *(continued next page)*

2. **Two-letter mailing abbreviations:** BC (British Columbia), MB (Manitoba), NL (Newfoundland and Labrador), YT (Yukon)
3. **Compass points:** NE (northeast), SW (southwest)
4. **Technical abbreviations:** kph (kilometres per hour), SS (sum of squares), SD (standard deviation)

Remember: Do not use periods with postal abbreviations for provinces or territories, compass points, technical abbreviations, and established organizations.

 For step-by-step discussion, examples, and practice of this common error, go to **www.pearsoned.ca/faigley/256**.

47c NUMBERS

In formal writing spell out any number that can be expressed in one or two words, as well as any number, regardless of length, at the beginning of a sentence. Also, hyphenate two-word numbers from twenty-one to ninety-nine.

My office is **twenty-three** blocks from my apartment—too far to walk but a perfect bike riding distance.

When a sentence begins with a number that requires more than two words, revise it if possible.

CORRECT BUT AWKWARD
Fifteen thousand six hundred runners left the Hopkinton starting line at noon in the Boston Marathon.

BETTER
At the start of the Boston Marathon, **15 600** runners left Hopkinton at noon.

The exceptions.   In scientific reports and some business writing that requires the frequent use of numbers, using numerals more often is appropriate. Most styles do not write out in words a year, a date, an address, a page number, the time of day, decimals, sums of money, phone numbers, rates of speed, or the scene and act of a play. Use numerals instead.

In **2001** only **33%** of respondents said they were satisfied with the City Council's proposals to help the homeless.

The **17** trials were conducted at temperatures **12–14°C** with results ranging from **2.43** to **2.89** mg/dl.

When one number modifies another number, write one out and express the other in numeral form.

In the last year all **four 8th** Street restaurants have begun to donate their leftovers to the soup kitchen.

Only after Meryl had rowed with **12 four**-person crews did she reach the finals in a regatta.

12 IF ENGLISH IS NOT YOUR FIRST LANGUAGE

If you are not a native speaker of English, the idea of writing academically and professionally in English may be intimidating. The challenges, however, are not insurmountable, especially if you understand what is involved in writing in a second language and make conscious and continuous efforts to develop your literacy.

MyCanadianCompLab Multimedia Resources

If English is not your first language, you may need an occasional review of some of the more difficult areas of English usage. Visit the MyCanadianCompLab website at **www.pearsoned.ca/highered/mycanadiancomplab/** for explanations, examples, and practice on the following topics:

- Differences among languages
- Writing for diverse audiences
- Verb tenses and forms
- Passive voice
- Troublesome words

Visit *The Brief Penguin Handbook* Companion Website at
www.pearsoned.ca/faigley/

MyCanadianCompLab
Where writing and research help is a click away.
MyCanadianCompLab may be packaged with your textbook.
If not, it can be purchased from your college or university's bookstore.
Go to **www.pearsoned.ca/highered/mycanadiancomplab/**
for a tour.

CHAPTER 48

Writing in a Second Language

Writing well takes hard work and years of practice even in your native language; writing in a second language is harder still. If you are not a native speaker of English, the idea of writing academically and professionally in English may be intimidating. The challenges, however, are not insurmountable, especially if you understand what is involved in writing in a second language and make conscious and continuous efforts to develop your literacy.

48a UNDERSTAND HOW LANGUAGES DIFFER

Many writers say that the main challenges of writing in a second language are grammar and vocabulary. While grammar and vocabulary are important, sometimes too much focus on the details of writing can take your attention away from other issues that affect your ability to communicate effectively. If English is not your first language, you may have noticed some differences between writing in English and in your native language. Some of the differences are relatively easy to identify, such as the direction of writing (left to right instead of right to left or top to bottom), the uses of punctuation (€ 2500.00 instead of € 2.500,00), or conventions of capitalization and spelling. Other differences are more subtle and complex, such as the citation of sources, uses of persuasive appeals, and the level of directness expected in a given situation. Readers of business correspondence in English, for example, expect communication to be direct, concise, and explicit, and they often become impatient with the indirect style of address sometimes preferred in business writing in other languages.

Since the sources of the differences are often varied, complex, and constantly changing, it is not always possible to make generalized statements such as "people in Canada write this way while people in China write in that way." Such generalizations can even lead to unproductive stereotypes about different languages, cultures, and ways of thinking.

When you write in an unfamiliar situation, it may be helpful to find a few examples of the type of writing you are trying to produce. If you are writing a cover letter to accompany a resumé, for example, ask your friends to share similar cover letters with you and look for the various ways they

WRITING IN THE WORLD

Differences within and between languages

Good writing is not a simple concept because the effectiveness of writing depends on the context and audience. Even within the same language, the clear and concise style of writing preferred in business letters may not be the top priority in legal writing, where being precise is more important. When you move from one language community to another, differences in the rhetorical situation and your readers' expectations may be even greater. In Japanese, for example, it is customary to begin a business letter with a paragraph-long seasonal greeting, while in English, business letter writers are encouraged to state the main point in the first paragraph.

While different conventions have evolved in different communities of writers, these conventions do not remain the same forever or in all contexts. Partly because of the influence of North American business conventions, simplified Japanese business letters that do not have seasonal greetings are becoming more common. Similarly, within North America, business letters in some situations—such as letters of rejection—do not necessarily state the main point in the first paragraph.

present themselves in writing in that situation. Ask them to read their letters out loud, and to explain the decisions they made as they wrote and revised their letters. In talking with them about how and why they wrote their cover letters, you will develop a better understanding of the ways writers in English respond to a given writing situation than you may be able to get from simply studying the format of a cover letter in a textbook.

Throughout the process of writing, try to focus on the overall effectiveness of your writing. If you find your concerns about grammar and vocabulary to be interfering with your writing process, consider setting aside some time at the end of the writing process to address these concerns. Many of the revision and editing strategies discussed in Chapter 5 may be applied to writing in a second language. The writing classroom and the writing centre provide practical and handy settings for peer review. Ask a peer to respond to your first draft by focusing on your main ideas and purpose. If your reader can summarize your main idea and purpose, then you can move on to consider the organization and content of your draft. Issues of grammar, vocabulary, and mechanics are best addressed in editing and proofreading after you are comfortable that your main ideas are clear (see Sections 5c and 5d).

48b USE YOUR NATIVE LANGUAGE AS A RESOURCE

As you continue to develop your ability to write in English, you will find that many of the strategies you developed in your native language are useful in English as well. The ability to think critically, for example, is important in any language, although what it means to be "critical" may differ from one context to another. You probably have developed the ability to tell stories and to organize your ideas in your native language. Imagery, metaphors, and expressions adapted from your native language may give your writing originality and uniqueness. It may make your writing culturally richer and more interesting to read.

You can also use your native language to develop your texts. While some writers find it more efficient to draft directly in English, others find it easier to develop an outline or even a rough draft in their native language first. Many people, when they cannot find an appropriate word in English, write down a word, a phrase, or even a sentence in their native language and consult a dictionary or a handbook later; it helps to avoid interrupting the flow of thought in the process of writing. Incorporating key terms from your native language is also a possible strategy. Here, for example, is the way a term from Japanese may be used to add flavour and perspective to a sentence: "Some political leaders need to have *wakimae*—a realistic idea of one's own place in the world."

Some people believe that using your own native language may interfere with your ability to write sentences that sound natural to native English speakers. Some readers may find words, concepts, or lines of argument from your native language distracting, especially when there are too many of them. To avoid miscommunication, incorporate non-English elements sparingly, revise and edit rigorously, and ask your classmates or writing tutors for feedback when possible and appropriate.

48c USE DICTIONARIES

You can use regular English dictionaries for definitions, but most English dictionaries designed for native English speakers do not include all of the information that many non-native English speakers find useful. For example, you may know the word *audience* but not whether and when *audience* can function as a count noun. Learner's dictionaries, such as the *Longman Dictionary of American English*, include information about count/non-count nouns and transitive/intransitive verbs (see Chapters 49 and 50). Many of them also provide sample sentences to help you understand how the word is used.

Some non-native English speakers also find a bilingual dictionary useful. Bilingual dictionaries are especially useful when you want to check your understanding of an English word or when you want to find equivalent words for culture-specific concepts and technical terms. Some bilingual dictionaries also provide sample sentences. When sample sentences are not provided, check the usage in another dictionary or by searching the word or phrase on the web (see Section 18c).

CHAPTER 49

Nouns and Articles

Hurdlers in track races try to clear every hurdle, yet it is not unusual to see even the most experienced runners clip one or two—and sometimes several—in a single race. If English is not your native language, you have probably "clipped" some of the rules governing English more than once. Throughout Chapters 49 through 51, you will see references to a website that is designed to help non-native speakers with some of the more difficult customs of English language usage. There, in addition to explanatory text, you will find many practice exercises to reinforce the guidelines in Chapters 49–51.

Perhaps the most troublesome conventions for non-native speakers are those that guide usage of the common articles *the, a,* and *an.* To understand how articles work in English, you must first understand how the language uses **nouns**.

49a KINDS OF NOUNS

There are two basic kinds of nouns. A **proper noun** begins with a capital letter and names a unique person, place, or thing: *Stephen Harper, Russia, Eiffel Tower.* In the following list, note that each word refers to someone or something so specific that it bears a name.

PROPER NOUNS

Beethoven	Michael Jordan	South Korea
Concorde	Toronto Blue Jays	Africa
B.C. Place	Picasso	Stockholm
Honda	Queen Elizabeth	Lake Superior
Thanksgiving	Margaret Laurence	New Brunswick

The other basic kind of noun is called a **common noun**. Common nouns do not name a unique person, place, or thing: *man, country, tower*. Note that the words in the following list are not names and so are not capitalized.

COMMON NOUNS

composer	athlete	country
airplane	baseball team	continent
building	painter	city
company	queen	lake
holiday	writer	province

Common nouns can also refer to abstractions, such as *grace, love*, and *power*. In English, proper nouns are names and are always capitalized while common nouns are not names and are not capitalized.

49b COUNT AND NON-COUNT NOUNS

Common nouns can be classified as either *count* or *non-count*. **Count nouns** can be made plural, usually by adding *-s* (*finger, fingers*) or by using their plural forms (*person, people; datum, data*). **Non-count nouns** cannot be counted directly and cannot take the plural form (*information*, but not *informations*; *garbage*, but not *garbages*). Some nouns can be either count or non-count, depending on how they are used. *Hair* can refer to either a strand of hair, when it serves as a count noun, or a mass of hair, when it becomes a non-count noun.

CORRECT USAGE OF *HAIR* AS COUNT NOUN
I carefully combed my few **hairs** across my mostly bald scalp.

CORRECT USAGE OF *HAIR* AS NON-COUNT NOUN
My roommate spent an hour this morning combing his **hair**.

In the same way, *space* can refer to a particular, quantifiable area (as in *two parking spaces*) or to unspecified open area (as in *there is some space left*).

If you are not sure whether a particular noun is count or non-count, consult a learner's dictionary. Count nouns are usually indicated as [C] (for "countable") and non-count nouns as [U] (for "uncountable").

49c SINGULAR AND PLURAL FORMS

Count nouns usually take both singular and plural forms, while non-count nouns usually do not take plural forms and are not counted directly. A count noun can have a number before it (as in *two books, three oranges*) and can be qualified with adjectives such as many (as in *many books*), some (as in *some schools*), a lot of (as in *a lot of people*), a few (several, as in *I ate a few apples*), and few (almost none, as in *few people volunteered*).

WRITING IN THE WORLD

Non-count nouns in English

In some languages, all nouns can take singular and plural forms. In English, non-count nouns refer to a collective mass that, taken as a whole, does not have a particular or regular shape. Think of the non-count noun as a mass that can be subdivided into smaller parts without losing its identity. Non-count nouns like *information, garbage, bread,* and *sand* can be broken down into smaller units and remain unchanged in essence: *bits* of information, *piles* of garbage, *slices* of bread, *grains* of sand. Count nouns like *train, finger,* and *ocean* cannot be subdivided without becoming something else: a wheel on a train, a knuckle on a finger, but no longer simply a train or a finger.

Non-count nouns can be counted or quantified in only two ways: either by general adjectives that treat the noun as a mass (*much* information, *little* garbage, *some* news) or by placing another noun between the quantifying word and the non-count noun (two *kinds* of information, three *piles* of garbage, a *piece* of news).

COMMON ERRORS

Singular and plural forms of count nouns

Count nouns are simpler to quantify than non-count nouns. But remember that English requires you to state both singular and plural forms of nouns consistently and explicitly. Look at the following sentences.

INCORRECT   The three **bicyclist** shaved their **leg** before the big race.

CORRECT   The three **bicyclists** shaved their **legs** before the big race.

In the first sentence, readers would understand that the plural form of *bicyclist* is implied by the quantifier *three* and that the plural form of *leg* is implied by the fact that bicyclists have two legs. (If they didn't, you would hope that the writer would have made that clear already!) Nevertheless, correct form in English is to indicate the singular or plural nature of a count noun explicitly, in every instance.

Remember: English requires you to use plural forms of count nouns even if a plural number is otherwise indicated.

For more help using count and non-count nouns, see the exercises at **www.pearsoned.ca/faigley/257**.

49d ARTICLES

Articles indicate that a noun is about to appear, and they clarify what the noun refers to. There are only two kinds of articles in English, definite and indefinite:

1. **the:** *The* is a **definite article**, meaning that it refers to (1) a specific object already known to the reader, (2) one about to be made known to the reader, or (3) a unique object.

2. **a, an:** The **indefinite articles** *a* and *an* refer to an object whose specific identity is not known to the reader. The only difference between *a* and *an* is that *a* is used before a consonant sound (*man, friend, yellow*), while *an* is used before a vowel sound (*animal, enemy, orange*).

Look at these sentences, identical except for their articles, and imagine that each is taken from a different newspaper story:

Rescue workers lifted **the** man to safety.
Rescue workers lifted **a** man to safety.

By use of the definite article *the*, the first sentence indicates that the reader already knows something about the identity of this man and his needing to be rescued. The news story has already referred to him. The sentence also suggests that this was the only man rescued, at least in this particular part of the story.

The indefinite article *a* in the second sentence indicates that the reader does not know anything about this man. Either this is the first time the news story has referred to him, or there are other men in need of rescue. When deciding whether to use the definite or indefinite article, ask yourself whether the noun refers to something specific or unique, or whether it refers to something general. *The* is used for specific or unique nouns; *a* and *an* are used for non-specific or general nouns.

A small number of conditions determine when and how count and non-count nouns are preceded by articles.

1. *A* or *an* is not used with non-count nouns.

INCORRECT   The crowd hummed with **an** excitement.
CORRECT   The crowd hummed with excitement.

2. *A* or *an* is used with singular count nouns whose particular identity is unknown to the reader or writer.

The security guard was reading **a** book.

3. *The* is used with most count and non-count nouns whose particular identity is known to the reader.
The noun may be known for one of several reasons:

- The noun has already been mentioned.

  I bought a book yesterday. **The** book is about Iraq.

- The noun is accompanied by a superlative, such as *highest, lowest, best, worst, least interesting,* or *most beautiful,* that makes its specific identity clear.

  This is **the most interesting book** about Iraq.

- The noun's identity is made clear by its context in the sentence.

  The book I bought yesterday is about Iraq.

- The noun has a unique identity, such as *the moon.*

  This book has as many pages as **the Bible**.

4. *The* is not used with non-count nouns meaning "in general."

INCORRECT   **The** war is hell.

CORRECT   War is hell.

COMMON ERRORS

Articles with count and non-count nouns

Knowing how to distinguish between count and non-count nouns can help you decide which article to use. Non-count nouns are never used with the indefinite articles *a* or *an*.

INCORRECT   Maria jumped into **a** water.

CORRECT   Maria jumped into **the** water.

No articles are used with non-count and plural count nouns when you wish to state something that has a general application.

INCORRECT   **The** water is a precious natural resource.

CORRECT   Water is a precious natural resource.

INCORRECT   **The** soccer players tend to be quick and agile.

CORRECT   Soccer players tend to be quick and agile.

Remember:

1. **Non-count nouns are never used with *a* and *an*.**
2. **Non-count and plural nouns used to make general statements do not take articles.**

 For more help using articles, see the exercises at
www.pearsoned.ca/faigley/258.

CHAPTER 50

Verbs

You cannot write a complete sentence in English without using a verb. As the heart animates the body, verbs animate sentences: without them, nothing—either real or imagined, past or present—happens. Though both native and non-native speakers of English encounter problems with verbs, this chapter focuses on the conventions of the verb system that are particularly challenging to non-native English speakers. See also Chapters 34 and 35.

50a TYPES OF VERBS

The verb system in English can be divided between simple verbs like *run, speak,* and *look,* and verb phrases like *may have run, have spoken,* and *will be looking.* In the examples of verb phrases, the words that appear before the main verbs—*may, have, will,* and *be*—are called **auxiliary verbs** (also called **helping verbs**). Helping verbs, as their name suggests, exist to help express something about the action of main verbs: for example, when the action occurs (tense), whether the subject acted or was acted upon (voice), or whether or not an action occurred.

50b *BE* VERBS

Indicating tense and voice with *be* verbs

Like the other auxiliary verbs *have* and *do, be* changes form to signal tense. In addition to *be* itself, the **be verbs** are *is, am, are, was, were,* and *been.* To show ongoing action, *be* verbs are followed by the present participle, which is a verb with an *-ing* ending:

INCORRECT	I **am think** of all the things I'd rather **be do**.
CORRECT	I **am thinking** of all the things I'd rather **be doing**.
INCORRECT	He **was run** as fast as he could.
CORRECT	He **was running** as fast as he could.

To show that an action is being done to, rather than by, the subject, follow *be* verbs with the past participle (a verb usually ending in *-ed, -en,* or *-t*):

INCORRECT	The movie **was direct** by John Woo.
CORRECT	The movie **was directed** by John Woo.
INCORRECT	The complaint **will be file** by the victim.
CORRECT	The complaint **will be filed** by the victim.

WRITING IN THE WORLD

Verbs that express cognitive activity

English, unlike Chinese, Arabic, and several other languages, requires a form of *be* before the present or past participle. As you have probably discovered, however, English has many exceptions to its rules. Verbs that express some form of cognitive activity rather than a direct action are not used as present participles with *be* verbs. Examples of such words include *know, like, see,* and *believe.*

INCORRECT   You **were knowing** that I would be late.

CORRECT   You **knew** that I would be late.

But here's an exception to an exception: a small number of these verbs, such as *considering, thinking,* and *pondering,* can be used as present participles with *be* verbs.

I **am considering** whether to finish my homework first.

50c MODAL AUXILIARY VERBS

Modal auxiliary verbs—*will, would, can, could, may, might, shall, must,* and *should*—are helping verbs that express conditions like possibility, permission, speculation, expectation, obligation, and necessity. Unlike the helping verbs *be, have,* and *do,* modal verbs do not change form based on the grammatical subject of the sentence (*I, you, she, he, it, we, they*).

Two basic rules apply to all uses of modal verbs. First, modal verbs are always followed by the simple form of the verb. The simple form is the verb by itself, in the present tense, such as *have,* but not *had, having,* or *to have.*

INCORRECT   She should **studies** harder to pass the exam.

CORRECT   She should **study** harder to pass the exam.

The second rule is that you should not use modals consecutively.

INCORRECT   If you work harder at writing, you **might could** improve.

CORRECT   If you work harder at writing, you **might** improve.

50d VERBS AND INFINITIVES

Several verbs are followed by particular verb forms. An **infinitive** is *to* plus the simple form of the verb. Here are some common verbs that are followed by an infinitive:

afford	expect	promise
agree	fail	refuse
ask	hope	seem
attempt	intend	struggle
claim	learn	tend
consent	need	wait
decide	plan	want
demand	prepare	wish

INCORRECT You **learn playing** the guitar by practising.

CORRECT You **learn to play** the guitar by practising.

Some verbs require that a noun or pronoun come after the verb and before the infinitive:

advise	instruct	require
cause	order	tell
command	persuade	warn

INCORRECT I would **advise to watch** where you step.

CORRECT I would **advise you to watch** where you step.

A few verbs, when followed by a noun or pronoun, take an *unmarked infinitive*, which is an infinitive without *to*.

have	let	make

INCORRECT I will **let** her **to plan** the vacation.

CORRECT I will **let** her **plan** the vacation.

50e VERBS AND *-ING* VERBALS

Other verbs are followed by **gerunds**, which are verbs ending in *-ing* that are used as nouns. Here are some of the more common verbs that are followed by a gerund.

admit	discuss	quit
advise	enjoy	recommend
appreciate	finish	regret
avoid	imagine	risk
consider	practice	suggest

INCORRECT	She will **finish to grade** papers by noon.
CORRECT	She will **finish grading** papers by noon.

A smaller number of verbs can be followed by either gerunds or infinitives (see Section 50d).

begin	hate	love
continue	like	start

WITH GERUND	She **likes working** in the music store.
WITH INFINITIVE	She **likes to work** in the music store.

 For more help using gerunds and infinitives, see the exercises at **www.pearsoned.ca/faigley/259**.

50f CONDITIONAL SENTENCES

Conditional sentences express *if-then* relationships: they consist of a **subordinate clause** beginning with *if*, *unless*, or *when* that expresses a condition, and a **main clause** that expresses a result. The tense and mood of the verb in the main clause and the type of conditional sentence determine the tense and mood of the verb in the subordinate clause.

┌─SUBORDINATE CLAUSE─┐ ┌──────MAIN CLAUSE──────┐
When the wind stops, the sea becomes calm.

Conditional sentences fall into three categories: **factual**, **predictive**, and **hypothetical**.

Factual conditionals

Factual conditional sentences express factual relationships: if this happens, that will follow. The tense of the verb in the conditional clause is the same as the tense of the verb in the result clause:

INCORRECT	If it rains, the ground **would become** wet.
CORRECT	If it rains, the ground **becomes** wet.

Predictive conditionals

Predictive conditional sentences express predicted consequences from possible conditions. The verb in the conditional clause is present tense, and the verb in the result clause is formed with a modal (*will, would, can, could, may, might, shall, must,* and *should*) plus the base form of the verb.

INCORRECT	If you **take** the long way home, you **enjoy** the ride more.
CORRECT	If you **take** the long way home, you **will enjoy** the ride more.

Hypothetical conditionals

Hypothetical conditional sentences express events that are neither factual nor likely to happen. For hypothetical events in the past, the conditional clause verb takes the past perfect tense. The main clause verb is formed from *could have, would have*, or *might have* plus the past participle.

INCORRECT	If we **had fed** the dog last night, he **would not run** away.
CORRECT	If we **had fed** the dog last night, he **would not have run** away.

For hypothetical events in the present or future, the conditional clause verb takes the past tense and the main clause verb is formed from *could, would*, or *might* and the base form.

INCORRECT	If we **paid** off our credit cards, we **can** buy a house.
CORRECT	If we **paid** off our credit cards, we **could** buy a house.

For more help using conditionals, see the exercises at
www.pearsoned.ca/faigley/260.

50g PARTICIPIAL ADJECTIVES

The present participle always ends in *-ing* (*boring, exciting*), while most past participles end in *-ed* (*bored, excited*). Both participle forms can be used as adjectives.

When participles are used as adjectives, they can either precede the nouns they modify or they can come after a connecting verb.

It was a **thrilling** book. [*Thrilling* modifies *book*.]

Stephanie was **thrilled**. [*Thrilled* modifies *Stephanie*.]

Present participles like *thrilling* describe a thing or person causing an experience, while past participles like *thrilled* describe a thing or person receiving the experience.

INCORRECT	Students were **exciting** by the lecture.
CORRECT	Students were **excited** by the lecture.

CHAPTER 51

English Sentence Structure

Performing musicians are not judged by the number of songs they know. Likewise, multilingual speakers understand that a good vocabulary is not enough to communicate effectively. Words derive much of their meaning from context, and the basic contextual unit is the **sentence**. Your ability to understand and convey information accurately in English depends largely on your understanding of how sentences are put together.

51a   SUBJECTS

With the exception of **imperatives** (commands such as *Be careful!* and *Jump!*) and informal expressions (such as *Got it?*), sentences in English usually contain a subject and a predicate. A **subject** names who or what the sentence is about; the **predicate** contains information about the subject.

> ⌐SUBJECT⌐ ⌐PREDICATE⌐
> The lion is asleep.

Many languages allow the writer to omit the subject if it's implied, but formal written English requires that each sentence include a subject, even when the meaning of the sentence would be clear without it. In some cases, you must supply an **expletive** (also known as *a dummy subject*), such as *it* or *there*, to stand in for the subject.

INCORRECT	Is snowing in Edmonton.
CORRECT	It is snowing in Edmonton.
INCORRECT	Won't be enough time to climb Giant's Head.
CORRECT	There won't be enough time to climb Giant's Head.

Both main and subordinate clauses within sentences require a subject and a predicate. A main clause can stand alone as a sentence, while subordinate clauses can only be understood in the context of the sentence of which they're a part. Still, even subordinate clauses must contain a subject. Look at the underlined subordinate clauses in the following two correct sentences.

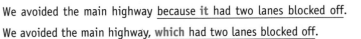

We avoided the main highway <u>because it had two lanes blocked off.</u>

We avoided the main highway, <u>**which** had two lanes blocked off.</u>

In the first example, the subject of the subordinate clause is *it*, a pronoun representing the highway. In the second sentence, the relative pronoun *which*—also representing the highway—becomes the subject. When you use a relative pronoun, do not repeat the subject within the same clause.

INCORRECT   We avoided the highway, which it had two lanes blocked off.

In this sentence, *it* repeats the subject *which* unnecessarily.

51b ENGLISH WORD ORDER

All languages have their own rules for sentence structure. In English, correct word order often determines whether or not you succeed in saying what you mean. The basic sentence pattern in English is subject + predicate. A **predicate** consists of at least one main verb (see Section 32a). Although it is possible to write single-verb sentences such as *Stop!* most English sentences consist of a combination of several words. A simple English sentence can be formed with a noun and a verb.

Birds fly.

In the above sentence, the subject (birds) is taking the action *and* receiving the action. There is no other object after the verb. The type of verb that can form a sentence without being followed by an object is called an **intransitive verb**. If the verb is intransitive, like *exist*, it does not take a direct object.

Some verbs are **transitive**, which means they require a **direct object** to complete their meaning. The direct object receives the action described by the verb.

INCORRECT   The bird saw.

CORRECT   The bird saw a cat.

In this sentence, the subject (the bird) is doing the action (saw) while the direct object (a cat) is receiving the action. A sentence with a transitive verb can be transformed into a passive sentence (*A cat was seen by the bird.*). See Chapter 26 for active and passive sentences.

Some verbs (*write, learn, read,* and others) can be both transitive and intransitive, depending on how they are used.

INTRANSITIVE   Pilots fly.

TRANSITIVE   Pilots fly airplanes.

Most learners' dictionaries and bilingual dictionaries indicate whether a particular verb is transitive or intransitive. See Section 48c on the use of dictionaries.

In another simple pattern, the transitive verb is replaced by a linking verb that joins its subject to a following description.

The tallest player was the goalie.

Linking verbs like *was, become, sound, look*, and *seem* precede a *subject complement* (in this example, *the goalie*) that refers back to the subject.

At the next level of complexity, a sentence combines a subject with a verb, direct object, and indirect object.

               INDIRECT   DIRECT
                 OBJ   OBJ

The goalie passed her the puck.

Passed is a transitive verb, *puck* is the direct object of the verb, and *her* is the indirect object, the person for whom the action was taken. The same idea can be expressed with a prepositional phrase instead of an indirect object:

             DIRECT   PREP
             OBJ   PHRASE

The goalie passed the puck to her.

Other sentence patterns are possible in English. (See Chapter 32.) However, it is important to remember that altering the basic subject + verb + object word order often changes the meaning of a sentence. If the meaning survives, the result may still be awkward. As a general rule, try to keep the verb close to its subject, and the direct or indirect object close to its verb.

51c   PLACEMENT OF MODIFIERS

The proximity of a modifier—an adjective or adverb—to the noun or verb it modifies provides an important clue to their relationship. Modifiers, even more than verbs, will be unclear if your reader can't connect them to their associated words. Both native and non-native speakers of English often have difficulty with misplaced modifiers.

Clarity should be your first goal when using a modifier. Readers usually link modifiers with the nearest word. In the following examples, the highlighted words are adjective clauses that modify nouns.

UNCLEAR   Many pedestrians are killed each year by motorists **not using sidewalks**.

CLEAR   Many pedestrians **not using sidewalks** are killed each year by motorists.

UNCLEAR   He gave an apple to his girlfriend **on a silver platter**.

CLEAR   He gave an apple **on a silver platter** to his girlfriend.

An **adverb**—a word or group of words that modifies a verb, adjective, or another adverb—should not come between a verb and its direct object.

AWKWARD	The hurricane destroyed completely the city's tallest building.
BETTER	The hurricane completely destroyed the city's tallest building.

While single-word adverbs can come between a subject and its verb, you should avoid placing adverbial phrases in this position.

AWKWARD	Toronto, following the SARS scare of 2003, created an emergency response network to prepare for future health epidemics.
BETTER	Following the SARS scare of 2003, Toronto created an emergency response network to prepare for future health epidemics.

As a general rule, try to avoid placing an adverb between *to* and its verb. This is called a **split infinitive**.

AWKWARD	The water level was predicted to not rise.
BETTER	The water level was predicted not to rise.

Sometimes, though, a split infinitive will read more naturally than the alternative. Note also how the sentence with the split infinitive is more concise:

WITHOUT SPLIT INFINITIVE	Automobile emissions in the city are expected to increase by more than two times over the next five years.
WITH SPLIT INFINITIVE	Automobile emissions in the city are expected to more than double over the next five years.

Certain kinds of adverbs have special rules for placement. Adverbs that describe how something is done—called **adverbs of manner**—usually follow the verb.

The student listened closely to the lecture.

These adverbs may also be separated from the verb by a direct object:

She threw the ball well.

Adverbs of frequency usually are placed at the head of a sentence, before a single verb, or after an auxiliary verb in a verb phrase.

Often, politicians have underestimated the intelligence of voters.

Politicians have often underestimated the intelligence of voters.

It's common practice in English to combine two or more nouns to form a compound noun. Where two or more adjectives or nouns are strung together, the main noun is always positioned at the end of the string:

12-speed road **bike**, tall oak **tree**, computer **table**

COMMON ERRORS

Dangling modifiers

A dangling modifier does not seem to modify anything in a sentence; it dangles, unconnected to the word or words it presumably is intended to modify. Frequently, it produces some funny results:

When still a girl, my father joined the army.

It sounds like *father* was once a girl. The problem is that the subject, *I*, is missing:

When I was still a girl, my father joined the army.

Dangling modifiers usually occur at the head of a sentence in the form of adjective clauses, with a subject that is implied but never stated.

INCORRECT   After lifting the heavy piano up the stairs, the apartment door was too small to get it through.

CORRECT   After lifting the heavy piano up the stairs, we discovered the apartment door was too small to get it through.

Whenever you use a modifier, ask yourself whether its relationship to the word it modifies will be clear to your reader. What is clear to you may not be clear to your audience. Writing, like speaking, is an exercise in making your own thoughts explicit. The solution for the dangling modifier is to recast it as a complete clause with its own explicit subject and verb.

Remember: Modifiers should be clearly connected to the words they modify, especially at the beginning of sentences.

For more help with modifiers, see the exercises at **www.pearsoned.ca/faigley/261**.

GLOSSARY OF GRAMMATICAL TERMS AND USAGE

The glossary gives the definitions of grammatical terms and items of usage. The grammatical terms are shown in blue. Some of the explanations of usage that follow are not rules but guidelines to keep in mind for academic and professional writing. In these formal contexts, the safest course is to avoid words that are described as *non-standard, informal,* or *colloquial.*

a/an Use *a* before words that begin with a consonant sound (*a train, a house*). Use *an* before words that begin with a vowel sound (*an airplane, an hour*).

a lot/alot *A lot* is generally regarded as informal; *alot* is non-standard.

absolute A phrase that has a subject and modifies an entire sentence (see Section 32d). *The soldiers marched in single file, their rifles slung over their shoulders.*

accept/except *Accept* is a verb meaning "receive" or "approve." *Except* is sometimes a verb meaning "leave out," but much more often, it's used as a conjunction or preposition meaning "other than."

active A clause with a transitive verb in which the subject is the doer of the action (see Section 26a). See also **passive.**

adjective A modifier that qualifies or describes the qualities of a noun or pronoun (see Sections 32b, 37a, and 37b).

adjective clause A subordinate clause that modifies a noun or pronoun and is usually introduced by a relative pronoun (see Section 32c). Sometimes called a *relative clause.*

adverb A word that modifies a verb, another modifier, or a clause (see Sections 32b, 37a, and 37c).

adverb clause A subordinate clause that functions as an adverb by modify-

ing a verb, another modifier, or a clause (see Section 32c).

advice/advise The noun *advice* means a "suggestion"; the verb *advise* means to "recommend" or "give advice."

affect/effect Usually, *affect* is a verb (to "influence") and *effect* is a noun (a "result"). Less commonly, *affect* is used as a noun and *effect* as a verb. In this usage, *affect* means an "emotional state or expression," and *effect* means "to bring about."

agreement The number and person of a subject and verb must match—singular subjects with singular verbs, plural subjects with plural verbs (see Chapter 34). Likewise, the number and gender of a pronoun and its antecedent must match (see Section 36b).

all ready/already The adjective phrase *all ready* means "completely prepared"; the adverb *already* means "previously."

all right/alright *All right,* meaning "acceptable," is the correct spelling. *Alright* is non-standard.

allude/elude *Allude* means "refer to indirectly." *Elude* means "evade."

allusion/illusion An *allusion* is an indirect reference; an *illusion* is a false impression.

among/between *Between* refers to precisely two people or things; *among* refers to three or more.

amount/number Use *amount* with things that cannot be counted; use *number* with things that can be counted.

an See **a/an**.

antecedent The noun (or pronoun) that a pronoun refers to (see Section 36b). *Jeff* is the antecedent of *his* in the following sentence. *Jeff picked up his coat.*

anybody/any body; anyone/any one *Anybody* and *anyone* are indefinite pronouns and have the same meaning; *any body* and *any one* are usually followed by a noun that they modify.

anymore/any more *Anymore* means "now," while *any more* means "no more." Both are used in negative constructions.

anyway/anyways *Anyway* is correct. *Anyways* is non-standard.

appositive A word or a phrase placed close to a noun that restates or modifies the noun (see Section 32d). *Dr. Lim, my physics professor, is the best.*

articles The words *a*, *an*, and *the* (see Section 32b).

as/as if/as though/like Use *as* instead of *like* before dependent clauses (which include a subject and verb). Use *like* before a noun or a pronoun.

assure/ensure/insure *Assure* means "promise," *ensure* means "make certain," and *insure* means to "make certain in either a legal or financial sense."

auxiliary verb Forms of *be*, *do*, and *have* combine with verbs to indicate tense and mood (see Section 32b). The modal verbs *can*, *could*, *may*, *might*, *must*, *shall*, *should*, *will*, and *would* are a subset of auxiliaries.

bad/badly Use *bad* only as an adjective. *Badly* is the adverb. *He was a bad dancer. Everyone agreed that he danced badly.*

being as/being that Both constructions are colloquial and awkward substitutes for *because*. Don't use them in formal writing.

beside/besides *Beside* means "next to." *Besides* means "in addition to" or "except."

between See **among/between**.

bring/take *Bring* describes movement from a more distant location to a nearer one. *Take* describes movement away.

can/may In formal writing, *can* indicates ability or capacity, while *may* indicates permission.

case The form of a noun or pronoun that indicates its function. Nouns change case only to show possession: the *dog*, the *dog's* bowl (see Section 32b). See **pronoun case** (Section 36a).

censor/censure To *censor* is to edit or ban on moral or political grounds. To *censure* is to reprimand publicly.

cite/sight/site To *cite* is to "mention specifically"; *sight* as a verb means to "observe" and as a noun refers to "vision"; *site* is most commonly used as a noun that means "location," but is also used as a verb to mean "situate."

clause A group of words with a subject and a predicate. A main or independent clause can stand as a sentence. A subordinate or dependent clause must be attached to a main clause to form a sentence (see Section 32c).

collective noun A noun that refers to a group or a plurality, such as *team, army,* or *committee* (see Section 34d).

comma splice Two independent clauses joined incorrectly by a comma (see Section 33c).

common noun A noun that names a general group, person, place, or thing (see Sections 32b and 46a). Common nouns are not capitalized unless they begin a sentence.

complement A word or group of words that completes the predicate (see Section 32c). See also **linking verb**. *Juanita is my aunt.*

complement/compliment To *complement* something is to complete it or make it perfect; to *compliment* is to flatter.

complex sentence A sentence that contains at least one subordinate clause attached to a main clause (see Section 32e).

compound sentence A sentence that contains at least two main clauses (see Section 32e).

compound-complex sentence A sentence that contains at least two main clauses and one subordinate clause (see Section 32e).

conjunction See **coordinating conjunction** and **subordinating conjunction**.

conjunctive adverb An adverb that often modifies entire clauses and sentences, such as *also, consequently, however, indeed, instead, moreover, nevertheless, otherwise, similarly,* and *therefore* (see Sections 32b and 37c).

continual/continuous *Continual* refers to a repeated activity; *continuous* refers to an ongoing, unceasing activity.

coordinate A relationship of equal importance, in terms of either grammar or meaning (see Section 28c).

coordinating conjunction A word that links two equivalent grammatical elements, such as *and, but, or, yet, nor, for,* and *so* (see Section 32b).

could of Non-standard. See **have/of**.

count noun A noun that names things that can be counted, such as *block, cat,* and *toy* (see Section 49b).

dangling modifier A modifier that is not clearly attached to what it modifies (see Section 37e).

data The plural form of *datum*; it takes plural verb forms.

declarative A sentence that makes a statement (see Section 32a).

dependent clause See **subordinate clause**.

determiners Words that initiate noun phrases, including possessive nouns (*Pedro's violin*); possessive pronouns (*my, your*); demonstrative pronouns (*this, that*); and indefinite pronouns (*all, both, many*).

differ from/differ with To *differ from* means to "be unlike"; to *differ with* means to "disagree."

different from/different than Use *different from* where possible.

direct object A noun, pronoun, or noun clause that names who or what receives the action of a transitive verb (see Section 32c). *Antonia kicked the ball.*

discreet/discrete Both are adjectives. *Discreet* means "prudent" or "tactful"; *discrete* means "separate."

disinterested/uninterested *Disinterested* is often misused to mean *uninterested.* Disinterested means "impartial." A judge can be interested in a case but disinterested in the outcome.

double negative The incorrect use of two negatives to signal the same negative meaning. *We don't have no money.*

due to the fact that Avoid this wordy substitute for *because*.

each other/one another Use *each other* for two; use *one another* for more than two.

effect See **affect/effect**.

elicit/illicit The verb *elicit* means to "draw out." The adjective *illicit* means "unlawful."

emigrate from/immigrate to *Emigrate* means to "leave one's country"; *immigrate* means to "settle in another country."

ensure See **assure/ensure/insure**.

enthused Non-standard in academic and professional writing. Use *enthusiastic* instead.

etc. Avoid this abbreviation for the Latin *et cetera* in formal writing. Either list all the items or use an English phrase such as *and so forth*.

every body/everybody; every one/everyone *Everybody* and *everyone* are indefinite pronouns referring to all people under discussion. *Every one* and *every body* are adjective-noun combinations referring to all members of a group.

except See **accept/except**.

except for the fact that Avoid this wordy substitute for *except that*.

expletive The dummy subjects *it* and *there* used to fill a grammatical slot in a sentence.

explicit/implicit Both are adjectives; *explicit* means "stated outright," while *implicit* means just the opposite, "unstated."

farther/further *Farther* refers to physical distance; *further* refers to time or other abstract concepts.

fewer/less Use *fewer* with what can be counted and *less* with what cannot be counted.

flunk In formal writing, avoid this colloquial substitute for *fail*.

fragment A group of words beginning with a capital letter and ending with a period that looks like a sentence but lacks a subject or a predicate or both (see Section 33a).

further See **farther/further**.

gerund An *-ing* form of a verb used as a noun, such as *running, skiing,* or *laughing* (see Section 32b).

good/well *Good* is an adjective and is not interchangeable with the adverb *well*. The one exception is health. Both she feels *good* and she feels *well* are correct.

hanged/hung Use *hanged* to refer only to executions; *hung* is used for all other instances.

have/of *Have*, not *of*, follows *should, could, would, may, must,* and *might*.

he/she; s/he Try to avoid language that appears to exclude either gender (unless this is intended, of course) and awkward compromises such as *he/she* or *s/he*. The best solution is to make pronouns plural (the gender-neutral *they*) wherever possible (see Section 36c).

helping verb See **auxiliary verb**.

hopefully This adverb is commonly used as a sentence modifier, but many readers object to it.

illusion See **allusion/illusion**.

immigrate See **emigrate from/immigrate to**.

imperative A sentence that expresses a command (see Section 32a). Usually the subject is implied rather than stated.

implicit See **explicit/implicit**.

imply/infer *Imply* means to "suggest"; *infer* means to "draw a conclusion."

in regards to Avoid this wordy substitute for *regarding*.

incredible/incredulous *Incredible* means "unbelievable"; *incredulous* means "not believing."

independent clause See **main clause**.

indirect object A noun, pronoun, or noun clause that names who or what is affected by the action of a transitive verb (see Section 32c). *Antonia kicked Mario the ball.*

infinitive The word *to* plus the base verb form: *to believe, to feel, to act*. See also **split infinitive**.

infinitive phrase A phrase that uses the infinitive form of a verb (see Section 32d).

interjection A word expressing feeling that is grammatically unconnected to a sentence, such as *cool, wow, ouch,* or *yikes*.

interrogative A sentence that asks a question (see Section 32a).

intransitive verb A verb that does not take an object, such as *sleep, appear,* or *laugh* (see Sections 32c and 35c).

irregardless Non-standard for *regardless*.

irregular verb A verb that does not use either *-d* or *-ed* to form the past tense and past participle (see Section 35b).

it is my opinion that Avoid this wordy substitute for *I believe that*.

its/it's *Its* is the possessive of *it* and does not take an apostrophe; *it's* is the contraction for *it is*. *Its tail is missing. It's an unusual animal.*

-ize/-wise The suffix *-ize* changes a noun or adjective into a verb (*harmony, harmonize*). The suffix *-wise* changes a noun or adjective into an adverb (*clock, clockwise*). Some writers are tempted to use these suffixes to convert almost any word into an adverb or verb form. Unless the word appears in a dictionary, don't use it.

kind of/sort of/type of Avoid using these colloquial expressions if you mean *somewhat* or *rather*. *It's kind of hot* is non-standard. Each is permissible, however, when it refers to a classification of an object. Be sure that it agrees in number with the object it is modifying.

lay/lie *Lay* means "place" or "put" and generally takes a direct object (see Section 35c). Its main forms are *lay, laid, laid. Lie* means "recline" or "be positioned" and does not take an object. Its main forms are *lie, lay, lain*.

less See **fewer**.

lie See **lay/lie**.

linking verb A verb that connects the subject to the complement, such as *appear, be, feel, look, seem,* or *taste* (see Section 32c).

lots/lots of Non-standard in formal writing; use *many* or *much* instead.

main clause A group of words with a subject and a predicate that can stand alone as a sentence (see Section 32c). Also called an *independent clause*.

mankind This term offends some readers and is outdated. Use *humans, humanity,* or *people* instead.

may/can See **can/may**.

may be/maybe *May be* is a verb phrase; *maybe* is an adverb.

media This is the plural form of the noun *medium* and requires a plural verb.

might of See **have/of**.

modal A kind of auxiliary verb that indicates ability, permission, intention, obligation, or probability, such as *can, could, may, might, must, shall, should, will,* or *would* (see Section 32b).

modifier A general term for adjectives, adverbs, phrases, and clauses that describe other words (see Chapter 37).

must of See **have/of**.

non-count noun A noun that names things that cannot be counted, such as *air, energy,* or *water* (see Section 49b).

non-restrictive modifier A modifier that is not essential to the meaning of the word, phrase, or clause it modifies and should be set off by commas or other punctuation (see Section 38c).

noun The name of a person, place, thing, concept, or action (see Section 32b). See also common noun and proper noun (see Section 49a).

noun clause A subordinate clause that functions as a noun (see Section 32c).

number See **amount/number**.

object Receiver of the action within the clause or phrase (see Sections 32c and 32d).

OK, O.K., okay Informal; avoid using in academic and professional writing. Each spelling is accepted in informal usage.

owing to the fact that Avoid this wordy, colloquial substitute for *because*.

parallelism The principle of putting similar elements or ideas in similar grammatical form (see Sections 28c, 28d, and 28e).

participle A form of a verb that uses *-ing* in the present (*laughing, playing*) and usually *-ed* or *-en* in the past (*laughed, played*). See Section 35a. Participles are either part of the verb phrase (*She had played the game before*) or used as adjectives (*the laughing girl*).

participial phrase A phrase formed either by a present participle (for example, *racing*) or by a past participle (for example, *taken*). (See Section 32d.)

parts of speech The eight classes of words according to their grammatical function: nouns, pronouns, verbs, adjectives, adverbs, prepositions, conjunctions, and interjections (see Section 32b).

passive A clause with a transitive verb in which the subject is being acted upon (see Section 26a). See also active.

people/persons *People* refers to a general group; *persons* refers to a collection of individuals. Use *people* over *persons* except when you're emphasizing the idea of separate persons within the group.

per Try to use the English equivalent of this Latin word except in technical writing or familiar usages like *miles per gallon.*

phenomena This is the plural form of *phenomenon* ("observable fact" or "unusual event") and takes plural verbs.

phrase A group of words that does not contain both a subject and predicate.

plenty In academic and professional writing, avoid this colloquial substitute for *very.*

plus Do not use *plus* to join clauses or sentences. Use *and, also, moreover, furthermore,* or another conjunctive adverb instead.

precede/proceed Both are verbs but they have different meanings: *precede* means "come before," and *proceed* means "go ahead" or "continue."

predicate The part of the clause that expresses the action or tells something about the subject. The predicate includes the verb and all its complements, objects, and modifiers (see Section 32a).

prejudice/prejudiced *Prejudice* is a noun; *prejudiced* is an adjective.

preposition A class of words that indicate relationships and qualities (see Section 32b).

prepositional phrase A phrase formed by a preposition and its object, including the modifiers of its object (see Section 32d).

pronoun A word that stands for other nouns or pronouns. Pronouns have several subclasses, including personal pronouns, possessive pronouns, demonstrative pronouns, indefinite pronouns, relative pronouns, interrogative pronouns, reflexive pronouns, and reciprocal pronouns (see Section 32b and Chapter 36).

pronoun case Pronouns that function as the subjects of sentences are in the **subjective** case (*I, you, he, she, it, we, they*). Pronouns that function as direct or indirect objects are in the **objective** case (*me, you, him, her, it, us, them*). Pronouns that indicate ownership are in the **possessive** case (*my, your, his, her, its, our,* their) (see Section 36a).

proper noun A noun that names a particular person, place, thing, or group (see Sections 32b and 49a). Proper nouns are capitalized.

question as to whether/question of whether Avoid these wordy substitutes for *whether.*

raise/rise The verb *raise* means "lift up" and takes a direct object. Its main forms are *raise, raised, raised.* The verb *rise* means "get up" and does not take a direct object. Its main forms are *rise, rose, risen.*

real/really Avoid using *real* as if it were an adverb. *Really* is an adverb; *real* is an adjective.

reason is because Omit either *reason is* or *because* when explaining causality.

reason why Avoid using this redundant combination.

relative pronoun A pronoun that initiates clauses, such as *that, which, what, who, whom,* or *whose* (see Section 32b).

restrictive modifier A modifier that is essential to the meaning of the word, phrase, or clause it modifies (see Section 38c). Restrictive modifiers are usually not set off by punctuation.

rise/raise See **raise/rise**.

run-on sentence Two main clauses fused together without punctuation or a conjunction, appearing as one sentence (see Section 33b).

sentence A grammatically independent group of words that contains at least one main clause (see Section 32a).

sentence fragment See **fragment**.

set/sit *Set* means "put" and takes a direct object; its main forms are *set, set, set. Sit* means "be seated" and does not take a direct object; its main forms are *sit, sat, sat. Sit* should not be used as a synonym for *set.*

shall/will *Shall* is used most often in first person questions, while *will* is a future tense helping verb for all persons. British English consistently uses *shall* with first person: *I shall, we shall.*

should of See **have/of.**

sit/set See **set/sit.**

some time/sometime/sometimes *Some time* means "a span of time," *sometime* means "at some unspecified time," and *sometimes* means "occasionally."

somebody/some body; someone/some one *Somebody* and *someone* are indefinite pronouns and have the same meaning. In *some body, body* is a noun modified by *some,* and in *some one, one* is a pronoun or adjective modified by *some.*

sort of See **kind of/sort of/type of.**

split infinitive An infinitive with a word or words between *to* and the base verb form, such as *to boldly go, to better appreciate* (see Section 37d).

stationary/stationery *Stationary* means "motionless"; *stationery* means "writing paper."

subject A noun, pronoun, or noun phrase that identifies what the clause is about and connects with the predicate (see Sections 32a and 32c).

subject-verb agreement See **agreement.**

subordinate A relationship of unequal importance, in terms of either grammar or meaning (see Section 28a).

subordinate clause A clause that cannot stand alone but must be attached to a main clause (see Section 32c). Also called a *dependent clause.*

subordinating conjunction A word that introduces a subordinate clause. Common subordinating conjunctions are *after, although, as, because, before, if, since, that, unless, until, when, where,* and *while* (see Section 32b).

such Avoid using *such* as a synonym for *very.* It should always be followed by a *that* and a clause that contains a result.

sure A colloquial term used as an adverb to mean "certainly." Avoid using it this way in formal writing.

> You **were certainly** [not *sure were*] correct when you said August would be hot.

sure and/sure to; try and/try to *Sure to* and *try to* are correct; do not use *and* after *sure* or *try.*

take See **bring/take.**

that/which *That* introduces a restrictive or essential clause. Restrictive clauses describe an object that must be that particular object and no other. Though some writers occasionally use *which* with restrictive clauses, it is most often used to introduce non-restrictive clauses. These are clauses that contain additional non-essential information about the object.

transition A word or phrase that notes movement from one unit of writing to another.

transitive verb A verb that takes a direct object (see Sections 32c and 35c).

verb A word that expresses action or characterizes the subject in some way. Verbs can show tense and mood (see Section 32b and Chapter 35).

verbal A form of a verb used as an adjective, adverb, or noun (see Section 32b). See also **gerund, infinitive, participle.**

well/good See **good/well.**

which/that See **that/which.**

who/whom *Who* and *whom* follow the same rules as other pronouns: *who* is the subject pronoun; *whom* is the object pronoun (see Section 36a).

will/shall See **shall/will.**

-wise/-ize See **-ize/-wise.**

would of See **have/of.**

you Avoid indefinite uses of *you.* It should only be used to mean "you, the reader."

your/you're The two are not interchangeable. *Your* is the possessive form of "you"; *you're* is the contraction of "you are."

574

INDEX